Niranjan Kumar

Niranjan Kumar works for Cognizant Technology Solutions (www.cognizant.com) in Chennai, India. He's been working in the IT industry since mid-1997. His career started with C on Unix platforms, and then migrated to C++ and Visual C++. He is a co-author of *Data-Centric .NET Programming with C#*, and has contributed many articles to www.csharptoday.com and www.c-sharpcorner.com. Apart from official work, Niranjan is exploring C# and .NET technologies. He likes swimming, diving, playing guitar, and solving 2D picture puzzles. He loves to roam around Europe and has a great passion for Italy and all things Italian. He can be reached at kniranja@chn.cognizant.com.

My first thanks go to the Wrox team for making this book a big success. I would also like to thank Jon Hill and all the reviewers for correcting and guiding me.

I take this opportunity to remember and thank all my close friends in Sella Synergy India Ltd, India and Banca Sella, Italy (www.sella.it), where I learned the basics of programming.

To my mother, Thirupurasundari, and to my close friends for their support at every stage of this work.

Scott McLean

Scott McLean started programming when he was in high school on an Atari 400 computer that had an 8-bit 6502 Microprocessor with 16 kilobytes of RAM and three registers. He taught himself Atari Basic and then moved on to 6502 assembler when his parents granted his Christmas wish, giving him the Atari Assembler/Editor cartridge so that he could get down to the metal of the machine. Fast-forward twenty years.

Since then, he served six years in the United States Navy, working as a "Nuke" Machinist Mate on a fast attack submarine. After the Navy, he earned a Bachelor of Science degree in Computer Science from the University of Georgia and went to work at Motorola, Inc. in Chicago as a software engineer. He learned about SS7, IS-41, and various interacting network agents that allow cellular phone networks to operate. Originally from Florida, one winter in Chicago was quite enough so he moved to the warmer climate of Atlanta, Georgia and worked at NCR developing ActiveX controls for point-of-sale peripherals: bar code scanners, signature capture devices, magnetic stripe readers, etc.

Presently, he is a software engineer at XcelleNet, Inc., enhancing the server communications function of the Afaria product. He programs in C++, COM, ATL, C#, and just about anything else that comes along. He is a cofounder of www.thinkdotnet.com, an online resource for .NET development. Check out some of his articles there, or drop him a line at scott@thinkdotnet.com.

I am indebted to my lovely wife, Nancy, for her unfailing support in my quest for computer nirvana.

Simon Robinson

Simon Robinson lives in Lancaster in the UK, where he shares a house with some students. He first encountered serious programming when he was doing his PhD in physics, modeling all sorts of weird things to do with superconductors and quantum mechanics. The experience of programming was nearly enough to put him off computers for life (though, oddly, he seems to have survived all the quantum mechanics), and he tried for a while being a sports massage therapist instead. But he then realized how much money was in computers compared to sports massage, and rapidly got a job as a C++ programmer/researcher instead. Simon is clearly the charitable, deep, spiritual type, who understands the true meaning of life.

Programming eventually led him into writing, and he now makes a living mostly from writing great books for programmers. His work has taken him through many different aspects of Windows programming and he routinely writes code in C++, C#, and VB. He is very enthusiastic about the .NET framework, which he firmly believes is set to revolutionize programming. His spare time is spent either at dance classes (he loves performing arts and is studying the subject in his spare time) or on his pet project: writing a computer strategy game.

You can visit Simon's web site at www.simonrobinson.com.

Dr P. G. Sarang

With more than 20 years of IT experience, Dr Sarang specializes in architecting and designing solutions based on various technologies. A CEO of ABCOM Information Systems Pvt, Ltd., Dr Sarang specializes in training and project development on Java, CORBA, and Microsoft platforms. During his long career, Dr Sarang has developed a number of successful products and has completed several industry projects. He is a regular speaker at many international conferences and regularly contributes technical articles to reputed international journals and magazines. He has co-authored several books for Wrox on Java, J2EE, e-commerce, and .NET.

My special thanks to Chandan Parulkar and Rahul Bhirud for providing valuable assistance in code development.

I dedicate the chapters to my mother.

Visual C++ .NET: A primer for C++ developers

Aravind Corera
Stephen Fraser
Sam Gentile
Niranjan Kumar
Scott McLean
Simon Robinson
Dr P. G. Sarang

Wrox Press Ltd. ®

Visual C++ .NET: A primer for C++ developers

Printing History

First Published March 2002

Published by Wrox Press Ltd,
Arden House, 1102 Warwick Road, Acock's Green,
Birmingham, B27 6BH, UK
Printed in the United States
ISBN 1-861005-96-2

Trademark acknowledgements

Credits

Authors
Aravind Corera
Stephen Fraser
Sam Gentile
Niranjan Kumar
Scott McLean
Simon Robinson
Dr P. G. Sarang

Technical reviewers
Panangipally Anand
Jay Cook
Billy Cravens
Edgar D'Andrea
Damien Foggon
Brian Hickey
Mark Horner
Kester Neal
Phil Powers de George
Ranga Raghunathan
Tomas Restrepo
Juan Ramon Rovirosa
Kenn Scribner
Scott Seely
Chris Sells
Marc Simkin
Vignesh Srinivas
Gavin Smyth
Helmut Watson
James Weiss

Technical architect
Julian Skinner

Technical editors
Jon Hill
Victoria Hudgson

Managing editor
Louay Fatoohi

Project manager
Beth Sacks

Author agent
Chris Matterface

Production coordinator
Natalie O'Donnell

Indexers
Michael Brinkman
Andrew Criddle

Proofreader
Lisa Stephenson

Cover
Chris Morris

About the authors

Aravind Corera

Aravind Corera is an independent software developer who lives and works in Chennai, India, and is currently working on a project for a document management and workflow software company. He has been working on Microsoft-based technologies for the past six years, particularly in designing and developing systems based on Microsoft's Component Object Model (COM). Aravind's areas of special interest include concurrent programming, distributed systems, and transaction processing monitors. He holds a degree in Computer Science and Engineering from the Coimbatore Institute of Technology. You can reach him at aravind@netluminosity.com.

I'd like to thank my family and friends for being extremely supportive and for sharing my highs and lows during the writing.

Stephen Fraser

Stephen Fraser is the Managing Principal for Fraser Training, a corporate training company focusing on .NET technologies. Stephen has over 15 years of IT experience working for a number of consulting companies, ranging from the large consulting firms of EDS and Andersen Consulting (Accenture), to a number of smaller e-business companies. His IT experience covers all aspects of application and web development and management, ranging from initial concept all the way through to deployment.

Stephen currently resides with his beautiful wife and daughter, Sarah and Shaina, in sunny Tustin Ranch, southern California.

Sam Gentile

Sam Gentile is currently a .NET consultant/principal software engineer at a major product firm with a large COM architecture. He is currently performing advanced work on generating .NET runtime callable wrappers (RCW), COM and native C++ interop, Managed C++ and C#, and Visual Studio .NET integration. Before that, Sam was a tech lead/principal software engineer at NaviSite, where he successfully led a team that, utilizing .NET technologies like ASP.NET, web services, ADO.NET, SOAP, C#, and more was able to deploy two production applications based on .NET Beta 2. A member of Microsoft's Early Adopter Program, Sam has been a software engineer for 17 years and has spent most of his time working with and becoming expert with Microsoft technologies. While not geeking out with software, Sam enjoys literary science fiction. You can visit Sam at his site on the Web (which includes .NET content) at www.project-inspiration.com/sgentile.

Besides his ever-patient and brilliant editor at Wrox, Victoria Hudgson, Sam would like to thank the following people at Microsoft: Sara Williams (who was instrumental in Sam getting into EAP and getting builds), Mark Hall of the C++ compiler team, Ronald Laeremans of the C++ team, Stan Lippman for his helpful emails, and Adam Nathan (who at one deadline helped find a crucial namespace bug!). Sam would especially like to acknowledge the gracious help of Don Box, Brent Rector, and John Lam who provided invaluable answers to questions about PInvoke internals. Without your help, my writing would be much less. You guys rock! Sam would also like to thank Tomas Restrepo and Chris Sells, not only for their reviews, but also for their overall help with questions above and beyond, and their friendship. Sam would also like to thank his beautiful wife Susan for all her love, support, and understanding, as well as his wonderful son Jonathan (Daddy will have time now!). And last but not least, Sam would like to thank his hard-working parents Mario and Catherine Gentile who emigrated from Italy and put him through university, without which none of this would be possible.

Table of contents

Table of contents

Table of contents

Table of contents

Table of contents

Introduction

In all of the noise surrounding the introduction of Microsoft's .NET, you'd be forgiven for beginning to wonder whether the time you've spent learning C++ was a good investment after all. Visual C++, the flagship of previous Visual Studio releases (remember those "Created With Visual C++" graphics that accompanied version 6.0?), goes almost unmentioned in the bulletins that introduce ASP.NET, Visual Basic .NET, and – in particular – C#. Could it really be the case that C++ has no useful part to play in the next wave of Windows development? In this book, we'll demonstrate that idea to be no closer to the truth now than it would have been had we suggested it five years ago.

For a start, it's important not to forget that when you think about the uses for Visual C++, you don't have to think about .NET, or even about Windows programming. The Standard Edition in particular is a popular choice for those seeking to learn "standard" C++ programming, either on a course or at home. In Visual C++ .NET, Microsoft has made further improvements to the IDE, and continued its policy of tracking the ISO/ANSI standard for C++ – Visual C++ .NET has a very high degree of standard compliance.

Second, there are significant innovations in COM and ATL. The development of the latter as a library that extends beyond COM programming, which began with the introduction of CWindow and related functionality in version 3.0, continues: there are more utility classes, and there's ATL Server – a brand new set of classes for the creation of highly optimized web applications and services that builds on the existing ISAPI framework. Furthermore, COM programming itself receives a boost with the introduction of attributes, which save you from having to manage separate IDL files and provide an alternative to writing detailed but repetitive code.

Finally, Microsoft has introduced extensions to the C++ language that turn it into a good .NET citizen. While it's likely that the majority of .NET code will be written using Visual Basic .NET or C#, there's a lot of existing work that will need to be integrated into these new applications in the short and medium term. Visual C++ .NET offers the only way of making legacy code work together with new code, and there are features of the product with exactly this purpose in mind.

What does this book cover?

At heart, this book is pragmatic: its purpose is to tell experienced C++ programmers what they need to know about Visual C++ .NET. To do that properly necessitates a detailed discussion of the .NET Framework itself, but that's certainly not the sole focus. In these pages, you'll also learn about the new features of COM and ATL, and about web services and C++'s role in implementing them.

To be more specific, the first half of the book is spent talking exclusively about .NET and its consequences for C++ programmers. After Chapter 1, which offers a quick guide to the features of .NET that make it worth targeting in your development efforts, we look at the changes Microsoft has made to the C++ language in order to access those features. Armed with knowledge of this "Managed" C++, we then explore some key areas of .NET in C++ terms, starting with assemblies, attributes and metadata, and ending with an analysis of the Framework as a class library to place alongside MFC, and even STL.

In the second half of the book, we deal with "unmanaged" C++, first in the context of arranging for 'legacy' code to interoperate with new code that's been written for the .NET Framework – something of which no other programming language is capable. Thereafter, we look at attribute-driven COM programming, at new features of ATL (which is now in version 7.0), at ATL Server, and at ATL web services. If you need to understand the vital role that C++ still plays in software development for Microsoft platforms, this book is for you.

What you need to use this book

This book and the code it contains have been checked against the release version of Microsoft Visual Studio .NET. Its minimum requirements are therefore the same as those for that product: a PII-450 CPU, Microsoft Windows NT 4.0 (or a later OS), at least 128 MB of RAM, and around 3GB of free space on your hard drive. The majority of code examples will work with the standard edition of Visual C++ .NET, and you'll certainly get full value from the book if you own that product, but there are a couple of illustrative examples that also use Visual Basic .NET and Visual C# .NET.

Style conventions

We've used a number of different styles of text and layout in this book to help differentiate between the different kinds of information. Code, for example, comes in a number of different guises. If we're talking about it in the text – when discussing a `while` loop, perhaps – it will be in `this font`. Alternatively, if it's a block of code that could be typed in, it looks like this:

```
<?xml version 1.0?>
```

On other occasions, you'll see code in a mixture of styles, like this:

```
<?xml version 1.0?>
<invoice>
   <part>
      <name>Widget</name>
      <price>$10.00</price>
   </part>
</invoice>
```

Here, the code with a white background is either something you're already familiar with, or something that's not terribly important to the discussion at hand. The converse is true of the code with a gray background.

Advice, hints, and background information come in this style.

Important pieces of information come in boxes like this.

Bullets appear indented, with each new bullet marked as follows:

- ❑ **Important words** are in a bold font.
- ❑ Words that appear on the screen, or in menus like File or Window, are in a similar font to the one you'd see on a Windows desktop.
- ❑ Keys that you press on the keyboard, like *Ctrl* and *Enter*, are in italics.

Finally, commands that you might need to type in on the command line are shown with a > for the prompt, and the input in **bold**, like this:

```
> something to type on the command line
```

Customer support and feedback

We value hearing from our readers, and we want to know what you think about this book: what you liked, what you didn't like, and what you think we can do better next time. You can send us your comments by either returning the reply card in the back of the book, or sending e-mail to feedback@wrox.com. Please be sure to mention the ISBN and the title of the book in your message.

Source code and updates

All of the source code for this book is available at the wrox.com web site. When you arrive at http://www.wrox.com/, locate the title through our search facility or by using one of the title lists. Then, click on the Download Code link on the book's detail page, and you can obtain the code.

The files that are available for download from our site have been archived using WinZip. When you've saved them to your hard drive, you'll need to extract the files they contain using a decompression program such as WinZip or PKUnzip. When you extract the files, ensure that your software has the Use folder names (or some equivalent) option switched on.

Errata

We have made every effort to ensure that there are no errors in the text or the code. However, no one is perfect and mistakes do occur. If you find an error in this book, we'd be very grateful if you'd tell us about it. By sending in errata, you may save another reader hours of frustration, and you'll be helping us to provide information of even higher quality. Simply e-mail your discovery to support@wrox.com; your information will be checked and, if found correct, posted to the errata page or used in subsequent editions of the book.

To find errata on the web site, log on to http://www.wrox.com, and locate the title through the search facility. Then, on the book's detail page, click on the Book Errata link. On this page you'll be able to view any errata that have been already submitted and verified. You can also click the Submit Errata link to notify us of any errata that you may have found.

Technical support

If you need to discuss a problem in the book with an expert who knows it in detail, send e-mail to support@wrox.com with the title of the book and the last four numbers of the ISBN in the subject line. A typical e-mail should include the following things:

❑   The **name** of the book, the **last four digits of its ISBN**, and the **page number** of the problem in the subject line.

❑   Your **name**, your **contact information**, and the **problem** in the body of the message.

We *won't* send you junk mail. We need the details to save your time and ours. When you send an e-mail message, it will go through the following chain of support:

❑   **Customer support**: Your message is delivered to our customer support staff, who are the first people to read it. They have files on most frequently asked questions and will answer general questions about the book or the web site immediately.

❑   **Editorial**: Deeper queries are forwarded to the technical editor responsible for the book in question. These people have experience with the subject matter, and are able to answer detailed technical questions on the subject. Once an issue has been resolved, the editor can post the solution to the web site.

❑   **The authors**: Finally, in the unlikely event that the editor cannot answer your problem, he or she will forward the request to the author. We do try to protect our authors from casual distractions, but they and we are quite happy to deal with specific requests. All Wrox authors help to support their books. They will mail the customer and the editor with their response, and again all readers should benefit.

The Wrox support process can only offer support to issues that are directly pertinent to the content of a published title. Answers to questions that fall outside the scope of normal book support may be found via the community lists of our http://p2p.wrox.com forum.

p2p.wrox.com

For author and peer discussion, join the **P2P mailing lists**. Our unique system provides **programmer to programmer**™ contact on mailing lists, forums, and newsgroups, all *in addition* to our one-to-one e-mail support system. Be confident that your query is being examined by the many Wrox authors, and other industry experts, who are present on our mailing lists. At p2p.wrox.com you will find a number of different lists that will help you not only while you read this book, but also as you develop your own applications.

To subscribe to a mailing list, just follow this these steps:

1.   Go to http://p2p.wrox.com

2.   Choose the appropriate category from the left menu bar

3. Click on the mailing list you wish to join

4. Follow the instructions to subscribe, and fill in your e-mail address and password

5. Reply to the confirmation e-mail you receive

6. Use the subscription manager to join more lists and set your mail preferences

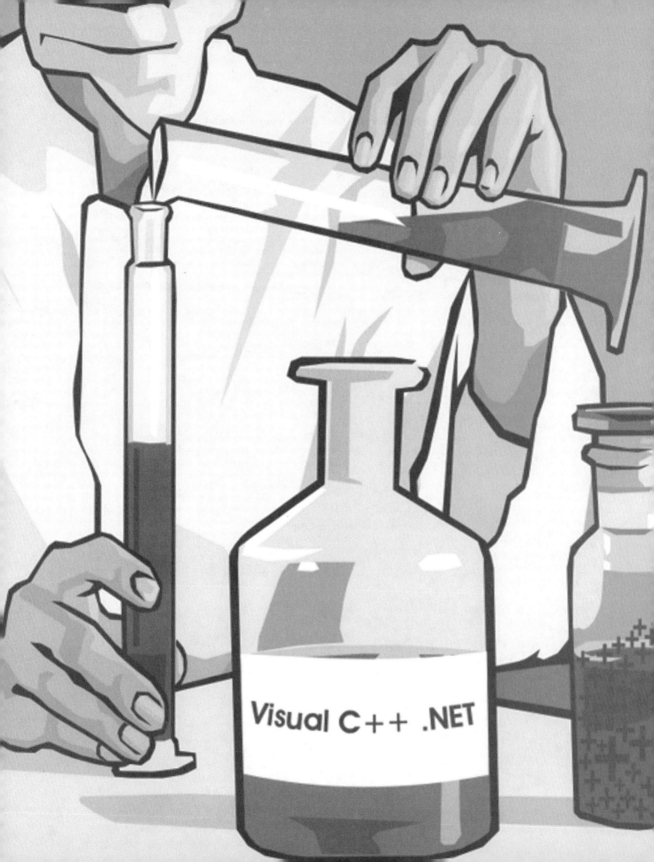

1

What's new in Visual C++?

For many years, C++ has been the most popular language for the development of highly optimized applications and components. Despite the enormous recent successes of Java, when it comes to the development of performance code, C++ is still the first choice of millions of programmers worldwide.

The release of the new version of Visual Studio has been timed to coincide with the release of Microsoft's new .NET Framework, which provides a language-neutral, robust environment for the creation of applications both for the World Wide Web and for standalone computers. To accompany this development, Visual Basic has been upgraded, and is now known as Visual Basic .NET. ASP has been upgraded to ASP.NET, and an altogether new language called C# has been introduced. And for the droves of C++ programmers, there is Visual C++ .NET.

Because so much code has been developed in Visual C++ over the years, Microsoft wanted to ensure that whatever advances it made would allow for backward compatibility. At the same time, though, it recognized that C++ programmers should be able to take advantage of the new platform. In this chapter, we have two goals: to assess the .NET Framework from a moderate height, and to examine the changes in Visual Studio – now named Visual Studio .NET – that will have an impact on the way you create your applications in C++.

As we mentioned in the introduction, and for reasons that will become increasingly apparent as we progress, it's actually quite unlikely that you'll want to develop brand new .NET applications in C++ – for that purpose, there are better options. In .NET, the important role of C++ is to provide the crucial interoperation between the tried and tested code that was written before .NET came along, and the new applications that will be written to use the Framework. In order to fulfill that role, though, we need to understand exactly how .NET works, and that's a process that we'll begin here.

In addition, and despite its name, not everything that's new in Visual C++ .NET is related to the .NET Framework. In the final third of this book, we'll be looking at the changes and improvements that have been made to COM and ATL programming, and we'll touch on a couple of those here, too.

This chapter, then, comes in three fairly distinct parts that you might decide to skim through, depending on your previous exposure to .NET and Visual C++. First of all, we'll take a high-level tour of the .NET Framework, outlining the key features that will be examined in more depth over the course of the book. Second, we'll look at some of the changes that have taken place in the Visual Studio IDE – some of these are cosmetic, but others are rooted in the new or different functionality that's available. Third, we'll walk through a quick example that uses some of the features of .NET that we talked about in the first section, and provides an opportunity to test the debugging ability of Visual Studio .NET.

The .NET Framework

Microsoft says that the .NET Framework "is a new computing platform that simplifies application development in the highly distributed environment of the Internet". In practical terms, what this means is that every computer on which the .NET Framework is installed shares a consistent execution environment in terms of performance, appearance, and security. In addition, via a number of mechanisms, the .NET Framework makes the relative locations of code storage and execution unimportant, and simplifies the thorny issues of deployment and versioning. As if that weren't enough, it also provides a development environment that absolves the programmer from several traditional but tedious responsibilities.

The .NET Framework is made up of two distinct but related parts: the **common language runtime** (**CLR**) and the **class library**. Broadly speaking, these can be summarized as "The services that it provides" and "The things that it makes possible". Most of the features of ".NET" that you've heard about – garbage collection, version control, thread management, and so forth – come courtesy of the CLR, through means that we'll discuss in more depth shortly. On the other hand, when people say that ".NET" enables Windows Forms applications and XML web services, they're talking about functionality that's embodied by the class library. Let's start by looking at the CLR.

The common language runtime

When you compile your source code (an application, a library, a control, etc.) for the .NET Framework, the object code you generate does not target the instruction set of the CPU of the machine you're working on. Compiling for .NET means compiling for the CLR, and that means that the result of compilation is code in a new language called **Microsoft Intermediate Language** (**MSIL**, or simply **IL**). MSIL defines an instruction set for a 'virtual' CPU – code that's compiled to IL must be further compiled into the native instruction set of a target CPU before it will run on that CPU.

The CLR provides a **just-in-time** compiler that compiles IL code into native machine code. Once compiled, the code is cached; when the application terminates, the compiled code may be removed from the system. Furthermore, compilation of the entire program may not take place at one time. Rather, the code is likely to be compiled piecemeal, as and when required. A running program may not require all the code during its lifetime – on any given run, a user may not use all the features of an application.

Now, regardless of how well this process is optimized, it's unlikely to be as efficient as going straight from source code to native code. That being the case, we need some good reasons for wanting to target the CLR. Of course, there are a number of these (we've hinted at a couple of them already), and we'll describe them in a little more detail in the following sections.

Garbage collection

C++ programmers have always been plagued by the memory leaks that can arise as a result of failing to deallocate resources properly when they are no longer required in applications. And if that weren't bad enough, you can also run into problems if you're too eager to deallocate your resources – you run the risk of attempting to access an invalid area of memory. The .NET Framework's CLR has solutions for both of these problems.

The CLR provides garbage collection (and, by extension, lifetime management). It assumes responsibility for keeping track of valid references, and for reference counting. It periodically checks all references to all objects; if an object is not currently referenced, it is freed from memory. When the garbage collector has finished freeing objects, it cleans up after itself by compacting the heap, providing contiguous memory for new allocations that are more efficient as a result.

Code portability

The CLR's provision for code portability falls out naturally from the description above: because the source code of a .NET application always compiles to IL, the compiled (IL) code may be run on *any* platform that provides a .NET CLR. Today, the CLR is available only on the Windows platform, but that's likely to change – the Mono Project (www.go-mono.com) that seeks to bring .NET to Linux is already well underway.

Language interoperability

In order to become .NET-compliant, and to ensure interoperability between applications, all .NET languages must follow Microsoft's specifications. A .NET language *must* be object-oriented, and it *must* use a standard set of data types defined by the **common type system** (**CTS**). In addition to the modifications that Microsoft has made to its 'own' languages, third parties have modified languages to support the .NET Framework too – these include COBOL, Eiffel, Perl, Python, and SmallTalk.

From the CLR's point of view, therefore, all languages are equal: as long as there's a compiler that can generate IL, that's all that matters. By the same token, once an application or a library has been compiled to IL, its original language is irrelevant. This fact makes it possible to take a library written in one language and call it from another with no difficulty at all – the types used for passing arguments and return values are always compatible.

Another benefit that accrues from the combination of IL and the CTS is improved debugging – not only can you use code from multiple .NET languages in the same application, but also you can debug multilingual code in the same session, using a consistent interface.

Code security

The CLR 'trusts' IL code to different degrees, depending on a number of criteria (not least of which is where the code has come from – the local machine, a LAN, or the Internet). The degree of trust can result in limitations on what a particular piece of code can do in terms of accessing the resources available to the computer on which the application is actually being executed.

As the IL code is compiled, the CLR gets a chance to verify it prior to execution on the real CPU. Permission for this code to use code that's been written by third parties or other team members may or may not be granted, depending on the user's current privileges. The CLR ensures the implementation of application-level security for a running program.

Access to the .NET Framework class library

Finally in this list, writing C++ code that targets the CLR automatically provides you with quick, easy access to the .NET Framework class library – a set of classes so rich that it dwarfs the functionality of ATL, and even of MFC. There are types in the library that represent every aspect of Windows programming, and we'll discuss just a few of its implications shortly. Before we do that, however, we'll dwell for a moment on just what it is about the *nature* of code that targets the CLR that makes it able to offer the benefits we've listed.

Properties of managed code

Code that's written for and uses the services of the CLR is called **managed code**; predictably, code that doesn't use the CLR's services (in other words, all that stuff you've been writing for years) is now called **unmanaged code**. As we've already discussed, compiling code to target the CLR results in the production of intermediate language (IL) code; what we haven't yet discussed is how this code is then distributed.

When you build a **Managed C++** application in Visual C++ .NET, the result is an EXE file; when you build a Managed C++ library, you get a DLL. There, however, the similarity between what you *actually* have and what you used to get ends. These files are in **portable executable** (**PE**) format, and contain not only the compiled MSIL code, but also **metadata** that describes everything about it: the types that it uses; the classes it contains (along with their methods and properties); the other files whose types it makes use of. These PE files are called **assemblies**, and we'll have much more to say about them in Chapter 3. However, even the little we've said about assemblies so far helps to explain just how the CLR is about to offer some of the services we've listed above, plus a couple of others.

Deployment

Under the .NET Framework, application deployment becomes much simpler. Because assemblies carry complete descriptions of the functionality they embody, there's no need to register that information elsewhere on the system. Installing a .NET application is often as simple as dragging the files from one location to another. If one of the libraries you bring with you happens to be incompatible with one that's already installed... there's no problem, as we'll discuss next.

Versioning

One of the key selling points of .NET is that it solves the problem popularly known as "DLL Hell", in which one version of a library overwrites another (usually a new one over an old one, though not always), instantly rendering numerous installed applications unusable. In .NET, assemblies carry their version numbers with them as part of the metadata, and the CLR is 'aware' of them to the extent that if necessary, two versions of the same library can be loaded simultaneously to service clients old and new.

We'll be expanding on these features of managed code in Chapters 2, 3, and 4. Let's move on now to talk about the second part of the .NET Framework: the class library.

The .NET Framework class library

The .NET Framework class library defines a set of reusable classes for the development of an incredibly wide variety of applications. The classes in the library provide standard services such as database access, networking, diagnostics, security, etc. They provide support for networking, enabling the development of standalone, distributed, and web-based applications. Also, they support XML and WSDL (Web Service Description Language), enabling us to develop web applications and services based on standard protocols.

The same set of classes is shared by all .NET applications, and like any good example of its kind, the .NET class library places all of the classes it contains inside a namespace. Where the C++ STL has std (and, as you'll discover later, ATL now has ATL), the .NET Framework defines the System namespace. This in turn contains many second- and third-level namespaces; a few of these, and the functionality they encompass, are listed here:

- ❑ System::Data defines the ADO.NET architecture that's used for accessing and managing data sources

- ❑ System::Xml defines support for XML

- ❑ System::Diagnostics is used for debugging, tracing, creating logs, and monitoring system performance

- ❑ System::DirectoryServices defines classes for accessing Active Directories

- ❑ System::Net defines networking support classes

- ❑ System::Drawing defines access to GDI+ graphics

- ❑ System::Windows::Forms defines classes for creating Windows-based applications

- ❑ System::Security provides the CLR's security system, and includes classes for security policy resolution, permissions, and stack walks

- ❑ System::Security::Cryptography defines classes for cryptographic services like data encoding/decoding, hashing, random number generation, message authentication, and formation of digital signatures

- ❑ System::Web provides core infrastructure for ASP.NET and Web Forms support

- ❑ System::Web::Services provides support for SOAP-based web services

Looking over that list, it seems that we keep talking about the enormous range of possible applications for the .NET Framework without ever being specific about it. Let's fix that now by running through a list of the four areas most likely to be targets of .NET development. Remember that for the most part, you won't be doing this development in C++, which has other ways to achieve the same functionality that we'll be discussing later in the book. What you're more likely to find is that one of these application types will need to make use of some 'old' code – and that's where C++ comes in.

ASP.NET applications

Microsoft has modified its ASP model. ASP.NET can be used for creating both the 'traditional', web-based applications of ASP 2.0 and 3.0 – now using Web Forms – and the latest web services, which we'll mention in their own right in a moment.

An application based on Web Forms is a typical ASP construction that uses HTML to render data on the client, HTTP for communication between the client and the server. Using Web Forms, a client may inherit the look and feel of a Visual Basic form, and use ActiveX components and cookies for state management.

Windows applications

Although .NET is primarily about the easy interoperation of components and applications across networks, it's quite possible to create a .NET application that consists of a standalone, Windows-based executable that runs on the .NET Framework under the control of the CLR. Apart from that last point, these are the kinds of applications that all of us have been developing for years.

Console applications

Old-fashioned they may be, but console applications are ideal for basic code testing, and support for generating them is enshrined in the .NET Framework class library's `System::Console` namespace. Where would we be without them?

Web services

A **web service** may be defined as a programmable application component that provides services and data to remote clients via standard web protocols. It uses two XML-based technologies – WSDL (Web Service Description Language) and SOAP (Simple Object Access Protocol) – as means of supplying information about the services it provides, andof passing data and method calls, respectively. Through these techniques, access to a web service is entirely independent of its implementation.

New features of Visual Studio .NET

Having taken our first look at the subject that will be occupying us in the chapters ahead, let's generalize a little and take a look at the bigger picture. With all of the changes that have taken place in the field of Windows programming, you might reasonably expect Visual Studio to have undergone some changes too – and of course, you'd be quite right. To match the fact that all the features of the .NET Framework are available to programmers of all Microsoft's languages, the latter now all share the same IDE. There's no longer a separate environment for developing Visual Basic applications, as there was in version 6.0.

Quite apart from aesthetics and convenience, though, there are sound reasons for this integration. Remember: the components of a .NET application can be created using different languages, and it follows that cross-language debugging can sometimes be necessary too. As you'll see later, this need (along with a number of others) has been addressed in the new version.

Our main interest in this book lies in the changes that affect the way we create Visual C++ applications. Leaving aside (for a moment) the cosmetic changes to the GUI, heading for the File | New | Project... menu reveals a dialog box containing more different project types than ever before, including the new Visual Basic and Visual C# types. If you select Visual C++ Projects from the Project Types pane, you'll see the following window at the top of the opposite page.

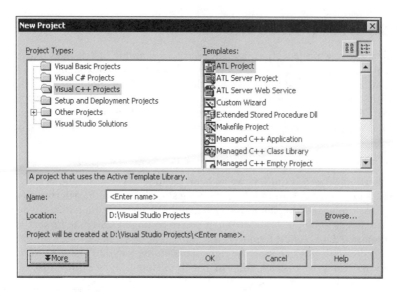

In the right-hand pane, there are a total of fifteen options for creating Visual C++ projects. Some of these will appear familiar to you, while others are new. The complete list is:

- ATL Project
- **ATL Server Project**
- **ATL Server Web Service**
- Custom Wizard
- Extended Stored Procedure Dll
- Makefile Project
- **Managed C++ Application**
- **Managed C++ Class Library**
- **Managed C++ Empty Project**
- **Managed C++ Web Service**
- MFC ActiveX Control
- MFC Application
- MFC DLL
- MFC ISAPI Extension Dll
- Win32 Project

We're not going to cover every one of these templates exhaustively here – indeed, there are some that address concerns beyond the scope of this book – but we will at least take a quick look at each of them. In each case, we'll examine what's new and the extent to which they'll play a part in the projects we create in future chapters.

Old Wizards with new looks

Before we look at the new project types, it makes sense to examine the changes that have been made to the Wizards that were available in Visual C++ 6.0. All of these have taken on a new look, and many have new options available. In addition, some of the underlying technologies have changed, and we'll address that point here too. Finally, looking at how the appearance of the Wizards has changed in Visual C++ .NET seems to provide a good opportunity for looking at how the appearance of the IDE has changed, and we can do that best by investigating probably the most familiar Wizard of all.

MFC Application

The MFC Application Wizard is the way we've been creating MFC applications for years – the Wizard generates the files necessary to start building an application based on the Microsoft Foundation Classes. But before we fire it up to see how things have changed, there's something that, if you're anything like this author, really needs to be put straight! When you're coding in C++, the Project Workspace window (or, as it's now known, the Solution Explorer) is supposed to be on the left side of the screen – but the default Visual Studio settings place it on the right. Thankfully, you don't have to sift through the menus to find the windows you want. Instead, you can just go to Help | Show Start Page:

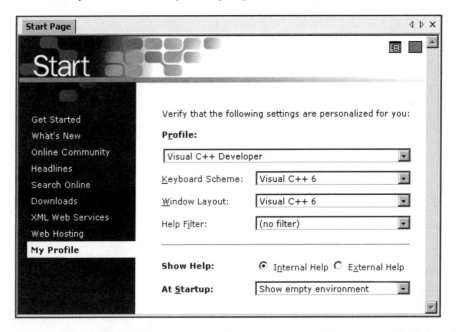

With the settings shown above, the environment will start to look more like home – and once you begin to feel comfortable with it, you'll find that there are a number of substantial improvements. Assuming that you'll discover those as we go along, though, we'll get back to the matter in hand and look at the Wizard.

The Wizard dialog

When you invoke the MFC Application Wizard in Visual Studio .NET, you get the following dialog:

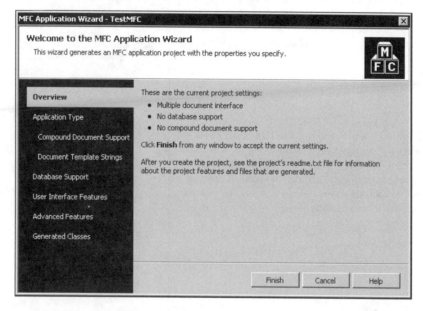

Clearly, this is a complete revision of the user interface compared with what we had under Visual Studio 6.0. Instead of leading you by the hand through a series of steps, all of the available options are listed on the left-hand side of a dialog that was created using DHTML (as you'll discover if you ever decide to create a custom Wizard). When you select a category, the various settings that relate to it appear in the main area of the Wizard.

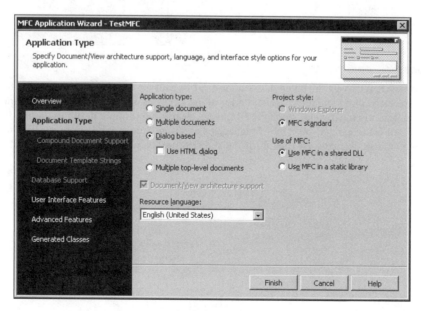

With a couple of minor exceptions, however, the options and settings themselves are very similar to the way things used to be in earlier versions of Visual C++. In the example above, we've chosen to create a dialog-based application, resulting in some of the categories becoming unavailable – just as choosing this option in Visual C++ 6.0 would reduce the number of steps in the Wizard.

Class View

After hitting Finish and watching the IDE wrap itself around your new project, some familiar sights will roam into view. The Class View is as ever it was, although it's now 'aware' of more things, making navigation around your project just a little easier. Maps and enumerations, for example, are now 'expandable' items, as you can see from this screenshot.

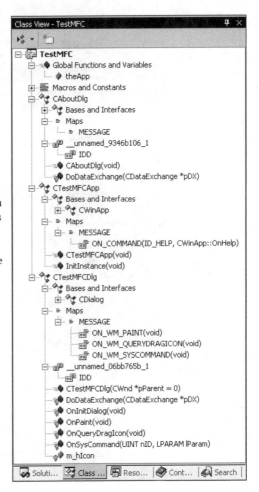

Controls, properties, and events

If the Class View is relatively unchanged, the same can't be said for the ClassWizard, whose functionality has been largely factored into a number of separate locations, or the WizardBar, which has disappeared entirely. Without going into too much detail here, these changes clearly stem from a desire to standardize the user's experience when developing in any of the languages that Visual Studio .NET supports. In place of the classic Visual C++ interfaces, we have a Visual Basic 6.0-style Properties window, shown opposite.

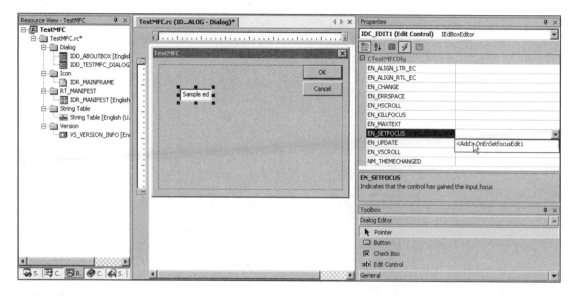

Here, we've opened up the Resource View and added an edit control to the main dialog of the MFC application. This in turn has resulted in the appearance of the Properties window, here listing the events that this control can fire to its parent. Selecting the option currently highlighted would result in the addition of a method called OnEnSetfocusEdit1() to the main dialog class (CTestMFC). The button to the left of the events' lightning bolt, on the other hand, provides a common home for the properties of any and all of the entities in your project – source files, variables, classes, controls, you name it. In this particular instance, it makes for a nice improvement over the old-style property windows that you had to remember to 'pin down' in order to prevent them from disappearing (screenshot overleaf).

This is not the place for a highly detailed discussion of the changes to the Visual C++ IDE, but hopefully this quick tour will have given you a feel for the kinds of changes that have been made, and why they were considered necessary. Broadly speaking, they're a mixture of straightforward improvements to functionality, and adaptations to fit in with the other programming languages. With that in mind, we'll continue our survey of the old Wizards in rather less detail.

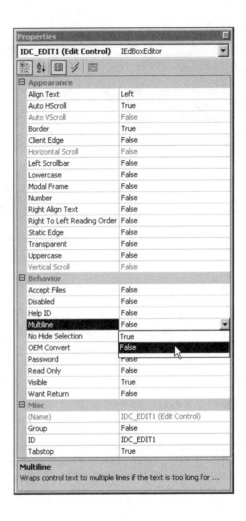

MFC DLL

If you're creating a DLL based on MFC, you will naturally use the MFC DLL option. Once again, the looks of this Wizard have been changed, but little else. You can configure all of the settings for your project simply by selecting the Application Settings category; the generated DLL may be a regular DLL that uses the shared MFC DLL, a regular DLL that has MFC statically linked, or an MFC extension DLL. Support for Automation and Windows sockets may be added, too.

MFC ActiveX Control

If you wish to create ActiveX controls using MFC, then the MFC ActiveX Control Wizard is the one you'll want to use: it generates the MFC control class and the property page class.

Under the Application Settings option, you may request the generation of help files and include support for a run-time license. Under the Control Names option, you can specify names for your control and property pages classes, and the files that will implement them. Under Control Settings, you can give additional features to your control, such as invisibility at runtime, flicker-free activation, windowless activation, and so forth.

MFC ISAPI Extension DLL

It's possible to extend the functionality of Internet Information Server (IIS) by creating extension DLLs, and the MFC ISAPI Extension DLL Wizard is one way of creating them. Under the Object Settings option, you may opt to generate a filter for an ISAPI extension, and specify the class name and description for the filter class. You can also specify the name and description for your server extension object. Under the Notifications option, you may select the notification priority, connection types, etc. The Wizard generates a filter object, filter object notifications, and a server extension class.

Makefile Project

If you're fond of compiling and building your projects from the command line, the option to do so is available to you. Under the Application Settings option of the Makefile Application Wizard, you can specify the Build command line complete with attendant switches, the name of the Output file, any Clean commands, and the Rebuild command line.

Win32 Project

One of the things most obviously missing from the list in the New Project window is everyone's favorite test client, the Win32 console application. Thankfully, it's still with us – it just doesn't get top billing anymore. The Win32 Application Wizard provides support for creating this and a couple of other much-loved project types:

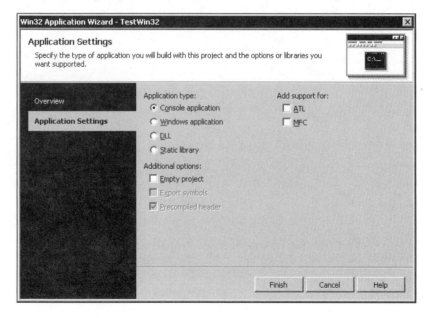

As you can see, this Wizard can also generate Windows applications, DLLs, and static libraries, with the option to add support for ATL where appropriate. We'll be making use of that option in particular when we turn our attention to developing with ATL 7.0 later in the book.

Custom Wizard

The Custom Wizard template allows you to create your own Wizard for creating projects appropriate to your problem domain. After deciding how many pages your Wizard should present to the user, the Wizard creates a DHTML page for each of the pages you have requested. Each generated page can then be customized to incorporate the actions you require; note that because the dialogs are now in DHTML, the language you use to implement custom Wizards is now JavaScript rather than C++.

Extended Stored Procedure DLL

The last of the 'old' Wizards is the Extended Stored Procedure DLL template, which is used for creating an extended stored procedure dynamic-link library project. It creates one .cpp file that contains the named stored procedure, and another that defines an entry point for the DLL.

The new Wizards

Having looked at the old Wizards, we can turn our attention to those that are new (or at least, heavily modified in one way or another) in Visual C++ .NET. These deal with the application types that we'll be using most frequently over the course of the rest of the book, so you'll have plenty of opportunity to become familiar with them as we progress.

Managed C++ Application

The ability to generate the skeleton of a Managed C++ application is, of course, a new feature of Visual C++ .NET. The Wizard asks for no project settings (other than the name), and generates a .cpp file to which Managed C++ code can be added. In case you're already curious, the contents of that file look like this:

```
// This is the main project file fora VC++ application project
// generated using an Application Wizard

#include "stdafx.h"

#using <mscorlib.dll>
#include <tchar.h>

using namespace System;

// This is the entry point for this application
int _tmain(void)
{
    // TODO: Please replace the sample code below with your own
    Console::WriteLine(S"Hello World");
    return 0;
}
```

This code simply displays a "Hello World" message in a console window. As you can see, the code is semantically similar to 'traditional' Visual C++ code, but it uses the .NET Framework class libraries to achieve the desired functionality. As you'd expect, we'll be discussing this code in more detail in the next chapter, and the rest of the book contains plentiful examples of using Managed Extensions for C++.

Managed C++ Class Library

If you wish to create a dynamic-link library (DLL) that uses Managed Extensions for C++, you'll use the Managed C++ Class Library Wizard, which generates the .cpp and .h files necessary for such an endeavor.

Managed C++ Empty Project

The Managed C++ Empty Project Wizard generates – you guessed it – an empty project. You'll need to add your own files to the project, and manage them as you see fit.

Managed C++ Web Service

If you wish to create a web service that uses Managed Extensions for C++, you use the Managed C++ Web Service template. This generates a file with the extension .vsdisco, which is the discovery file that describes the web service in WSDL. You may use the Web.config file to override the default configuration settings for the web service. The Wizard also generates a .asmx file that encapsulates the web service functionality.

If you're intrigued by the terminology, we'll be examining web services in Chapter 11, although we won't be using Managed C++ to write them. Instead, we'll be using ATL, which has gained this and several other new abilities in its version 7.0 incarnation.

ATL Project

Talking of ATL, the apparently superficial changes to the ATL Project Wizard are misleading. Alongside the usual options regarding the kind of server you'd like to create, and what additional features you wish to support, is the unassuming **Attributed** check box:

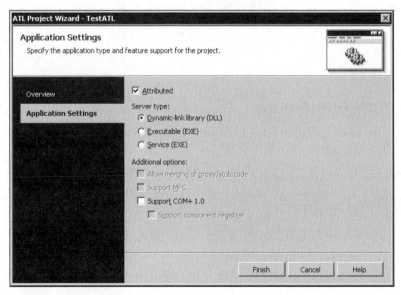

This option will be the subject of much discussion in Chapter 9. In short, it revolutionizes COM and ATL programming by allowing you to place IDL-style attributes in your C++ code that result in the inclusion of tracts of boilerplate code just before compilation, simplifying your development effort no end.

ATL Server Project

ATL Server is a set of ATL classes that facilitate the development of web application projects that are highly efficient and tightly coupled with IIS and ISAPI. The ATL Server Project Wizard provides the basis for creating such applications, as well as XML web services. Among others, the Wizard generates `.srf` and `.h` files; the former contains a starter for your web application, while the latter defines the ATL Server request handler class whose contents depend on the options you select in the Wizard. We'll be discussing the output of this Wizard, and ATL Server in general, in Chapter 10.

ATL Server Web Service

Last, and arguably least, is the ATL Server Web Service Wizard. It's not that web services aren't useful – we'll be covering them in Chapter 11 – but that this Wizard does nothing that's not already possible with the previous Wizard. As such, it's redundant, and there seems little point in discussing it further.

Cross-language development and debugging

As we outlined earlier, a key feature of .NET is its language neutrality. Developers can build components in any language they please, secure in the knowledge that whatever they develop will be compatible with other components created by other developers, even if they were using a different programming language. Clearly, this is a significant step forward from the world before .NET, when cross-language development was possible, but notoriously difficult – your code had to adhere to some very stringent guidelines. If you've ever written a COM component in C++ that was destined to be used from Visual Basic, the word "variant" is likely to bring you out in a cold sweat.

In the chapters to come, we'll be talking more about assemblies, MSIL, CTS, exception handling, and so on – all the things that allow managed code and the .NET Framework to behave the way they do. To round off this chapter, though, we can have a little fun and put together an example that at least proves all we've said so far to be true. We'll create a .NET application that's implemented in three different languages, and then demonstrate how Visual Studio .NET's debugging tools are quite happy to move seamlessly between them.

Cross-language example

The sample we'll throw together is a simple demonstration of multi-language inheritance. Basically, the program has the following flow:

- ❑ A C# console application instantiates a Visual Basic .NET class and then calls a method on it
- ❑ The Visual Basic .NET class inherits from a C++ class

And the outcome, assuming that everything goes to plan, will look something like this:

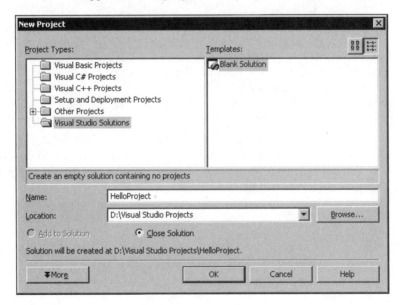

It might look like overkill, but it amply proves the point that it doesn't matter what language you choose to write your .NET code in. Each part of this application is purposely kept simple, but the principle remains the same regardless of how complex your application becomes. All that matters is that your assembly must adhere to the common language specification for any exposed variable, method, or property.

To get things started, head into Visual Studio .NET and create a **Blank Solution** called `HelloProject`. This way we can build our application language neutrally right from the beginning:

Writing a class using C++

The first thing that we need to add to the `HelloProject` solution is a Managed C++ Class Library called `HelloMCPP` (or anything else you'd like to call it):

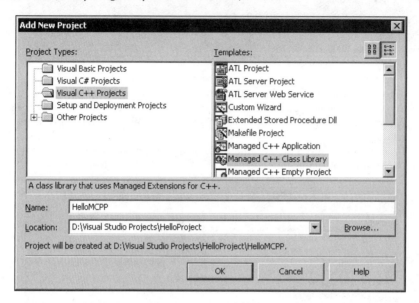

Ignoring for now some new elements that we'll be examining in detail in the next chapter, the Wizard has created a class called `Class1` in a namespace called `HelloMCPP`. The only alteration we'll make to these settings is to change the name of the class to `HelloMCPP` too, and since the implementation is beyond easy, we'll place our code right in the header file, `HelloMCPP.h`:

```cpp
// HelloMCPP.h

#pragma once

using namespace System;

namespace HelloMCPP
{
    public __gc class HelloMCPP
    {
    public:
        virtual void Hello()
        {
            Console::WriteLine(S"Hello from Managed C++!");
        }
    };
}
```

Here, the `Class1::Hello()` method uses a function from the .NET Framework class library –
`System::Console::WriteLine()` – to display Hello from Managed C++! in a console window. That's all we have to do for now, so once you've compiled the project, we can move on to the second phase.

Writing a class using Visual Basic .NET

Phase two means Visual Basic .NET, and we can kick it off by creating another new project. This time, we'll get Visual Studio .NET to generate a Visual Basic Class Library project called HelloVB:

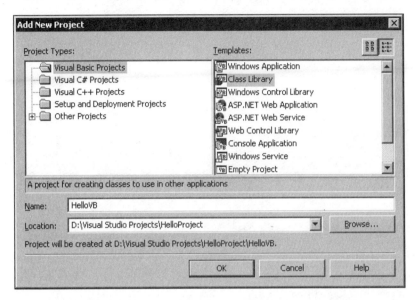

Even if you don't know Visual Basic, the simple code we'll add here should be easy to understand. It defines a class called HelloVB that inherits from the Managed C++ class, HelloMCPP. It overrides the virtual method Hello() with its own version that first calls the parent class's version of the Hello() method, and then writes Hello from VB.NET! to the console.

```
Public Class HelloVB
    Inherits HelloMCPP.HelloMCPP

    Public Overrides Sub Hello()
        MyBase.Hello()
        System.Console.WriteLine("Hello from VB.NET!")
    End Sub
End Class
```

Now, the blue underlining in this screenshot means that Visual Basic doesn't recognize some of the names we've used, but that's probably not too surprising. If you let the cursor hover over the Inherits line for a moment, a tool tip will tell you exactly what the problem is:

Type 'HelloMCPP.HelloMCPP' is not defined.

We need to tell Visual Basic where the assembly that defines this type is located, but this is not a difficult thing to do. Select Project | Add Reference..., choose the Project tab of the resulting dialog box, and find your way to the HelloMCPP project, as shown overleaf:

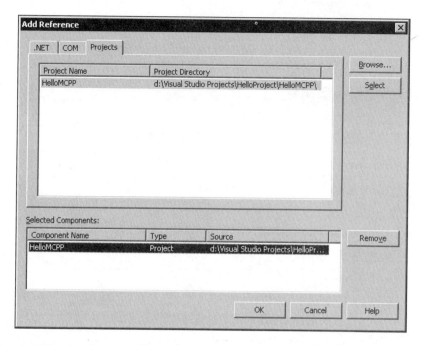

When this operation completes, you'll see those nasty blue lines disappear. Build this part of the project, and we can move on to stage three.

Writing a class using C#

If we're finished with Visual Basic .NET, it must be time to do some work in C#. This time, we need to add a Visual C# Console Application called HelloCSharp, as shown below:

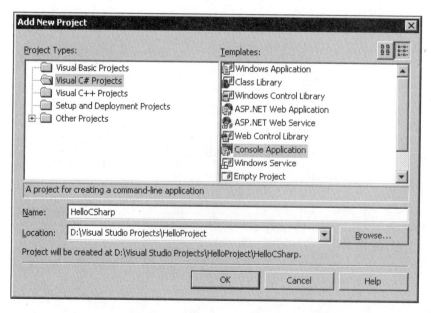

You should have little difficulty reading the C# code below – it has a lot of similarities to C++. The listing defines a class called `HelloCSharp` with a static method called `Main()` that will be the entry point for this application. `Main()` creates a new object of our `HelloVB` class and calls its `Hello()` method before adding its own contribution to the console output: Hello from C#!

```
using System;

namespace HelloCSharp
{
    /// <summary>
    /// Summary description for Class1.
    /// </summary>
    class HelloCSharp
    {
        /// <summary>
        /// The main entry point for the application.
        /// </summary>
        [STAThread]
        static void Main(string[] args)
        {
            HelloVB.HelloVB hello = new HelloVB.HelloVB();
            hello.Hello();
            Console.WriteLine("Hello from C#!");
        }
    }
}
```

Like our Visual Basic project before it, though, this class will not compile as it stands – it doesn't know what `HelloVB.HelloVB` is. This time, we have to add references to both `HelloVB` and `HelloMCPP` to the project, as shown:

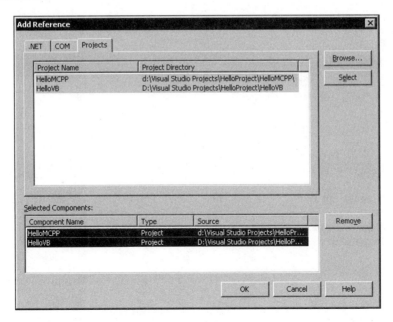

Finally, you should set the C# project to be the 'startup project' in your solution (right-click on the project name in the Solution Explorer and choose **Set as StartUp Project**), compile and build the whole solution, and try it out. With the amount of effort you've put in, you might not think this example is much of a big deal – but just try doing that with COM!

Debugging

When you're programming for the .NET Framework, cross-language debugging is every bit as easy as cross-language developing. Visual Studio .NET doesn't care which language is 'responsible' for the code being debugged, so long as it's .NET-compliant. Let's set a breakpoint and navigate through the example we just built:

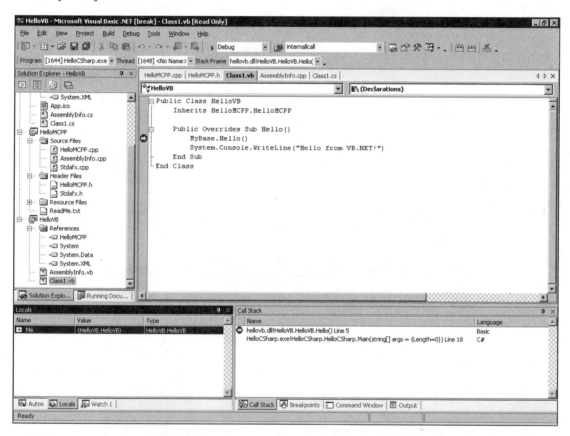

First, we place a breakpoint in the Class1.vb file, where it calls the MyBase.Hello() method. When we run the application in the debugger, it stops exactly where we'd expect. Notice that the **Call Stack** window reports correctly that we're nested within the Main() method of the C# console application. This demonstrates already that Visual Studio can handle a breakpoint outside of the initial application language.

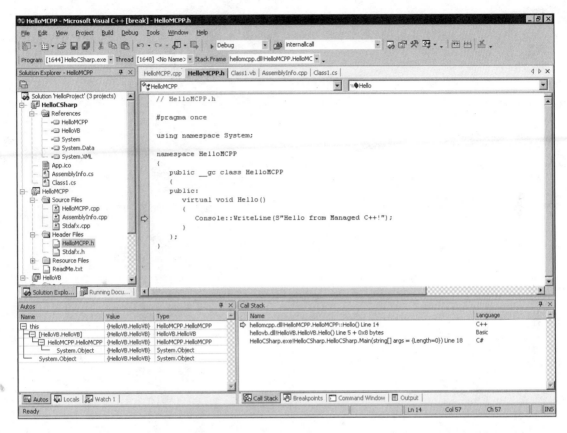

Next, step into the `MyBase.Hello()` method by pressing *F11* or selecting Step Into from the Debug menu. Lo and behold, it displays `HelloMCPP`, our original Visual C++ class. Once again, the Call Stack window describes exactly what's going on.

Even from this simple example, it's clear that the development language chosen by you or the members of your team doesn't matter to Visual Studio .NET's debugging facilities. If you go ahead and play around with the debugger for a while, you'll find that the look and feel of the debugging tools remain constant as well. Multi-language development is now a reality.

Summary

In this chapter, we've introduced the changes that have taken place in Visual C++ .NET, and explained some of the reasons behind them. We've also begun to explore the .NET Framework by examining what makes it such an attractive proposition for developers and users alike, and we've considered the role that C++ has to play in its development.

In the rest of the book, we'll be building on the quick descriptions given here, and we'll explore both .NET and the new features of 'unmanaged' C++ in depth. In the very next chapter, we'll begin that process by looking at the changes that Microsoft has made to C++ in order to make it a good .NET citizen.

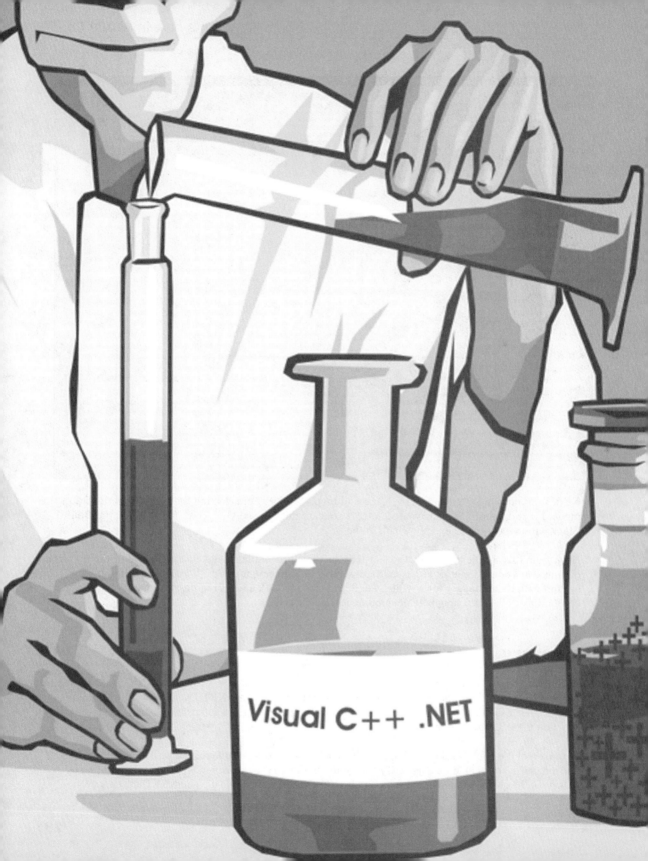

2

Introduction to Managed C++

At this point, we have learned about the Common Language Runtime (CLR), and we've seen an example of cross language compatibility. We have seen that managed code brings the benefits of garbage collection and code security, and the ability to use the .NET Framework class library, among others.

Now it is time to discuss how we can use C++ in the .NET managed environment. Because C++ has been around for a long time, and was developed long before anyone had even dreamed up .NET, clearly it is not designed to target the .NET platform. Microsoft needed to make some additions to the language – these have come in the form of several new keywords known as **Managed Extensions** to Visual C++. These keywords allow us to take advantage of the .NET Framework in our existing and future C++ projects. You'll have to use Managed Extensions if you need to:

- ❑ Migrate existing C++ code to a managed environment
- ❑ Consume .NET Framework classes in your C++ code
- ❑ Allow existing C++ code to be consumed by .NET languages

We'll start this chapter by examining the major factors we need to consider when writing C++ code to target the CLR. In particular, we need to think about what kinds of in-built types we can use, how we create custom types, and how we are going to generate the necessary metadata. The main focus of this chapter, however, will be an in-depth study of the Managed Extensions for C++. By the end of this chapter, you will have enough understanding of this area to begin developing managed C++ applications.

Language interoperability

One of the major goals of the .NET Framework is to enable seamless integration of cross-language components. As we saw in the last chapter, .NET enables components written in different languages to call each other's methods, to pass data, and even to inherit from one another. There are two important factors that enable this to work:

- ❑ Metadata
- ❑ Common Type System

In this section, we'll be examining how the use of metadata and the CTS enable language interoperability, and what the implications are for writing C++ for .NET. We won't look in detail at the Managed Extensions yet, but we'll see why they are important for creating managed, interoperable components.

Metadata

If you have done a lot of COM programming, then you'll be familiar with IDL files and the type libraries they generate. Metadata is a similar concept – it fully describes a type in a language neutral manner. Any language that targets the CLR can consume that type. This means that you can write a class in managed C++, which can be used as a base class for a VB.NET or C# type, or vice versa. Metadata not only enables cross-language component interoperability, but also cross-language inheritance.

Unlike the type library implementation in COM, however, metadata is embedded within the PE (portable execution file) alongside the code that implements the types described by the metadata. With .NET, there is no need to keep separate type libraries and implementation files, which means fewer headaches for the developer. Because the metadata is bundled with the code that depends on it, there is no chance that it can become out of synch with the code.

A third aspect of metadata is its extensibility via attributes: you can actually create your own attributes that will generate custom metadata to provide additional information about your code. We'll see how this works in detail in Chapter 4.

The focus of this chapter is the collection of keywords known as the Managed Extensions for C++. The C++ purist might see these extensions as ugly and unnecessary, but they are absolutely crucial to enable us to specify that a certain class or structure targets the CLR, and also to make that class or structure accessible from code written in other .NET languages.

> **The keywords defined by the Managed Extensions for C++ result in the generation of metadata that fully describes the code in terms the CLR can understand, and therefore allows it to interact with other code written in any other .NET language.**

Common Type System (CTS)

All languages that target the CLR need to use types that conform to the CTS in order to be compatible with other languages. This shared type system enables easy exchange of data between languages; if we want to pass a Double or a String (or even a more complex type) between managed C++ and Visual Basic .NET, we can do so freely, with none of the overhead involved in marshaling between types written in different languages.

> The keywords defined by the Managed Extensions for C++ allow you to write your own types that conform to the CTS, and are therefore interoperable with other .NET languages.

The .NET Framework class library

When writing managed code, we'll need to make use of the set of classes defined by the .NET Framework class library. We'll look at this in a little more detail in Chapter 5, when we see how to use some of the common utility classes, but in order to get started with managed code, it will be useful to take a look at some of the basic data types. Specifically we'll look at the String type, as this is so ubiquitous, we're going to need it as soon as we start writing any kind of managed code.

The table below lists the .NET Framework basic data types that correspond to the C++ primitive types you'll be familiar with:

C++ primitive type	.NET class library type
char	SByte
signed char	SByte
short	Int16
int	Int32
long	Int32
__int64	Int64
unsigned char	Byte
unsigned short	UInt16
unsigned int	UInt32
unsigned long	UInt32
unsigned __int64	UInt64
float	Single
double	Double
void	Void
bool	Bool

The good news here is that, when writing your managed C++ code, you can simply use the C++ primitive version of the type. This is compatible with the CTS, because these types are directly interchangeable with their corresponding .NET Framework type. Care needs to be taken, however, if you are overloading a function with two different C++ types that correspond to the same .NET type. Note that these types are all defined in the System namespace.

Strings

String processing is pervasive throughout most applications. We pass strings to functions, return strings from functions, output strings to files and streams, and so on. Historically, dealing with strings on the Windows platform has been the bane of a programmer's existence, due to the myriad string types that have been introduced over the years. As well as the standard C++ types, we also have LPTSTR, CString, and CComBSTR, to name but a few! In managed code, though, there's only one string type: System::String.

In this section, we'll just stick to using string literals, but we do need to be aware of how to convert between System::String and the unmanaged types we're already familiar with. In Chapter 7, we'll look in more detail at how to marshal between String and the unmanaged string types.

C++ string literal to System::String*

There are two forms of string literals in C++:

❑ Single-byte strings, specified using double quotation marks that enclose the string

❑ Double-byte strings, specified in the same way with the addition of a preceding letter L

In managed C++, String* automatically accepts both forms of the C++ string literal:

```
String* s1 = "Hello World!";
String* s2 = L"Hello World!";

Console::WriteLine("s1 = {0}", s1);
Console::WriteLine("s2 = {0}", s2);

if(s1 == s2)
    Console::WriteLine("s1 and s2 point to a single String instance");
else
    Console::WriteLine("s1 and s2 point to different String instances");
```

Execution of this code results in the following output:

```
s1 = Hello World!
s2 = Hello World!
s1 and s2 point to different String instances
```

The code shown here is an extract from a managed C++ project called Strings, *which is available for download from the Wrox web site, along with the rest of the code for this chapter.*

S string literals

Managed C++ introduces a third form of string literal known as an S string literal. This form is preferred in managed C++ code, since it's more efficient than the single-byte and double-byte string literals. This is because all String instances created from identical S string literals will point to the same instance. Furthermore, all String instances are double-byte Unicode strings, and when initializing from a single-byte string literal, the String constructor will perform a conversion to Unicode, and then copy the string to a new location and maintain a pointer to it. In contrast, when initializing from an S string literal, there is no constructor call and therefore no conversion or copying. Here's an example illustrating the use of S string literals:

```
String* s3 = S"Hello World!";
String* s4 = S"Hello World!";

Console::WriteLine(S"s3 = {0}", s3);
Console::WriteLine(S"s4 = {0}", s4);

if(s3 == s4)
    Console::WriteLine(S"s3 and s4 point to a single String instance");
else
    Console::WriteLine(S"s3 and s4 point to different String instances");
```

Execution of this code results in the following output:

```
s3 = Hello World!
s4 = Hello World!
s3 and s4 point to a single String instance
```

Comparing strings

The String class overrides the Object::Equals() method to provide a comparison of the *values* of the Strings, rather than determining whether two *instances* are the same:

```
if(String::Equals(s1, s2))
    Console::WriteLine(S"Using Equals(), s1 and s2 string values identical");
else
    Console::WriteLine(S"Using Equals(), s1 and s2 string values different");
```

The output here is:

```
Using Equals(), s1 and s2 string values identical
```

Similarly, if you want to perform a value comparison on types you create, you should override the Object::Equals() method.

Another way to compare strings is to use the IComparable interface, which is implemented by String. This interface has only one method, CompareTo():

```
if(0 == s3->CompareTo(s4))
    Console::WriteLine(S"Using CompareTo(), s3 and s4 string values identical");
else
    Console::WriteLine(S"Using CompareTo(), s3 and s4 string values different");
```

The output here is:

Using CompareTo(), s3 and s4 string values identical

IComparable is a standard interface, which should be implemented by types that need to support ordering. CompareTo() returns an integer value, which is positive or negative depending on whether the instance is greater than or less than the value passed for comparison, respectively. If the two values are the same, then CompareTo() returns 0.

> *String also implements ICloneable, IEnumerable, and IConvertible. We'll look at ICloneable shortly, but for full details on all of these interfaces, you should consult the documentation.*

Three common operations that we perform with strings are concatenation, copying, and cloning. The following sections describe the methods that support these operations and how to use them. Be aware, though, that this is just a taster of the support String has for common string handling operations, such as trimming and padding, splitting strings, formatting, and much more.

Concatenation

The String type supports concatenation using the Concat() method:

```
String* s5 = S"Hello";
s5 = String::Concat(s5, S" World", S"!");
Console::WriteLine(S"s5 = {0}", s5);
```

This method is static, and has a number of overloads that allow concatenating String instances together, as well as the string representation of System::Object instances.

Copying

String instances can be copied using Copy(), another static method. This takes the string to be copied as a parameter and returns a new string instance with the same value:

```
Console::WriteLine(S"Copying...");
String* s6 = String::Copy(s5);
Console::WriteLine(S"s6 = {0}", s6);

if(s5 == s6)
    Console::WriteLine(S"s5 and s6 point to a single String instance");
else
    Console::WriteLine(S"s5 and s6 point to different String instances");

// Use static String::Compare() method...
if(0 == String::Compare(s5, s6))
    Console::WriteLine(S"Using Compare(), s5 and s6 string values identical");
else
    Console::WriteLine(S"Using Compare(), s5 and s6 string values different");
```

Execution of this code results in the following output:

```
s5 = Hello World!
Copying...
s6 = Hello World!
s5 and s6 point to different String instances
Using Compare(), s5 and s6 string values identical
```

Note that although the instance returned by Copy() is *distinct* from the instance being copied, the *values* of the two instances are identical.

Cloning

System::String implements the ICloneable interface. This has just one method, Clone(), which takes no parameters, and returns an Object*, a reference to the cloned object:

```
Console::WriteLine(S"Cloning...");
String* s7 = __try_cast<String*>(s6->Clone ());
Console::WriteLine(S"s7 = {0}", s7);

if(s7 == s6)
    Console::WriteLine(S"s6 and s7 point to a single String instance");
else
    Console::WriteLine(S"s6 and s7 point to different String instances");

// Use static String::Compare() method...
if(0 == String::Compare(s7, s6))
    Console::WriteLine(S"Using Compare(), s6 and s7 string values identical");
else
    Console::WriteLine(S"Using Compare(), s6 and s7 string values different");
```

Execution of this code results in the following output:

```
Cloning...
s7 = Hello World!
s6 and s7 point to a single String instance
Using Compare(), s6 and s7 string values identical
```

Unlike the previous example that used Copy(), in the case of Clone(), the same *instance* is returned.

Note that we need to cast the clone reference to a String, as Clone() returns an Object*.
__try_cast<>() is a managed version of the familiar C++ dynamic_cast<>(), and we'll
be looking at it in more detail later on in the chapter.*

The managed environment

In vanilla C++, we have two locations from which to allocate objects: the run-time stack and the heap. Local variables get allocated on the run-time stack, while type instances created with the C++ new operator are allocated on the heap. It is the responsibility of the programmer to delete dynamically allocated instances when they are no longer needed. In COM development, the complexity increases, with the need to implement proper reference counting. Managing object lifetime in this way can cause many difficulties for the developer, such as memory leaks and access violations.

Things are dramatically different in .NET. The CLR implements garbage collection, a scheme that automatically tracks an application's references to an object. As long as the object is being referenced by the application, it lives. When the object is no longer being referenced by the application, it will die, although maybe not immediately. The runtime achieves this by providing an additional location from which to allocate objects: the **managed heap**. The managed heap is similar to the C++ heap – that is, it is a large chunk of memory where type instances are created – but it is under the control of the garbage collector. Only **managed types** can exist on the managed heap.

Managed code and managed data

At this point, it is important to differentiate between **managed data** and **managed code**. Managed code can be written in a number of languages, for example, Visual Basic .NET, C#, or C++. It is compiled to IL (Intermediate Language) and is executed on the CLR. As we learned in the last chapter, the CLR uses metadata to provide important services such as exception handling, security, automatic life management, and more. Managed C++ is an annotated subset of C++ that compiles to target the CLR and can take advantage of these run-time features. Unmanaged code is the traditional native x86 code found in your pre-.NET applications, as well as in Win32 OS libraries. This includes native C/C++ code, as well as COM components. It has no notion of the .NET runtime, and does not need it to run, nor can it take advantage of its services directly.

Managed data is under the control of the garbage collector. In the managed world, all dynamically allocated memory from the managed heap is managed data. All objects must be self-describing; the garbage collector must be able to examine the metadata at runtime and be able to discover the exact type of the object, as well as verify that none of the operations performed on this data violate or corrupt memory. The layout of managed data is automatically provided by the CLR, but can be modified via metadata (for example with the StructLayout attribute, which we will see in Chapter 4). The lifetime of managed data is also managed by the CLR.

Allocations on the managed heap are faster than those on the C++ heap, and almost as fast as allocation from the run-time stack. This is due to the structure and layout of the managed heap, which is simply a contiguous block of memory with a base pointer and a pointer to the next free memory address to be used when allocating the next object. Each time an object is allocated, the pointer to the next free memory address is incremented accordingly. Contrast this to the operation of the unmanaged heap, in which the heap must be walked searching for a suitably sized block of memory. It goes without saying that as long as memory is available on the managed heap, allocation will succeed. Garbage collection takes place to compact the working set of memory and maximize the available memory on the managed heap. The mechanics of this process should be seamless to the programmer, but it's worth taking a look at this process in more detail, as it helps us gain a better understanding of the managed environment.

Garbage collection

When the remaining unused memory on the managed heap is insufficient to satisfy an allocation request, a garbage collection will occur. Any application reference to a managed type instance allocated on the managed heap is known as a root. The runtime tracks all roots for each type. During a collection, the runtime builds a graph of all reachable objects allocated on the heap from the application's roots. (By *reachable*, we mean an object that still has a reference to it elsewhere in the application.) If it finds an object that is not reachable, that object is a candidate for compaction. If during the course of a collection enough unreachable objects are discovered, each reachable object will be relocated in managed heap memory. Once compaction is complete, the application's roots are updated to reflect the relocation of the objects. This means that we can't use ordinary C++ pointers to reference data in the managed heap: the memory addresses will change. Instead, we need to use **managed pointers**, whose addresses are updated automatically. These are discussed later in this chapter.

The garbage collection algorithm uses a technique called generations to organize all objects into separate regions of the managed heap based on how many garbage collections they have survived. Each time an object makes it through a garbage collection unscathed, it's promoted into the next generation. The .NET garbage collection algorithm uses three generations – 0, 1, and 2 – where new objects are allocated from generation 0. Subsequent collections will promote any surviving objects to generation 1. Objects that have been around the longest end up in generation 2, and stay there until they are no longer reachable from an application's roots. Generations help garbage collection performance because during a collection of a generation, only that generation's region will be considered for compaction, rather than the entire heap.

Reference types and value types

If we want to create our own types that are automatically under the control of the garbage collector, then we need to write C++ code to target the CLR.

> **The keywords defined by the Managed Extensions for C++ allow you to create managed types that are capable of being allocated on the managed heap.**

All .NET types that are garbage collected – whether user-defined or from the Framework class library – exist on the managed heap. They are all **reference types**, and we access them via **managed pointers**.

If the data type is just very small and short-lived, however, it may not make sense to allocate it on the managed heap – garbage collection would just be too costly. In this case, the type may be allocated on the run-time stack, and it is referred to as a **value type**.

The .NET Framework classes that represent the C++ primitive classes fall into this category; they are all value types. String, on the other hand, is a far more complex type, and is defined as a reference type. There are special keywords to specify whether your code is a garbage-collected type or a value type, and we'll be looking at these in detail later on.

Creating managed code

In order to make your code run on the CLR and to give your code access to the .NET Framework classes, you need to make use of some new compiler options that themselves form a subset of the Managed Extensions.

Compiler options

To specify that your C++ code should be compiled to MSIL, rather than to native executable code, you should add the /clr option to the list of those used. This option makes your code compile into an assembly. We'll be looking at assemblies in detail in the next chapter, but for now it's not unreasonable to think of them as being like DLLs, which contain metadata in addition to compiled code. The assembly is dependent on the CLR being present at runtime, but it doesn't automatically mean that it will contain managed data. Managed types must be explicitly marked as such – we'll see how to do this shortly.

The screenshot below shows this option being set in the Project | Properties dialog box; if you use one of the wizards to create your project, it will have been set for you automatically:

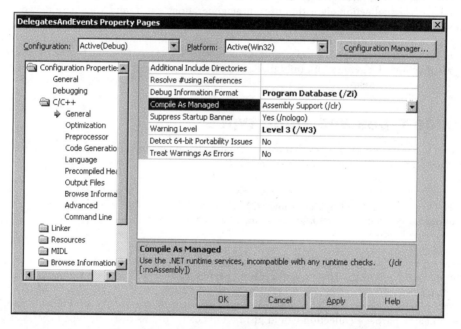

Another new compiler option, /Fu, can be used as a substitute for the #using preprocessor directive, which we'll look at more closely in a moment. It forces the compiler to reference the metadata in the file that you specify. If you need to reference multiple files, you need one occurrence of the option for each file:

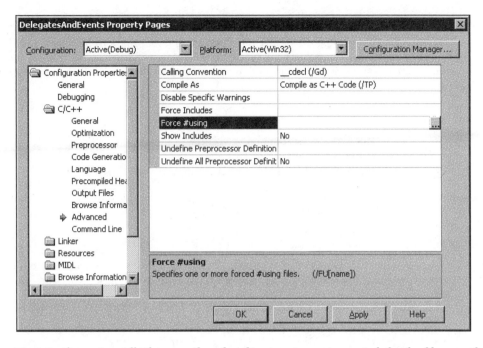

The /AI compiler option tells the compiler what directory to use in a search for the files specified by /Fu (or #using). Again, the option only allows one path to be specified, so if you need to search multiple paths, you will need to use multiple occurrences:

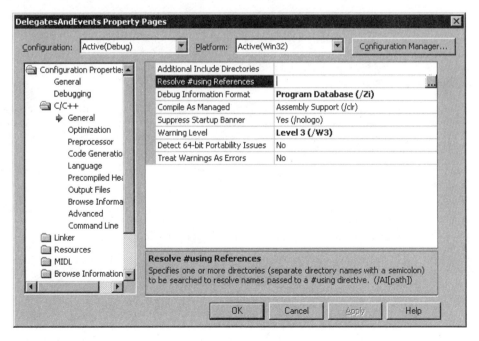

#using preprocessor directive

C++ programmers have been using the #include directive in their programs for years, and C++ COM programmers are now almost as familiar with #import. The Managed Extensions for C++ add a new preprocessor directive – #using – which is used to make the types defined in other assemblies accessible in the current program:

```
#using <mscorlib.dll>
```

The code snippet above shows the most common invocation of the #using directive – it's being used to import the metadata from mscorlib.dll. This DLL defines the core types used by managed applications, and a reference to it is required by all but the most trivial managed C++ code.

If you use the Visual C++ .NET wizard to generate a managed C++ project for you, you'll see that this line is automatically added to the main .cpp file of the application.

Simple example

Let's put the things we've looked at so far into context by taking a very simple, unmanaged C++ application and converting it to a managed application. You can probably just about work out what this program does:

```
#include <iostream>

int main(void)
{
    std::cout << "Hello World!" << std::endl;
    return 0;
}
```

Assuming that you created it initially as an unmanaged console application in Visual Studio .NET, it's fairly simple to convert this program so that it runs as a managed C++ application. In fact, if you create an empty new managed C++ project, and add this .cpp file to it, then it should compile and run straight away, as managed code.

Alternatively, you can change an unmanaged project to a managed one by adding the /clr flag, as discussed above. However, in this case, there are some incompatibility problems that arise when using some existing compiler options together with /clr. If you have specified any of the options listed in the table below, then you may need to disable or change these in order to compile your application as managed code:

Compiler option	Compatibility issues with .NET
/RTC, /RTCc, /RTCs, /RTCu, /RTC1	The run-time checks are unneeded in managed code because the CLR already does the checks for you. (The compiler currently doesn't support it for some unmanaged functions in a managed module.)
/Gm	Enables minimal rebuilds and causes the compiler to track dependencies. However, the method it uses to do this is incompatible with that of the #using directive.
/ZI	Enables the 'edit and continue' debugging feature, which is not supported by the CLR.

Compiler option	Compatibility issues with .NET
/MLd, /ML	Directs the compiler to link with the single-threaded version of the C runtime library. Needs to be changed to a multi-threaded version (/MTd, /MDd, /MT, /MD), because all .NET applications are inherently multithreaded.
/GL	This directive causes the linker to further optimize the code by inlining across modules (.obj files), a task that in .NET is left to the JIT engine.
/Zd	This produces COFF style debugging information, which the .NET runtime doesn't support.

Finally, once compiler option incompatibilities are dealt with, we can simply rebuild the project, and the resulting .exe file will be compiled into an assembly, containing IL and metadata, which will run on the CLR. Note that we have made no changes to code at all to achieve this. The application is now managed.

Let's now convert the use of std::cout to a call to its .NET Framework equivalent – that is, the System::Console::WriteLine() method. All managed applications that use managed types must reference mscorlib.dll; we can make our code do this by including a #using directive:

```
#using <mscorlib.dll>

int main(void)
{
    System::Console::WriteLine(S"Hello World!");
    return 0;
}
```

Our application now uses the #using preprocessor directive to import the types included in the mscorlib.dll module, and it executes on the CLR, but it's not a terribly impressive demonstration of what managed code has to offer. To start doing some more advanced programming with managed C++, it's time we looked in more depth into the Managed Extensions for C++.

Using Managed Extensions

The rest of this chapter is focused around the new keywords introduced by the Managed Extensions for C++. All of the keywords are easily identifiable, because they all start with a double underscore (__). We'll look at how to use these keywords to declare and use different reference types, including classes, interfaces, arrays, and pointers. After that, we'll move on to the various value types and look at the boxing technique, which is used to pass value types in the place of reference types. Towards the end of this section, we'll see how to handle managed exceptions and how to use managed C++ for properties, delegates, and events.

__gc types

At the beginning of this chapter, we talked at length about what is meant by managed code and data, and the workings of the garbage collector. We saw the need for a separate managed heap to allow the garbage collector to do its job, and the conditions that it necessarily places upon us. Now, we're going to consider how to use C++ to create objects on the managed heap – objects that the CLR will manage on our behalf.

The Managed Extensions for C++ introduce the notion of __**gc types** – garbage-collected types. There is no need to delete these types – the CLR looks after their lifetime management. If we want our types to be consumed by other CLR-compatible languages, we need to declare them using __gc.

Visual C++ .NET allows the creation of four different __gc types:

❑ Classes

❑ Structures

❑ Interfaces

❑ Pointers

Classes and structures

There are several differences between unmanaged C++ classes and __gc classes, but the main two are that the latter are garbage collected and can only derive from one other class. Multiple implementation inheritance is not supported in __gc classes, although they may implement any number of __gc interfaces. If no other base class is specified, then a __gc class or structure will inherit implicitly from System::Object.

> **System::Object is the base class for all classes in .NET.**

This means that an Object* can be thought of as the managed equivalent of void*, since a pointer to any managed type can be up-cast to Object* (we saw this earlier in our string example). Let's take a look at the members of System::Object, since all .NET classes inherit these methods:

Member name	Access	Description
Equals	public	Virtual method that performs comparison of this instance to another instance. By default, it performs reference comparison – returning true if both instances are actually the same instance. Can be overridden to provide a value comparison if needed. Also provided as a static method that takes two object parameters.
GetHashCode	public	Returns an integer used as a hash value by some of the System.Collection classes. We'll see more of these in Chapter 5.

Member name	Access	Description
GetType	public	Returns a Type instance that describes the run-time type of this object instance. We'll see more of this, along with the __typeof keyword, in Chapter 4.
ReferenceEquals	public	Static method that takes two object parameters and determines whether they actually reference the same object instance. This is necessary if the Equals() method is overridden to provide value comparison.
ToString	public	Virtual method that can be overridden to provide a user-friendly text string representation of the object instance.
Finalize	protected	Plays a part in garbage collection. This method is discussed in more detail later on.
MemberwiseClone	protected	Performs a shallow copy of the instance. This method is discussed in more detail later on.

A __gc class or structure can be declared by preceding the keyword class or struct with __gc:

```
__gc struct SomeStruct
{
};

__gc class SomeClass
{
};
```

There are a few constraints on the kinds of data members that a __gc class may contain. It is perfectly legal for a data member to be a pointer to an unmanaged type, but it can't be an instance of an unmanaged type, except for the POD types, which have equivalent .NET classes defined, as described in the table earlier.

Construction

All garbage-collected types must be created on the managed heap using the __gc new operator:

```
SomeStruct* somestruct = __gc new SomeStruct;
SomeClass* someclass = new SomeClass;              // Implicit __gc new
```

The second line here demonstrates that it's not actually necessary to include the __gc keyword – if the type being instantiated is a __gc type, then the compiler will automatically invoke the __gc new operator. There is no 'placement' version of the __gc new operator, which makes sense because the type is allocated on the managed heap, and we are prevented from knowing its exact memory location – such things are left to the control of the CLR.

Static class constructors

Like any other C++ class, __gc classes can define a constructor. In managed C++, this is known as an **instance constructor**, since all instances will invoke this constructor when instantiated. Something new for C++ programmers is the **static class constructor**, which will only be called once, before the first instance of its type is constructed. This might be useful in situations where all instances of a class share some resource that needs to be initialized only once, such as a file, but prior to any instances being created. The shared resource could be initialized in the static constructor ready for use by new instances. This is where we should initialize all static class members:

```
__gc class SomeClass
{
public:
    static SomeClass()
    {
        Console::WriteLine(S"In static class constructor");
        m_lInstanceCount = 0;
    }

    SomeClass()
    {
        m_lInstanceCount++;
        m_lInstance = m_lInstanceCount;
        Console::WriteLine(S"In instance {0} constructor. Total instances = {1}",
                        m_lInstance.ToString(), m_lInstanceCount.ToString());
    }

private:
    static long m_lInstanceCount;
    long m_lInstance;
};

int _tmain(void)
{
    SomeClass* pA1 = new SomeClass;
    SomeClass* pA2 = new SomeClass;
    SomeClass* pA3 = new SomeClass;
    return 0;
}
```

Note that although the static member, m_lInstanceCount, is declared as a C++ long type, we can still call ToString() on this type, because it is treated as a System::Int32 type in managed code and therefore inherits all the methods of System::Object.

Execution of the above code results in the following output, demonstrating that the static constructor executes just once, prior to the execution of the instance constructors:

```
In static class constructor
In instance 1 constructor. Total instances = 1
In instance 2 constructor. Total instances = 2
In instance 3 constructor. Total instances = 3
```

Copying objects

__gc classes follow a different form of copy semantics from traditional C++ classes. A __gc class *cannot* define a copy constructor. This is because the .NET runtime does not support the notion of copy constructors, and if you implemented them, your classes would not be able to be used by languages other than managed C++. Instead, we can use the MemberwiseClone() method of System::Object to perform a shallow copy of the object.

Recall that a shallow copy performs a bit-wise copy of all data members. For example, instance A has a member m_p, which points to instance C. If we perform a shallow copy of instance A to instance B, the m_p members of both instances A and B point to C. In unmanaged C++, the default copy constructor performs shallow copy semantics, and the developer can provide an implementation of the copy constructor that performs deep-copy semantics, which in our example would result in instance B's m_p member pointing to a copy of instance C.

In managed C++, things work differently. MemberwiseClone() cannot be overridden, and it's a protected method, which means that it can only be called from code within System::Object itself or from a deriving class. It's therefore impossible for *client* code to use it to make a copy of the object. Instead, the .NET Framework provides a different copying paradigm from that of the C++ copy constructor. If you want to allow copying of your objects, you should implement the ICloneable interface, which defines one member: a method named Clone().

Continuing with our SomeClass example, we can make the class cloneable by having it implement the ICloneable interface:

```
__gc class SomeClass : public ICloneable
{
public:
    // Code removed for brevity
    Object* Clone()
    {
        Console::WriteLine( S"Cloning instance {0}. Total instances = {1}",
                m_lInstance.ToString(), (++m_lInstanceCount).ToString());
        return MemberwiseClone();    // Shallow copy
    }
    // Code removed for brevity
};
```

In order to test this Clone() method, we need to override the Object::Equals() method:

```
    bool Equals(Object* o)
    {
        return (this->m_lInstance == static_cast<SomeClass*>(o)->m_lInstance);
    }
```

We can test this with the following code:

```
    SomeClass* pA4 = __try_cast<SomeClass*>(pA3->Clone());
    if (pA3->Equals(pA4))
    {
        Console::WriteLine(S"Shallow copy successul");
    }
```

The SomeClass implementation of the Clone() method simply calls the MemberwiseClone() method, which performs a shallow copy of the object and returns a __gc pointer to the cloned object instance.

Suppose we had a class that needed deep-copy semantics. We could implement deep-copy semantics in the Clone() method as the following example shows:

```
#using <mscorlib.dll>
using namespace System;

__gc class DeepCopy : public ICloneable
{
public:

    Object* Clone()
    {
        DeepCopy* p = new DeepCopy();
        if ( m_p != NULL )
        {
            // deep-copy
            p->m_p = static_cast<DeepCopy*>(m_p->Clone());
        }
        return p;
    }
    DeepCopy*   m_p;
};
```

The DeepCopy class implements ICloneable and thus supports cloning. In this case, however, its implementation of the Clone() method performs deep-copy semantics by cloning the instance pointed to by its member m_p. Here is the code that tests our DeepCopy class:

```
int _tmain (int argc, _TCHAR* argv[])
{
    DeepCopy* dcC = new DeepCopy();
    DeepCopy* dcA = new DeepCopy();
    dcA->m_p = dcC;

    DeepCopy* dcB = static_cast<DeepCopy*>(dcA->Clone());

    if ( ! Object::ReferenceEquals(dcB->m_p, dcC) )
    {
        Console::WriteLine(S"Deep copy successul");
    }
    return 0;
}
```

Destruction

Just as in unmanaged code, classes in managed C++ can declare a destructor. You might question why you would need to write a destructor – doesn't the runtime clear up all memory for us? The answer is that you still need to implement a destructor to clean up any resources that the garbage collector won't, such as closing connections to files, and so on.

Unlike unmanaged C++, however, the destructor is called during garbage collection, and so exactly when this happens is unpredictable. The programmer can force destruction by using delete, but although this calls the destructor, the memory isn't freed until garbage collection. This technique can be useful when you want to ensure that the destructor code is executed at a specific time, rather than waiting until it's garbage-collected. Note that if you want to call delete on a managed object instance, you *must* define a destructor or the compiler will emit an error.

When a managed object is 'collected' by the garbage collector, the destructor is not *actually* called. Rather, the garbage collector calls a method called Finalize(). However, in the case of Visual C++ .NET, this Finalize() method is generated by the compiler and performs whatever action is specified in the real destructor. The compiler also adds code to call the Finalize() method of any base object. It's important to note that we can't define the Finalize() method ourselves – it is generated by the compiler. The developer needs to provide any necessary implementation in the form of a C++ destructor.

The following sample code continues the previous example, and illustrates how destructors get called via delete and the garbage collector:

```
__gc class SomeClass : public ICloneable
{
public:
    // Code removed for brevity

    ~SomeClass()
    {
       m_lInstanceCount--;
       Console::WriteLine(S"In instance {0} destructor. Total instances = {1}.",
                    m_lInstance.ToString(), m_lInstanceCount.ToString());
    }

    // Code removed for brevity
};

int _tmain(void)
{
    // code removed for brevity

    Console::WriteLine(S"Removing reference to instance 1");
    pA1 = 0;

    Console::WriteLine(S"Forcing Garbage Collection");
    GC::Collect();

    Console::WriteLine(S"Deleting remaining instances");
    delete pA2;
    delete pA3;
    delete pA4;

    return 0;
}
```

We remove the reference to the first instance by setting pA1 to point to 0 – this means the first instance is available for garbage collection. We can force garbage collection to happen by invoking System::GC::Collect(). Finally, we delete the remaining instances.

Forcing garbage collection is a potentially expensive proposition, and should rarely be performed. We do it here simply to demonstrate the principles of destruction as applied to managed types.

Execution of this code results in the following output:

```
In static class constructor
In instance 1 constructor. Total instances = 1
In instance 2 constructor. Total instances = 2
In instance 3 constructor. Total instances = 3
Cloning instance 3. Total instances = 4
Shallow copy successful
Deep copy successful
Removing reference to instance 1
Forcing Garbage Collection
Deleting remaining instances
In instance 2 destructor. Total instances = 2
In instance 3 destructor. Total instances = 1
In instance 3 destructor. Total instances = 0
In instance 1 destructor. Total instances = 3
```

What is really interesting about the output is the sequence of the last few lines of output during destruction, which seems to be out of order from what we would expect. The destructor output for instance 1 appears last in the output even though we forced a garbage collection prior to deleting the remaining instances. This is because the garbage collector is performing finalization on a separate thread than the main thread of execution, and, therefore, the ordering of the output for the destruction of instance 1 may vary.

Abstract classes

The creation of abstract classes in *unmanaged* C++ revolves around pure virtual methods that prevent a class from being instantiated – such classes can only be used as base classes. In managed C++, this implicit creation of abstract classes is made explicit by the __abstract keyword, which states quite clearly that the class or struct it's attached to cannot be instantiated.

Using the __abstract keyword doesn't prevent us from declaring virtual and pure virtual methods in a class; nor does it imply that a class is garbage collected. Here's a simple example of the keyword in action:

```
__abstract class MyAbstractClass
{
public:
    virtual void Foo()
    {
        Console::WriteLine(S"In MyAbstractClass::Foo()");
    };
};

class MyConcreteClass : public MyAbstractClass
{
public:
    void Foo()
    {
        Console::WriteLine(S"In MyConcreteClass::Foo()");
    };
};
```

This code declares a class called MyAbstractClass that defines a virtual member function called Foo(). It then declares a second class, MyConcreteClass, derived from MyAbstractClass, which overrides the virtual method. This is perfectly ordinary C++ behavior, and were it not for the new keyword, it would be possible to instantiate both classes.

Because MyAbstractClass was declared using the __abstract keyword, however, it *isn't* possible to instantiate it directly. Any attempt to do so will result in an error at compile time. It's worth noting, though, that declaring a class to be abstract in this fashion allows you to write default implementations for *all* the methods of an abstract class, something that's not possible using unmanaged C++'s pure virtual syntax. Note that __abstract can only be applied to a __gc class or interface.

Sealed classes

Whereas an abstract class cannot be instantiated (and therefore *must* always be derived from), a sealed class (declared with the keyword __sealed) *must not* be used as a base class. Conceptually speaking, __sealed is the opposite of __abstract. Here's a simple example of using the __sealed keyword:

```
__sealed __gc class MyNonDerivableClass
{
};
```

MyNonDerivableClass may not be a base to any other class. For example, given the following code:

```
class Derived1 : public MyNonDerivableClass
{
};
```

The compiler will emit the following error message:

error C3246: 'Derived1' : cannot inherit from 'MyNonDerivableClass' as it has been declared as '__sealed'

The __sealed keyword can also be used to prevent deriving classes from overriding non-pure virtual methods of managed classes. This might prove useful in cases where you are deriving from a base class that exposes one or more virtual methods that you want to override *and* you want to prevent future deriving classes from overriding these methods further. It is rare that you would need to use this in practice. __sealed can only be applied to __gc classes.

Interfaces

The __interface keyword allows us to declare an **interface** – effectively, a structure comprising *only* pure virtual functions that can be implemented by deriving classes. So, why do we need this new keyword? A common idiom in unmanaged C++ is to declare an interface by declaring a class with only pure virtual functions. As with most of the other new keywords, the reason is more than just making a C++ idiom an explicit part of the language. When we declare an **interface** using the __interface keyword, the compiler emits metadata describing the interface. This means that other .NET compatible languages and code can then use the interface.

We can declare an interface using syntax like this:

```
__interface IBasicIntegerMath
{
    int Add(int x, int y);
    int Subtract(int x, int y);
    bool LessThan(int x, int y);
};
```

This declares an interface named `IBasicIntegerMath`, each method of which is implicitly public and pure virtual. We can't declare interface members with any access specifier other than `public`. You could add the "= 0" syntax, but it's unnecessary, since the methods are pure virtual by default. Similarly, it's legal to use the __abstract keyword, but there's nothing to gain. To use the interface, you need only derive from it, and implement the pure virtual functions:

```
class CIntegerCalculator: public IBasicIntegerMath
{
public:
    // Implement IBasicIntegerMath
    int Add(int x, int y) {return (x + y);}
    int Subtract(int x, int y) {return (x - y);}
    bool LessThan(int x, int y) {return (x < y);}
};
```

Interfaces can't contain declarations of classes or structures, but they *can* contain __value enum declarations, which we'll cover in the *__value types* section later in the chapter. Equally, they can contain neither data members nor static members, though they *may* include property declarations, which we'll cover in the *Properties* section.

If we have a class that implements several interfaces, sometimes we might find that two or more interfaces declare a method that has the same signature in each of the interfaces. This results in an ambiguity, so we need to qualify each member declaration/definition with the interface identifier. In the calling code, we need to cast the object reference to the appropriate interface to avoid an ambiguous call.

Pointers

On being confronted with the .NET Framework, C++ programmers tend to fall into two camps. One camp will ask, "With all the hype about the garbage collector handling memory allocation and de-allocation for us, why do we need pointers at all?" The other camp is asking, "Cool, a managed heap; how can we get a pointer into the thing and play around?"

Unfortunately, both are going to be somewhat disappointed. The first camp will probably have realized already that in Managed Extensions, *every* managed type is accessed via a pointer. Secondly, since we'll eventually be dealing with interoperability between the unmanaged and managed worlds, we will definitely need to continue to use pointers, to some extent at least.

As for the second camp, it's a simple fact that Manage Extensions places constraints on pointers into the managed heap and strictly controls how pointers to managed objects are declared and used.

__gc*

All the managed types you've seen so far have been declared and accessed via pointers, and, in fact, this is true for the majority of the managed types you'll encounter. What may not have been quite so clear, though, is that the pointers we've been using were *not* ordinary C++ pointers. Because managed objects are allocated on the managed heap, we need __gc pointers (or managed pointers) to point to them.

As with the __gc new operator, the Visual C++ .NET compiler automatically detects when you're creating a pointer to a managed type and produces __gc pointers as and when appropriate – that's why you haven't seen any deviations from standard C++ syntax. It's quite possible, though, to specify much more clearly that you're using __gc pointers:

```
CLivesOnManagedHeap __gc* pManagedHeapObject;
pManagedHeapObject = __gc new CLivesOnManagedHeap;
pManagedHeapObject->m_s = S"This is fun!";
```

The first two lines here simply declare a pointer to a managed class of type CLivesOnManagedHeap and set it equal to the address of a new instance of CLivesOnManagedHeap, as returned by the __gc new operator. We then use the pManagedHeapObject variable to assign a string to the m_s member of the CLivesOnManagedHeap instance.

The compiler assumes that a pointer to a managed type is automatically a __gc pointer, and that a pointer to an unmanaged type is automatically a __nogc pointer. The only way to get a __nogc pointer to a managed type is by pinning the __gc pointer. We'll discuss pinning in more detail in Chapter 7.

__gc* __gc*

It is possible to have a __gc pointer to a __gc pointer – it just means that the top level pointer points to another __gc pointer on the managed heap. Usually, this will be a sub-object of a managed object. The code shown below illustrates this:

```
// Declare a __gc* __gc*
CLivesOnManagedHeap __gc* __gc* p;

// Point the pointer to a __gc pointer sub-object
p = &(pManagedHeapObject->m_pObj);

// Point the pointer on the heap to the object on the heap
*p = pManagedHeapObject;
```

The first line declares the pointer to a pointer, called p, and initializes it to zero. Don't be concerned that we haven't set the pointer to zero (or that we didn't do so in the last example) – the compiler automatically initializes __gc pointers to zero. The next line sets p to the address of the m_pObj member of the object that pManagedHeapObject points to. The last line points the m_pObj member to the object pointed to by pManagedHeapObject. In effect, the object's m_pObj pointer points back on the object itself.

Address-of

When taking the address of a type instance, the resulting pointer *might* point into the managed heap, in which case the pointer is a __gc pointer. Alternatively, it may point to an instance that was allocated outside the managed heap – on the stack or the unmanaged heap – in which case the pointer is a __nogc pointer.

A __nogc pointer can automatically be converted to a __gc pointer. This allows a __gc pointer to point to any type, wherever it was allocated. The garbage collector ignores any __gc pointers that don't point into the managed heap, so letting __gc pointers point to __nogc instances is not a problem.

Casting

Standard C++ provides the following casts to handle situations where one type needs to be converted to another:

- ❑ static_cast<>()
- ❑ dynamic_cast<>()
- ❑ reinterpret_cast<>()
- ❑ const_cast<>()

The semantics of these four casts are not changed by the introduction of managed C++, although there's a new issue with reinterpret_cast<>() that we'll look at in a moment. In addition to these four, though, the Managed Extensions for C++ provide the __try_cast<>() operator.

__try_cast

The __try_cast<>() operator is an alternative (perhaps even a replacement) to dynamic_cast<>(). As you know, the latter performs a run-time check when casting, in order to ensure that the conversion being attempted is possible. It returns zero (a null pointer) if the cast can't be made. __try_cast<>() has the same basic functionality, with the important difference that in the case of failure it will throw a System::InvalidCastException exception. Exceptions are the standard mechanism for handling error conditions in managed code, so it makes sense to use __try_cast<>() in place of dynamic_cast<>():

```
CLivesOnManagedHeap* pManagedHeapObject = new CLivesOnManagedHeap;

try
{
    // Up-cast
    Object* pObj = __try_cast<Object*>(pManagedHeapObject);

    // Down-cast
    pManagedHeapObject = __try_cast<CLivesOnManagedHeap*>(pObj);
}
catch(InvalidCastException* e)
{
    Console::WriteLine(e->Message);
}
```

The above sample should work without complaint, but the next listing contains an unsafe cast, which will cause an exception to be thrown:

```
CLivesOnManagedHeap* pManagedHeapObject = new CLivesOnManagedHeap;

try
{
    // Unsafe down-cast, not allowed. pObj doesn't point to a CLivesOnManagedHeap
    Object* pObj = new Object;
```

```
        pManagedHeapObject = __try_cast<CLivesOnManagedHeap*>(pObj);
        Console::WriteLine(S"__try_cast<CLivesOnManagedHeap*>(pObj) succeeded.");
    }
    catch(InvalidCastException* e)
    {
        Console::WriteLine(e->Message);
    }
```

Executing this code results in the output:

```
Specified cast is not valid
```

Using exception handling like this can save us from the sizable if structures that can be involved with checking for null pointers when using dynamic_cast<>().

reinterpret_cast

In unmanaged C++, the reinterpret_cast<>() operator can be used to cast between apparently unrelated types, such as integers and pointers. It retains this functionality in managed C++, with the proviso that reinterpret_cast<>() *won't* allow us to remove the __gc-ness of a __gc pointer, even when casting from a pointer to an integer type. For example, we can't do this:

```
// Declare a pointer to a Byte
Byte* pb;

// Convert from Byte __gc* to integer
UInt32 nn = reinterpret_cast<UInt32>(pb);
```

Here, we're trying to convert from a reference type to a value type, and the compiler will issue the following error:

error C2440: 'reinterpret_cast' : cannot convert from 'unsigned char __gc *' to 'unsigned int'
Cannot cast a __gc pointer to an integral type

References

Managed Extensions allow the use of references to __gc objects. It can sometimes be more convenient to use references than to use pointers, and it's up to programmers to decide what they would like to use in a particular situation. References to __gc objects follow the same rules as standard C++ references; as one would expect, taking the address of a __gc reference results in a __gc pointer.

Arrays

The Managed Extensions provide a garbage-collected array type. This can be extremely useful; it provides many methods for manipulating and getting information from arrays. Functionality includes sorting, searching, and copying, and information about the array, such as the length, the type, the bounds, and so on, is easily accessible via a set of GetXXX() methods. This makes managed arrays very straightforward to work with. Managed arrays also support multiple dimensions.

Before we get going, it's worth taking a quick look at how to declare a standard, no-frills C++ array in managed code. To do this, we use __nogc in the array declaration:

```
char ch_array __nogc [5] = {'A', 'B', 'C', 'D', 'E'};
```

To declare a managed array, the syntax is similar to C++ (in that the array brackets follow the identifier), but the size is specified in the call to __gc new, or by the number of elements in the initializer list. The following code declares a managed array of type System::Char, initialized using an initializer list:

```
Char c1 __gc [] = {'A', 'B', 'C', 'D', 'E'};
```

Although we explicitly used __nogc and __gc in the above examples, it's not strictly necessary because the compiler will determine whether the array should be managed or unmanaged based on the type of the array elements.

Usage

Here's an example of declaring an array of String pointers:

```
String* s1[] = {S"This", S" is", S" a", S" string", S" array.\n"};
for(int i = 0; i < s1->Length; i++)
{
    Console::Write(s1[i]);
}
```

Notice here that we didn't include '__gc' in the array declaration. Because the array is of type String* – a managed type – the array is managed by default. After initializing the array, we output each element to the console in a for loop, using Write() rather than WriteLine() in order to suppress undesirable carriage returns.

System::Array

Any managed array that you create is an object derived from System::Array, which provides a number of methods for array manipulation. Above, we've used the Length property and the [] operator to iterate over the elements in the array. Also notice that specifying an array index for managed arrays is not the same as for unmanaged arrays. In unmanaged arrays, the array variable can be treated as a pointer to the first element in the array, and so pointer arithmetic can be used to access the elements in the array as offsets from the base pointer. This is not true for managed arrays.

Array contains methods for sorting, searching, and obtaining information regarding the size characteristics of the array, such as the upper bound, lower bound, and number of elements in the array. You should consult the documentation for a full list. One common function that we might like to perform is to copy one or more elements from one array to another; Array provides the Copy() method for just this purpose:

```
String* s2[] = {S"Wrox", S"Professional", S"Visual C++ .NET"};
String* s3[] = new String*[s2->Length];
Array::Copy(s2, s3, 3);
```

The above code declares and initializes an array of String pointers called s2. It then creates a new empty array, called s3, which is equal in size to s2. Finally, it uses the Copy() method to copy three elements from s2 to s3. We can display the results of the copy using the following function:

```
void DumpArrayElements(Array* a)
{
    for(int i = 0; i < a->Length; i++)
    {
        Console::WriteLine(S"a[{0}] = {1}", i.ToString(), a->GetValue(i));
    }
}
```

The DumpArrayElements() function takes a single Array* argument. It uses a simple for loop to iterate over the array's elements and output them to the console – but note that this function can *only* handle one-dimensional arrays. Also note that instead of using the more traditional array notation for element access, the GetValue() method must be used to access elements in the array. This is because we can't do pointer arithmetic with array indexes, as we do in unmanaged code, to loop through an array. Passing the s3 array to the DumpArrayElements() function results in the following output:

```
a[0] = Wrox
a[1] = Professional
a[2] = Visual C++ .NET
```

> *System::Array implements several interfaces, one of which is the IList interface that we'll look at later in Chapter 5.*

Arrays of arrays

It's possible to create a managed array whose elements are also arrays, by using an array of Object* as the topmost array, and then assigning each sub-array to an element of the Object* array. Here's an example of this technique:

```
Object* object_array[] = new System::Object*[2];

String* planets[] = {S"Mercury", S"Venus",  S"Earth",   S"Mars",   S"Jupiter",
                     S"Saturn",  S"Uranus", S"Neptune", S"Pluto", S"Wrox"};

Int32 moons[] = {0, 0, 1, 2, 16, 18, 21, 8, 1, 100};

object_array[0] = planets;
object_array[1] = moons;
```

The above code declares an array that's capable of holding two Object*. It then declares a String* array, called planets, which contains the names of our Solar System's nine planets, plus a recently discovered rogue planet called "Wrox". Next, an Int32 array called moons is declared and initialized with the count of each planet's moons, paired by index. Finally, the planets and moons arrays are stored in the object_array.

We can use the `DumpArrayElements()` function we defined earlier to display the array elements to the console:

```
DumpArrayElements(object_array);
DumpArrayElements(__try_cast<Array*>(object_array[0]));
DumpArrayElements(__try_cast<Array*>(object_array[1]));
```

Executing this code results in the following output, which also shows that the elements of the `object_array` are actually arrays themselves, and that the `Array::ToString()` method displays a string representation of the type of the array:

```
a[0] = System.String[]
a[1] = System.Int32[]

a[0] = Mercury
a[1] = Venus
a[2] = Earth
a[3] = Mars
a[4] = Jupiter
a[5] = Saturn
a[6] = Uranus
a[7] = Neptune
a[8] = Pluto
a[9] = Wrox

a[0] = 0
a[1] = 0
a[2] = 1
a[3] = 2
a[4] = 16
a[5] = 18
a[6] = 21
a[7] = 8
a[8] = 1
a[9] = 100
```

Multidimensional arrays

The Managed Extensions also support multidimensional arrays:

```
String* state_abbr_names[] = {S"FL", S"Florida",
                              S"GA", S"Georgia",
                              S"NY", S"New York",
                              S"OH", S"Ohio",
                              S"CA", S"California"};

String* stateabbr2name[,] = new String*[50, 2];

for(int j = 0; j < state_abbr_names->Length; j += 2)
{
    stateabbr2name[j / 2, 0] = state_abbr_names[j];       // Abbreviation
    stateabbr2name[j / 2, 1] = state_abbr_names[j + 1];   // Name
}
```

The code declares and initializes a one-dimensional array of String pointers called state_abbr_names. In it, the elements with even indices contain a state abbreviation, while the elements with odd indices contain the state name for each of the abbreviations. For brevity, we've only included five states.

The next array, stateabbr2name, is a two-dimensional array. When declaring multidimensional arrays, the dimension count is equal to the number of commas between the array brackets plus one.

The for loop then copies each of the state abbreviations and names from the one-dimensional array into the two-dimensional array. Finally, we dump the elements of the array with the help of a slightly modified version of the DumpArrayElements() function that can handle the extra dimension, which looks like this:

```
void DumpArrayElements2(System::Array* a)
{
    for( int j=0; j < a->Rank; ++j)
    {
        for( int i=0; i < a->Length / a->Rank; ++i )
        {
            Console::WriteLine(S"a[{0},{1}] = {2}", i.ToString(),
                               j.ToString(), a->GetValue(i,j));
        }
    }
}
```

Passing the stateabbr2name array to the DumpArrayElements2() function will produce the following output:

```
a[0,0] = FL
a[1,0] = GA
a[2,0] = NY
a[3,0] = OH
a[4,0] = CA
a[5,0] =
...
a[49,0] =

a[0,1] = Florida
a[1,1] = Georgia
a[2,1] = New York
a[3,1] = Ohio
a[4,1] = California
a[5,1] =
...
a[49,1] =
```

Note that the array elements that are not assigned a string are initialized to the empty string.

__value types

So far, we've been looking at managed types that are allocated on the garbage-collected heap. Now, we will look at a mechanism in managed C++ that allows us to define **value types**. __value types can be structures or classes whose declarations are preceded by the new __value keyword, rather than the __gc keyword. Instances of these types will be allocated on the stack, rather than the CLR's managed heap. We can also allocate them on the *unmanaged* C++ heap, via the __nogc new operator. We use __value to improve performance for types that are small in size with short lifetimes, which are not worth the overhead of garbage collection. This is why the .NET Framework classes that represent the primitive types are all __value types.

__value structures and __value classes both derive from System::ValueType. This class forms the root of all value types and inherits from System::Object. It overrides the following methods inherited from System::Object:

Member name	Description
Equals	Overridden to provide a value comparison of this instance with another instance of the same type.
GetHashCode	Returns a 32-bit integer used as a hash value by some of the System.Collection classes.
ToString	Returns a fully qualified string representation of the type name for this instance.

If __value types inherit at all, they can *only* do so from __gc interfaces. Furthermore, they may not be derived from, as they are implicitly sealed. They can override virtual methods from System::ValueType, but they can't define new ones.

Like __gc objects, __value objects can declare instance constructors and static constructors, and can contain properties, which we'll discuss later in this chapter.

Declaring __value classes and structures

__value classes and structures are declared by preceding the class or struct keyword with the __value keyword:

```
__value struct PersonInfo
{
    char* m_FirstName;
    char* m_MiddleInitial;
    char* m_LastName;
};
```

When this code is compiled, the compiler will emit code causing a type called PersonInfo to be created that inherits from System::ValueType. Because the PersonInfo structure doesn't contain any __gc pointers, it can be allocated on either the unmanaged heap or the stack, just like an ordinary, unmanaged C++ type. Note that the members of this structure are just ordinary unmanaged pointers. It is also perfectly legal for it to contain instance of unmanaged POD types.

To allocate an instance of `PersonInfo` on the stack, we use standard C++ syntax:

```
PersonInfo person_info;                          // Allocated on the stack
person_info.m_FirstName = "John";
person_info.m_MiddleInitial = "W";
person_info.m_LastName = "Smith";
```

To allocate an instance of `PersonInfo` on the unmanaged C++ heap, we have to use the `__nogc` new operator:

```
PersonInfo* pperson_info = __nogc new PersonInfo;   // Allocated on the C++ heap
pperson_info->m_FirstName = "George";
pperson_info->m_MiddleInitial = "M";
pperson_info->m_LastName = "Jones";
```

Note that we can't create a freestanding `__value` type on the managed heap. Not that we would want to, since the main point of `__value` types is to allow the creation of lightweight types that are allocated on the stack for better run-time performance.

Now, our `PersonInfo` structure contained nothing but unmanaged pointers. Suppose we declare a `__value` type that includes `__gc` pointers:

```
__value struct PhoneNumber
{
    String* m_AreaCode;
    String* m_Prefix;
    String* m_LastFour;
};
```

This limits the creation of instances of this structure to the stack:

```
// This is allocated on stack
PhoneNumber phone_number;
phone_number.m_AreaCode = S"212";
phone_number.m_Prefix = S"555";
phone_number.m_LastFour = S"WROX";
```

So far, we have seen how to create `__value` types on the stack and on the unmanaged heap. If we want to use the managed heap, then we need to embed the `__value` type inside of a `__gc` type, since only `__gc` types can be allocated on the managed heap:

```
__gc class PhoneNumberObject
{
public:
    PhoneNumber m_PhoneNumber;
};
```

The above code declares a `__gc` class called `PhoneNumberObject` that contains a `__value` member of type `PhoneNumber`, called `m_PhoneNumber`. Because instances of the `PhoneNumberObject` class are allocated on the managed heap, the embedded `__value` member `m_PhoneNumber` will be allocated there too.

Boxing and unboxing

So far, we've seen how to declare and allocate __value types on the stack, the C++ unmanaged heap, and the CLR's managed heap – and discovered that in the last case, the __value type had to be embedded within a __gc type in order for the operation to work.

This need to 'wrap' __value types can be a problem when we want to pass an instance of a __value type to a function that accepts a pointer to a System::Object instance, a common scenario (recall that an Object* is like a void*). There is no way to 'cast' from a __value type to a __gc type.

Following on from the PhoneNumber example, suppose we wanted to pass an instance of our PhoneNumber __value type to the following function:

```
void DumpObject(System::Object* o)
{
    System::Console::WriteLine(o->ToString());
}
```

We could create an instance of the __gc PhoneNumberObject class that wraps the __value struct, cast the pointer to it to an Object*, and then pass this to the DumpObject() method. That would work, but it would be a real pain if we had to do that every time we wanted to pass a __value type instance to a method that takes a pointer to a System::Object instance.

What we *can* do, however, is to use a process called **boxing** that makes this process a whole lot easier.

Enter the box

The Managed Extensions include a keyword called __box that performs the work necessary to wrap any type of __value type with a __gc class. This wrapper class allows members to be accessed just like an ordinary __value instance, but in this case, instances of the wrapper class are allocated on the managed heap, just like all other __gc classes.

The following code uses the __box keyword to create an instance of a boxed PhoneNumber type:

```
PhoneNumber phone_number;
phone_number.m_AreaCode = S"212";
phone_number.m_Prefix = S"555";
phone_number.m_LastFour = S"2122";
```

```
__box PhoneNumber* bxPN = __box(phone_number);
DumpObject(bxPN);
```

Note the use of __box in the declaration *and* assignment of bxPN. When the first line of code is compiled, the compiler creates a wrapper class that derives from System::ValueType; it emits code to create an instance of the wrapper class, copy the phone_number instance to the PhoneNumber member of the wrapper, and return a pointer to the wrapper class instance.

Leave the box

An important thing to realize here is that any change you happen to make to the boxed instance *won't* be reflected in the original __value type instance. This is because the two instances are distinct: one lives on the stack, and the other on the managed heap as part of the wrapper class:

```
bxPN->m_AreaCode = S"888";

Console::WriteLine(S"Stack instance area code = {0}", phone_number.m_AreaCode);
Console::WriteLine(S"Boxed instance area code = {0}", bxPN->m_AreaCode);
```

This displays the following output:

```
Stack instance area code = 212
Boxed instance area code = 888
```

In order to make the local stack instance reflect the changes, we must 'unbox' the boxed instance:

```
phone_number = *(__try_cast<__box PhoneNumber*>(bxPN));
Console::WriteLine("Stack instance area code = {0}", phone_number.m_AreaCode);
```

Here, we are simply casting the boxed object to obtain the __gc pointer to the object stored on the managed heap, and dereferencing it to obtain a copy of the original __value type.

This displays the following output:

```
Stack instance area code = 888
```

In Managed Extensions, the programmer must explicitly perform all boxing operations – there are no implicit boxing conversions. Incidentally, it's also possible to pass boxed versions of __value types as parameters to functions:

```
void DumpBoxedPhoneNumber(__box PhoneNumber* bxPN)
{
    DumpObject(bxPN);
}
```

A call to the above method requires the caller to box the value type:

```
DumpBoxedPhoneNumber( __box(phone_number) );
```

__value enums

The Managed Extensions for C++ extend the C++ enum type with __value enum. These can be used just like C++ enum types, but they offer more capability in managed applications. One important difference is that they allow the programmer to specify the underlying type that's used to represent the enumeration:

```
__value enum Planets : Byte {Mercury, Venus, Earth, Mars,
                             Jupiter, Saturn, Uranus, Neptune, Pluto};
```

This declares a __value enum type called Planets that has an underlying type of System::Byte and members called Mercury, Venus, and so on. Byte corresponds to C++'s unsigned char type. The underlying types of __value enum types must be C++ integer types, or any System::xyz type where xyz has a C++ integral counterpart.

An occasional problem in C++ is that enum declarations can collide with other identifiers in the same scope, such as other enum declarations. For the following example, the compiler will spit out redefinition errors for each of the enumerated identifiers in the declaration of RomanGods, because they've already been defined in the declaration of GasGiants:

```
enum GasGiants {Jupiter, Saturn, Uranus, Neptune};
enum RomanGods {Jupiter, Saturn, Uranus, Neptune};
```

__value enum types solve this problem by forcing the programmer to qualify the enumerator name explicitly in the case of ambiguity. Alternatively, if a non-enumeration identifier is declared with the same name as a member of an enumeration, then the compiler chooses the non-enumeration identifier ahead of the enumeration member:

```
__value enum InnerPlanets : Byte {Mercury, Venus, Earth, Mars};
__value enum Metals {Nickel, Gold, Mercury, Titanium};

int Gold = 0;
```

The above code declares some __value enum types that both contain Mercury as one of the enumerated members. Also, a variable called Gold is declared that matches one of the identifiers in the declaration of Metals. This compiles quite happily under managed C++. The following code uses these enumerations:

```
InnerPlanets ClosestToSun = InnerPlanets::Mercury;
Metals LiquidAtRTP = Metals::Mercury;
int n = Gold;
```

We must fully qualify Mercury with the enumerated type names: InnerPlanets and Metals. Also, because an identifier named Gold was declared in the same scope as the declaration of Metals, the compiler uses the non-enumerated Gold when assigning to the integer variable n.

Like other __value types, __value enum types can be boxed, in which case the boxed version inherits from System::Enum. They can also be declared in __gc interfaces. Finally, like all other managed types, it's quite possible for other .NET languages to consume the enumerations you create in managed C++.

So far, we've been focusing on the managed __gc and __value types. Now let's move on to some concepts related to object-oriented programming, which until now have not been directly implemented in C++. In order to implement our managed types in a way that makes them interoperable with other languages, they need to support features such as properties and events, and the metadata that describes them needs to include information about these properties and events. The Managed Extensions provide us with some new keywords to achieve this.

Properties

Properties are methods that are accessed by clients as though they were member variables. In other words, when client code specifies the property, a method is called depending on how the property is being accessed. The methods allow clients to interact with the object in well-defined and syntactically simplified ways.

Scalar properties

The __property keyword allows you to declare a pair of methods that implement the property mechanism. A **scalar property** is one that declares 'get' and 'set' methods according to the following signature rules:

❑ The return type of a scalar property's 'get' method is the same as the property type. The method takes no parameters.

❑   The return type of a scalar property's 'set' method is void. The method takes a single
     parameter whose type is the same as the property type.

Here's an example:

```
__gc class IceCream
{
public:

    __property String* get_Flavor(void)
    {
        return m_Flavor;
    }

    __property void set_Flavor(String* s)
    {
        m_Flavor = s;
    }

private:

    String* m_Flavor;
};
```

This declares a __gc class called IceCream and a member variable that we'll use to implement the
property methods. The above code declares a property called Flavor using the __property keyword.
The presence of a 'get' method distinguishes this as a readable property, and the 'set' method
distinguishes it as a writable property. When the compiler encounters this code, it uses the part
following the underscore as the property name: Flavor, whose type is String*. This is the name that
will appear in the IDE as a property, and this is the name by which client code will access the property.

The set_Flavor() method accepts a single parameter of type String* and returns void. The
method is then implemented using the m_Flavor member.

Here's how clients of this class can use the Flavor property:

```
IceCream*    ic=new IceCream;
ic->Flavor = S"Chocolate";
Console::WriteLine(S"The flavor of the day is {0}", ic->Flavor);
```

The first of the statements that access the properties assigns the string "Chocolate" to the Flavor
property; note that the client accesses the property as if it were a member of the class, and not as a
method call. Next, we display the value of the property to the console. Once again, the client code
simply accesses the Flavor property as if it were a member of the class. Here's the output that results
from executing this code:

```
The flavor of the day is Chocolate
```

Indexed properties

It can sometimes be useful for properties to allow indexing behavior – that is, for the entity that's accessed through a property to depend on some criteria. Continuing with the previous example, an object might provide a property called `FlavorOfTheDay` that's indexed based on the day of the week that we provide. Here's how such a property might be accessed:

```
IceCream* flavorToday = obj->FlavorOfTheDay["Tuesday"];
```

Used as in the above code, the `FlavorOfTheDay` property would return a pointer to an `IceCream` instance.

Indexed properties are defined using the following signature rules:

❑   The 'get' method should return the type of the property and take any number of parameters that together form the index.

❑   The 'set' method should return `void` and take any number of parameters that together form the index, followed by a parameter of the property type that is to be assigned to the property, based on the index parameters.

We can extend the previous example by adding a new class called `IceCreamVendor` that defines an **indexed property** called `FlavorOfTheDay`:

```
using namespace System::Collections;

__gc class IceCreamVendor
{
public:

    IceCreamVendor()
    {
        m_FlavorOfTheDay = new Hashtable();
    }

    __property IceCream* get_FlavorOfTheDay(String* index)
    {
        return static_cast<IceCream*>(m_FlavorOfTheDay->Item[index]);
    }

    __property void set_FlavorOfTheDay(String* index, IceCream* value)
    {
        m_FlavorOfTheDay->Item[index] = value;
    }

private:
        Hashtable*    m_FlavorOfTheDay;
};
```

The `IceCreamVendor` class implements the `FlavorOfTheDay` property using a `Hashtable` class from the `System::Collections` namespace. We map the day of the week string to a pointer to an `IceCream` instance.

Client code can use the indexed property like this:

```
IceCreamVendor* icv = new IceCreamVendor;

IceCream* icVanilla = new IceCream;
icVanilla->Flavor = S"Vanilla";

IceCream* ic2xChocChip = new IceCream;
ic2xChocChip->Flavor = S"Double Chocolate Chip";

IceCream* icStrawberry = new IceCream;
icStrawberry->Flavor = S"Strawberry";

icv->FlavorOfTheDay[S"Monday"] = icVanilla;
icv->FlavorOfTheDay[S"Tuesday"] = ic2xChocChip;
icv->FlavorOfTheDay[S"Wednesday"] = icStrawberry;

Console::WriteLine(S"Tuesday's flavor of the day is {0}",
                       icv->FlavorOfTheDay[S"Tuesday"]->Flavor );
```

First, we create an instance of the IceCreamVendor class. Then we create some instances of IceCream and set the Flavor property of each to some tasty flavor. Next, we assign each IceCream instance to the IceCreamVendor instance's FlavorOfTheDay property indexed by a day of the week. Finally, we display Tuesday's flavor of the day using the indexed property. Executing the above code displays the following output:

```
Tuesday's flavor of the day is Double Chocolate Chip
```

Keep in mind that the 'get' and 'set' methods of an indexed property may make use of any number of parameters to form the index. For example, we could have used a day of the week and some other value, such as a price, as an index pair, to achieve a two-dimensional indexing scheme. Indexed property methods can also be overloaded.

Delegates

If you were concentrating hard, you may have noticed something missing from the *Pointers* section: function pointers. The reason for this is that .NET makes use of an object-oriented version of a function pointer, called a **delegate**. Delegates are full-blown objects, with methods that allow us to do some very useful things. Unsurprisingly, we declare a delegate with the __delegate keyword. The syntax looks pretty similar to a function declaration:

```
__delegate void DelegateOne();
__delegate int DelegateTwo(int x, String* s);
```

Here, DelegateOne can 'point' to any function that returns void and takes no parameters. DelegateTwo, on the other hand, can 'point' to any function that returns int and takes two parameters: an int and a String*, in that order. The following class definition includes some functions that can be used as targets of the delegates we just declared.

```
__gc class Functions
{
public:
  Functions(String* s)
  {
    m_s = s;
  }

  void Foo()
  {
    Console::WriteLine(S"Functions {0} - Foo()", m_s);
  }

  int Bar(int x, String* s)
  {
    Console::WriteLine(S"Functions {0} - Bar({1}, {2})", m_s, x.ToString(), s);
    return x;
  }

  static int Zoo(int x, String* s)
  {
    Console::WriteLine(S"Functions::Zoo({0}, {1})", x.ToString(), s);
    return x;
  }

private:
  String* m_s;
};
```

The `Functions` class contains three member functions: `Foo()`, `Bar()`, and `Zoo()`. These functions don't really do anything exciting – they're just meant to act as targets of the two delegates we declared above, and to output some diagnostic code to the console, so that we can see what's happening. Let's look at how we can use the `Functions` class and the delegates we just defined:

```
Functions* f1 = new Functions(S"Instance 1");
Functions* f2 = new Functions(S"Instance 2");

DelegateOne* d1 = new DelegateOne(f1, Functions::Foo);
```

This creates two instances of the `Functions` class, passing a different string to each instance at instantiation. The more interesting line creates a `DelegateOne` instance. The delegate constructor takes two parameters that define the delegate's **target**:

❑ The first parameter is a pointer to an object, and determines which object will receive the function call. (In the case of a static method, this parameter should be set to zero.)

❑ The second parameter is the address of the function to be invoked.

Note that a target method must be a member of an object, though it may be a static method or an instance method. In the above code, we pass `f1` as the first parameter and the `Functions::Foo` method as the second parameter. This means that when the delegate is invoked, `f1->Foo()` will be called:

```
d1();
```

This might look like a regular function call, but, in fact, it causes the target method of the delegate instance d1 to be invoked.

Multicasting

If this were all they did, delegates wouldn't be much to write home about, but they also support an interesting ability called **multicasting**. This allows us to use a *single* delegate instance to target *multiple* methods. Here's how we can add an additional target method to the d1 delegate instance:

```
DelegateOne* d1 = new DelegateOne(f1, Functions::Foo);
d1 += new DelegateOne(f2, Functions::Foo);
d1();
```

By using the += operator, we add a new DelegateOne instance to the one already pointed to by d1. Notice that the new delegate instance's target method is again Functions::Foo, but that the target object is f2. When the above code is executed, the target methods are called in the order they were added to the delegate. In this case, f1->Foo() is called first, followed by f2->Foo(). Here's the output after running this code:

```
Functions Instance 1 - Foo()
Functions Instance 2 - Foo()
```

As you'd expect, you can use the -= operator to remove a target method from a delegate.

As mentioned earlier, the target method of a delegate can be either a static or an instance method:

```
DelegateTwo* d2 = new DelegateTwo(f1, Functions::Bar);
d2 += new DelegateTwo(0, Functions::Zoo);
d2 += new DelegateTwo(f2, Functions::Bar);
d2 += new DelegateTwo(0, Functions::Zoo);

d2(5, "Hello");
```

The Functions::Zoo() method is static, so we pass a zero as the first parameter to the DelegateTwo constructor. Functions::Bar() is an instance method, so it requires an object pointer to be passed as the first argument to the DelegateTwo constructor. Finally, we invoke the delegate d2, passing it the two required parameters. Here's the output that results from executing this code:

```
Functions Instance 1 - Bar(5, Hello)
Functions::Zoo(5, Hello)
Functions Instance 2 - Bar(5, Hello)
Functions::Zoo(5, Hello)
```

Not only are the target methods invoked in the order they were added to the delegate, but also each method receives the same parameter values that were passed to the delegate at the time it was invoked.

Events

Delegates form the basis of the 'publish-subscribe' event model defined in .NET. Essentially, this model is characterized by the existence of one event sender, and one or more event receivers. The mechanism is similar to the event model used in COM, with the event sender being a source and an event handler being a sink. An object can subscribe to an event by attaching an event handler to the event. When the event is published, each event handler attached to the event is invoked. The event publisher notifies all event receivers that an event has occurred.

Events are declared with the __event keyword, using a delegate that's been declared elsewhere in the application. The following code declares a delegate called WarningHandler. In terms of the event-handling architecture, we're specifying the signature of the functions we'll eventually write to handle the events we fire:

```
__delegate void WarningHandler(Object* sender, WarningEventArgs* e);
```

This signature follows the standard event-handling signature recommended by the .NET event model. This does not mean that you can't define events in terms of delegates with other signatures, but be aware that if you do that, then it may cause confusion for other developers more familiar with the conventional event model. The two parameters are a pointer to the object that sent (or 'fired') the event, and a pointer to an instance of the System::EventArgs class (or a derived class thereof).

The System::EventArgs class is used in situations where the event being sent does not have any additional state information related to it, and the mere occurrence of the event conveys all the information needed for the event receiver to perform its work. However, if additional state information is required by the event handler, we must derive a class from System::EventArgs to holds this information. In the example above, we've used a WarningEventArgs class that derives from System::EventArgs to hold a message that conveys information related to our event:

```
__gc class WarningEventArgs : public System::EventArgs
{
public:
    WarningEventArgs(String* s) : m_WarningMessage(s){}
    String* m_WarningMessage;
};
```

This is a simple class that contains a public member that will contain a description of the cause of the warning event. Now we can define the OnWarning event in terms of the WarningHandler delegate:

```
__gc class SendsWarningEvent
{
public:
    __event WarningHandler* OnWarning;

    void FireWarning(WarningEventArgs* e)
    {
        OnWarning(this, e);
    }
};
```

The `SendsWarningEvent` class uses the `__event` keyword to declare an event called `OnWarning`. In the model, `SendsWarningEvent` is considered the **event publisher**, while `WarningHandler` is the **event subscriber**'s event handler method. The `FireWarning()` method accepts a pointer to a `WarningEventArgs` instance and passes it as the second argument to the `OnWarning` event. If this seems a little tricky, perhaps an example will help clarify things.

```
__gc class ReceivesWarningEvent
{
public:
    ReceivesWarningEvent(String* s): m_s(s){}

    void Handler(Object* sender, WarningEventArgs* e)
    {
        Console::WriteLine(S"Warning event rec'd by {0} - Warning message: {1}",
                           m_s, e->m_WarningMessage);
    }

private:
    String* m_s;
};
```

First, we define a class called `ReceivesWarningEvent` that defines a method called `Handler()`, with the requisite signature for participating as an event subscriber in the .NET event model. All the `Handler()` method does is to output a message to the console containing this instance's `String` member, `m_s`, and the message conveyed in the `WarningEventArgs` instance.

Now we need to use the above code to hook up some subscribers to the event publisher and raise the event:

```
ReceivesWarningEvent* wh1 = new ReceivesWarningEvent(S"email");
ReceivesWarningEvent* wh2 = new ReceivesWarningEvent(S"console");

SendsWarningEvent* w = new SendsWarningEvent;
```

First, we instantiate two `ReceivesWarningEvent` instances – we pass "email" to the constructor of one and "console" to the other. This is to illustrate two separate agents 'listening' to the `OnWarning` event: one agent (in a real situation) would send an email for each occurrence of the event, and the other agent would display a message to the console. Next, we instantiate a `SendsWarningEvent` class instance; this is the class that contains the `OnWarning` event.

Now all we need to do is to get the two `ReceivesWarningEvent` instances to subscribe to the event:

```
w->OnWarning += new WarningHandler(wh1, ReceivesWarningEvent::Handler);
w->OnWarning += new WarningHandler(wh2, ReceivesWarningEvent::Handler);
```

Here, we're creating two new instances of the `WarningHandler` delegate, setting the target of each to the `Handler()` method of the "email" and "console" `ReceivesWarningEvent` instances we created earlier. We add these delegate instances to the `OnWarning` event in the same way as we added multiple targets to a delegate instance, when we looked at multicasting behavior.

All that's left to do now is to fire the event by calling the `FireWarning()` method:

```
w->FireWarning(new WarningEventArgs(S"System overload!"));
```

Executing this code results in the following output:

```
Warning event rec'd by email - Warning message: System overload!
Warning event rec'd by console - Warning message: System overload!
```

Exceptions

In the .NET Framework, **exceptions** are *the* error handling mechanism. It's possible for a type defined in one language to throw a managed exception that can be caught by a type defined in a different .NET compatible language.

Throwing, try/catch, and __finally

Managed Extensions support both C++ exception handling and structured exceptions – but to standard C++ exception handling, it adds the __finally keyword. An added bonus to cross-language exception handling is that HRESULTs are no longer needed – which can only be good news for the developer.

Typically, we wrap code that may throw an exception in a try block, and define one or more exception handlers in catch blocks:

```
try
{
    // Force out of memory condition...
    SomegcClass* pa[] = new SomegcClass* __gc[1000000000];
}
catch(OutOfMemoryException* e)
{
    Console::WriteLine(e->Message);
    Console::WriteLine(e->StackTrace);
}
```

The above code attempts to allocate a managed __gc array of some 1,000,000,000 SomegcClass object instances. On my test system, the call to new results in a System::OutOfMemoryException being thrown. The catch block handles this exception and outputs some information about the exception to the console.

> *The MSDN documentation does a fairly good job at listing exceptions thrown by a given method. There is also a mapping of HRESULTs to .NET Framework exception classes, which you can find by searching for "HRESULTs and Exceptions".*

Something new provided by the Managed Extensions is the __finally keyword. This is used to declare a __finally block of code after a try/catch block. Code within the __finally block will *always* be executed regardless of whether an exception was thrown (caught or uncaught). To demonstrate __finally, here's a function that will throw an exception of an unmanaged type called nogcWroxException:

```
void Foo()
{
    SomeClass nogcObj(S"Foo() on stack");
    SomeClass* pObj = new SomeClass(S"Foo() on unmanaged heap");
    SomegcClass* pgcObj = new SomegcClass(S"Foo() on managed heap");
```

```
    try
    {
       Console::WriteLine(S"Throwing nogcWroxException!");
       throw new nogcWroxException;

    }
    __finally
    {
       Console::WriteLine(S"Foo() in __finally block");
       if(pObj)
       {
          delete pObj;
       }
       if(pgcObj)
       {
          // Force destructor and finalization of __gc object
          delete pgcObj;
       }
    }
}
```

For demonstration purposes, this code allocates two instances of a __nogc class called SomeClass –
one on the stack and one on the unmanaged heap. Then, it allocates an instance of a __gc class called
SomegcClass on the managed heap.

> *Note that* nogcWroxException *and* SomeClass *are declared elsewhere in the code – for the*
> *full listing, see the code download.*

This function demonstrates the use of the __finally block to clean up any resources still held by the class
after throwing the nogcWroxException exception. Since there's no catch clause, the exception will
continue to propagate up the call stack to a higher-level handler *after* execution of the __finally block.

Here's some code that calls the Foo() method and provides a catch block:

```
// Catch unmanaged
try
{
   Console::WriteLine(S"main() calling Foo()");
   Foo();
}
catch(nogcWroxException*)
{
   Console::WriteLine(S"main() in catch(nogcWroxException*) block!");
}
__finally
{
   Console::WriteLine(S"main() in __finally block!");
}
```

Executing this code yields the following screen output:

```
main() calling Foo()
SomeClass() created by Foo() on stack
SomeClass() created by Foo() on unmanaged heap
```

```
SomegcClass() created by Foo() on managed heap
Foo() Throwing nogcWroxException!
Foo() in __finally block
~SomeClass() created by Foo() on unmanaged heap
~SomegcClass() created by Foo() on managed heap
~SomeClass() created by Foo() on stack
main() in catch ( nogcWroxException* ) block!
main() in __finally block!
```

Look at the order of events after Foo() throws the nogcWroxException. First, the __finally block in Foo() is called – this block deletes both the managed and unmanaged heap-based instances. Then, the stack-based instance is destroyed automatically as the stack is unwound. Stack unwinding destroys all stack-based instances between the catch clause that handles the exception and the point that the exception is thrown. Because __gc objects are allocated on the managed heap, they won't take part in the unwinding and need to be destroyed explicitly (unless of course we let the garbage collector take care of them).

The use of __finally is important when you're dealing with managed objects that hold onto system resources and must be disposed of in a timely manner. For example, if we have a heap-based object that has a file handle open, we can structure our code so that if an *uncaught* exception is thrown, the __finally clause will ensure the file handle is closed. The system is returned to a known state even in the face of uncaught exceptions.

The previous example demonstrated using the __finally keyword with unmanaged C++ exception handling. Let's look at another example that demonstrates throwing a managed C++ class and follow that up with an example and discussion on mixing managed and unmanaged types in exception handling:

```
void Bar()
{
    SomeClass nogcObj(S"Bar() on stack");
    SomeClass* pObj = new SomeClass(S"Bar() on unmanaged heap");
    SomegcClass* pgcObj = new SomegcClass(S"Bar() on managed heap");

    try
    {
        Console::WriteLine(S"Bar() Throwing gcWroxException!");
        throw new gcWroxException();
    }
    __finally
    {
        Console::WriteLine(S"Bar() in __finally block");
        if(pObj)
        {
            delete pObj;
        }
        if(pgcObj)
        {
            // Force destructor and Finalization of gc object
            delete pgcObj;
        }
    }
}
```

This code defines a function called `Bar()` that's almost identical to the `Foo()` function we defined earlier – the only difference is that this function throws an instance of a *managed* class called `gcWroxException` that derives from `System::Exception`:

```
__gc class gcWroxException : public System::Exception {};
```

It's possible to mix `catch` blocks that handle unmanaged exceptions with those that handle managed exceptions. Here's some code that calls the `Bar()` method:

```
try
{
    Console::WriteLine(S"main() calling Bar()");
    Bar();
}
catch(gcWroxException*)
{
    Console::WriteLine(S"main() in catch(gcWroxException*) block!");
}
catch(nogcWroxException*)
{
    Console::WriteLine(S"main() in catch(nogcWroxException*) block!");
}
__finally
{
    Console::WriteLine(S"main() in __finally block!");
}
```

Executing this code yields the following output:

```
main() calling Bar()
SomeClass() created by Bar() on stack
SomeClass() created by Bar() on unmanaged heap
SomegcClass() created by Bar() on managed heap
Bar() Throwing gcWroxException!
Bar() in __finally block
~SomeClass() created by Bar() on unmanaged heap
~SomegcClass() created by Bar() on managed heap
~SomeClass() created by Bar() on stack
main() in catch ( gcWroxException* ) block!
main() in __finally block!
```

Execution of the above code is basically the same as the previous example. Object instances are created on the stack, the unmanaged heap, and the managed heap, the exception is thrown, the __finally block in `Bar()` is executed, stack unwinding occurs, and the exception is caught in `main()`, after which the __finally block in `main()` is executed.

We have seen examples in this section illustrating that it is possible to throw both managed and unmanaged C++ exceptions in managed code. When an unmanaged C++ instance is thrown, the .NET runtime wraps it in an instance of the System::Runtime::InteropServices::SEHException class. When searching for a handler, if the catch block specifies an unmanaged class, the SEHException class is unwrapped to reveal its unmanaged class – the latter is then compared to the type specified in the catch block and caught if there is a match. If, on the other hand, the catch block specifies an SEHException class or one of its bases, then the class is not unwrapped, and the exception is caught by the handler as an SEHException class (or one of its bases). For this reason, it's important that all catch clauses for *unmanaged* C++ classes are placed before those for an SEHException class (or one of its bases).

The following example demonstrates what happens when an unmanaged class is thrown, and a catch block for an SEHException appears prior to one for the unmanaged class:

```
try
{
    Console::WriteLine(S"main() calling Foo()");
    Foo();
}
catch(System::Runtime::InteropServices::SEHException*)
{
    Console::WriteLine(S"main() in catch(SEHException*) block!");
}
catch(gcWroxException*)
{
    Console::WriteLine(S"main() in catch(gcWroxException*) block!");
}
catch(nogcWroxException*)
{
    Console::WriteLine(S"main() in catch(nogcWroxException*) block!");
}
__finally
{
    Console::WriteLine(S"main() in __finally block!");
}
```

Executing this code results in the following output:

```
main() calling Foo()
SomeClass() created by Foo() on stack
SomeClass() created by Foo() on unmanaged heap
SomegcClass() created by Foo() on managed heap
Foo() Throwing nogcWroxException!
Foo() in __finally block
~SomeClass() created by Foo() on unmanaged heap
~SomegcClass() created by Foo() on managed heap
~SomeClass() created by Foo() on stack
main() in catch ( SEHException* ) block!
main() in __finally block!
```

Notice that the exception is caught by the catch(SEHException*) block. This is because the unmanaged nogcWroxException is wrapped in an SEHException class as it's passed up the stack, and the system searches for a suitable handler. If you re-organize the catch blocks so that the SEHException is last, then this code should work as intended.

The __identifier keyword

We've now covered most of the new keywords from the Managed Extensions, but there's one more interesting one that we should mention here. __identifier is necessary if you ever find yourself importing a type (probably created in a different language) that has the same name as a Visual C++ keyword. For example, imagine that we're using an assembly called friend.dll that was produced in C# and defines a class called friend within a namespace called nsFriend. In order to use this class in managed C++, we must use the __identifier keyword. Here's some code that demonstrates this:

```
#using "friend.dll"

using namespace nsFriend;

void Foo()
{
    __identifier(friend)* p = new __identifier(friend);
}
```

Since friend is a keyword in C++, this code would not compile if we wrote it 'normally'. The language extension is helping to make possible one of the promised benefits of the .NET Framework, by providing a way round one of the barriers in the way of true cross-language development.

Summary of keywords

The Managed Extensions for Visual C++ include fifteen keywords, most of which we've seen in practice throughout this chapter. The following table summarizes all of the available keywords:

Keyword	Description
__abstract	When attached to a class or structure, declares that the type cannot be instantiated
__box	Used to create a managed object from a __value object
__delegate	Used to declare a kind of 'smart' function pointer known as a delegate
__event	Used to declare an event (in different ways) in unmanaged, managed, and COM code
__finally	Declares a 'finally' block that will take part in exception handling
__gc	Declares a type that will be garbage collected
__identifier	Can be used to handle types (declared elsewhere) that share names with C++ keywords
__interface	When attached to a class or structure, forces all members to be pure virtual functions

Keyword	Description
__nogc	Declares a type that will not be garbage-collected (that is, an ordinary C++ type)
__pin	Used to prevent an object from being collected or moved by the garbage collector
__property	Used to declare a method of a class that will be exposed as a property
__sealed	When attached to a class or structure, declares that the type cannot be derived from
__try_cast	A potential replacement for dynamic_cast that throws an exception on failure
__typeof	An operator that returns the type of any managed object you care to specify
__value	Used to declare a __value type

There are a couple that we've not looked at in this chapter – __typeof and __pin. These are examined later on in the book, in Chapters 4 and 7, when we cover reflection and interoperability issues, respectively.

Summary

This chapter has taken you through a wide-ranging discussion of development in managed C++. We started by examining the requirements for developing in a managed environment, where our data is garbage collected and our code needs to be interoperable with code written in other languages. This led us into a detailed study of the Managed Extensions for C++. We looked at most of the new keywords and have seen how they're used to create __value and __gc types.

We studied various aspects of programming with managed code for the .NET world. We saw how the Managed Extensions allow us to create properties for our managed types. We looked at the .NET event model and how it makes use of delegates and events. Finally, we discussed using managed exceptions.

In short, Managed Extensions provide the necessary mechanism to allow C++ code to play in the .NET world. We can use managed C++ to allow our existing C++ code to make use of the .NET Framework classes or expose our existing C++ code to .NET components. As we saw in this chapter, there are a few new keywords and idioms to learn, but for the most part it's surprisingly easy to develop managed applications and components using managed C++.

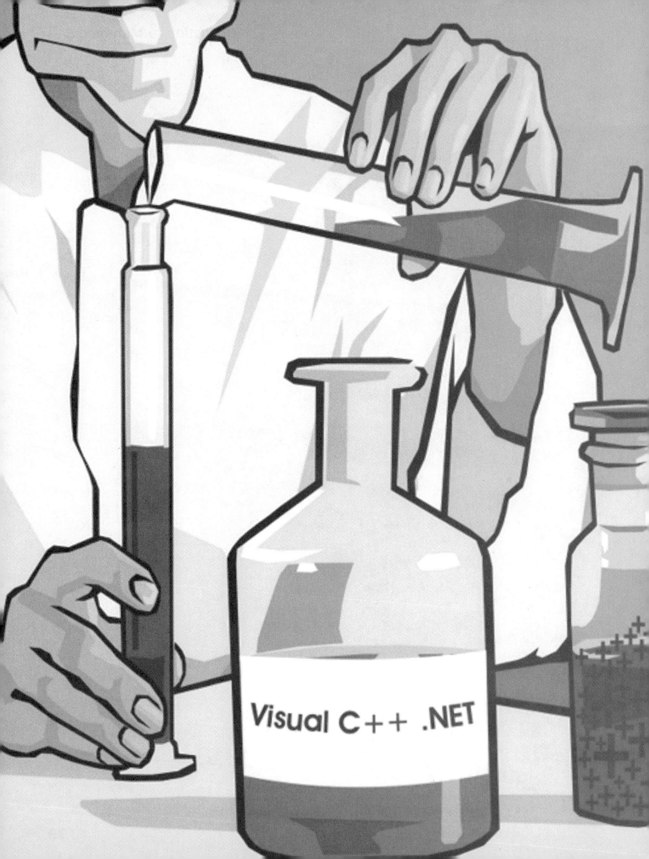

Visual C++ .NET

3

Assemblies

This chapter looks in great detail at the .NET **assembly**. We'll cover a lot of ground, starting with a general overview of assemblies, moving on to examine their internals, and finally looking at building and using them. More specifically, we will examine:

- ❑ What assemblies are, what they're made of, what advantages they offer, and the basics of creating and using assemblies

- ❑ Viewing assemblies using `ildasm.exe`

- ❑ The distinction between private and shared assemblies, how to create a shared assembly, and how to install it in the global assembly cache (GAC)

- ❑ Creating resources and working with resources in assemblies

- ❑ Deploying assemblies

Let's start the ball rolling by looking at what assemblies are, what features they offer, and how they form a fundamental part of the .NET architecture.

What are assemblies?

Quite simply, assemblies are the central building block for all .NET Framework application distribution and execution. Every executable, library, or resource file that you develop with .NET is an assembly – you have no choice in the matter. Not only are they a fundamental component for application deployment, they're also the construct from which version control, the scope of types and resources, dependencies, and security permissions all hang. This is a big change from the world before .NET, where the executables or DLL files you created stored only the actual application and library code, while external files stored the metadata that described the contents. In fact, the internal organization of a .NET assembly is nothing like the internal organization of a classic executable or DLL. The only obvious similarities that remain between the .NET and the classic cases are their purpose and that they both use files whose names end in .exe and .dll.

Assembly structure

Essentially, an assembly is a collection of elements that together make up a segment of an application; it requires multiple assemblies to make up an application. An assembly can be made up of four different managed element types:

❑   The **assembly manifest** contains metadata that describes the complete assembly. This includes information on all the other elements that make up the assembly and how they relate to each other. It also contains information on versioning, security, and so on.

❑   The **metadata** provides information about the types defined in the assembly – their names, visibilities, base classes, and the interfaces they implement. The metadata and the assembly manifest mean that the assembly is completely self-describing.

❑   Application code, compiled to the **Microsoft Intermediate Language** (MSIL), that implements the types described in the metadata.

❑   Other resources, such as bitmaps, cursors, and static text.

In addition to this, an assembly can also contain unmanaged code and data. There are many ways to group these four elements together in an assembly. (The only *required* element is the assembly manifest, but without metadata, application code, or resources, an assembly won't serve much purpose.) Note that an assembly does not have to be one physical file; each of the above element types except the assembly **manifest** can be distributed across multiple files. The most common approach, though, is to use a single file:

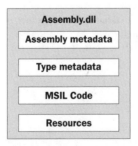

This is known as a **portable executable** file or **PE**. Frequently, single file assemblies – the only type we have created so far – will only be made up of the manifest, the metadata, and the MSIL code.

If an assembly is made up of multiple files, elements of the assembly are placed in separate **modules**. Modules can be composed of compiled MSIL code, resources such as `.bmp` or `.jpeg` files, or other resource files. The modules that make up a multi-file assembly appear as separate files to the file system and are not physically linked in any way. Rather, they are linked logically through the assembly manifest, which contains details of all the files that make up the assembly, although the individual files don't 'know' that they are part of an assembly. All files must reside in the same physical directory, and we can use them to generate the manifest using the **Assembly Linker** (`AL.exe`) tool. The CLR manages the multi-file assembly as a unit.

Only one module in an assembly can contain the manifest. It's possible to have a standalone module that contains *only* the manifest, but it's more likely to be packaged in one of the related modules. This example of a multi-file assembly shows a single assembly that's spread across four files; note that only `Assembly.exe` contains the manifest:

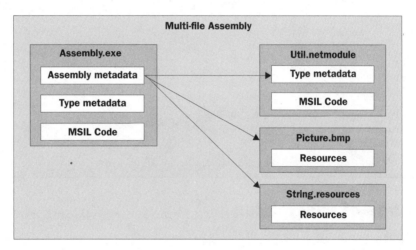

Multi-file assemblies come in handy when you're building large applications composed of components built in different languages – you can place each language in its own module and assign them to different members of your development team. They're also helpful when you're trying to optimize downloads – you can place seldom-used types and methods in their own modules, and download them only when needed.

Linker options

When we use the wizard to create a managed C++ application, then we get a single file assembly by default. However, you can control how the linker packages managed code using some of the new linker options that are part of the Managed Extensions for C++:

❑ `/NOASSEMBLY` causes the output file not to include assembly information, producing a module DLL that can then be used or packaged by other assemblies.

❑ `/ASSEMBLYMODULE` allows a module DLL (produced using the `/NOASSEMBLY` option or by some other .NET-compatible language compiler) to be imported into the current project without making the types defined in the module available to the importing assembly.

A possible use of this latter option would be to produce an assembly from a few module files that were generated using /NOASSEMBLY. Each of these modules defines a subset of some library you're providing that will eventually be packaged in a single assembly DLL. Using the /ASSEMBLYMODULE option allows you to package two modules together into one assembly that you then ship to end-users. The screenshot below illustrates how you can add a module to an assembly using the property pages for the project:

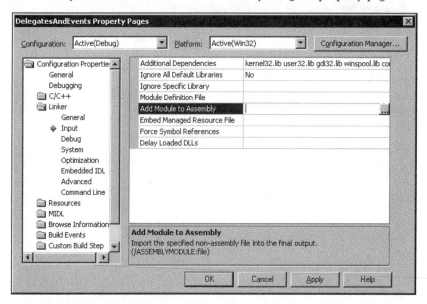

Key features of assemblies

Summarized below are some of the key features of assemblies that make them easy to use, install, and distribute:

❑ Assemblies define the security boundaries for an application – they specify the set of permissions that are required by the runtime for the application to run correctly.

❑ Assemblies prevent type conflicts, because the full name of any type that you create includes the name of the assembly in which it's defined.

❑ The assembly manifest contains information to resolve all external reference requirements. It also specifies all of the types and resources that are exposed by the assembly.

❑ An assembly will specify exactly what versions of any referenced assemblies it requires.

❑ Assemblies are self-describing – all of the information needed for execution of the assembly is contained within the assembly itself.

❑ As a result of assembly versioning, it's possible for two assemblies within an application to reference two different versions of a third assembly side-by-side, without conflict. We'll see a practical example of this later.

❑ Assemblies benefit from zero impact installation and uninstallation. Installation often just involves dragging and dropping the application directory to the location of your choice; for automated installation, a simple xcopy can usually suffice. We'll look at deployment in more detail at the end of the chapter.

Building assemblies

We have already been building assemblies in this book, as all .NET applications are assemblies. In this section, we'll build a couple more, but now we'll focus on them as assemblies and not just programs. We'll start with a (very) simple library assembly, and then we'll create a console application assembly that calls it. Both the library and the application are assemblies. The only difference between a library assembly and an application assembly is that the application assembly has an initial entry point from which the program will run.

Creating a class library

The library we'll build will contain a stopwatch class called `Stopwatch` that lives inside a namespace called `MyClock`. Create a new project, and select **Managed C++ Class Library**:

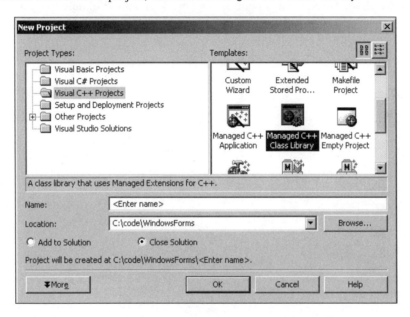

When the Wizard finishes doing its thing, add the following code to the generated `MyClock.h` header file:

```
#pragma once

using namespace System;

namespace MyClock
{
    public __gc class Stopwatch
    {
    public:
        Stopwatch();

        void Start();
        void Stop();
```

```
        __property int get_ElapsedTime();

    private:
        TimeSpan elapseTime;
        DateTime startTime;
    };
}
```

The `Stopwatch` class's two private member variables, `elapseTime` and `startTime`, are of types that come straight from the .NET Framework class library's `System` namespace. The `TimeSpan` structure represents a time interval, while the `DateTime` structure represents an instant in time, typically represented by a date and a time of day.

Along with these variables, `Stopwatch` declares a public constructor and two public methods, `Start()` and `Stop()`, which we'll examine in a moment. Finally, there's the read-only `ElapsedTime` property, which returns `TimeSpan`'s `TotalMilliseconds` property, which in turn contains the total time span in milliseconds.

Next, add the following code to the `MyClock.cpp` definition file:

```
#include "stdafx.h"

#include "MyClock.h"

MyClock::Stopwatch::Stopwatch()
{
    elapseTime = TimeSpan::Zero;
    startTime = DateTime::MinValue;
}

void MyClock::Stopwatch::Start()
{
    startTime = DateTime::Now;
}

void MyClock::Stopwatch::Stop()
{
    if(startTime != DateTime::MinValue)
        elapseTime = DateTime::Now - startTime;
}

int MyClock::Stopwatch::get_ElapsedTime()
{
    return Convert::ToInt32(elapseTime.TotalMilliseconds);
}
```

In the constructor, we initialize the `elapseTime` member to `TimeSpan::Zero`, so that the `ElapsedTime` property will return zero milliseconds if it's accessed before `Start()` has been called. We also initialize the `startTime` member variable to `DateTime::MinValue`, so that if `Stop()` is called before `Start()`, we don't get a garbage result in `elapseTime`.

Start() simply sets startTime to the current date and time, while Stop() (after checking to make sure that Start() has been called) subtracts the time stored in startTime from the current time and stores it in elapseTime. When you compile the project, you'll have a library assembly called MyClock.dll in your output directory.

Type accessibility

The types defined within assemblies have **accessibility**, in much the same way that the members of a C++ class do. By default, all of the classes in an assembly are private, which means that only the types defined within the same assembly can use them. To make a class visible to *other* assemblies, you need to mark the *class* as public. The following code demonstrates both public and private class declarations:

```
public __gc class LookAtMe {};
private __gc class CantTouchMe {};
```

Because public classes are visible to external assemblies, there must also be a mechanism to define the accessibility of class *members* to code within the assembly, and to code outside the assembly. The Managed Extensions for C++ achieve this by allowing *two* access specifiers to be used instead of one. The more restrictive of the two designates the *external* visibility, while the less restrictive designates the *internal* visibility. For example:

```
public __gc class LookAtMe
{
private private:

    // Private internal and external
    void PrivatePrivate() {}

private protected:

    // Protected internal and private external
    void PrivateProtected() {}

public private:

    // Public internal and private external
    void PrivatePublic() {}
};
```

The PrivatePrivate() method has private accessibility both internally within the assembly and externally to other assemblies. The PrivateProtected() method has protected accessibility internally within the assembly, but private accessibility externally, to other assemblies. This means that types defined within the same assembly as the LookAtMe class can derive from the LookAtMe class and access the protected member, but types defined in an external assembly that derive from the LookAtMe class don't have access to the protected member. Thirdly, the PrivatePublic() method has public *internal* accessibility and private *external* accessibility. Remember, the order of the access specifiers is irrelevant; it's simply that the more restrictive is used for external accessibility, and the less restrictive for internal accessibility.

The class visibility specifier overrides the member access specifier if the class access specifier is more restrictive. So even if a class declared as private has members that are declared to be externally public, the members will be made private when the code is compiled.

The last thing you need to know about using two access specifiers on class members is that using just one specifier is the same as using the same specifier twice. In other words, the PrivatePrivate() method need only have been specified as private (rather than private private), while to make a member accessible both inside and outside the assembly (class visibility specifiers permitting) requires you simply to specify it as public, as though nothing had changed.

Creating an application

That little departure aside, let's get back to the Stopwatch class we created earlier. On its own, the class is really quite useless, as it doesn't have an entry point. Next, then, we'll create an application that uses it, giving us the opportunity to check that everything works as expected. Create a new managed C++ application called TestStopwatch. This will simulate a poor man's profiling tool by using the Stopwatch class to find out how long it takes to run different sections of code.

When the new, empty project is ready, update the generated TestStopwatch.cpp file with the following code:

```cpp
#include "stdafx.h"

#using <mscorlib.dll>
#using "MyClock.dll"

#include <tchar.h>

using namespace System;
using namespace MyClock;

// This is the entry point for this application
int _tmain(void)
{
    Stopwatch &watch = *new Stopwatch;  // Reference to Stopwatch
    watch.Start();

    for(__int64 i = 0; i < 100000000; i++);
    watch.Stop();
    Console::WriteLine(S"Interval time in milliseconds: {0}",
                       watch.ElapsedTime.ToString());

    for(__int64 i = 0; i < 100000000; i++);
    watch.Stop();
    Console::WriteLine(S"End time in milliseconds: {0}",
                       watch.ElapsedTime.ToString());
    watch.Start();

    for(__int64 i = 0; i < 100000000; i++);
    watch.Stop();
    Console::WriteLine(S"Reset stopwatch elapsed time in milliseconds: {0}",
                       watch.ElapsedTime.ToString());
    return 0;
}
```

The main() function creates an instance of the Stopwatch class, which resides in the namespace MyClock. We call the Start() method to start the stopwatch and execute some code (in this case, a simple for loop), before calling Stop() and outputting the result to the console. Then, to make things interesting, we repeat this sequence a couple more times.

Before you compile the code, however, you'll need to make sure that you've told Visual Studio where it can find the assembly you've referenced with the #using directive at the top of the file. Right-click on the project node in Solution Explorer, and choose the Properties option from the context menu. In the project properties dialog box that appears, choose the C/C++ folder in the left pane, and then click on the General properties node. In the corresponding property grid that appears in the right pane, use the Resolve #using References property to add the folder path that contains the assembly that you've referenced with the #using directive:

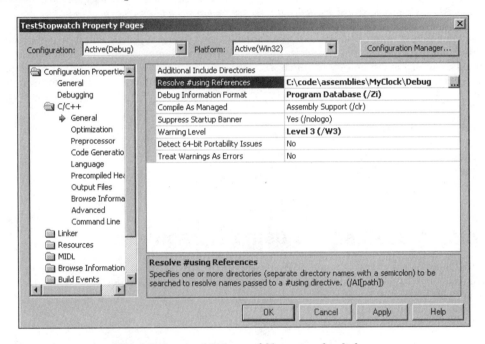

You might want to add both Debug and Release folders using this dialog.

You're now ready to build the application. Note that if you forget to add the reference for the right folder, then you'll get the following error when you try to build the code:

fatal error C1107: could not find assembly 'MyClock.dll': please specify the assembly search path using /AI or by setting the LIBPATH environment variable

However, we still can't run the application successfully yet. If you try, you'll find that the application crashes with a System.IO.FileNotFoundException – the CLR can't find the right file, namely, MyClock.dll.

> **The CLR only looks in three places for assemblies: the global assembly cache (GAC), the directory in which the application resides, or a subdirectory of that directory.**

The problem is that `MyClock.dll` is in none of these places, so the CLR can't find it. Adding the reference as described above only helped *Visual Studio .NET* find it. To help the *CLR* find it, we need to place it in one of the three places that the CLR will look. For now, it's easiest to simply move it to the `Debug` subdirectories of the `TestStopwatch` directory – we'll see how to use the GAC later on in the chapter.

You may be wondering why we didn't come across this problem in Chapter 1, in our cross-language example. The reason is that when you are using Visual Basic .NET or C#, Visual Studio .NET automatically copies across the assembly DLL for you, when you add reference to a project.

While in this simple example it's easy to move the file across using Windows Explorer, this is clearly not a good option for large, complex projects. In general, it's much better to add some commands to the pre-build event of `TestStopwatch`, which will execute every time `TestStopwatch` is recompiled. You can do this easily from the project's property pages – just select the **Pre-Build Event** from the **Build Events** folder.

Now you should be able to run the `TestStopwatch` application. The output will look something like this:

```
Interval time in milliseconds: 1432
End time in milliseconds: 2844
Reset stopwatch elapsed time in milliseconds: 1722
```

Examining assemblies using ILDasm

The .NET Framework comes with an **MSIL disassembler** called **ILDasm** that will allow us to examine the contents of an assembly. Using this tool, it's possible to disassemble a portable executable (PE) file that ends with `.exe`, `.dll`, `.obj`, or `.lib`.

You can run `ILDasm` from the command prompt:

```
> ildasm [options] [PEfilename] [options]
```

Note that you'll first need to set up your environment variables for Visual Studio .NET. All of `ILDasm`'s parameters are optional, and as is traditional for command-line tools, you can get a list of them by specifying "`ildasm /?`". If you don't enter any parameters, you'll be presented with an empty window on the desktop, from which you can retrieve the file you want to disassemble by selecting it via the **File | Open** menu item.

An easier way of running `ILDasm` is to add it to Visual Studio .NET's **Tools** menu. As in previous versions of Visual Studio, you can add any number of your own commands to this menu. Select **External Tools...** from the **Tools** menu, click **Add**, and then fill in the dialog as shown.

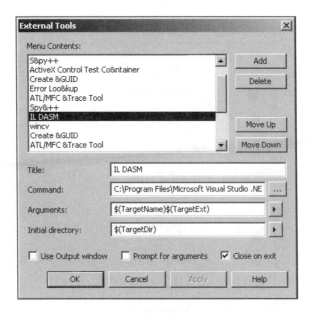

What these settings do is call ILDasm, passing it the output filename of the current project, and setting the current directory to this file's location. If you open up the MyClock project that you created earlier in this chapter and then select IL DASM from the Tools menu, MyClock.dll and an initial directory of Debug will be sent to ILDasm.exe, which in turn will generate the following window:

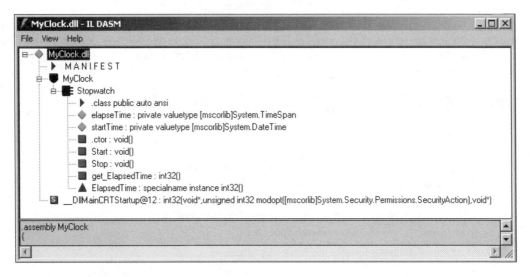

To make the breakdown of the disassembly easier to follow, ILDasm uses a tree structure not unlike the one that's shown by the Class View in Visual Studio .NET. Each element of the tree provides details about the assembly that the CLR will use later, during execution. As you'd expect, the symbols in the tree view all have specific meanings:

Symbol	Meaning
▶	More information about parent
⬛	Namespace
▤	Class
▣	Interface
▤	Value type
▣	Enum
■	Method
⑤	Static method
◆	Field
◈	Static field
▼	Event
▲	Property

If you think back to when you wrote MyClock.dll, you should notice a striking resemblance between the code you wrote and the output of ILDasm. The full details of MyClock.dll are here in plain view. In fact, if you double-click on any element in the tree, you'll get even more detail. Try clicking on the Start() method for example; you should see a window pop up that contains the IL version of this method:

```
Stopwatch::Start : void()                                                    _ □ ×
.method public instance void  Start() cil managed
{
  // Code size       22 (0x16)
  .maxstack  2
  .locals ([0] valuetype [mscorlib]System.DateTime V_0,
           [1] valuetype [mscorlib]System.DateTime V_1)
  IL_0000:  call       valuetype [mscorlib]System.DateTime [mscorlib]System.DateTime::get_Now()
  IL_0005:  stloc.0
  IL_0006:  ldloc.0
  IL_0007:  stloc.1
  IL_0008:  ldarg.0
  IL_0009:  ldflda     valuetype [mscorlib]System.DateTime MyClock.Stopwatch::startTime
  IL_000e:  ldloca.s   V_1
  IL_0010:  cpobj      [mscorlib]System.DateTime
  IL_0015:  ret
} // end of method Stopwatch::Start
```

The assembly manifest

When you double-click on M A N I F E S T, for example, you should see something like the screenshot below:

```
/ MANIFEST                                                              _|□|×|
.assembly extern mscorlib
{
    .publickeytoken = (B7 7A 5C 56 19 34 E0 89 )                // .z\U.4..
    .hash = (98 31 71 95 B3 A4 51 E8 E2 0D 25 55 57 E7 6E 9E    // .1q...Q...%UW.n.
             54 8C EF C9 )                                       // T...
    .ver 1:0:3300:0
}
.assembly extern Microsoft.VisualC
{
    .publickeytoken = (B0 3F 5F 7F 11 D5 0A 3A )                // .?_....:
    .hash = (EC 47 1C 7B E2 10 BB EE 15 E2 3B 4E FB 55 44 9D    // .G.{......;N.UD.
             E2 D0 4D B7 )                                       // ..M.
    .ver 7:0:3300:0
}
.assembly MyClock
{
    .custom instance void [mscorlib]System.Reflection.AssemblyKeyFileAttribute::.ctor(string) = ( 01
    .custom instance void [mscorlib]System.Reflection.AssemblyDescriptionAttribute::.ctor(string) = (
    .custom instance void [mscorlib]System.Reflection.AssemblyDelaySignAttribute::.ctor(bool) = ( 01
    .custom instance void [mscorlib]System.Reflection.AssemblyCompanyAttribute::.ctor(string) = ( 01
    .custom instance void [mscorlib]System.Reflection.AssemblyCopyrightAttribute::.ctor(string) = ( (
    .custom instance void [mscorlib]System.Reflection.AssemblyKeyNameAttribute::.ctor(string) = ( 01
    // --- The following custom attribute is added automatically, do not uncomment -------
    //  .custom instance void [mscorlib]System.Diagnostics.DebuggableAttribute::.ctor(bool,
    //                                                                    bool) = ( 01 0(
```

Once you know what you're looking for, you'll find that the manifest provides the following information:

❑   Assembly name – a text string containing the name of the assembly. In our case this is MyClock.

❑   Version number – a version number in `<major>:<minor>:<build>:<revision>` format.

❑   Culture – information about the culture (language, currency, number formatting, and so on) supported by this assembly.

❑   Strong name information – a fancy name for the public key from the publisher of the assembly. This is incorporated into the "strong name" of the assembly, which is a unique name and allows the publisher of the assembly to be identified. We'll see more on this later.

❑   List of files that make up the assembly.

❑   List of all referenced assemblies – all names, version numbers, and strong names of assemblies that are accessed by this assembly.

❑   Type reference information – information used by the CLR to map a type reference to the file that contains its declaration and implementation. This is used for types that are exported from the assembly.

❑   List of all assembly permissions – all the permissions required by the assembly that the CLR will have to allow for the assembly to run successfully.

In the MyClock manifest above, you can see that the assembly will reference the mscorlib and Microsoft.VisualC shared assemblies. To make sure that it accesses the *correct* assemblies, the manifest contains .publickeytoken to identify the assembly, .hash to verify that it has not been changed, and finally .ver to specify the version number needed for execution.

93

Next you see in the manifest above that this assembly is called `MyClock`. The `MyClock` assembly has several attributes associated with it, which contain information about the assembly. We can access this information programmatically, using a technique known as reflection, which we'll see in the next chapter. The `AssemblyInfo.cpp` file (generated by the Wizard) is used to set the manifest's attributes.

At the end of the manifest (not visible on the screenshot above) are a number of assembler directives used by the CLR to JIT compile the assembly. `.module` specifies the names of all the files that make up the assembly, in this case only one file, `MyClock.dll`:

```
.module MyClock.dll
```

AssemblyInfo.cpp

The details about the assembly that are found in the manifest come directly from the `AssemblyInfo.cpp` file, which was auto-generated by the project Wizard:

```
#include "stdafx.h"

using namespace System::Reflection;
using namespace System::Runtime::CompilerServices;

//
// General information about an assembly is controlled through the following
// set of attributes. Change these attribute values to modify the information
// associated with an assembly.
//
[assembly:AssemblyTitleAttribute("")];
[assembly:AssemblyDescriptionAttribute("")];
[assembly:AssemblyConfigurationAttribute("")];
[assembly:AssemblyCompanyAttribute("")];
[assembly:AssemblyProductAttribute("")];
[assembly:AssemblyCopyrightAttribute("")];
[assembly:AssemblyTrademarkAttribute("")];
[assembly:AssemblyCultureAttribute("")];


//
// Version information for an assembly consists of the following four values:
//
//      Major Version
//      Minor Version
//      Build Number
//      Revision
//
// You can specify all the values or you can default the Revision and Build
// numbers by using the '*' as shown below:

[assembly:AssemblyVersionAttribute("1.0.*")];


//
// In order to sign your assembly you must specify a key to use. Refer to the
// Microsoft .NET Framework documentation for more information on assembly
// signing.
```

```
//
// Use the attributes below to control which key is used for signing.
//
// Notes:
//   (*) If no key is specified, the assembly is not signed.
//   (*) KeyName refers to a key that has been installed in the Crypto Service
//       Provider (CSP) on your machine. KeyFile refers to a file that contains
//       a key.
//   (*) If the KeyFile and the KeyName values are both specified, the
//       following processing occurs:
//       (1) If the KeyName can be found in the CSP, that key is used.
//       (2) If the KeyName does not exist and the KeyFile does exist, the key
//           in the KeyFile is installed into the CSP and used.
//   (*) In order to create a KeyFile, you can use the sn.exe (strong name)
//       utility. When specifying the KeyFile, the location of the KeyFile
//       should be relative to the project directory.
//   (*) Delay Signing is an advanced option - see the Microsoft .NET Framework
//       documentation for more information on this.
//
[assembly:AssemblyDelaySignAttribute(false)];
[assembly:AssemblyKeyFileAttribute("")];
[assembly:AssemblyKeyNameAttribute("")];
```

During the compilation process, this file is compiled along with the other source files. However, unlike the other source files, this does not compile to MSIL, but instead is used to update the assembly manifest. If we need to update any of the manifest attributes, we simply fill in the quoted parameter. Valid values for the Culture attribute are defined by RFC 1766 *Tags for the Identification of Languages*. The AssemblyVersionAttribute allows us to specify a particular version number, which will become very important when we start to look at shared assemblies in a moment. The last three attributes – AssemblyDelaySignAttribute, AssemblyKeyFileAttribute, and AssemblyKeyNameAttribute – can each be used to add a strong name or public key to the assembly, and we'll be covering that soon, too. The following code extract illustrates how these attributes might be used:

```
[assembly:AssemblyTitleAttribute("Professional C++")];
[assembly:AssemblyDescriptionAttribute("")];
[assembly:AssemblyConfigurationAttribute("Retail Version")];
[assembly:AssemblyCompanyAttribute("Wrox Press")];
[assembly:AssemblyProductAttribute("Wrox Professional Series")];
[assembly:AssemblyCopyrightAttribute("Copyright (C) Wrox Press 2001")];
[assembly:AssemblyTrademarkAttribute("Wrox is a trademark of Wrox Press Ltd")];
[assembly:AssemblyCultureAttribute("en-US")];
```

Shared assemblies and private assemblies

Assemblies come in two flavors: private and shared. These highly imaginative names actually describe the situation quite well: both types are made up of one or more modules, and have one manifest. In fact, both types can provide exactly the same functionality. The only real difference lies in which assemblies can access them.

Private assemblies are exclusive to the application that uses them – all the assemblies we have created so far have been private assemblies. They must reside in the application's directory or in one of its subdirectories. (We saw this in practice earlier, when we had to copy the `MyClock` assembly to the `TestStopwatch` application directory.)

Since these assemblies can only be used within a single application, naming and versioning are no problem – you don't have to worry about conflicts with other applications. As long as you use and adhere to your own naming conventions, and make the assembly unique within the application, you will have no difficulties.

Shared assemblies, on the other hand, can be used by more than one application at the same time. Unlike private assemblies, shared assemblies are deployed to the **global assembly cache** (**GAC**), a machine-accessible location that's reserved only for assemblies. We'll cover the installation of shared assemblies later in this chapter. We have used shared assemblies already in our code – all of the assemblies that contain the implementations of the .NET Framework classes are shared assemblies and live in the GAC: for example, `mscorlib`.

Because they can be shared, these assemblies must be more careful about names and version numbers. It's possible, for example, that two different developers could create assemblies with the same name, with the potential for conflict. To combat this, shared assemblies also have a **strong name**, which is guaranteed to be unique.

It's also possible that two applications on the same machine could require two different versions of the same assembly; the use of shared assemblies allows this. Unlike COM, however, there is no necessity that assemblies should be backward compatible (though it doesn't hurt if they are). If an application were to access the wrong version of an assembly, it would be quite likely not to work as expected.

Creating shared assemblies

To create a shared assembly, you start by creating a private assembly, and then add a strong name, (optionally) set a specific version number, and place the assembly in the GAC. We've already got a private assembly (`Stopwatch`), so let's continue from there and convert it to a shared assembly.

Shared assembly names

A shared assembly requires two things. First, its name must be globally unique. Second, no one else must be allowed to steal the assembly name and use it (generally known as spoofing). In the old COM world, unique names were handled by using a globally unique identifier (GUID), but these only dealt with the first requirement of shared assemblies. In .NET, assemblies use **strong names**, which are made up of three parts: a simple text name, a public key, and a digital signature.

> *Public-key encryption is a very secure process. Anything encrypted by a private key can only be decrypted by the corresponding public key. As long as the private key remains unknown to the public, no one else can create anything that can be decrypted by the public key.*

The use of a key and a digital signature means that we can verify the author of an assembly and the fact that it has not been tampered with. First, the compiler creates an assembly and places the public key in the manifest for everyone to access. Then, it creates a hash of all the files belonging to the assembly, and encrypts the hash using the private key. Later, at runtime, the CLR loads the shared assembly and checks the hash signature using the public key. If the results are not valid, then it is known that the contents of the assembly have been changed – only the owner of the private key can create a valid hash.

Normally, you only create one public/private key pair for your company, which raises something of a problem during development: if all the programmers in the company have access to this key in order to test their shared assemblies, your security is already compromised. Instead, the developers should create their own keys; then, when the assembly is finished, it can be re-signed with the company key. We'll look at how to do this later on.

Generating a strong name

Creating a strong name is simplicity itself, although it does require the use of Microsoft's new strong name utility, SN. This tool has numerous command-line options, but for now we have only to concern ourselves with the -k option, which instructs SN to create an assembly key file containing a strong name. You can run sn.exe from the command prompt, or you can add it to the Tools menu. The naming convention for strong name key files is to end them with .snk, so to create a strong name key file, simply type the following at the command prompt:

```
> sn -k StrongName.snk
```

The file generated by sn.exe can only be referenced from your projects in two ways. You can specify its full filename, including the path, or you can specify it relative to the project directory.

> *If you've created shared assemblies in C#, you need to be careful here, because its behavior differs from that of C++. In C#, SNK files are expected to be found in the* `%ProjectDirectory%\obj\<configuration>` *directory.*

Signing the assembly

Now that we've got a key pair, all we need to do is update the AssemblyInfo.cpp file with it. Simply change the AssemblyKeyFile attribute to StrongName.snk, instead of the default empty string. Then set AssemblyDelaySignAttribute to false. What this means is that the assembly is fully signed when created. If you were to set this to true then space would be reserved in the assembly for the signature, which will be later filled by a signing tool such as the sn.exe utility. Finally, leave the AssemblyKeyNameAttribute empty. We'll see why in a second. The code should end up looking something like this:

```
[assembly: AssemblyDelaySignAttribute (false)];
[assembly: AssemblyKeyFileAttribute ("StrongName.snk")];
[assembly: AssemblyKeyNameAttribute ("")];
```

The AssemblyKeyNameAttribute attribute allows you to get your key pair from a Cryptographic Service Provider (CSP). It specifies the name of a key container within the CSP containing the key pair used to generate the strong name. An example of the syntax is:

```
[assembly: AssemblyDelaySignAttribute (false)];
[assembly:AssemblyKeyFileAttribute("")];
[assembly:AssemblyKeyNameAttribute("myKeyContainer")]
```

There is also a third way of assigning a strong name to an assembly. If you are using the AL.exe tool to link together different modules and/or resources to form an assembly manifest, then you simply specify the key name using the /keyf[ile]:*filename* option.

After completing any one of the preceding three methods of inserting a strong key, you should find that the public key contained in the SNK file has been added to the manifest:

```
/ MANIFEST                                              _ □ ×
                    72 00 6D 00 69 00 73 00 73 00 69 00 6F 00 6E 00  ▲
                    53 00 65 00 74 00 3E 00 0D 00 0A 00 )
   .publickey = (00 24 00 00 04 80 00 00 94 00 00 00 06 02 00 00   // .$....
                 00 24 00 00 52 53 41 31 00 04 00 00 01 00 01 00   // .$..RSf
                 FF 48 D8 2B 0E 11 C0 00 9A 53 E5 89 F8 E3 EC 13   // .H.+..
                 67 13 BF 03 06 FF FD FE 62 16 73 25 3B 38 77 1B   // g.....
                 3E 0B BB 29 A9 25 E8 42 E2 60 19 CE 21 75 86 26   // >..).%.
                 70 E3 AD 00 C2 30 B1 C8 B7 D9 29 64 2B 98 FA 4A   // p....0.
                 B2 DD 4E 4D BA DE D4 53 15 F1 EE CF 08 54 25 87   // ..NM..
                 0B 56 B8 19 0F 91 DE 1B 1C 1E 09 53 15 F5 44 38   // .U.....
                 E8 00 C8 3F F8 13 85 17 5C 1B BC 95 92 20 AF 41   // ...?..
                 84 FB E5 F1 2D BE 11 FF 7A CA A4 0D 3D 59 58 B4 ) // ....-.
   .hash algorithm 0x00008004
   .ver 1:0:764:24274
 }

 .module MyClock.dll
 // MVID: {64506626-A091-45CB-A1C1-DBF947DF83EA}
 .imagebase 0x10000000
 .subsystem 0x00000002
 .file alignment 4096
 .corflags 0x0000000a
 // Image base: 0x030a0000
```

Signcode digital signature

A strong name for your assembly will guarantee that it will have a unique name and prevent name spoofing. It allows an administrator to determine whether an assembly is authentic. On the other hand, no level of trust can be associated with a strong name.

Signcode.exe is a utility that allows you to sign an assembly with an authentic digital certificate, obtained from a third party certification authority. This digital signature will specify who created the assembly, allowing an administrator to decide if the assembly can be trusted.

You can add either, neither, or both a strong name and a signcode to an assembly, but if you have a strong name it must be added first. Signcode can sign only one file at a time. If you are using multi-file assemblies then you need to sign the file that contains the assembly manifest.

Setting the version number

If you're watching *very* closely, you may have noticed that the version number in the assembly manifest has also increased. This is because the AssemblyInfo.cpp file controls the version number of the assembly as well.

As we saw earlier, the version number of an assembly is made up of four parts: major, minor, build, and revision. In the MyClock assembly shown above, the version number is 1:0:764:24274. Typically, changes to the major and minor version numbers mean that some incompatibility has been introduced. A change to the build number means that incompatibility *may* have been introduced, while a change to the revision number means that the assembly is still guaranteed to be compatible with earlier versions.

You can set the version number to anything you desire by changing AssemblyVersionAttribute in AssemblyInfo.cpp, like this:

```
[assembly:AssemblyVersionAttribute("1.2.3.4")];
```

You can also allow the compiler to generate the revision and/or build number automatically, by using the default:

```
[assembly:AssemblyVersionAttribute("1.2.*")];
```

or:

```
[assembly:AssemblyVersionAttribute("1.2.3.*")];
```

When the compiler generates the last two portions of the version number automatically, it uses the number of days since January 1, 2000 as the build number, and the number of seconds since midnight divided by two (using the computer's clock) for the revision number.

Getting the version number programmatically

To get access to the version number of the MyClock assembly from the TestStopwatch assembly, we need to add a new property to the Stopwatch class called AssemblyVersion. This property will return a Version class, which has some handy properties to retrieve the four parts of the version.

The first thing you have to do is add the System::Reflection namespace and the definition of the new property to Stopwatch.h:

```
using namespace System::Reflection;

namespace MyClock
{
    public __gc class Stopwatch
    {
    public:
        __property Version *get_AssemblyVersion();

        // rest of code
    };
}
```

The System::Reflection namespace contains classes that facilitate programmatic access to metadata, such as versioning information. We'll be seeing lots more of this in the next chapter. Now, add the implementation of the property to Stopwatch.cpp:

```
Version *MyClock::Stopwatch::get_AssemblyVersion()
{
    Char del[] = new Char[1];
    del[0]= ',';

    Assembly *assembly = Assembly::GetExecutingAssembly();
    String *name[] = assembly->FullName->Split(del);

    return new Version(name[1]->Substring(name[1]->IndexOf('=')+1));
}
```

The `AssemblyVersion` property looks more complicated then it actually is. First we grab the executing assembly and then get the full name of the assembly. The full name contains a comma-delimited string of all the pieces that make up the name of the assembly. The second piece is the version number, in the form `Version=<major>.<minor>.<build>.<revision>`. So, after we get the full name, we `Split()` off the versions and then we `Substring()` the actual number. Finally we create a new `Version` using its constructor.

Now to access the version number in `TestStopwatch`, you simply have to get the number from the `AssemblyVersion` property:

```
int _tmain(void)
{
    Stopwatch &watch = *new Stopwatch;  // Reference to Stopwatch
    // rest of code
    Console::WriteLine(watch.AssemblyVersion);
}
```

If you build and run this code then you should see that – in addition to the output we saw earlier – this code also now outputs the version of the `MyClock` assembly.

The global assembly cache

As the name suggests, the **global assembly cache** (**GAC**) is a cache for assemblies, which sounds quite impressive until you realize that it's actually just a location-fixed, publicly accessible directory that stores shared assemblies. It has three ways of storing assemblies:

- ❑   In a machine-independent fashion – that is, as MSIL code.
- ❑   In native machine code – we'll cover native assemblies a little later.
- ❑   ASP.NET allows assemblies to be downloaded so that they can be used within HTML pages. Since ASP.NET does not readily support C++ we will not cover it in this book.

The location at which this directory is fixed is `<WINDIR>\assembly`; on most systems, this is the `C:\WinNT\assembly` directory. Because this location is guaranteed, the CLR will have no problem locating a shared assembly when it comes to execute an application that requires one.

Global assembly cache viewer

To view all the shared assemblies on your system, you can simply use Windows Explorer to navigate to the `assembly` directory:

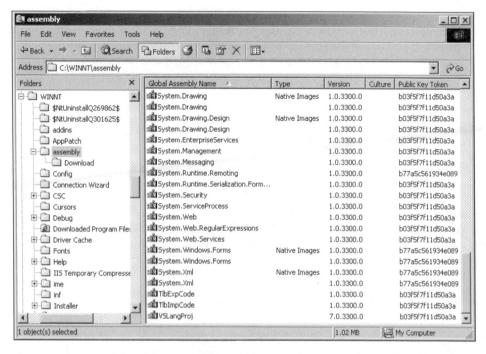

If the GAC viewer doesn't appear, it means that your system has had trouble installing the shell extension COM DLL, `shfusion.dll`, which Windows Explorer uses to generate the viewer. To fix this problem, simply register `shfusion.dll` using `regsvr32`.

The cache viewer allows you to see the assembly's name, type, version, culture, and public token. If you right-click on any assembly, you are given the option to delete the assembly or to view its properties. Here are the properties for the `System.Xml` assembly:

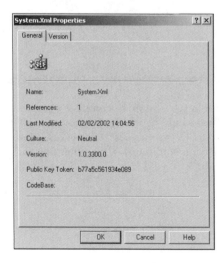

The assembly viewer is kind of neat, but unfortunately it also hides many of the details of the assembly (and the true directory structure) from the user. We'll need these details shortly, but the only way to see the real directory structure of the GAC is to use the command line. Fortunately, the actual directory structure, and the real location of a shared assembly, is easy to figure out based on the information provided by the viewer:

```
<WINDIR>\assembly\GAC\<assembly name>\<version>__<key token>
```

For the System.Xml assembly on my system, the shared assembly will be placed at:

```
C:\WINNT\assembly\GAC\System.XML\1.0.3300.0__b77a5c561934e089
```

There are two other major directories under <WINDIR>\assembly. The first is called Download and stores all download assemblies for HTML use. The second is a Native Image directory to store assemblies that have been compiled into native code (note that this is not visible in Explorer). You should never have to work with either of these directory structures directly. ASP.NET handles the first, and the native image generator, which we'll discuss below, handles the second.

Installing a shared assembly into the GAC

After you've signed an assembly with a strong name, there are two ways of installing it into the GAC (and thereby creating a shared assembly). The first, which I use exclusively, is simply to drag the assembly that you want to share into the GAC viewer. Nothing could be easier. (As a side note, deleting a shared assembly is just as easy: select the shared assembly in the viewer and press the *Delete* key.)

The second way is to use the global assembly cache utility, gacutil.exe. This tool doesn't provide any additional functionality over the GAC viewer, but since it's command-line driven, it can be used in batch routines. The gacutil.exe tool provides a few options, but the two you'll likely use most often are for installation and uninstallation. To install an assembly, use:

```
> gacutil /i <assembly name>.dll
```

To uninstall an assembly, use:

```
> gacutil /u <assembly name>,Version=<version number>
```

You might think that things start to get a bit more complex when you try to move multi-file assemblies to the GAC. Believe it or not, you would be wrong. To move a multi-file assembly, you either drag and drop the assembly DLL (that contains the manifest) to the GAC viewer, or call gacutil.exe for that same assembly DLL. When the command finishes, the other files that make up the assembly move automatically to the GAC as well.

Native image generation

Precompiled assemblies are assemblies that have been compiled to the native machine code of the platform on which they are to be executed. Since these images don't need to be compiled before being executed, they start a lot faster when called upon by the CLR. If you need the faster startup times provided by being precompiled, then this is a good option. However, it does use up a little more disk space, as the GAC requires that any assembly in the native image cache (the place in the GAC where the native image generator places its precompiled assemblies) *must* also have a copy in the regular GAC. This extra copy is used to extract metadata from and also gets JITed for cases where security changes or versions checks fail.

There currently is no automatic way of precompiling assemblies. You must do it manually, when you install them into the GAC. To generate native images, you use the native image generator utility, ngen.exe. As usual, this utility can take several options, but specifying the name of the assembly alone will generate the native image automatically within the GAC:

```
> ngen MyClock
```

Now you should be able to see two versions of MyClock in the GAC, where one has its Type specified as Native Image. The native image will remain in the GAC until it is deleted; to do this, simply run ngen.exe again, specifying the /delete option along with the name of the assembly:

```
> ngen /delete MyClock
```

Using a shared assembly

Let's now use the TestStopwatch application assembly to reference a shared version of the MyClock library assembly. The first thing you need to do is delete MyClock.dll from the project's Debug and Release directories – if you don't, TestStopwatch.exe will try to reference it there, rather than from the GAC. Also, you must delete (or comment out) any build events you created earlier in the TestStopwatch project that would copy MyClock.dll back again!

Now if you compile and execute TestStopwatch, you'll see virtually the same output as we had when executing the private assembly version:

```
Interval time in milliseconds: 1863
End time in milliseconds:3916
Reset stopwatch elapsed time in milliseconds: 12363
1.0.764.24896
```

Replacing the strong name key for delivery

When at last the shared assembly is fully tested and ready to be deployed, it's time to sign the assembly with the company's key pair. (Until now, all development has been done with the developer's key pair.) Creating the company's key pair is no different from creating the developer's; the difference between the two lies in who has access to those keys.

```
> sn -k CompanyStrongNameKey.snk
```

Now that the privileged developer has both the shared assembly and the company key, all they have to do is to run the strong name utility `sn.exe` one more time, this time using the replace option:

```
> sn -R <assembly name> <key file name>
```

The -R option states that you plan on replacing the strong name in the assembly that follows. Now all that needs to be done with the newly signed, shared assembly is to install it into the GAC – and we've already covered that. With this newly signed assembly, the CLR can now be assured that the assembly is the one expected and that it has not been altered in any way.

Versioning support

Now that we have covered the GAC, we can come back and see .NET versioning support in action. The main thing you need to understand is that assemblies reference each other using a specific version. Since we already have one copy of `MyClock.dll` assembly in the GAC, which is referenced by the `TestStopwatch.exe` assembly, all we need do now is move another version of `MyClock.dll` into the GAC and have it referenced by another assembly. The easiest way to do this is to simply recompile both projects in Release mode, rather than Debug mode. Start with the `MyClock` project, and copy the newly generated `MyClock.dll` assembly to the GAC; using the GAC viewer, you should see two copies of `MyClock.dll`, with two different versions:

Global Assembly ...	Type	Version	Culture	Public Key Token	
mscorcfg		1.0.3300.0		b03f5f7f11d50a3a	
mscorlib	Native Images	1.0.3300.0		b77a5c561934e089	
MSDATASRC		7.0.3300.0		b03f5f7f11d50a3a	
MSDDSLMP		7.0.3300.0		b03f5f7f11d50a3a	
MSDDSP		7.0.3300.0		b03f5f7f11d50a3a	
MyClock		1.0.764.26049		f64921db005adfcb	
MyClock		1.0.764.24896		f64921db005adfcb	
Office		7.0.3300.0		b03f5f7f11d50a3a	
Regcode		1.0.3300.0		b03f5f7f11d50a3a	
SoapSudsCode		1.0.3300.0		b03f5f7f11d50a3a	

Next, recompile the client application `TestStopwatch`, making sure that you are referencing the release version of `MyClock`. To see .NET versioning in action, run the debug and release version of `TestStopwatch.exe`; you will see that they both access different version numbers. These assembly versions happen to be the version that they were compiled against:

```
Command Prompt                                              _ □ x
C:\>cd C:\code\assemblies\TestStopwatch\Debug

C:\code\assemblies\TestStopwatch\Debug>TestStopwatch
Interval time in milliseconds: 1873
End time in milliseconds: 3765
Reset stopwatch elapsed time in milliseconds: 2303
1.0.764.24896

C:\code\assemblies\TestStopwatch\Debug>
```

```
Command Prompt                                                    _ □ X
C:\>cd C:\code\assemblies\TestStopwatch\Release

C:\code\assemblies\TestStopwatch\Release>TestStopwatch
Interval time in milliseconds: 1853
End time in milliseconds: 3705
Reset stopwatch elapsed time in milliseconds: 2283
1.0.764.26049

C:\code\assemblies\TestStopwatch\Release>
```

Working with resources

The .NET Framework base classes provide great support for working with resources – that is, pictures, icons, cursors, strings, and so on. Unfortunately for C++ programmers, and unlike some of the other .NET languages, it takes a little work up front in order to get things started. There are three ways to work with resources in .NET:

❑   Embed the resource file(s) directly into an assembly.

❑   Have the resource file(s) external to the assembly. This allows you to have *dynamic* resource files – you can create and then use an external resource file while an application is executing.

❑   Have resources as satellite assemblies – assemblies that contain only resources. These can be used to handle localization or provide language specific resources based on the culture implementing the assembly.

Creating a resource file

There are two editable text file formats that can be used to create resource files: XML and name/value pairs. XML resource files take the extension .resX, while name/value files can have pretty much any extension you like – although the convention is to use .txt.

As a C++ programmer, you will have little need to deal with .resX files – they're used to store the Windows Forms and Web Forms resources that can be created within Visual Studio .NET. Visual C++ .NET doesn't support Web Forms, and Windows Forms can only be created manually, with little help from the IDE (as we'll see in Chapter 6). Since the format of .resX files is quite complex – certainly, much more so than name/value files – and not supported by the C++ IDE, we won't be discussing them any further here.

It's possible to place pictures, string tables, and many other objects into .resources files. You can create .resources files comprising only one type of resource or made of many different types. The simplest type of resource you can create is a string table, used predominantly for multi-language applications (human languages, this time). To create a string table resource, simply create a text file comprising name/value pairs, like this:

```
name = value
```

Spaces are allowed in both the name and the value, but you need to be careful if you plan on lining up all the equal signs – the extra spaces will become part of the name. It's also quite safe to embed an equal sign in the value, as only the first such sign is significant.

ResGen

In itself, a text file is not a resource file – it needs to be converted to a binary .resources file that will be used by the CLR. The .NET Framework provides a utility called resgen.exe to do this conversion for you; to use it on a resource text file called test.txt, for example, you can simply type the following at the command line:

```
> resgen test.txt
```

When the utility finishes executing, you'll have a resource file called test.resources in your current directory. This file can be embedded into an application or library assembly, accessed as it stands, or placed in a satellite assembly. We'll examine how to embed a .resources file into an assembly later on in this chapter.

ResourceWriter

Unfortunately, the resgen.exe utility doesn't support pictures or other non-text objects, but adding non-text objects is still quite easy to do; we use the ResourceWriter class, which can be found in the .NET Framework base classes. The code for creating a .resources file containing images couldn't be much easier. Here, for example, is all the code you need to create a resource file containing an image of the Wrox logo:

```
#using <mscorlib.dll>
#using <System.Drawing.dll>

using namespace System;
using namespace System::Resources;
using namespace System::Drawing;

int main(void)
{
    ResourceWriter* rw = new ResourceWriter(S"WroxLogo.resources");
    rw->AddResource(S"WroxLogo", Image::FromFile(S"wroxlogo.gif"));
    rw->Close();

    return 0;
}
```

We simply create an instance of a ResourceWriter, add resources to it using its AddResource() method, and then close it. The first parameter of the overloaded AddResource() method is always the name of the resource, while the second is the resource itself – it can be a string, an array of bytes, or a generic object. This built-in versatility means that you can put almost anything into a resource file using this method, provided that the total size of the file does not exceed 2 GB. If you build and execute this code, a CLR binary called WroxLogo.resources is generated.

Using Visual Studio .NET to build .resources files

Going to the command line to handle all of your resource file activities can become quite a hassle. However, although Visual Studio .NET won't handle resources for you automatically, you can force it to do so with just a few minor property changes.

Let's go ahead and build an application that shows all the resource types in action. We will start with simple embedded resources, then make a little side step to see how localization works, and finally we will use some dynamic external `.resources`. The external resource will be an image file that will be displayed in a Windows Form.

First, start up Visual Studio .NET and create a **Managed C++ Application** called ResourceDemo. Next, add three new *text* files called test_1.txt, test_1.fr.txt, and test_2.txt to the project. You can do this by right-clicking on the project and selecting **Add | Add New Item...** from the context menu:

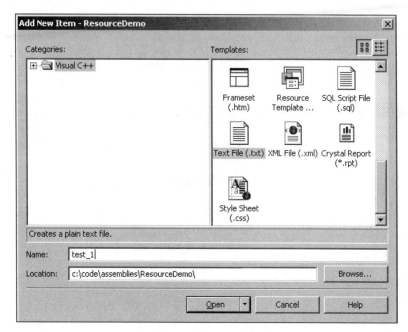

These will hold the resource file name/value pairs. We will need to convert them into `.resources` files before they will get the benefits of the resource management provided by .NET. Obviously, there is nothing stopping you from using these files as ordinary text files. To test_1.txt, add the following:

```
First = The first text.
Second = The second text = Equals included (works!).
Third = The third text.
Fourth = The fourth text.
```

We will embed test_1.txt into the ResourceDemo assembly. To test_1.fr.txt, add the following:

```
First = Le texte premiere.
Second = Le texte deuxieme.
Third = Le texte troisieme.
Fourth = Le texte quatrieme.
```

We will be converting this into a satellite assembly. Finally, enter the following into `test_2.txt`:

```
Fifth = The fifth text.
Sixth = The sixth text.
Seventh = The seventh text.
Eighth = The eighth text.
```

This file will be converted to an external `.resources` file called `test_2.resources`.

To get Visual Studio .NET to convert these files automatically whenever they are changed takes a little effort on the part of the developer. The idea, though, is quite simple; we need to run `resgen.exe` in the custom build step of each of the `.txt` files. Select `test_1.txt`, and bring up its **Properties** dialog box. Then select **General** from within the **Custom Build Step** folder, and update the **Command Line** edit box to read **ResGen.exe $(InputFileName)** and the **Outputs** box to read **$(InputName).resources**:

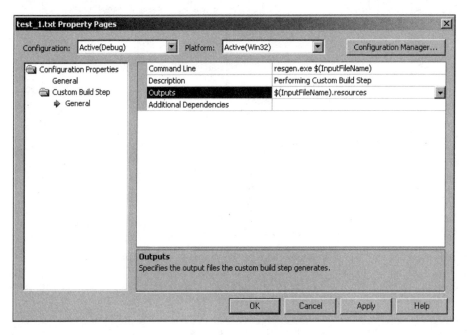

Finally, repeat this same process for the `test_1.fr.txt` and `test_2.txt` files. Now we have three text files that get converted to `.resources` files on each build. Next, we need to embed the `test_1.resources` file into the `ResourceDemo.exe` assembly. We can do this from the **Properties** dialog box for the application – select **Input** from within the **Linker** folder. From here, add `test_1.resources` to the **Embed Managed Resources File** edit box:

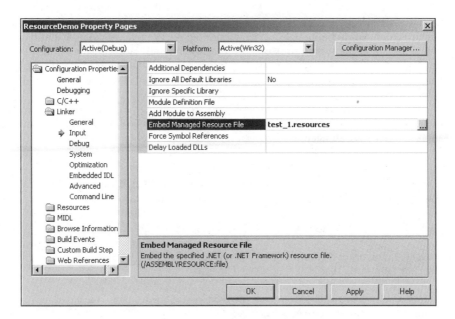

You'll be able to verify that this has been done successfully, because after rebuilding the project, you'll find the following entry in the assembly manifest of the ResourceDemo assembly:

```
.mresource public test_1.resources
{
}
```

Localization

We've already created a .resources file that contains the French equivalent of test_1.resources. Wouldn't it be good to be able to have the application change automatically to French if you have set up you computer to use the French culture? This is known as localization. Unfortunately, it is not quite as easy to do this in C++ as it is in Visual Basic .NET or C#. For those languages it is simply a matter of changing a property, setting the culture to the one you want to develop in, and then finally changing the UI just like you did for your default language. The IDE handles all the resources stuff in the background and you don't have to worry about it. For C++, on the other hand, none of this functionality exists. You have to handle the resources yourself. However, you end up doing it in exactly the same way as the other languages do behind the scenes.

We will see how to access the resources a little later, but first let's see how we need to set up the resources files so that localization will work. We start by creating a .txt file that contains all the same name/value pairs as the default culture, except, of course, all the values are translated. If you don't translate all the values, the localization process will automatically default to the default culture's values; if you deleted the second name/value pair from the above test_1.fr.txt file, then the default English text would be displayed. In fact, to see this is action a little later, go ahead and delete that name/value pair now.

Localizations are handled by creating a subdirectory where the application assembly is located. The name of the directory should be the RFC 1766 culture tag for French – that is, "fr". Add an `fr` directory to the debug directory of the `ResourceDemo` project directory structure. Inside of this directory we need to place one satellite assembly associated with that culture. The name of the assembly will be `ResourcesDemo.resources.dll`.

Building a satellite assembly requires the Assembly Linker (`AL.exe`) command. This command takes a number of parameters to build the satellite assembly: first, the name of the assembly to create, followed by its version. Obviously, you need to set the culture for the assembly and finally embed the resource into the assembly:

```
> al /out:fr/ResourceDemo.resources.dll /version:1.0.0.0 /culture:fr
/embedresource:test_1.fr.resources,test_1.fr.resources,Private
```

We could add this as a post-build event to the project, which would contain the following command:

```
al /out:$(OutDir)/fr/ResourceDemo.resources.dll /v:1.0.0.0 /c:fr
/embed:test_1.fr.resources,test_1.fr.resources,Private
```

This will automatically take the `.resources` file that Visual Studio .NET built earlier and build a satellite assembly right into the correct directory.

Accessing resource files

Now that we have resources embedded into an assembly, or just saved in a `.resources` file, we're going to want to give be able to access them. The .NET Framework provides two classes for doing this:

❑   `ResourceManager` – reads the resources directly out of an assembly

❑   `ResourceReader` – iterates through a resource file, extracting resources from it

ResourceManager

We need to determine the assembly being executed, and use it along with the name of the `.resources` file we want to access, in order to create an instance of the `ResourceManager` class. Then, using the `ResourceManager`, we request the resource value we need by name. The hardest part is getting the name of the executing assembly. Fortunately, the .NET Framework provides a static method called `GetExecutingAssembly()` (from the `System::Reflection::Assembly` class) that handles this for us. The following listing shows how easy it is to code:

```
// ResourceDemo.cpp

#include "stdafx.h"
#using <mscorlib.dll>

using namespace System;
using namespace System::Reflection;
using namespace System::Resources;
```

```
int main(void)
{
    // Accessing resources from within assembly
    Assembly* assembly = Assembly::GetExecutingAssembly();
    ResourceManager* rm = new ResourceManager(S"test_1", assembly);

    Console::WriteLine(rm->GetObject(S"First"));
    Console::WriteLine(rm->GetObject(S"Second"));
    Console::WriteLine(rm->GetObject(S"Third"));
    Console::WriteLine(rm->GetObject(S"Fourth"));

    // rest of code - explained in the following sections
}
```

Localization with ResourceManager

The ResourceManager class has an added bonus in that it handles localization automatically based on the CurrentUICulture property of the current thread, which we can obtain using the static method Threading::Thread::CurrentThread().To change the value of the CurrentUICulture property, we assign it with an instance of a CultureInfo object (from the System::Globalization namespace), which we initialize with a string value of the tag for the culture. Once this is done, we can get the objects out of the .resources file as above:

```
// Accessing resources from satellite assembly
Globalization::CultureInfo* cultureInfo =
                            new Globalization::CultureInfo(S"fr");
Threading::Thread::CurrentThread->CurrentUICulture = cultureInfo;

Console::WriteLine(rm->GetObject(S"First"));
Console::WriteLine(rm->GetObject(S"Second"));
Console::WriteLine(rm->GetObject(S"Third"));
Console::WriteLine(rm->GetObject(S"Fourth"));
```

The application will abort if it can't find a satellite assembly of the culture expected. However, you do not need to replicate all object types. If the resource manager is unable to find the resource object in the satellite it will then grab it from the default .resources file.

ResourceReader

If you plan on using external .resources files, then you have two options:

❑   Use the static method of the ResourceManager class, CreateFileBasedResourceManager(), to create the ResourseManager

❑   Use the ResourceReader class

We'll focus on the ResourceReader class in this section. ResourceReader allows you to treat a .resources file like any other sequential file, reading through the name/value pairs one at a time. A potential problem is that the order read might not be the same as the order in which it was written – we'll see this happening later in this chapter.

The basic sequence of operations for using ResourceReader is the same as for any other stream file. (In fact, you can use a stream instead of a .resources file, if you want to.) You open the .resources file, create an enumerator, read or MoveNext() through the name/value pairs, and close the .resources file. This is demonstrated in th code overleaf.

```
// Accessing external resource files
ResourceReader* rr = new ResourceReader(S"test_2.resources");
Collections::IDictionaryEnumerator* de = rr->GetEnumerator();
while(de->MoveNext())
{
   Console::Write(de->Key);
   Console::Write(S" = ");
   Console::WriteLine(de->Value);
}
rr->Close();
```

We'll cover enumerating through lists and collections using the .NET Framework collection classes in Chapter 5.

Dynamic resources

We finish up the `ResourceDemo` example by dynamically creating a `.resources` file containing an image and then displaying that image in a simple Windows Form. We have already seen the code to create a `.resources` file dynamically. The new thing here is the call to create a Windows Form:

```
ResourceWriter *rw = new ResourceWriter(S"test_3.resources");
rw->AddResource(S"WroxLogo", Image::FromFile(S"wroxlogo.gif"));
rw->Close();

// Accessing dynamically generated resource file (with an image)
Application::Run(new WinForm());
```

Shown below is the code for the `WinForm` class, derived from the `Form` class. In its constructor, we get the `.resources` file, and then create a picture box, setting its properties appropriately to display the image. Finally, we resize the form and add the picture to it:

```
__gc class WinForm: public Form
{
public:
   WinForm()
   {
      ResourceManager *rm =
         ResourceManager::CreateFileBasedResourceManager(S"test_3", "", 0 );

      PictureBox *pictureBox = new PictureBox();
      pictureBox->Image = dynamic_cast<Image*>(rm->GetObject(S"WroxLogo"));
      pictureBox->Location = Point(16, 8);
      pictureBox->Size = Drawing::Size(64, 72);

      this->ClientSize = Drawing::Size(100, 80);
      this->Controls->Add(pictureBox);
   }
};
```

In order to use the classes that allow us to create Windows Forms, we need to import a couple of new assemblies, and add some using namespace directives at the top of the file:

```
#include "stdafx.h"

#using <mscorlib.dll>
#include <tchar.h>
#using <System.dll>
#using <System.Windows.Forms.dll>
#using <System.Drawing.dll>

using namespace System;
using namespace System::Resources;
using namespace System::Windows::Forms;
using namespace System::Drawing;
```

From the above code, you can see that the process of creating a form or window is considerably easier in .NET than with traditional C++. We'll see a lot more examples of this in Chapter 6.

> *Note that we need to qualify the* Size *class with* Drawing, *even though we have declared the* System::Drawing *namespace, in order to distinguish it from the* Size *property of the* Form *class.*

Now that we've finally completed the ResourceDemo, it's time to build and run the project. Here is what the final output should look like:

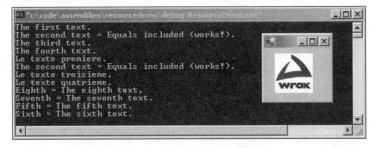

Note that there is potential 'gotcha' when using ResourceReader. The last four text entries are not in the order that they were placed into the .resources file. Because of this, you should check the object's name before assuming it is the object that you want.

Deploying assemblies

The first thing to consider when deploying the applications and controls that you've written for .NET is that they require the .NET Framework to be installed on the computer on which they are to be executed. There are two free distributable versions of the .NET Framework:

- ❑ The full version consists of the entire .NET Framework, excluding the design-time elements. This version is used for full-featured applications and controls.

- ❑ The control version is a minimal subset of the .NET Framework designed solely to allow the operation of .NET controls hosted within a browser.

Only the full version is relevant for us, as C++ does not support Web Forms or controls. The console applications, Windows Forms applications, and web services that can be made using C++ code all require the full version.

Once a target machine has the .NET Framework installed, application deployment may be as simple as copying the assemblies required to execute the application to the target machine. This can be done in one of three ways, depending on the method of distribution and the complexity of the application. The first and easiest way is to use `xcopy.exe` or `unzip.exe` to get the application's directory to the target machine. This directory can be placed *anywhere* on the target machine, as the only requirement for private assemblies is that they should be located in the application's directory or a culture specific subdirectory. Admittedly, this solution can be used only if no shared assemblies need to be placed in the GAC, but then there's nothing stopping you from writing a simple batch command to accomplish this.

The second way to deploy an application is to make it available for download over the Web. This is most conveniently accomplished using CAB files, which are subject to the following restrictions:

❑   Only one assembly can be placed into a CAB file.

❑   The CAB file has to have the same name as the assembly (apart from the extension, of course). If the assembly were called `lotafunc.dll`, then the CAB file would be called `lotafunc.cab`.

> *The CLR does not search CAB files for referenced assemblies, so your installation process must expand the CAB files.*

It is important to note that copying assemblies onto the target machine only really works in the case of pure managed code. It is likely that the majority of managed C++ applications will also include *unmanaged* code. After all, one of the main motivating factors behind using managed C++ is that it provides you with a way to interface between existing unmanaged code and the managed world of .NET. Once you introduce unmanaged code, you are likely to introduce dependencies on external libraries, and also have other additional requirements, such as COM component registration. In such cases, you would need a more sophisticated method of installation, such as using the Windows Installer and deploying on a CD-ROM or DVD.

This latter method provides by far the most functionality – you can automate the entire process, including the repair and removal of all assemblies at a later date. You can also add other installation requirements. The person installing the software just needs to place the CD-ROM or DVD into their drive and answer a few simple questions.

Using the Windows Installer, you can automate the copying of all shared assemblies, be they local to the application or located in the GAC. If an assembly is destined for the GAC, the Windows Installer will run `gacutil.exe` automatically. Building an installation file is simply a matter of adding a **Setup Project** to your current project, as shown opposite:

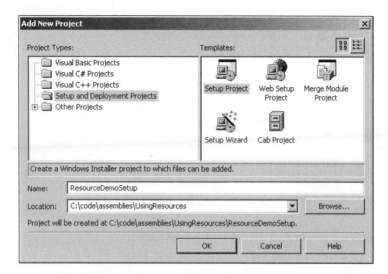

Then, depending on what you want to add, you select Project Output from the Add menu item of the Application Folder or Global Assembly Cache Folder:

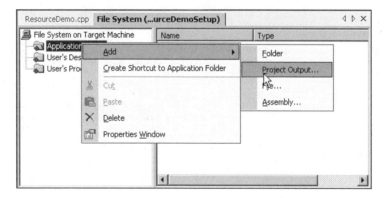

This will bring up the **Add Project Output Group** dialog box. First, select the startup project (that is, the project that contains the application's entry point) in the **Project** drop-down box. Then select **Primary Output**. This will cause all of this application's assemblies to be moved to the setup file.

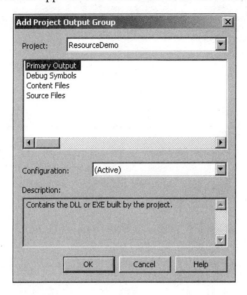

To add a satellite assembly, simply create a sub-directory off of `Application Folder` with the RCF 1766 culture tag as its name (in this case "fr") and then add the satellite resource to this subdirectory:

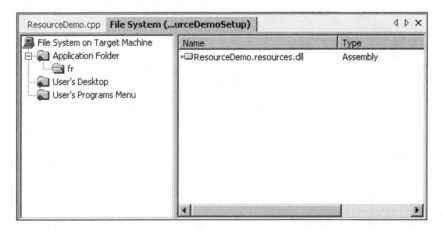

To add an assembly to the GAC, you need to add a special folder. Right-click on the **File System on Target Machine** folder, select **Add Special Folder**, and then select **Global Assembly Cache Folder**. Now all you have to do is move all shared assemblies destined to the GAC into this folder.

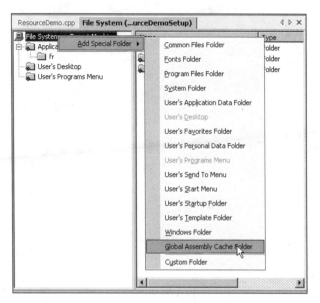

There are many other properties that you can change as well, but to cover them all would require another book!

Summary

In this chapter, we have carried out a thorough examination of assemblies, the key to all .NET Framework application execution and distribution. Assemblies are crucial in fulfilling the main design goals of .NET – they are platform and language independent, are self-describing, and have zero impact installations. They can interoperate with assemblies written in any other .NET-compatible language.

We have seen how assemblies work in action by building class library and application assemblies, and we saw how they referenced one another. We then delved into the internals of our assembly by examining its structure – in particular, its manifest – using the ILDasm utility.

Having covered the basics, we continued by contrasting private assemblies with shared assemblies. We saw how to create strong names and versions, and how to install an assembly in the global assembly cache (GAC). Along the way, we looked at a couple of useful utilities for working with the GAC:

- ❑ gacutil.exe – for installing and uninstalling assemblies in the GAC
- ❑ ngen.exe – generates a native image for faster startup times

We examined resource files, both embedded into assembles and external in a .resources file. We covered how to create them with a text file and resgen.exe and the ResourceWriter class. After this, we looked at how to access them with the ResourceManager and ResourceReader classes. We then went ahead and created a simple example showing resources in action, and learned how simple text resources can be used to implement localization.

Finally, we had a brief overview of deployment assemblies, using xcopy.exe, unzip.exe, CAB files, or Windows Installer.

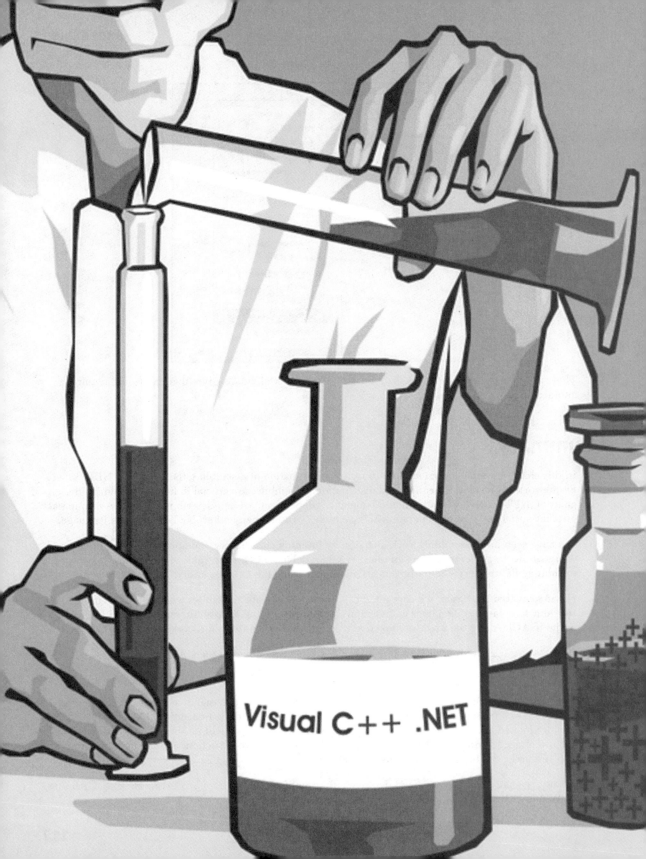

4

Attributes and reflection

In the book so far, and especially in the last chapter, we've made much of how .NET's assemblies provide a way of distributing not only executable code, but also information about that code: metadata. At this stage, the metadata you've seen has been almost exclusively to do with things like data types and version numbers – useful, but nothing you couldn't have achieved using more traditional techniques, if you'd put your mind to it. In this chapter, we're going to look at how to add information to your code that actually changes the way it behaves, and at how to read all of these kinds of information programmatically. The .NET technologies in question are attributes and reflection.

Attributes are extra pieces of information about the entities in your code (classes, methods, properties, and so on) that you include in your source code using a special syntax. They may either modify the behavior of those entities, or simply be stored as extra information in the metadata of the emitted assemblies. If that sounds a bit vague, you'll begin to get a clearer idea just as soon as we start looking at some examples!

Reflection is the ability to gain programmatic access to the information in the metadata. This means that a program can examine the classes, methods, and other items in an assembly, or even examine itself in this way. This means that certain tasks that were very difficult (or even impossible) to code with traditional languages are now easy to implement.

Although attributes and reflection are two very different technologies, it's likely that you can already start to see the potential of using them together. They're related at the level of metadata: attributes can emit it, and reflection is about examining it. You can use attributes to add extra information that describes the classes, methods, etc. in your code, and programmatically examine that information later on, before taking actions based on it. To give an idea of why this is useful, we've listed some possible applications overleaf.

❑ Developer tools can make use of reflection to provide details about the classes, methods, and parameters in libraries automatically.

❑ The WinCV documentation tool uses reflection to provide information about the classes in the .NET Framework class library.

❑ If your organization sells class libraries to other software companies, you could use attributes to indicate the date that each class or method in your code was last modified, or which group in your organization was responsible for that piece of code. Your customers could then use reflection to retrieve the information, and so speed up software support or maintenance calls.

❑ If your application relies on a library that contains an unknown number of similar classes, it can use reflection to determine exactly what classes are available for it to use. We'll see an example of this later in this chapter, when we develop a musical instruments library.

❑ An application that provides a user interface for a database could use attributes to indicate which members of a class correspond to which tables and fields in the database, simplifying the code necessary to read from and write to the database.

❑ If you ship several versions of an application ("professional", "enterprise", etc.), you could use attributes to indicate what features of your application should be available in what version. Similarly, if your application involves some administration, you could use attributes to indicate what types of user should be permitted access to which features. (Actually, in the last case you may find that .NET's inbuilt security facilities can do what you need more easily.)

With all of these facilities available, there's a fair amount of ground to cover, and we need to deal with things in a sensible order. The remainder of this chapter is broadly divided into three sections:

❑ Attributes – we'll examine some of the more useful attributes that Microsoft has defined, as well as how to define your own.

❑ Reflection – we'll develop a small example that demonstrates how you can use reflection to discover the properties of a class.

❑ Putting the two technologies together – we'll assemble a short sample based on a music software package that uses attributes and reflection to enumerate the different instruments it defines.

Attributes

At the beginning, we said that attributes "may either modify the behavior of entities [in your code], or simply be stored as extra information in the metadata of the emitted assemblies". These apparently unrelated aspects of attributes' behavior come from the fact that attributes actually come in two flavors:

❑ Attributes that, rather like some preprocessor directives, cause extra C++ code to be added to your programs immediately before compilation. These attributes are new in Visual C++ .NET, but actually have nothing to do with the .NET Framework – for the most part, they've been introduced in order to simplify COM programming. Because they're not related to .NET, they don't emit metadata, and it's not possible to use reflection with these attributes.

❑ Attributes that are recognized by the .NET Framework. These do not cause C++ code to be added to your program, but they do normally cause additional metadata to be added to assemblies, and *can* be used in conjunction with reflection.

Whereas the COM-related attributes are entirely a feature of the new C++ compiler (and are therefore C++-specific), the .NET-related attributes are supported from within the .NET Framework itself. This means that they're also available in the other .NET-compatible languages, including C# and Visual Basic .NET. Because the .NET Framework supports the definition of new attributes as well as the use of existing ones, we can further subdivide the .NET-related attributes into:

- ❑ .NET attributes that have been defined and implemented by Microsoft as part of the .NET Framework. These attributes are recognized by the various .NET compilers and can result in some additional compilation actions, as well as causing extra metadata to be emitted.

- ❑ Custom attributes that are (usually) defined in third-party code.

Syntactically, there are no differences between the three categories of attributes. You simply apply the attributes you need, and you don't need to worry about where they came from. You will find, however, that the names of COM attributes tend to be lower case (coclass, uuid), while .NET attributes are usually Pascal-cased (that is, the first letter of each word is capitalized, as in StructLayout or AttributeUsage). Because of the very different effects of the different attribute types, we will continue to examine them separately.

C++ attributes

If you've ever done any COM component programming, and needed to examine Interface Definition Language (IDL) files, then you'll already be familiar with attributes – they form an integral part of IDL. Since attributes in C++ work in much the same way as they do in IDL, we can learn a lot by reminding ourselves how attributes work in IDL. For example, look at this COM interface definition:

```
// NB. This is IDL code, not C++ code
[
    object,
    uuid(82CB2B10-DD33-4B05-A0D1-E199EF32AEB8),
    dual,
]
interface ISomeInterface : IDispatch
{
    [id] HRESULT DoSomething([in] BSTR bstrData);
};
```

The attributes are the entities between square brackets, and they get *everywhere*. The object attribute tells the IDL compiler that this interface is part of a COM class definition, the uuid attribute supplies the IID of the interface, and the dual attribute indicates that the interface is derived from IDispatch (and so supports Automation). These three attributes apply to the whole interface, and therefore – according to IDL syntax – must be placed immediately before the interface definition. Similarly, the id attribute (giving the dispatch ID) is applied to the interface's method, while the method's one parameter is modified by the in attribute, indicating that the parameter is used to accept a value from the client, rather than to pass one back. The IDL compiler relies on the information supplied by the attributes – it wouldn't be possible to write an IDL file without them.

In Visual C++ .NET, attributes are a Microsoft-specific extension to ANSI C++, and the C++ compiler now recognizes a number of attributes. The syntax is exactly the same as for IDL – one of the attributes is coclass, which serves much the same function in C++ as it does in IDL. (It informs the compiler that the class being declared is actually intended to be a COM object, so the compiler generates code for a COM object instead of a plain C++ class.) The following code declares a C++ class that will also be compiled into a COM object. It uses the coclass attribute along with a number of others whose rough meaning you can probably guess:

```
// This really is C++ code, even though it might not look like it!
[
    coclass,
    threading("apartment"),
    vi_progid("ATLAttribs.MyCOMAttribObject"),
    progid("ATLAttribs.MyCOMAttribObject.1"),
    version(1.0),
    uuid("BC7DCB98-67E6-4BA3-AC58-BEE653E56C29"),
    helpstring("MyCOMAttribObject Class")
]
class ATL_NO_VTABLE CMyCOMAttribObject : public IMyCOMAttribObject
{
    // Code for class
};
```

If you're doing COM programming, you'll find that coclass and other attributes make life much easier – they replace many of the old ATL macros, and even remove the need for you to maintain a separate IDL file at all. If you're not doing COM programming, though, you're not likely to encounter so many attributes at once, and nor do you need to learn these particular ones. You can learn more about programming COM using attributes in Chapter 9.

.NET attributes

We've now seen the syntax for attributes in general. To see an example of how they work with .NET, we'll take a quick look at the Obsolete attribute, which you can use to indicate that a method is now deprecated:

```
[Obsolete(S"BoardPlane() deprecated. Use CheckSecurityAndBoardPlane().")]
void BoardPlane()
{
    // etc.
}
```

The use of this attribute with the BoardPlane() method means that if you attempt to call it, the C++ compiler will emit a warning at build time, outputting the warning text as above. We'll examine Obsolete in more detail soon, when we come to look at some selected .NET attributes.

You should be aware that due to some bugs in the release version of the Visual C++ .NET compiler, some of the attributes described here do not function correctly from C++, though they work fine in other languages such as C# and Visual Basic .NET. Microsoft has indicated that these problems will be fixed in service packs, but in this section we'll explain how the various attributes are supposed to work, and add background notes that point out where your code may not work quite as expected if you have an early version of Visual Studio .NET. Obsolete is one such affected attribute.

We should also mention that because the .NET-related attributes are a part of the .NET Framework, you'll only be able to use them in projects that compile to managed code. (In fact, you'll normally find they only make sense when applied to managed objects within that code.) The following will cause a compilation error:

```
__nogc class Airport
{
    [Obsolete(S"Warning text here")]
    void BoardPlane()
    {
        // etc.
    }

    // etc.
}
```

Conversely, since COM objects are not the same as .NET objects, it would not make sense to apply C++ COM-related attributes like coclass to a managed object.

The predefined .NET attributes

Microsoft has already defined a large number of .NET attributes, and it's quite possible that more will be added in the future. For those reasons, it would be impossible to give an exhaustive list of .NET attributes here. Instead, we'll work through some of the more important ones, to give you an idea of how they work.

Obsolete

System::Obsolete tells the compiler that a class, or a structure, or one of its members is deprecated – you apply it to an entity in your code when you don't want other developers to use that entity any more. It can take zero, one, or two parameters. If you supply two parameters, the first is a string containing the message that the compiler should emit if it detects an attempt to use that member, while the second is a Boolean that – if set to true – indicates that any attempted use should cause a compilation *error*, rather than a warning. The code extract shown below is identical to our earlier example, except that a compilation error will occur if BoardPlane() is called from anywhere in your code:

```
[Obsolete(S"BoardPlane() deprecated. Use CheckSecurityAndBoardPlane().", true)]
void BoardPlane(void)
{
    // etc.
}
```

The zero- and one-parameter versions of this attribute simply assume default values for the remaining parameters – compiler warning rather than error, and a default message.

At the time of writing, the warning or error will only be generated if the obsolete method is called from code in a different project, and not if it is called from within the same project. This is not the case in C# or Visual Basic .NET, in which Obsolete works correctly.

Conditional

The `System::Diagnostics::Conditional` attribute provides an alternative to the `#ifdef` preprocessor directives that are used to compile code that you only wish to be available in certain versions of your application (such as diagnostic code that you only want to be compiled in 'debug' versions). For example:

```
[Conditional(S"_DEBUG")]
void WriteUserDiagnostics()
{
    Console::Write(S"g_nUsers = ");
    Console::WriteLine(g_nUsers);
}
```

In this case, we've applied `Conditional` to a diagnostic method that displays the value of what we assume here is a global variable, g_nUsers.

Although the intended use of the `Conditional` attribute is described here, this attribute is ignored by the version of the C++ compiler available at the time of writing, other than for emitting metadata. This should be fixed in a service pack, and you should note that `Conditional` does work correctly in C# and Visual Basic .NET.

The `Conditional` attribute can only be applied to methods, and it takes one parameter: a string. When the compiler encounters the attribute, it examines the parameter, and compares it to the preprocessor symbols that are currently defined. The method in question will only be compiled if the parameter matches a current preprocessor symbol. If no such symbol is found, then not only will the compiler ignore the method definition, but it will also ignore any calls to that method that occur anywhere else in the source code. Continuing the above example, we can just write:

```
int _tmain(void)
{
    g_nUsers = 2;
    WriteUserDiagnostics();
    Console::WriteLine(S"Hello World");
    return 0;
}
```

This code will compile even if we choose to do so in 'release' mode, in which the _DEBUG preprocessor symbol is not defined (and so the `WriteUserDiagnostics()` method doesn't exist). With the old method of using `#ifdef` preprocessor directives to force conditional compilation, you would've had to add `#ifdef` directives to every call to your diagnostic method, making your code look pretty ugly and hard to read. You could get round this to some extent by defining macros similar to MFC's `ASSERT`, but the results were still syntactically untidy. If you weren't using the `Conditional` attribute, the best you could do to achieve the same effect as in the example above would probably look something like this

```
// Equivalent code not using attributes
#ifdef _DEBUG
void WriteUserDiagnostics()
{
    Console::Write(S"g_nUsers = ");
    Console::WriteLine(g_nUsers);
}
```

```
#define WRITEUSERDIAGNOSTICS WriteUserDiagnostics()
#else
#define WRITEUSERDIAGNOSTICS
#endif

int _tmain(void)
{
    g_nUsers = 2;
    WRITEUSERDIAGNOSTICS;
    Console::WriteLine(S"Hello World");
    return 0;
}
```

It's also possible to apply `Conditional` more than once to a member function, in which case the function will be compiled if any one of the conditions is true.

```
[Conditional(S"Professional"), Conditional(S"Enterprise")]
void DoSomething()
{
    // Code here will be compiled if either Professional or Enterprise is defined
}
```

Clearly, the idea of conditional compilation implemented in this way can only work syntactically if the method in question returns `void` – you'll get a compilation error if you try to apply `Conditional` to a method that returns anything else. Also, for obvious reasons, the method should not be an override.

StructLayout

`System::Runtime::InteropServices::StructLayout` provides a way to implement C/C++-style unions, which .NET doesn't support directly – if you try to define a union in a managed type, you'll get a compilation error. However, `StructLayout` is actually far more powerful than C/C++ unions: where a union could allow you to indicate that two or more members of a structure occupy memory starting at the same location, `StructLayout` actually allows you to specify the relative offsets of each member from the start of the structure instance. There are two main reasons why you might want to use this:

❑   To code a C/C++-style union within managed code.

❑   To define a structure for passing to an unmanaged API function using the P/Invoke mechanism (see Chapter 7), where you need to ensure that the .NET structure has exactly the memory layout that the unmanaged API function is expecting. (You *could* use a plain C++ structure here, but then you wouldn't be able to use that structure for any method calls that expect a managed structure. `StructLayout` gives you the flexibility to use the same structure in calls to both managed and unmanaged code.)

In the second case above, you'll most likely be using `StructLayout` in conjunction with two other attributes: `DllImport` and `MarshalAs`. We'll look briefly at the `DllImport` attribute later in this chapter, but we'll look at both of these attributes in more detail in Chapter 7.

It's possible to use `StructLayout` for managed structures – that is, for __value structures and classes. It's not possible to apply `StructLayout` to __gc types, because the .NET Framework itself always chooses how to arrange these types in memory.

In this chapter, we'll illustrate the use of `StructLayout` through a quick sample called `ComplexTypes`, in which we'll define two structures that hold complex numbers. (For our purposes, a complex number is simply a pair of `doubles`.) We'll define two complex number types: `Complex`, a structure defined in the normal way; and `ReImComplex`, defined using `StructLayout`. `ReImComplex` will contain two unions, because there are two popular pairs of names for the two `doubles` contained in a complex number: *x* and *y*, and *Re* and *Im* (in mathematics, the two `doubles` in a complex number are referred to as the real and imaginary parts). Using `StructLayout` allows us to access the same data efficiently using both pairs of names.

The code we use looks like this. (For simplicity, I placed the class definitions and a quick piece of test harness code in the same file in a console application.) First, we define a normal complex number without using `StructLayout`, just for comparison:

```
#include "stdafx.h"

#using <mscorlib.dll>
#include <tchar.h>

using namespace System;
using namespace System::Runtime::InteropServices;

__value struct Complex
{
    double x;
    double y;
};
```

This code demonstrates our intended idea for a complex number. Adding the `using` directive for the `System::Runtime::InteropServices` namespace is important, as that's where the `StructLayout` attribute is located. However, it's still defined in the `mscorlib.dll` assembly, so there's no need to reference any other assemblies.

> **Just like the .NET Framework classes, .NET attributes are defined in namespaces, so you need to make sure that you refer to the appropriate namespace in order to use them.**

Next, we define our complex number using `StructLayout`:

```
[StructLayout(LayoutKind::Explicit)]
__value struct ReImComplex
{
    [FieldOffset(0)] double x;
    [FieldOffset(8)] double y;
    [FieldOffset(0)] double Re;
    [FieldOffset(8)] double Im;
};
```

This is where things get interesting. We can see from this code that `StructLayout` takes one compulsory parameter, which is a `__value` enumeration of type `LayoutKind`. The possible values for the parameter are listed in the table opposite.

Parameter value	Description
LayoutKind::Explicit	Indicates that we are going to tell the compiler explicitly how to lay out the structure in memory.
LayoutKind::Sequential	The fields are arranged sequentially in memory. Specifying this option also means that we get the chance to specify how closely packed the fields should be in memory.
LayoutKind::Auto	The CLR determines the layout of the structure in memory.

We will examine LayoutKind::Sequential soon, while specifying LayoutKind::Auto is the same as not using the StructLayout attribute at all, so we won't consider that any further.

LayoutKind::Explicit

As you can see from the above example, if we use LayoutKind::Explicit, then we need to use another attribute, FieldOffset, to indicate the actual location of each field. The FieldOffset attribute is applied to each member of the structure and takes a single integer parameter that specifies the number of bytes from the start of the structure at which the member should be placed. Since a double occupies eight bytes, we give x (the first member of the structure) an offset of zero, and y an offset of eight, so that it immediately follows x. Then we define the members Re and Im, specifying their offsets so that they occupy the same memory as x and y respectively. Note that there is no requirement to list the members in the same order as they appear in memory.

Now let's test our new types. We'll assign values to the x and y members of a ReImComplex instance, and check to ensure that the Re and Im members have also been assigned. We'll also display the sizes of our two structures, which in both cases should be 16 bytes. The code to do this is shown below:

```
int _tmain(void)
{
    ReImComplex c1;
    c1.x = 23.5;
    c1.y = 10.0;
    Console::WriteLine(S"c1.x = {0}", c1.x.ToString());
    Console::WriteLine(S"c1.y = {0}", c1.y.ToString());
    Console::WriteLine(S"c1.Re = {0}", c1.Re.ToString());
    Console::WriteLine(S"c1.Im = {0}", c1.Im.ToString());
    Console::Write(S"sizeof(ReImComplex) = ");
    Console::WriteLine(sizeof(ReImComplex));
    Console::Write(S"sizeof(Complex) = ");
    Console::WriteLine(sizeof(Complex));
    return 0;
}
```

Running this code produces the following output:

```
c1.x = 23.5
c1.y = 10
c1.Im = 23.5
c1.Re = 10
sizeof(ReImComplex) = 16
sizeof(Complex) = 16
```

By using `StructLayout` and `FieldOffset`, we really do have total control over the location in memory of each member. In our example, we chose to ensure that `Im` (y) immediately followed `Re` (x). However, if we'd wished to add eight bytes of padding between them, we could easily have done so, like this.

```
[FieldOffset(0)] double x;
[FieldOffset(16)] double y;
[FieldOffset(0)] double Re;
[FieldOffset(16)] double Im;
```

We can even make members partially overlap by choosing the field offsets appropriately – this used to be done in Windows programming in order to represent a `LARGE_INTEGER` with two smaller integers.

LayoutKind::Sequential and the packing size

By using `LayoutKind::Sequential` with the `StructLayout` attribute, it's possible to specify a sequential rather than an explicit layout for the structure, and in that case to specify a packing size. (This is *often* what happens if you don't specify the `StructLayout` attribute, but you shouldn't count on it.) Even if the members follow sequentially, though, they still might not occupy successive memory locations. Depending on the types of the fields, there may be some padding (unoccupied memory) between them. This is because by default, for performance reasons, the system aligns elementary types so that they occupy memory locations starting at integer multiples of their sizes. If a member contains fields of different sizes, this packing distance is determined by the size of the largest field, and that's when some padding can occur. Consider the following structure:

```
__value struct TestPackStruct
{
    Byte c;
    double x;
    Byte y;
};
```

`System::Byte` has size one, while `double` has size eight, which on the face of it makes for a total size for the structure of ten. However, because of the presence of the `double`, the system will align all the fields on eight-byte boundaries. The **packing size** is eight, which means that the total size of the structure will actually be 24. If we want to, we can override this behavior, like this:

```
[StructLayout(LayoutKind::Sequential, Pack = 1)]
    __value struct TestPackStruct
{
    Byte c;
    double x;
    Byte y;
};
```

This ensures that the packing size is set to one, which will result in the structure having size ten. It will occupy less memory, although there's a possible performance cost due to system hardware considerations.

The possible values that `Pack` can be set to are 1, 2, 4, 8, 16, and 32... or zero, which makes the system select a default packing level (usually 8).

Due to a bug in the C++ compiler at the time of writing, the Pack *parameter is ignored in C++, though it works correctly in C# and Visual Basic .NET. This is likely to be fixed in a future service pack.*

Notice here that instead of simply giving the value of the parameter to the attribute, we've actually named the parameter in our attribute declaration: Pack = 1. In general, you'll find that different attributes will make use of one or other of these techniques. There's no rule – it's just a question of how each attribute has been defined. If you're not sure, check the documentation.

DllImport

DllImport is an extremely useful attribute, and it's one of the few that you can apply to unmanaged methods as well as managed ones. It's used to refer to an external method that can be found in a named dynamic-link library, and which should be accessed using the PInvoke mechanism for calling into unmanaged code. Typical usage looks something like this.

```
[DllImport(S"user32.dll", EntryPoint = S"MessageBox", CharSet = Unicode)]
int MessageBox(void* hWnd, wchar_t* lpTxt, wchar_t* lpCptn, unsigned int uType);
```

The MessageBox() function has been chosen to illustrate the syntax here because it's so well known, but in practice you're unlikely to need to call it from a managed application, since the MessageBox::Show() method in the System::Windows::Forms namespace will do the job just as well (see Chapter 6). However, if you choose to access features of the Windows API that are *not* available via the .NET Framework class library, or if you need to access third party code that's packaged in 'classic' DLLs, then you may choose to use the DllImport attribute to do so.

We won't discuss DllImport *or PInvoke further here, since the question of interoperability with legacy unmanaged code is covered in detail in Chapter 7.*

ThreadStatic

To demonstrate the versatility of attributes, here's a quick preview of a subject that we'll be looking at in more detail in the next chapter: threading. The System::ThreadStatic attribute marks a static member of a class as being a per-thread entity – that is, each thread that accesses the class will receive its own independent copy of the member that is immune from modifications by other threads. Here's an example of how you might use it, taken from a Chapter 4 project:

```
__gc class TestThreadStatic
{
public:

    // Method definitions omitted for brevity

private:
    [ThreadStatic] static int m_nThreadStatic;
    static int m_nNotThreadStatic;
};
```

Assembly attributes

The attributes that we've discussed so far have all been applied within the main body of a program – to methods, properties, classes, structures, and so on. However, it's also possible to apply attributes to an assembly as a whole. A number of attributes are defined by the .NET Framework that give information such as the title, description, and copyright information for an assembly, or supply important data to the compiler concerning assembly files that are to be placed in the Global Assembly Cache.

129

Assembly attributes are *always* prefixed by `assembly:`. If you create any Managed C++ application using Visual Studio .NET, you'll find a set of default assembly attributes declared and ready for you to edit in the `AssemblyInfo.cpp` file, as we saw in the last chapter.

```
[assembly:AssemblyTitleAttribute("")];
[assembly:AssemblyDescriptionAttribute("")];
[assembly:AssemblyConfigurationAttribute("")];
[assembly:AssemblyCompanyAttribute("")];
[assembly:AssemblyProductAttribute("")];
[assembly:AssemblyCopyrightAttribute("")];
[assembly:AssemblyTrademarkAttribute("")];
[assembly:AssemblyCultureAttribute("")];
[assembly:AssemblyVersionAttribute("1.0.*")];
```

Attributes as classes

Now that we've explored some of the more frequently used .NET attributes, we'll look a bit more closely at how attributes are implemented in the .NET Framework. The key concept to grasp here is that every .NET attribute is actually a class as well.

> **All .NET attributes are implemented as .NET classes.**

The easiest way to see this is to examine the class definition of one of the attributes we've already met – `Obsolete` – using the `WinCV` tool that comes with Visual Studio .NET (`Microsoft Visual Studio .NET\FrameworkSDK\Bin\WinCV.exe`). When using `WinCV`, you simply type in the name of a class and are quickly presented with some pseudo-code for its definition. Shown below is what `WinCV` comes up with for the `Obsolete` attribute, which is obtained by typing in **"obsolete"**, and then selecting `ObsoleteAttribute` from the classes in the tree view. The code is presented in C# rather than C++ syntax, but you should be able to see what's going on.

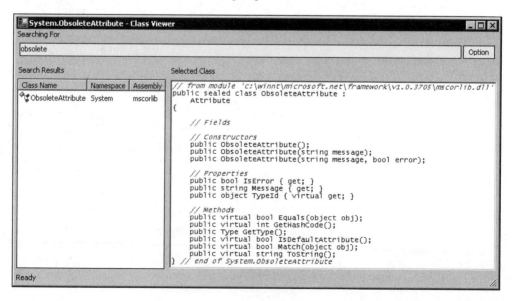

The first thing you'll notice is that the name of the class is not `Obsolete` but `ObsoleteAttribute`. It's generally recommended that the names of all classes that represent attributes should be appended with the word `Attribute`, although to make your code easier to read, the compiler automatically appends this part of the class name when it comes across an attribute in your code. If you want to do it, though, using the full name works just as well.

You may have noticed that when generating the blank assembly attributes for you to edit in the `AssemblyInfo.cpp` file, the Wizard wrote the attribute names in full.

`ObsoleteAttribute` is derived from `System::Attribute`, a .NET Framework base class. All attributes must derive from this class, as this is the mechanism by which compilers recognize them.

`System::Attribute` defines a few methods that are (of course) listed in the MSDN documentation, but they're not often used, and we'll speak no more of them here. They're mainly to do with retrieving information about whether the attribute in question is defined for certain classes, assemblies, etc.

Earlier, you saw that we could use the `Obsolete` attribute and pass in zero, one, or two arguments. If you look at the `ObsoleteAttribute` class's constructors, you'll see that that is exactly the choice they provide. The general rule is that the available constructors determine the parameters you need to supply.

When you use an attribute in your code, you can think of it as the compiler instantiating an object of the attribute's class, depending on the arguments you pass in. However, the attribute isn't *actually* instantiated, so the constructor isn't *actually* executed. Rather, the compiler will examine the arguments supplied (to make sure they are compatible with the available constructors for the corresponding attribute class) and place their values in the assembly metadata. Later in this chapter, you'll see that it's possible to instantiate an attribute object by using reflection, during which process the values in the metadata are passed to the constructor.

Attribute class members

Returning to the pseudo-code, you can also see that `ObsoleteAttribute` has two properties that will return the values of its arguments: `Message` and `IsError`. Later on, you'll discover that it's very important for properties like these to be defined – if they're not present, you'll be unable to use reflection to examine the values of these parameters.

`ObsoleteAttribute`'s remaining methods and property are of little concern to us here. For the most part, the methods we see listed above are simply those defined in `System::Object`, and therefore they are present for all .NET objects. There are also a couple of methods and properties that are inherited from `System::Attribute`, as mentioned above: `Match()`, `IsDefaultAttribute()`, and `TypeId`.

The properties we've seen defined for `ObsoleteAttribute` are read-only, but what happens if the property is writable? Writable properties allow you to specify a property by name when you use an attribute, and while `ObsoleteAttribute` doesn't contain any of these, `StructLayout` has three: `Pack`, `CharSet`, and `Size`. Here's the `WinCV` pseudo-code for `StructLayout`.

```
// from module 'c:\winnt\microsoft.net\framework\v1.0.3705\mscorlib.dll'
public sealed class System.Runtime.InteropServices.StructLayoutAttribute :
    Attribute
{
    // Fields
    public System.Runtime.InteropServices.CharSet CharSet;
    public int Pack;
    public int Size;

    // Constructors
    public StructLayoutAttribute(short layoutKind);
    public StructLayoutAttribute(
                    System.Runtime.InteropServices.LayoutKind layoutKind);

    // etc.
```

In this case, the relevant attribute parameters are actually defined as public members rather than properties, but for the purposes of using the attribute, that amounts to the same thing. For example:

```
[StructLayout(LayoutKind::Sequential, Pack = 1)]
    public __value struct TestPackStruct
```

Here, the *<property>* = *<value>* syntax is used, so the compiler looks for a public property or member of the corresponding attribute class with the given name. If it finds one, then it sets that member/property to the supplied value. If it can't find one, you'll get a compilation error.

The AttributeUsage attribute

We've now covered most of what we need to know in order to write our own attributes, but there's one more topic that we need to cover before finally doing so. When we define our own attributes, we have to tell the compiler a couple of things about how they are going to be used:

❑   What items the attributes can be applied to (classes, structures, methods, arguments to methods, or assemblies as a whole)

❑   Whether it is permissible for the same attribute to be applied to a given item more than once

❑   Whether the attribute should be passed on to derived classes automatically

The way we tell the compiler about all these things is by applying an attribute (yes, another one!) to our attribute definition: System::AttributeUsageAttribute (or, more simply, AttributeUsage). The next sample – a project called CustomAttributes – will illustrate the definition and use of a custom attribute called CompletionAttribute. We'll assume that CompletionAttribute can be applied to structures and classes, and that its intention is to allow code to be tracked as it is written, with an enumerated value of type CompletionStatus indicating what work needs to be done, and an optional comment. The syntax for the start of the CompletionAttribute definition looks like this:

```
[AttributeUsage(AttributeTargets::Class | AttributeTargets::Struct,
                        AllowMultiple = false, Inherited = false)]
__gc class CompletionAttribute : public Attribute
{
```

AttributeUsage can only be applied to classes, and it's intended only to be used for classes that will be used as attributes. It takes one mandatory and two optional arguments. The mandatory parameter is of type AttributeTargets and indicates where our new attribute can be used. AttributeTargets is a .NET enumeration and is defined like this:

```
[Flags]
_value enum AttributeTargets {
    Assembly    = 0x00000001,
    Module      = 0x00000002,
    Class       = 0x00000004,
    Struct      = 0x00000008,
    Enum        = 0x00000010,
    Constructor = 0x00000020,
    Method      = 0x00000040,
    Property    = 0x00000080,
    Field       = 0x00000100,
    Event       = 0x00000200,
    Interface   = 0x00000400,
    Parameter   = 0x00000800,
    Delegate    = 0x00001000,
    ReturnValue = 0x00002000,
    All         = 0x00003fff,
};
```

The possible values of this enumeration should be self-explanatory. In our code, we've used the bitwise OR operator to specify that CompletionAttribute can be applied to classes or structures. This means that we'll legitimately be able to write things like:

```
[Completion(CompletionStatus::ReadyToShip)]      // Applied to a managed class
__gc class MyClass
{
    // etc.
};
```

On the other hand, we'll get a compilation error if we try to write:

```
[Completion(CompletionStatus::ReadyToShip)]    // Illegally applied to a method
void DoSomething()
{
    // etc.
}
```

Incidentally, you may have noticed something else about the AttributeTargets enumeration – it's been decorated with another attribute! On this occasion, we have System::FlagsAttribute, which is used to indicate that an enumeration is actually a series of flags that might be combined using bitwise operators. This has no effect on the code for the enumeration, but it might be detected by developer tools and used to modify the user interface appropriately. Visual Studio .NET, for example, checks for the presence of the Flags attribute when deciding how to display IntelliSense pop-ups for enumerations.

The second parameter of the AttributeUsage attribute, AllowMultiple, is optional. It's a Boolean value that indicates whether the attribute can be applied more than once to the same item. In our example we've indicated false, which means that we can't legally write code like this:

```
// This code won't compile because AllowMultiple is set to false
[Completion(CompletionStatus::InProgress),
 Completion(CompletionStatus::ReadyToShip)]
__gc class MyClass
{
   // etc.
};
```

If `AllowMultiple` were set to `true`, then the above code would be fine. If `AllowMultiple` is left unspecified, the default setting is `false`. In our case, since it's hard to see what a class having more than one status could mean, it makes more sense to set this parameter to `false`.

The final optional parameter, `Inherited`, is also a Boolean value. If it's set to `true`, it indicates that the attribute will be propagated to derived classes, or to overrides of methods. Since different developers may have written derived classes, it makes more sense in our case to set this attribute to `false`. If it's not specified, `Inherited` defaults to `true`.

Writing custom attributes

Considering all of the attributes we've examined so far, each has had some effect on the build process, or on the code produced. If you define your own, custom attributes, it's not possible for the compiler to have any specific knowledge of them. Therefore, the *only* effect that your attributes can have is that they will cause extra information to be placed in the assembly metadata. Nevertheless, despite these apparent limitations, writing custom attributes is a very powerful technique.

> **Custom attributes can only be used to produce metadata. They do not affect the compilation process.**

In this section, we'll develop an attribute called `CompletionAttribute` that will be used to indicate the progress made so far in writing a class or structure. We'll assume the organization concerned has a quality control system that defines four phases in the writing of code, which we'll indicate by means of the following enumeration:

```
__value enum CompletionStatus {InProgress, Coded, Checked, ReadyToShip};
```

In real life, such an attribute would probably be applied at a fine granularity – to individual methods, constructors, and properties – but we'll keep things simple here. The attribute takes two parameters:

- ❑ A value from the `CompletionStatus` enumeration indicating progress made in writing the code (mandatory)

- ❑ An optional accompanying comment

We'll also follow the convention of writing the attribute so that the compulsory parameter must be supplied with this syntax:

```
[Completion(CompletionStatus::InProgress)]
__gc class SomeClass
{
   // etc.
};
```

While the optional parameter, if present, must be supplied with this syntax:

```
[Completion(CompletionStatus::InProgress,
            Comment = S"Methods not yet implemented")]
__gc class SomeClass
{
   // etc.
};
```

We must arrange for the compulsory parameter to be supplied via a constructor, and for the optional parameter to be available through a writable property or member. The full code that defines the CompletionAttribute attribute is as follows:

```
#pragma once

using namespace System;

__value enum CompletionStatus {InProgress, Coded, Checked, ReadyToShip};

[AttributeUsage(AttributeTargets::Class | AttributeTargets::Struct,
                            AllowMultiple = false, Inherited = false)]
__gc class CompletionAttribute : public Attribute
{
public:
   CompletionAttribute(CompletionStatus status) : m_Status(status),
                                                  m_pComment(S"")
   {
   }

   __property CompletionStatus get_Status()
   {
      return m_Status;
   }

   __property String* get_Comment()
   {
      return m_pComment;
   }

   // This property accessor allows us to supply
   //  an optional parameter in the constructor
   __property void set_Comment(String* pComment)
   {
      m_pComment = pComment;
   }

private:
   CompletionStatus m_Status;
   String* m_pComment;
};
```

Now that we've defined the attribute, we can try using it. The `CustomAttributes` sample contains the following code:

```
#include "stdafx.h"

#using <mscorlib.dll>
#include <tchar.h>
#include "CustomAttributes.h"

using namespace System;

[Completion(CompletionStatus::Checked)]
__gc class MyClass
{
    void DoSomething() {}
};

[Completion(CompletionStatus::InProgress,
            Comment = S"Methods not yet implemented")]
__value class MyBetterClass
{
    void DoSomething() {}
    void DoSomethingElse(int x) {}
};

// This is the entry point for this application
int _tmain(void)
{
    Console::WriteLine(S"Hello World");
    return 0;
}
```

If you compile the sample, you can verify that the attribute values have been placed in the assembly with the definitions of `MyClass` and `MyBetterClass` by using the `ILDasm` tool that you looked at in the previous chapter.

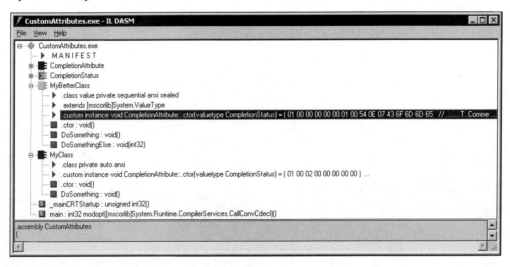

The information about our new attribute is contained in the lines that begin ".custom instance...". Unfortunately, ILDasm doesn't line wrap, which makes the output a little difficult to read, but if we dump the contents of the tree view to a file (by pressing *Ctrl-T*), we can see more of the contents. For MyBetterClass, the relevant line is:

```
.custom instance void CompletionAttribute::.ctor(valuetype CompletionStatus) =
( 01 00 00 00 00 00 01 00 54 0E 07 43 6F 6D 6D 65   // ........T..Comme ...
```

And for MyClass, the line is:

```
.custom instance void CompletionAttribute::.ctor(valuetype CompletionStatus) =
( 01 00 02 00 00 00 00 00 )  ...
```

Unfortunately, in both these cases, we get hit by ILDasm refusing to dump more than a certain number of characters per line, but at least we can see that the attribute information is there.

In terms of running this sample, that's as far as we're going to get. This might leave you feeling somewhat dissatisfied, since the code doesn't actually do anything – the main() function simply returns straight away, without actually using either of the classes we've defined. In fact, though, we can't yet *do* much more, because we haven't covered how to use the extra information we've placed in the metadata. Once we've seen how to write code that uses reflection, we'll develop a better sample that illustrates some of the other ways in which you can use custom attributes.

Reflection

To begin this section, we're going to leave attributes behind for a while. Although reflection and attributes can certainly be used together, the former has a broader range of application. Reflection allows your programs to examine *all* of the metadata that assemblies contain, as you'll begin to see in our first example.

The ListColors sample

We're going to jump in at the deep end with a quick sample called `ListColors` that will show you how to code up reflection, and illustrate why it is so powerful. It's a straightforward program that simply lists the names of some colors:

You're probably wondering – reasonably enough – what this has to do with reflection. Well, the colors our `ListColors` sample has come up with aren't just any old colors; they're the complete set of named colors that are defined by the .NET Framework. And the only way to find out what those colors are programmatically is to use reflection.

In the .NET Framework, colors are represented by the `System::Drawing::Color` structure, which is used for painting different colors in the user interface of an application. It implements a number of static properties that return different named colors. If, for example, you wanted to obtain a `Color` structure that represented a purple color, you might write:

```
Color* pPurple = Color::Purple;
```

Now, that's all very well if you specifically want purple, but what if you just want to find out all of the colors that are available to you? You could read the documentation and then code all the names into your application, but it's not a great solution, and you'd have your work cut out – there are 149 named colors implemented right now, and you'd need to rewrite your code if Microsoft added any more. We need a way of finding out programmatically what properties `Color` implements – and that's exactly the kind of problem that can be solved using reflection.

Actually, the colors are also named in the `System::Drawing::KnownColor` enumeration. If we used this, we wouldn't need to use reflection to find out the color names. However, `KnownColor` contains not only the 'actual' named colors, but also various system colors that map to different named colors depending on your PC's settings. (`ActiveBorder` maps to whatever the border of an active window is set to display as.) If we only require the names of the actual colors, then we must use reflection.

Although the next sample has some nuances that you may not see straight away, all will become clear when we examine the reflection-related classes more closely. In the meantime, here's the code for `ListColors`:

```
#include "stdafx.h"

#using <mscorlib.dll>
#using <System.Drawing.dll>
#include <tchar.h>

using namespace System;
using namespace System::Reflection;
using namespace System::Drawing;

int _tmain(void)
{
    Type* colorType = __typeof(Color);
    PropertyInfo* colorProps[] = colorType->GetProperties();

    // Iterate over properties
    for(int i = 0; i < colorProps.Length; i++)
    {
        PropertyInfo* colorProp = colorProps[i];
        if(colorProp->GetGetMethod()->IsStatic &&
                            colorProp->PropertyType == __typeof(Color))
        {
            Console::Write(colorProps[i]->Name);
            Console::Write(S"\t");
        }
    }

    return 0;
}
```

Quickly going over this code, you can see that we're using a couple of namespaces (System::Drawing for the Color structure, and System::Reflection for the reflection classes) and an extra library (System.Drawing.dll, again for the Color structure).

We start the main body of the program by defining a variable of type System::Type. This is a .NET base class that describes a named type, and it almost always acts as the entry point for reflection – we'll look at it in more detail shortly. Next, we use the __typeof() operator to acquire a Type object, and then use its GetProperties() method, which returns an array of PropertyInfo instances. Each PropertyInfo instance contains information about one of the properties implemented by the type – in this case, the Color structure. You'll find PropertyInfo in the System::Reflection namespace.

Once we have the PropertyInfo array, we're pretty much done (and all in just two lines of code!). We just have to display the names of those properties, using the Name property:

```
Console::Write(colorProps[i]->Name);
```

The Console::Write() statement is inside an if clause because Color defines some other properties besides the ones we're interested in. For example, Color::R returns the magnitude of the red component of a color – that it's not going to be of interest to us is given away by the fact that it returns a Byte (not a Color), and by the fact that it's an instance property, not a static one.

To make sure that we only pick up the properties that return named colors, we restrict ourselves to those that are static and those whose return type is `Color`:

```
if(colorProp->GetGetMethod()->IsStatic &&
                        colorProp->PropertyType == __typeof(Color))
{
    ...
}
```

`PropertyInfo::PropertyType` provides us with a `Type` object that describes the return type of the property. Finding out whether a property is static is slightly more complicated, since there's no `PropertyInfo` member that gives this information directly. Instead, we recall that a property is in reality nothing more than a pair of methods – get and set accessors – and use `PropertyInfo::GetGetMethod()` to return a `MethodInfo` instance that describes the 'get' accessor of the property. The `MethodInfo` class (in the `System::Reflection` namespace) is there to describe methods, just as `PropertyInfo` describes properties – and `MethodInfo` *does* have a property (called `IsStatic`) that returns a Boolean value indicating whether or not the method is static.

Invoking a member

The `ListColors` example should have given you a fair idea of the capabilities of reflection, but there's still something missing. Being able to get a list of the members of a class is one thing, but what if, having identified a particular property or method, you actually want to access it? Before we have a more detailed, theoretical look at reflection, we'll quickly extend `ListColors` to display the values of the red, green, and blue components of each color.

In this list, you can see that yellow (as you'd expect) is composed of the maximum possible values of red and green (255), but no blue: (255, 255, 0). The color called "WhiteSmoke", on the other hand, is apparently a kind of off-white. All of the colors are just off their maximum values: (245, 245, 245).

In order to find out this information, we need to instantiate a `Color` object that represents the required color and access its R, G, and B properties. Here's what the new code looks like, with the changes highlighted:

```
int _tmain(void)
{
    Type* colorType = __typeof(Color);
    PropertyInfo* colorProps [] = colorType->GetProperties();
```

```
    // Iterate over properties
    for(int i = 0; i < colorProps.Length; i++)
    {
        PropertyInfo* colorProp = colorProps[i];
        MethodInfo* pMethod = colorProp->GetGetMethod();
        if(pMethod->IsStatic && colorProp->PropertyType == __typeof(Color))
        {
            Object* colorAsObject = pMethod->Invoke(0, 0);
            Color* theColor = dynamic_cast<Color*>(colorAsObject);
            Console::Write(S"RGB: ({0, 3}, {1, 3}, {2, 3})",
                        theColor->R.ToString(), theColor->G.ToString(),
                        theColor->B.ToString());
            Console::WriteLine(S"    {0}", colorProps[i]->Name);
        }
    }

    return 0;
}
```

This time, as well as retrieving the name of the property, we actually invoke it – or more precisely, we invoke its 'get' accessor. We do this by calling the `Invoke()` method of a `MethodInfo` object that we again retrieve by using the `PropertyInfo::GetGetMethod()` method. `MethodInfo::Invoke()` takes two parameters:

❑ A pointer to the object against which we wish to invoke the method

❑ The set of parameters to be passed to the method, as an array of `Object`s

In our case, both the parameters are zero, because the properties that we're using to return the named colors are all static – there is no associated object, and there are no parameters to be passed in, because 'get' accessors never take parameters, by definition!

`Invoke()` returns the return value of the method that we invoked, but cast to type `Object*` – this is inevitable, since `Invoke()` could be used to call absolutely any method. The return value's actual type might be any managed type. We use the `dynamic_cast<>()` operator to cast the return value to the `Color*` that we know is what will actually be returned in this case:

```
        Object* colorAsObject = pMethod->Invoke(0, 0);
        Color* theColor = __try_cast<Color*>(colorAsObject);
```

Notice that although we used reflection to return the `Color` object representing the named color, we didn't have to use reflection to access its R, G, and B properties. We just did that in the normal way, since we knew exactly what calls we wanted to make at compile time.

```
        Console::Write(S"RGB: ({0,3}, {1,3}, {2,3})",
                    theColor->R.ToString(), theColor->G.ToString(),
                    theColor->B.ToString());
```

In the case of returning the `Color`s themselves, the determination of what methods were to be invoked was only made at runtime – when we use reflection, we don't necessarily know what we're going to find. The properties we were dealing with here included `Color::Yellow` and `Color::WhiteSmoke`, but we didn't put those names anywhere in the sample. Reflection allowed us to determine and access those properties at runtime, and that's its power.

The System::Type class

Access to reflection is granted through a number of .NET base classes. The most important of these (as you'll probably have gathered from the above example) is System::Type, which in many ways can be seen as the main programmatic entry point to reflection functionality. It's presumably because of its importance and widespread use that it's defined in the System namespace – almost all of the other reflection-related base classes are defined in the System::Reflection namespace.

> *Although it won't affect our use of System::Type, it's worth pointing out that it's part of a fairly complex class hierarchy. It derives directly from System::Reflection::MemberInfo, a class that can describe any member of a class or structure, and also implements the System::Reflection::IReflect interface, which defines various methods to obtain the members of a type.*

Obtaining a System::Type reference

You'll usually get a System::Type reference in one of two ways:

- ❑ Calling System::Object::GetType()
- ❑ Using the __typeof() operator

If you have access to an actual object instance, and you want information about its type, then you can use the GetType() method. For example, suppose we have the following class defined:

```
__gc class MyClass
{
   // etc.
};
```

Then we can write:

```
MyClass* pMine = new MyClass;
Type* pType = pMine->GetType();
```

Since GetType() is defined in System::Object, all managed objects automatically support this method. In other words, when you're writing a C++ class or structure, placing either __gc or __value in the definition will ensure that it supports a GetType() method, without you having to do anything else. Note, however, that __value types need to be boxed before you can call GetType(); supposing that we had a __value type, MyStruct, defined like this:

```
__value struct MyStruct
{
   // etc.
};
```

We would have to box it before calling GetType():

```
MyStruct myStruct;
ValueType* pmyObj = __box(myStruct);
Type* pType = pmyObj->GetType();
```

The advantage of using GetType() is that you don't need to know at compile time what the actual type of the object instance is – in the above samples, for example, the pMine pointer doesn't necessarily have to point to a MyClass instance; it could point to an instance of some class derived from MyClass instead. In that case, GetType() would correctly obtain a Type object describing the derived class.

If you don't have access to a particular object instance, but you know at compile time what the name of the class is, then you can instead use the __typeof() operator, just as we've been doing in our earlier examples:

```
Type* colorType = __typeof(Color);
```

Using __typeof() is a bit less flexible than using GetType(), because it requires knowing at compile time what the class is, but it saves you from having to instantiate an object. If you wish to obtain type information for an abstract class, then clearly __typeof() is the only option.

It's important to understand that you don't ever construct a Type instance directly – you can't, because System::Type is itself an abstract class. The implication – though it's not actually stated in the documentation – seems to be that for every managed type that is defined, the .NET Framework makes available (behind the scenes) a corresponding class derived from System::Type that describes the type in question. From your point of view, though, this is immaterial – you simply obtain your Type reference using one of the two techniques we just described.

Bear in mind that there is only ever one instance of a Type object describing each managed type. If you attempt to retrieve two Type objects that describe the same class, you'll find that you just get two pointers to the same object! As a result, it's possible to compare Type references directly, in order to find out whether they refer to the same class:

```
Type* pType = __typeof(MyClass);
Type* pAnotherType = __typeof(MyClass);
if(pType == pAnotherType)              // This condition will always be true
{
    // etc.
}
```

System::Type properties and methods

The Type object exposes a large number of methods and properties that provide information about the type it represents. The following tables give a non-exhaustive selection of the members available, starting with the properties:

Property	Purpose
Assembly	Returns an instance of the System::Assembly class, which describes the assembly in which the type was defined.
BaseType	The type from which this type inherits. (This returns another Type object. If you want to go further up the inheritance chain, you can access the BaseType of the returned object, and so on until you hit System::Object.)
IsAbstract	Indicates whether the type is abstract.

Table continued on following page

Property	Purpose
IsArray	Indicates whether the type is an array.
IsClass	Indicates whether the type is a __gc class.
IsEnum	Indicates whether the type is a __value enumeration.
IsInterface	Indicates whether the type is a .NET interface.
IsPrimitive	Indicates whether the type is a .NET primitive type (Double, Byte, Short, and so on).
IsSealed	Indicates whether the type is sealed.
Namespace	Returns the name of the namespace containing the type as a string.

Note that these properties are all read-only. It is not possible to use a Type instance to make any modifications to a type definition. You can only find out about the existing type definition.

Method	Purpose
GetConstructor()	Returns a ConstructorInfo reference with details of the constructor that takes the specified parameters.
GetConstructors()	Returns a ConstructorInfo array with details of all of this type's constructors.
GetEvent()	Returns an EventInfo object containing details of the named event.
GetEvents()	Returns an EventInfo array containing details of all the events defined within the type.
GetField()	Returns a FieldInfo reference that describes the named field.
GetFields()	Returns a FieldInfo array containing details of all the fields defined within the type.
GetInterface()	Returns an Object reference that describes the named interface.
GetInterfaces()	Returns an Object array containing details of all the interfaces defined within the type.
GetMember()	Returns a MemberInfo reference that describes the named member.
GetMembers()	Returns a MemberInfo array containing details of all the members defined within the type.
GetMethod()	Returns a MethodInfo reference that describes the named method.
GetMethods()	Returns a MethodInfo array containing details of all the methods defined within the type.
GetProperty()	Returns a PropertyInfo reference that describes the named property.

Method	Purpose
GetProperties()	Returns a PropertyInfo array containing details of all the properties defined within the type.
IsSubclassOf()	Indicates whether the type is derived directly or indirectly from another specified type.

You'll notice that many of these methods return instances of other classes, such as MethodInfo, MemberInfo, and PropertyInfo. We've already (briefly) encountered the PropertyInfo class, which is used to obtain information about a property, and the MethodInfo class, which serves the same purpose for a method. The classes with similar names have similar purposes too – EventInfo to supply information about an event, and so on. Since there are a large number of such classes, and as their uses are fairly intuitive, there's little point discussing them in detail here.

Listing types: the musical instruments sample

So far, we've used reflection to invoke the properties and methods of a given type, and even to instantiate an object of that type. In order to do this, however, we've had to have a type available in advance, obtained using either the __typeof() operator (with the fully qualified name of the type) or the System::Object::GetType() method (with an object instance). In this section, we'll examine a situation where we don't even have that information available. We'll develop an example in which the only information we have at the outset is the name of the assembly that we wish to examine. We'll need to find out at runtime what types it defines.

For the sample, we're going to assume that we're writing some music software. We'll have a set of musical instruments represented by a library of classes that are contained in an assembly, which may be updated independently of any client application. Each class represents one instrument, so we'll have types with names like Guitar and Clarinet. When the application is fully developed, these classes will have some sophisticated functionality, but for now each class will implement just one method, PlayNote(), which takes a string describing the note to be played. And because we don't want to get bogged down in coding DirectX audio, our idea of playing a note will consist of writing a line to the console that says something like "Guitar is playing note C".

Our music software will need to have some kind of user interface that allows the user to choose between all the available instruments. If the library gets updated, the UI should automatically accommodate any new instruments; this means that it will have to be able to read the assembly containing the library and determine programmatically what instruments are actually available. However, we can't just assume that every class in the library is a musical instrument – there could be some utility classes and structures, too. We'll need to establish which classes we're interested in by looking at their base class; in our case, all musical instruments will be derived from an abstract class called InstrumentBase.

Now that we've defined the problem, let's look at the library contained in the InstrumentLibrary sample that's available with the code for this chapter – it was created as a Managed C++ Class Library.

```
// InstrumentLibrary.h

#pragma once

using namespace System;
using namespace System::Collections;
```

```
namespace InstrumentLibrary
{
    public __gc __abstract class InstrumentBase
    {
    public:
        virtual void PlayNote(String* note) = 0;
    };

    public __gc class Guitar : public InstrumentBase
    {
    public:
        virtual void PlayNote(String* note)
        {
            Console::WriteLine(S"Guitar playing note {0}", note);
        }
    };

    public __gc class Saxophone : public InstrumentBase
    {
    public:
        virtual void PlayNote(String* note)
        {
            Console::WriteLine(S"Saxophone playing note {0}", note);
        }
    };

    public __gc class Clarinet : public InstrumentBase
    {
    public:
        virtual void PlayNote(String* note)
        {
            Console::WriteLine(S"Clarinet playing note {0}", note);
        }
    };

    public __gc class InstrumentCollection
    {
    private:
        ArrayList *pInstruments;
        // There will be various public methods to access the collection
    };
}
```

There are quite a few classes defined here, but they're all fairly simple. Our InstrumentBase class defines the abstract PlayNote() method, which is overridden in the derived classes Guitar, Saxophone, and Clarinet. Although we'll use reflection to find out about the derived classes, we'll assume that we know about InstrumentBase at compile time, so knowledge of that will be coded into our client application. If fully implemented, InstrumentCollection would represent a collection of musical instruments by using the System::Collections::ArrayList base class, which we'll see more of in the next chapter. We're not actually going to implement it here, though – at the moment, it's only present to make sure that there's a class in the library (besides InstrumentBase) that doesn't represent a type of instrument.

The next stage is to write our 'user interface' – and for now, this will just list the musical instruments, instantiate each one, and call the PlayNote() method against them all. To do so, we'll create a separate project called PlayInstruments as a **Managed C++ Application**. We must also ensure that the compiled InstrumentLibrary assembly is copied over to the folder in which the PlayInstruments assembly will reside, or else PlayInstruments won't be able to see it. (In some cases, it may be appropriate to register the library in the Global Assembly Cache, as described in the previous chapter. In our case, InstrumentLibrary is clearly designed for use with one specific application, so that wouldn't be a sensible choice here.) Here's the complete code for PlayInstruments:

```
#include "stdafx.h"

#using <mscorlib.dll>
#using "Debug\InstrumentLibrary.dll"
#include <tchar.h>

using namespace System;
using namespace System::Reflection;
using namespace InstrumentLibrary;

// This is the entry point for this application
int _tmain(void)
{
    Assembly* library = Assembly::Load(S"InstrumentLibrary");
    Type* instBaseType = library->GetType(S"InstrumentLibrary.InstrumentBase");
    Type* types[] = library->GetTypes();

    for(int i = 0; i < types->Count; i++)
    {
        Type* inst = types[i];
        if(inst->IsAbstract)
            continue;
        if(inst->IsSubclassOf(instBaseType))
        {
            Console::WriteLine(types[i]->Name);
            Object* instObj = Activator::CreateInstance(inst);
            InstrumentBase* pinst = dynamic_cast<InstrumentBase*>(instObj);
            pinst->PlayNote(S"C");
        }
    }

    return 0;
}
```

After the usual setup code, we load the assembly using the Assembly::Load() method:

```
    Assembly* library = Assembly::Load(S"InstrumentLibrary");
```

Assembly is a class defined in the System::Reflection namespace, and Load() is a static method that forces the named assembly to be loaded into the application, if it hasn't already been loaded. (In general, it will have been loaded implicitly if some call to a type defined in that assembly has already been made, although this is not the case in our particular sample.) Load() returns a pointer to an Assembly instance that describes the assembly in question, which we then use to call the non-static method Assembly::GetType():

```
Type* instBaseType = library->GetType(S" InstrumentLibrary.InstrumentBase");
```

GetType() has a number of overloads, but the simplest – and the one we use here – takes the fully qualified name of a type that's defined in the given assembly as a parameter, and returns a pointer to a Type object that describes the type in question. *We* obtain a Type object that describes the InstrumentBase class, and we'll need this because we're going to have to be able to test whether the other types we find in the library are derived from InstrumentBase (that is, whether they represent a musical instrument).

Note that the fully qualified name of the InstrumentBase class is given using .NET (C#) syntax, not C++ syntax, so namespace names are separated by periods rather than by double colons.

Next, we call Assembly::GetTypes(), which is similar to Assembly::GetType(), but instead of returning the Type object corresponding to a named type, it simply grabs all the types that are defined in the assembly and returns an array of Type objects:

```
Type* types[] = library->GetTypes();
```

Now we simply need to iterate through the array, checking which types are actually derived from InstrumentBase, instantiating an object of each of those types, and calling the PlayNote() method of each of those objects. We can find out whether a given type is derived from another given type by using the System::Type::IsSubclassOf() method, which returns a bool. We also check whether each class is abstract, and skip processing that class if it is. Obviously, if a class is abstract, we're going to run into problems instantiating it!

```
for(int i = 0; i < types->Count; i++)
{
    Type* inst = types[i];
    if(inst->IsAbstract)
        continue;
    if(inst->IsSubclassOf(instBaseType))
```

Instantiating an object is done using another static method, Activator::CreateInstance(). Activator is another class defined in System::Reflection, and its purpose is simply to provide a way of instantiating objects of other classes. The simplest CreateInstance() overload takes one parameter: a System::Type object that defines the type we want an instance of. This overload will work if the type in question has a no-parameter constructor available, which is the case here. If parameters need to be passed to the constructor, there are other overloads of CreateInstance() that take extra parameters and pass them on.

Once we have our object, it's just a question of calling its PlayNote() method. Do note, though, that because Activator::CreateInstance() returns an Object pointer, we need to cast it to InstrumentBase* to be able to access PlayNote():

```
    {
        Object* instObj = Activator::CreateInstance(inst);
        InstrumentBase* pinst = dynamic_cast<InstrumentBase*>(instObj);
        pinst->PlayNote(S"C");
    }
```

That completes the code for the `PlayInstruments` sample; running it gives this output:

```
Guitar
Guitar playing note C
Saxophone
Saxophone playing note C
Clarinet
Clarinet playing note C
```

As you can see, the client has correctly picked out only those classes that represent musical instruments from the library.

Combining attributes and reflection

For the final part of this chapter, we're going put together the two topics we've discussed so far by extending our musical instrument library to use attributes. As the application stands, it's possible to identify the musical instruments that are available in the library, and to instantiate them and invoke their methods. However, it's *not* possible to find out any more information about those instruments (other than the information available through the static properties of an instrument class, were it to have them). For example, musical instruments are normally grouped together according to the style of instrument – woodwind, string, brass, and so on – and it would be reasonable to expect that our musical application should recognize these categories. We're going to use attributes to add this functionality.

We'll be using two new sample projects: `InstrumentLibraryWithAttributes` and `PlayInstrumentsWithAttributes`. Unsurprisingly, these projects contain basically the same code as `InstrumentLibrary` and `PlayInstruments`, but with some new material added.

First, let's look at the library. We'll define an attribute called `InstrumentCategory`, which will take one parameter, to indicate the category an instrument falls into. We also need to define a .NET enumeration that contains the possible categories. The code for our new attribute looks like this:

```
public __value enum InstrumentCategory
    {Strings, Woodwind, Percussion, Piano, Brass};

public __gc class InstrumentCategoryAttribute : public Attribute
{
public:
    InstrumentCategoryAttribute(InstrumentCategory category)
    {
        Category = category;
    }

    InstrumentCategory Category;
};
```

This attribute has one constructor, which takes an enumerated value as its parameter. To keep things simple, we've not bothered to define a property for the category, but simply left it as a public data member.

Now that we've defined our new attribute, we need to modify the code for the class definitions in the instrument library by decorating them with the attribute. The new code looks like this, with the changes highlighted (the class definitions have been omitted for brevity):

```
public __gc __abstract class InstrumentBase
{
    // Class definition
};

[InstrumentCategory(InstrumentCategory::Strings)]
public __gc class Guitar : public InstrumentBase
{
    // Class definition
};

[InstrumentCategory(InstrumentCategory::Woodwind)]
public __gc class Saxophone : public InstrumentBase
{
    // Class definition
};

[InstrumentCategory(InstrumentCategory::Woodwind)]
public __gc class Clarinet : public InstrumentBase
{
    // Class definition
};

public __gc class InstrumentCollection
{
    // Class definition
};
```

As before, once we've made these changes, we need to compile the library and copy the assembly into the folder where the calling assembly is located (or a subfolder thereof).

Next, we cut and paste the PlayInstruments code into the PlayInstrumentsWithAttributes project, and modify it so that it's able to read the information about the InstrumentCategory attribute, and therefore display the category of each instrument:

```
int _tmain(void)
{
    Assembly* library = Assembly::Load(S"InstrumentLibrary");
    Type* instBaseType = library->GetType(S"InstrumentLibrary.InstrumentBase");
    Type* types[] = library->GetTypes();

    for(int i = 0; i < types->Count; i++)
    {
        Type* inst = types[i];
        if(inst->IsAbstract)
            continue;
```

```
        if(inst->IsSubclassOf(instBaseType))
        {
            Console::WriteLine(types[i]->Name);
            Object* pAttribs[] = inst->GetCustomAttributes(
                                    __typeof(InstrumentCategoryAttribute), true);
            for(int i = 0; i < pAttribs->Length; i++)
            {
                InstrumentCategoryAttribute* pCat =
                        dynamic_cast<InstrumentCategoryAttribute*>(pAttribs[i]);
                Console::WriteLine(__box(pCat->Category)->ToString());
            }

            Object* instObj = Activator::CreateInstance(inst);
            InstrumentBase* pinst = __try_cast<InstrumentBase*>(instObj);
            pinst->PlayNote(S"C");
        }
    }

    return 0;
}
```

In order to examine the attributes for a class, we use the `Type::GetCustomAttributes()` method, which returns an array of `Object` pointers. Each of these points to an actual instance of an attribute that has been used to decorate the type in question. There are a couple of overloads to this method, but the one we use takes two parameters: a `Type` object that describes the attribute we're interested in, and a `bool` that indicates whether we are to retrieve attributes inherited from base classes. Using this overload means that we only retrieve any `InstrumentCategory` attributes that a type has been decorated with. The other `GetCustomAttributes()` overload takes only the `bool` parameter and returns *all* the attributes used to describe the type. In both cases, however, an array is returned – even if we're only interested in one attribute, it may have been used more than once (if it was defined with the `AllowMultiple` flag set to `true`).

This is the point at which the `InstrumentCategoryAttributes` object actually gets instantiated, and so this is where we start to see the value of having our attribute types defined as classes. Once we have the attribute array, it's just a matter of iterating through it. We cast each object in the array to `InstrumentCategoryAttribute*`, and use the `Category` member of our attribute to display the category of the instrument. Here's the output:

```
Guitar
Strings
Guitar playing note C
Saxophone
Woodwind
Saxophone playing note C
Clarinet
Woodwind
Clarinet playing note C
```

Besides showing how to examine the data provided by custom attributes, this example also shows the importance of having the attributes defined as classes, and having the parameters available as public properties or members of those classes. The process of examining the attributes involves instantiating an `Attribute` object using reflection, and then using its properties to find out what the values of the parameters were.

Finally, you may have wondered whether we really needed custom attributes for this sample. Couldn't we have achieved the same effect by, for example, having all the `Instrument` classes implement a read-only property that indicates the instrument category – or perhaps even by having them derive from an interface that defines such a property? The answer is that, in principle, we could have done that. The idea of a custom attribute – at least, one applied to a class – is that it supplies more information about the class, and in a sense that's what an interface does too. Just about any solution involving applying a custom attribute to a class could equally be solved by some combination of interfaces and properties. To some extent, it's a matter of opinion as to which technique provides the neatest solution for a given problem – but quite often, you'll find that the best solution is to use attributes.

Summary

In this chapter, we started off by examining the syntax for decorating the items in your code with attributes, and saw how similar it is to the old IDL attribute syntax that we're familiar with. We also examined some of the uses for these attributes, including adding C++ code to unmanaged applications, modifying the compilation process, and adding metadata to managed applications. Turning specifically to .NET, we made a brief tour of some of the more commonly used attributes, and saw that the .NET Framework supports these attributes using classes derived from `System::Attribute`, which we can also use to define our own custom attributes. Custom attributes and their properties are always emitted into an assembly as metadata.

Next, we moved on to reflection, examining how it can be used to obtain information about a given type, and suggesting a number of possible uses, ranging from developer tools to – as in the musical instruments sample – customizing a user interface based on the types available in a library. We developed an example that used reflection to obtain information about the types defined in an assembly, and finally saw how it could be used to obtain information about the custom attributes that have been applied to any type.

When combined, attributes and reflection can be used for a variety of purposes, such as adding documentation to your code that can be examined programmatically by other applications, or finding out information about the types in an assembly so that the user can be given a choice of what types to instantiate. This is a powerful synthesis of technologies that quite simply had no parallel in pre-.NET C++.

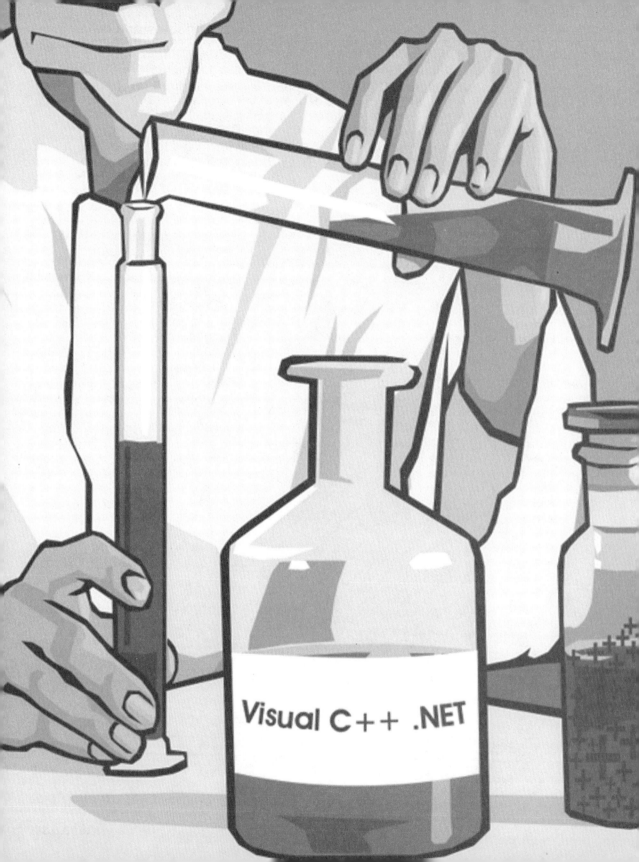

5

.NET Framework utility classes

The .NET Framework is not the first attempt to provide C++ developers with a set of classes for handling common tasks. MFC, ATL, STL, and the C++ Standard Library variously provide facilities for things like advanced mathematical operations, string handling, and the manipulation of regular expressions. However, if you're targeting the CLR with your C++ code, it makes sense to make the best use of the .NET Framework class library.

In this chapter, we'll examine some of the utility classes provided by the .NET Framework, and see how to use them in C++ applications. Specifically, we'll look at the support for file and text handling, for data structures, and for threading. This chapter does not comprise a comprehensive reference; rather, we'll be focusing on just a few classes and some of their more important members. For a complete list of classes, their members, and their functionality, you should of course refer to the MSDN documentation.

Text handling

The System::Text namespace provides classes for formatting String objects, encoding data, decoding data, and applying validation rules to data. In this section, we'll discuss:

- ❑ System::Text::StringBuilder – used for dynamically altering string content

- ❑ System::Text::RegularExpressions::Regex – used to validate complex data through the use of regular expressions

StringBuilder

You may be wondering why we're looking at another string class here – after all, we learned about the powerful `String` class in the last chapter. In some circumstances, however, using the `String` class can be very inefficient, particularly if we want to make a lot of text substitutions on a string, in order to alter it in some way. `String` is an *immutable* data type; we cannot alter it. What this means is that using methods such as `Concat()`, `Replace()`, and `Remove()` results not in the original string being changed, but rather in the creation of a new string entirely. In circumstances where repeated small changes are made, `String` can introduce a performance hit, and you should consider using `StringBuilder` instead.

`StringBuilder` is similar to `String`, but the way it is allocated is different. When you create an instance of a new `StringBuilder` class on the managed heap, you are actually allocated *more* memory than is required by the string itself. You can add characters and change the string without having to copy it to a new string in a different memory location.

By default, all of this work is done 'under the hood', but you can set the capacity of the string manually, using the `Capacity` property of the `StringBuilder` class. Note that this is distinct from the `Length` property, which is the length of the actual string contained by the class. In terms of utility, `StringBuilder` is not as powerful as the `String` class – it doesn't support nearly as much functionality – so when and how much you use it will depend on how you intend to use strings in your code.

Let's code an application that uses `StringBuider`:

```
using namespace System;
using namespace System::Text;

int _tmain(void)
{
    // Create a new StringBuilder
    StringBuilder* l_ptrSBValue = new StringBuilder;
    Console::WriteLine(S"Initial Capacity is {0}",
                       l_ptrSBValue->Capacity.ToString());
    Console::WriteLine(S"Initial Length is {0}",
                       l_ptrSBValue->Length.ToString());

    // Append some data
    l_ptrSBValue->Append(S"Hello!\n");
    l_ptrSBValue->AppendFormat(S"Name = {0}\nAddress = {1}",
                       S"Niranjan", S"No 226, Cathedral Road");

    DateTime l_dtCurrTime = DateTime::Now;
    l_ptrSBValue->Append(S"\nCurrent Date = ");
    l_ptrSBValue->Append(l_dtCurrTime.ToString(S"f"));

    // Output result
    Console::WriteLine(
            S"\nStringBuilder object now contains:\n{0}", l_ptrSBValue);

    Console::WriteLine(S"After appending data the Capacity is {0}",
                       l_ptrSBValue->Capacity.ToString());
```

```
        Console::WriteLine(S"After appending data the Length is {0}",
                           l_ptrSBValue->Length.ToString());

    // Alter the contents
    l_ptrSBValue->Remove(0, 7);
    l_ptrSBValue->Replace(S"Name = ", S"Welcome ");
    l_ptrSBValue->Insert(0, S"My Personal Details are shown below:\n");

        Console::WriteLine(S"\nContents of StringBuilder after modification:\n{0}",
                           l_ptrSBValue);

    // Reduce the capacity to Length of object
    l_ptrSBValue->Capacity = l_ptrSBValue->Length;
        Console::WriteLine(S"Finally the Capacity is {0}",
                           l_ptrSBValue->Capacity.ToString());

    return 0;
}
```

The initial capacity and length of the `StringBuilder` are output to the console using the `Capacity` and `Length` properties. We then append some data and output the result. Note that we use two different methods of `StringBuider` here:

❑   `AppendFormat()` takes a formatted string, containing format specifications. In this example, we replace the format specifications with strings for name and address information.

❑   `Append()` simply takes a `String*` as parameter, which points to the `String` object to append.

We call the `ToString()` method on the `DateTime` object in order to append it to our `StringBuilder`; we use `"f"` as an argument, which formats the date with the name, the month, and the current time.

Next, we alter the contents of the string using some other methods of the `StringBuilder` class, namely `Replace()`, `Remove()`, and `Insert()`. Although we only replace one instance of a string in our example, the `Replace()` method will replace all occurrences of the search string with the replacement string. `Remove()` takes two integers (a start position and the length) and removes the characters specified by these two values (the length provided here, 7, includes the newline character).

In this example, `Insert()` is to insert a string at the specified position, but there are overloads that take most of the basic types. While this method is similar to `String::Insert()` in usage, the behavior is different. The `String` version doesn't affect the calling object – it returns the result as a new `String*`. The `StringBuilder` version inserts the passed string into the calling object.

When these operations are carried out, the `StringBuilder` object automatically allocates the memory necessary, so we output the length and the capacity again to see how things have changed. If you build and run the code, you should see something like this:

```
Initial Capacity is 16
Initial Length is 0

The StringBuilder object now contains:
Hello!
```

```
Name = Niranjan
Address = No 226, Cathedral Road
Current date = 04 February 2002 12.56
After appending data the Capacity is 128
After appending data the Length is 93

Contents of StringBuilder after modification:
My personal details are shown below:
Welcome Niranjan
Address = No 226, Cathedral Road
Current date = 04 February 2002 12.56
Finally, the Capacity is 128
Finally, the Length is 124
```

We can see that the initial `Capacity` of the `StringBuilder` object is 16, although the string itself is empty. After adding lots of data, however, the `Capacity` has risen to 128 automatically, with no effort required on our part. After further modifications of the string data, the `Capacity` stays the same, while the `Length` increases.

We could try to reduce the `Capacity` to something shorter than the `Length` of the current string manually, with the line:

```
l_ptrSBValue->Capacity = 100;
```

However, this would result in an exception of type `ArgumentOutOfRangeException` being thrown. For this reason, you should take care when trying to control the `Capacity` property by hand.

Regex

The .NET Framework makes complex data validation easy by introducing a set of utility classes as part of the `System::Text::RegularExpressions` namespace. In this section, we'll restrict our focus to the main class, `Regex`, which performs regular expression matching on a `String` object. `Regex` has a number of overloaded methods to facilitate complex pattern matching techniques.

We can initialize a `Regex` object by passing a string to the constructor. The example below illustrates how to search for the string `"is"` inside another string:

```
String* myText = S"This is a big silver whistle.";
Regex* firstRegex = new Regex(S"is");
MatchCollection* myMatches = firstRegex->Matches(myText);
Console::WriteLine(S"Looking for \"is\": number of matches = {0}",
                    myMatches->Count.ToString());
```

The `Matches()` method returns a `MatchCollection` object – a collection of `Match` objects that each correspond to a match found in the string. (`Regex` has a similar method called `Match()` that returns one `Match` object, corresponding to the first match found.) We can find the number of matches by examining the `Count` property of the `MatchCollection` object, which is three in this example. We'll be looking at collections in more detail later on in the chapter.

It's also possible to call `Matches()` as a static method of the `Regex` object. In this configuration, we pass both a search string and a pattern to be used:

```
myMatches = Regex::Matches(myText, S"this");
Console::WriteLine(S"Looking for \"this\": number of matches = {0}",
                        myMatches->Count.ToString());
```

Since the regular expression is case sensitive by default, no matches are found here. However, we can tell it to ignore the case by using one of the enumerated values of RegexOptions – in this example, IgnoreCase:

```
myMatches = Regex::Matches(myText, S"this", RegexOptions::IgnoreCase);
Console::WriteLine(
            S"Looking for \"this\" (IgnoreCase): number of matches = {0}",
            myMatches->Count.ToString());
```

This time, we find the match for "this". Note that a RegexOptions enumerated value can also be passed as an additional parameter to the Regex constructor.

Perhaps we want to search for a whole word, rather than just a sub-string? Going back to the first example, we can set up the regular expression to specify "is" as a whole word:

```
Regex* secondRegex = new Regex(S"\\bis\\b");
myMatches = secondRegex->Matches(myText);
Console::WriteLine(S"Looking for \"is\" (whole word): number of matches = {0}",
                        myMatches->Count.ToString());
```

The escape character \b in a regular expression pattern indicates a word boundary. (Note that in C++, we need to use two backslashes in order for \b to get passed to the regular expression from the string.) There are lots of other escape characters we can use; here are some that you might find useful for matching on whitespace characters:

- ❑ \t – tab
- ❑ \n – newline
- ❑ \r – carriage return

The Regex class also provides methods for altering the search string depending on the result of matches. For example:

```
String* myNewText = Regex::Replace(myText, S"whistle", S"bell");
Console::WriteLine(myNewText);
```

Here, we're using the Replace() method, to which the first parameter is the input text, the second parameter is the search pattern, and the third parameter is the replacement text. The method returns the modified string. Again, there are many overloaded versions of this method, and you should consult the MSDN documentation for a full listing.

Pattern matching

So far, we've seen only quite simple regular expressions. Let's look at some more complicated pattern matching by developing an application that validates some input data – in this case, a name, a telephone number, an e-mail address, and a credit card number. If the input is invalid, the user will be asked to try again. Let's start with the name:

```
Console::Write(S"Enter your name: ");
strName = Console::ReadLine();
Regex* ptrREName = new Regex(S"^([A-Z][a-z]+[ ]?)+$");
while(!ptrREName->IsMatch(strName))
{
    Console::Write(S"Name is not valid! Try again: ");
    strName = Console::ReadLine();
}
```

We initialize the `Regex` object with the pattern `"^([A-Z][a-z]+[ ]?)+$"`. `[A-Z]` simply looks for a capital letter. After this, we look for one or more lower case letters, specified by `[a-z]+`, where + just means 'one or more'. This is followed by an optional space character, where ? means 'zero or one'. (If you want to specify 'zero or more', you can use *.) We place this whole expression in parentheses and add another +; this allows us to validate one or more words that begin with a capital letter and are separated by spaces – the usual form for writing a name. Finally, note that we include a ^ at the start of the pattern and $ at the end. These are special characters that allow us to specify where the pattern exists in the text: ^ means it is at the start, and $ means it is at the end. By using both of these in our pattern, we don't allow for any other text in the search string. This is a very useful technique for validation.

> *For the rest of this section, we'll just focus on the regular expressions themselves, rather than looking at all the code. For a full code listing, you can of course consult the code download.*

Shown below is the regular expression used to validate a telephone number:

```
Regex* ptrREPhone = new Regex(S"^\\d{3}[-\\s]?\\d{3}[-\\s)]?\\d{4}$");
```

Here, we're looking for a series of digits, specified by the escape character `\d`. We expect the phone number to be formatted as 3 digits, followed by 3 digits, followed by 4 digits, with optional separators of a space or a hyphen.

Next, we have the regular expression to validate an e-mail address:

```
Regex* ptrREEmail = new Regex("^\\w+(\\.\\w+)*@\\w+(\\.\\w+)+$");
```

The escape character `\w` indicates any word character – that is, a letter, a digit, or an underscore. Here, we assume that an e-mail address must contain one or more words separated by a period, followed by @, then two or more words separated by periods again. This means we can validate addresses such as:

❑   `bridget@wrox.com`
❑   `bridget.jones@mail.wrox.co.uk`

More complex validation could include checks on the last part of the address to ensure that it has the appropriate ending for a valid top-level domain.

Finally, we validate a credit card number with this regular expression:

```
Regex* ptrRECardNumber = new Regex("^\\d{4}-?\\d{4}-?\\d{4}-?\\d{4}$");
```

This expression allows a total of 16 digits, optionally separated into groups of 4 with a hyphen as a separator.

In this section, we've had just a taster of working with regular expressions, but even the simple examples presented here should give you an idea of the kinds of things you can do with the .NET regular expression classes. Other classes in the `System::Text::RegularExpressions` namespace provide functionality for working with **captures** – that is, objects representing previous matches – allowing for more complex matching and string manipulation.

File handling

Next, we're going to deal with the .NET classes that aid with file handling. We'll be discussing the classes `System::IO::File`, `System::IO::FileStream`, `System::IO::StreamReader`, and `System::IO::StreamWriter`.

File and FileStream

In the .NET Framework, the `System::IO` namespace provides classes that are necessary for managing input and output. It includes classes that can work on files, explore directories, handle byte arrays, deal with text and binary data, handle file related exceptions, and more. In this section, we'll focus on the `File` and `FileStream` classes.

We'll develop an application that accepts two file names as input and appends the content of the second file to the first. We'll just focus on the methods for handling files here – for the full code listing, you should consult the `FileCat` project in the code download.

Opening files

We can open files using static methods of the `File` class. We need to open the source file in read mode and the target file in append mode:

```
FileStream* l_fsSource = File::OpenRead(l_strSourceFileName);
FileStream* l_fsTarget = File::Open(l_strTargetFileName, FileMode::Append);
```

`File::OpenRead()` accepts the path to a file, opens it in read mode, and returns a `FileStream*`. (This is similar to opening a file in `"r"` mode in a call to the `fopen()` C language function.) The second argument to the `File::Open()` method specifies the mode in which the file should be opened (in our case, `Append`), and also returns a `FileStream*`. (This is equivalent to opening a file in `"a"` mode with `fopen()`.) If the input file passed to either of these methods is not present, a `FileNotFoundException` will be raised. For this reason, we need to put all this code inside a `try` block and add a `catch` block to handle such an exception.

Reading from and writing to files

In order to read and write data using `FileStream`, we need to use an array of type `unsigned char __gc[]`. The following code declares such an array, as well as an integer variable called `l_iBytesRead` that will be used while reading the source file. The preprocessor constant `MAX_VALUE` is defined as 255:

```
unsigned char l_arrContents __gc[] = new unsigned char __gc[MAX_VALUE];
int l_iBytesRead = 0;
```

To read data from a `FileStream` object, we call `FileStream::Read()`, passing the `__gc[]` array, the position in the array at which to begin writing, and the number of bytes to read as arguments. When the file is read successfully, this method returns the number of bytes read and stored in the array. When it reaches the end of the file, `Read()` returns zero. The next code fragment reads the whole source file in a `while` loop and writes into the target file using `FileStream::Write()`:

```
Console::WriteLine(S"Contents of the Source file\n***********");
while(l_iBytesRead = l_fsSource->Read(l_arrContents, 0, MAX_VALUE))
{
    // Convert unsigned char to String and print in the console
    String* l_strContents = Encoding::ASCII->GetString(l_arrContents);
    Console::Write(l_strContents);

    // Write to file
    l_fsTarget->Write(l_arrContents, 0, l_iBytesRead);
    l_fsTarget->Flush();

    // Initialize the array
    int iCtr = 0;
    for(; iCtr < MAX_VALUE; iCtr++)
    {
        l_arrContents->Item[iCtr] = '\0';
    }
}
```

`FileStream::Write()` is similar to its counterpart. It accepts the array, the offset into the array, and the number of bytes to write as arguments. In the `while` loop, we store the number of bytes read from the file in the integer variable `l_iBytesRead`. Also, the unsigned char `__gc[]` array is converted to a `String*` by using the `System::Text::Encoding` class, so that we can write the contents to the console. `Flush()` will write the buffered data and clears the contents of the stream. (This is similar to the `fflush(FILE*)` C function.) Finally, the array is initialized in a `for` loop so that it will be empty for the next `Read()` operation.

Closing files

The following code fragment shows how to close the open files by using `FileStream::Close()`:

```
l_fsSource->Close();
l_fsTarget->Close();
```

`FileStream::Close()` will write the buffered data (if any) and close the file. Note that before terminating the application, the runtime will close all the files that were opened by the program even if we *don't* call `File::Close()`, but it's good practice to close the file programmatically instead of depending on the system.

An alternative way of performing the above operation would be to perform all three steps inside the `while` loop, using the `FileStream::Length` property, which returns the length of the stream. We can declare the array accordingly, then perform read and write operations. The following code fragment illustrates this:

```
// Determine the length
__int64 l_len = l_fsSource->Length;
```

```
// Declare the array
unsigned char l_arrContents __gc[] =  new unsigned char __gc[l_len];

// Read the input file
l_fsSource->Read(l_arrContents,0,l_len);

// Write to output file
l_fsTarget->Write(l_arrContents,0,l_len);
```

The problem with this approach, however, is that if the input file is too big (megabytes), the program could fail to allocate that much memory. It's advisable to perform read and write operations in a loop, as we did earlier, rather than in one shot.

StreamReader and StreamWriter

When .NET provides the `FileStream` class for handling file input and output, why do we need `StreamReader` and `StreamWriter` to do the same job? The answer is that these classes handle the data in the form of strings, rather than bytes. It can be something of a nuisance to spend your time converting data from `String*` to `unsigned char __gc[]` and vice versa, so when it's appropriate, dealing with `String` objects from start to finish is a big help.

The two classes under discussion here derive from `System::MarshalByRefObject`. The class hierarchy is shown below:

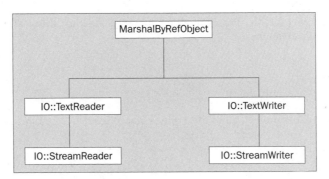

The `StreamReader` class is used to open a file in 'read' mode, while the `StreamWriter` class opens a file in 'write' mode. Both classes support encoding while reading and storing data, but we won't be using those facilities in this section. To illustrate these classes, we'll develop a utility that copies text files by taking two command-line arguments: the source file and the target file. You can find the full code listing in the `FileCopy` project.

In the following code, the file names are passed as arguments to the constructors, and the respective stream objects are created:

```
StreamReader* l_swSource = new StreamReader(l_strSourceFileName);
StreamWriter* l_swTarget = new StreamWriter(l_strTargetFileName);
```

The next step is to copy the files, which we do using `StreamReader::ReadLine()` and `StreamWriter::Write()`. We keep performing this operation until the end of the file is reached, as determined using `StreamReader::Peek()`, which returns the next available character in the stream (without updating the current position) or -1 when we reach the end of the file. The next listing implements the core logic of the application:

```
Console::WriteLine(S"Contents of the file\n***********");
String* l_strContents = S"";

for(; l_swSource->Peek() > -1; )
{
    // Read the line
    l_strContents = l_swSource->ReadLine();

    // Write to file
    l_swTarget->WriteLine(l_strContents);
    l_swTarget->Flush();

    // Write to console
    Console::WriteLine(l_strContents);
}

Console::WriteLine(S"\n************");
Console::WriteLine(S"The file '{0}' successfuly copied to '{1}'.",
                    l_strSourceFileName, l_strTargetFileName);
```

After we copy to the target file, we display the file's contents. The only thing left to do is to close the streams using the `Close()` method:

```
// Close files
l_swSource->Close();
l_swTarget->Close();
```

Again, in the downloadable project, all of this code is placed inside a `try` block, so we include appropriate `catch` blocks afterwards.

Collections

In this section, we'll look at some of the important collection classes that are provided by the .NET framework in the `System::Collections` namespace, and at the interfaces they implement. The important interfaces in this namespace are:

❑ `ICollection` – defines a collection of objects

❑ `IList` – represents a collection of objects that can be accessed like an array, using an index

❑ `IComparer` – used for comparison of two objects

❑ `IEnumerable` – allows a client to access an enumerator via its `GetEnumerator()` method

❑ `IEnumerator` – supports iteration over a collection

❑ `IDictionary` – represents a key-value pair collection

Later in this section we'll take a look at a couple of these interfaces – IComparer and IEnumerator – in more detail. First, however, we'll examine a useful class from the System::Collections namespace. System::Collections::ArrayList implements the IList interface.

ArrayList

ArrayList acts like a dynamic array. We can add any type of object to an ArrayList instance and then iterate through it. The ArrayList::Add() method takes an Object* argument that it adds to the array, while individual items in the array can be read using the ArrayList::Item property. There are two main differences between an ArrayList and a normal __gc[] array:

❑ In an ArrayList, elements can be added dynamically after creation. In __gc[] arrays, this is not possible.

❑ An ArrayList allows any type of data to be stored, while __gc[] arrays can store only data of their type. One cannot store a string value in an int __gc[] array.

The following example adds objects of different types (String, double, DateTime, and int) to an ArrayList object, using the Add() method. Note that we need to convert the __value types to Object* by using the __box keyword.

```
Collections::ArrayList* l_ptrALDetails = new Collections::ArrayList;

String* l_strName = S"Niranjan Kumar";
String* l_strAddress = S"KNiranja@chn.cognizant.com";
double l_dMonthlyInc = 7500.60;
DateTime l_dtDOB(1976, 05, 15, 16, 20, 00);
__box int* l_iNumber = __box(DateTime::Today.Day);

l_ptrALDetails->Add(l_strName);
l_ptrALDetails->Add(l_strAddress);
l_ptrALDetails->Add(__box(l_dMonthlyInc));
l_ptrALDetails->Add(__box(l_dtDOB));
l_ptrALDetails->Add(l_iNumber);
```

The next step is to read the values from the array by using the ArrayList::Item property:

```
Console::WriteLine(S"The values in the ArrayList are: ");
for(int l_iCtr = 0; l_iCtr < l_ptrALDetails->Count; l_iCtr++)
{
    Console::WriteLine(l_ptrALDetails->Item[l_iCtr]->ToString());
}
```

To *remove* an element from the array, one option is to use the Remove() method. This takes an Object* as an argument and removes the first occurrence of that argument type from the array. RemoveAt(), on the other hand, takes an index number as an argument and removes the item pointed to by that index. Note that after removing an item from the list, the rest of the items are repositioned, so their indexes change accordingly:

```
// Remove last element
l_ptrALDetails->Remove(l_iNumber);
```

Sorting

The `ArrayList` class implements another method, `Sort()`, that allows us to sort all the elements in the array. In order for this to work, however, the objects in the array need access to an implementation of the `IComparer` interface, which has a single method: `Compare()`. This method makes a value comparison of two objects and returns an integer whose value depends on whether one object is 'bigger' than the other.

We can control how our array is sorted by the three arguments we pass to `Sort()`:

❑   The starting index

❑   The number of elements to sort

❑   The implementation of the `IComparer` interface

If we don't pass a value for the third parameter, then the default implementation of `Sort()` is used; this is fine for objects that already support `IComparer`, such as `String`. In our sample application, we'll just sort the first two `String*` elements of the array and then display the list of items again:

```
l_ptrALDetails->Sort(0, 2, 0);

Console::WriteLine(S"\nThe ArrayList now contains: ");
for(int l_iCtr = 0; l_iCtr < l_ptrALDetails->Count; l_iCtr++)
{
    Console::WriteLine(l_ptrALDetails->Item[l_iCtr]->ToString());
}
```

Shown below is the entire output of the sample application. Note that the two `String*` objects (name and e-mail address) are sorted and displayed correctly at the end:

```
The values in the ArrayList are:
Niranjan Kumar
KNiranja@chn.cognizant.com
7500.6
5/15/76 4:20:00 PM
5

The ArrayList now contains:
KNiranja@chn.cognizant.com
Niranjan Kumar
7500.6
5/15/76 4:20:00 PM
```

SortedList

The `System::Collections::SortedList` class is very different from `ArrayList`. Every element is stored in the form of a key-value pair. `SortedList` behaves like a combination of an array and a hash table, and allows us to address its elements in two different ways. When the elements are accessed using the `Item` property, the class behaves like a hash table. When the elements are accessed using the `GetByIndex()` method, it behaves like an array.

In this section, we'll explore the SortedList class and write an application that uses it. To start with, we'll add an element to the list using SortedList::Add(), which accepts two Object* variables – the first is the key, while the second is the actual value. Note that the key must be unique; attempting to add a duplicate key will result in an exception of type ArgumentException. In our application, we'll accept and then output six names.

```
Collections::SortedList* l_ptrSLNames = new Collections::SortedList;
String* l_strName;
String* l_strKey;

Console::WriteLine(S"Capacity of SortedList = {0}",
                        l_ptrSLNames->Capacity.ToString());

// Add to the SortedList
for(int l_iCtr = 0; l_iCtr < 3; l_iCtr++)
{
    Console::Write(S"Enter Name: ");
    l_strName = Console::ReadLine();
    l_strKey = String::Concat(S"Name", l_iCtr.ToString());
    l_ptrSLNames->Add(l_strKey, l_strName);
}
```

In the above code fragment, before any input is accepted, the capacity of the list is printed using the SortedList::Capacity property. Initially the size is set to 16. If you know that you won't be using all the elements allocated by the runtime, you can remove the unused ones by calling SortedList::TrimToSize():

```
l_ptrSLNames->TrimToSize();
Console::WriteLine(S"Now the capacity is {0}",
                        l_ptrSLNames->Capacity.ToString());
```

Even after removing the unused elements, we can still add elements to the SortedList object simply by calling SortedList::Add(). The following code shows two elements being added, illustrating the dynamic ability of SortedList to decrease and increase its size when elements are removed and added:

```
// Add two more elements
l_strKey = String::Concat(S"Name", l_ptrSLNames->Count.ToString());
l_ptrSLNames->Add(l_strKey, S"Murali");
l_strKey = String::Concat(S"Name", l_ptrSLNames->Count.ToString());
l_ptrSLNames->Add(l_strKey, S"Murugan");
```

The GetKey() method returns the key associated with the index you pass, while GetByIndex() accepts an index number and returns the corresponding element:

```
Console::WriteLine(S"The keys and values of the SortedList using Index: ");
for(int l_iCtr = 0; l_iCtr < l_ptrSLNames->Count; l_iCtr++)
{
    Console::WriteLine(S"Key = {0}, Value = {1}",
            l_ptrSLNames->GetKey(l_iCtr), l_ptrSLNames->GetByIndex(l_iCtr));
}
```

When you use the `Item` property, the object behaves like a hash table:

```
Console::WriteLine(S"The values of the SortedList using Key: ");
for(int l_iCtr = 0; l_iCtr < l_ptrSLNames->Count; l_iCtr++)
{
    l_strKey = String::Concat(S"Name", l_iCtr.ToString());
    Console::WriteLine(l_ptrSLNames->Item[l_strKey]);
}

Console::WriteLine("Finally, the capacity = {0}",
                        l_ptrSLNames->Capacity.ToString());
```

When compiled and run, the output of the above listing is as shown below.

```
Capacity of SortedList = 16
Enter Name: Aruna
Enter Name: Roberto
Enter Name: Giacomo
Now the capacity is 3
The keys and values of the SortedList using Index:
Key = Name0, Value = Aruna
Key = Name1, Value = Roberto
Key = Name2, Value = Giacomo
Key = Name6, Value = Murali
Key = Name7, Value = Murugan
The values of the SortedList using Key:
Aruna
Roberto
Giacomo
Murali
Murugan
Finally, the capacity = 6
```

We first added three items, then we trimmed the size by calling `TrimToSize()`, leaving the capacity of the list at three. Later, we added two more items to the list, but rather than ending up with $3 + 2 = 5$ elements, we wound up with six. This is because whenever there is a need for more elements, `SortedList` allocates a number of items that's equal to its current capacity. When we started adding new elements, the capacity doubled to six.

The IComparer interface

We saw earlier that in order to compare two objects when `Array::Sort()` is called, we need to implement the `IComparer` interface. In our `ArrayList` sample, we sorted the first two `String*` elements by calling `ArrayList::Sort()`:

```
l_ptrALDetails->Sort(0, 2, 0);
```

Here, we passed 0 for the third parameter, which means that we didn't specify an implementation of `IComparer`. We could still sort the `String` elements because the `String` class already implements `IComparer`.

Implementing IComparer

Consider a C++ class called `Friend` that represents information about a person, holding information such as Name and Age. We could add an instance of this class to `ArrayList`, but we wouldn't be able to call `ArrayList::Sort()` to sort the items in the list. To achieve this, we need to pass a custom implementation of `IComparer` as the third parameter to the `Sort()` method.

Implementing `IComparer` is actually pretty simple – all we need to do is derive a class from `IComparer` and implement its members. `IComparer` has only one public method, `Compare()`, which accepts two `Object` pointers as parameters and performs a value comparison of the two objects. The possible return values of the method are as follows:

❑   0 – the value of both the parameters is the same

❑   < 1 – the value of the first object is less than the second

❑   > 1 – the value of the first object is greater than second

Let's start implementing the `Friend` class. (Note that you can find this code in the downloadable files as the `CustomCompare` project.) It will have two read-only properties: Name, of type `String*`, and Age, of type `int`. These will be implemented by private members called m_strName and m_iAge:

```
__gc class Friend
{
private:
    String* m_strName;
    int m_iAge;

public:
    Friend(String* l_strName, int l_iAge) : m_strName(l_strName),
                                            m_iAge(l_iAge)
    {}

    __property String* get_Name()
    {
        return m_strName;
    }
    __property int get_Age()
    {
        return m_iAge;
    }
};
```

The next step is to implement the `IComparer` interface in another class:

```
__gc class MyComparer : public IComparer
{
private:
    int m_iSortBy;

public:
    MyComparer() : m_iSortBy(0)
    {}
```

```
    // SortBy property
    __property int get_SortBy()
    {
        return m_iSortBy;
    }
    __property void set_SortBy(int l_iValue)
    {
        m_iSortBy = l_iValue;
    }

    // Compare the Objects
    int Compare(Object* l_ptr1, Object* l_ptr2)
    {
        int l_iRetval = 0;
        try
        {
            Friend* l_ptrFriend1 = dynamic_cast<Friend*>(l_ptr1);
            Friend* l_ptrFriend2 = dynamic_cast<Friend*>(l_ptr2);

            // Sort by Age
            if(m_iSortBy == 0)
            {
                if(l_ptrFriend1->Age < l_ptrFriend2->Age)
                    l_iRetval = -1;
                else if(l_ptrFriend1->Age > l_ptrFriend2->Age)
                    l_iRetval = 1;
            }
            else
            {
                // Sort by Name
                l_iRetval = String::Compare(l_ptrFriend1->Name, l_ptrFriend2->Name);
            }
        }
        catch(Exception* e)
        {
            Console::Write(e);
            return l_iRetval;
        }
        return l_iRetval;
    }
};
```

In the MyComparer class, we can decide whether we're sorting by name or by age, depending on the value of the SortBy property. The Compare() method takes two Object*s as parameters (as defined by the IComparer interface), which we cast to type Friend*. It returns an int, which is initialized to 0 at the start of the method. If the value of the SortBy property is 0, then we compare the Age properties of the Friend objects and set the return value accordingly. If, on the other hand, SortBy is 1, we sort on the Name property. Since Name is of type String, it's compared using the String::Compare() static method, which we can use to set the appropriate return value automatically. When any exception is raised, the method is terminated.

In order to see what's going on inside the list, we'll add a utility function that outputs the Name and Age properties from Friend instances stored in an ArrayList:

```
void PrintElements(ArrayList* l_ptrList)
{
   for(int l_iCtr = 0; l_iCtr < l_ptrList->Count; l_iCtr++)
   {
      Friend* l_ptrSorted = dynamic_cast<Friend*>(l_ptrList->Item[l_iCtr]);
      Console::WriteLine(S"Name = {0}, Age = {1}",
                    l_ptrSorted->Name, l_ptrSorted->Age.ToString());
   }
}
```

Now let's write some code to test the MyComparer class:

```
int _tmain(void)
{
   Friend* l_ptrFriend;
   ArrayList* l_ptrFriendList = new ArrayList;
   int l_iCtr = 0;

   // Add Friends to the ArrayList
   l_ptrFriend = new Friend(S"Roopa", 26);
   l_ptrFriendList->Add(l_ptrFriend);
   l_ptrFriend = new Friend(S"Zaratin", 24);
   l_ptrFriendList->Add(l_ptrFriend);
   l_ptrFriend = new Friend(S"Johnny", 32);
   l_ptrFriendList->Add(l_ptrFriend);

   Console::WriteLine(S"Before sorting the array");

   // Print before sorting
   PrintElements(l_ptrFriendList);

   // Sort elements on Age using MyComparer
   MyComparer* l_obj = new MyComparer;

   // Sort by Age
   l_ptrFriendList->Sort(0, 3, l_obj);

   // Print after sorting
   Console::WriteLine(S"After sorting the array on Age");
   PrintElements(l_ptrFriendList);

   // Sort elements on Name using MyComparer
   l_obj->SortBy = 1;
   l_ptrFriendList->Sort(0, 3, l_obj);

   // Print after sorting
   Console::WriteLine(S"After sorting the array on Name");
   PrintElements(l_ptrFriendList);

   return 0;
}
```

We create a few Friend instances, add them to an ArrayList object, and output the initial values of the unsorted list to the console. Next, we call Sort() on the array, passing it a pointer to a new instance of our MyComparer class for the third parameter, and output the results once again. Finally, we change the SortBy property of the MyComparer instance to 1, allowing us to sort the array by name, before outputting the results one last time. The output of the entire program is shown below:

```
Before sorting the array
Name = Roopa, Age = 26
Name = Johnny, Age = 32
Name = Robert, Age = 41
After sorting the array on Age
Name = Roopa, Age = 26
Name = Johnny, Age = 32
Name = Robert, Age = 41
After sorting the array on Name
Name = Johnny, Age = 32
Name = Robert, Age = 41
Name = Roopa, Age = 26
```

The IEnumerator interface

IEnumerator is an interface that defines a set of methods to facilitate the traversal of elements in a collection – it is the base interface for all enumerators. Before we begin to discuss it any further, though, it's important to point out that this interface doesn't support any modification of data – rather, it represents a snapshot. Classes that implement this interface can be used in a C# or Visual Basic .NET 'for each' loop.

A C# or VB 'for each' loop is similar to C's for loop, but 'for each' automatically handles initialization, conditional checking, advancing to the next element, and so on.

The members of IEnumerator are shown in the table below:

Member name	Member type	Description
MoveNext()	Public method	Advances the enumerator to the next element
Reset()	Public method	Resets the enumerator to its initial element
Current	Public property	Gets the current element from the list

Implementing IEnumerator

In this section, we'll develop a C++ class that implements the IEnumerator interface – it will store a list of names, with one name in each element. We will first create a Managed C++ Class Library called FriendArray inside a solution called MyFriends. (This will allow us to add a client project to the solution later.) In the FriendArrary library, we'll create a C++ class called MyFriends that implements IEnumerator:

```
// FriendArray.h

#pragma once

using namespace System;
using namespace System::Collections;

namespace Friendarray
{
    public __gc class MyFriends : public IEnumerator
    {
    private:
        ArrayList* m_ptrALNames;
        int m_iPos;

    public:
        MyFriends()
        {
            m_ptrALNames = new ArrayList;
            m_iPos = -1;
        }

        // Value property
        __property set_Value(String* l_strValue)
        {
            m_ptrALNames->Add(l_strValue);
        }

        // Method to extract an element
        String* GetValue(int l_iCount);
        {
            return dynamic_cast<String*>(m_ptrALNames->Item[l_iIndex]);
        }

        // Count property
        __property int get_Count()
        {
            return m_ptrALNames->Count;
        }

        // Returns IEnumerator implementor
        IEnumerator* GetEnumerator();

        // The IEnumerator interface
        bool MoveNext();
        __property Object* get_Current();
        void Reset();
    };
}
```

The MyFriends class has two private members: m_ptrALNames, which holds a list of names, and m_iPos, which will be used in iteration. We can add an element to the array using the 'set' method for the Value property and retrieve its value using the corresponding 'get' method. Note that we need to perform a cast in the 'get' method, since ArrayList::get_Item() returns an Object*. Count is a read-only property that returns the count of ArrayList members.

The next three methods allow clients written in C# or Visual Basic .NET to iterate through our collection using a 'for each' loop. In order to do this, the loop uses the implementation of the IEnumerator interface. If we want this functionality to be accessible from other languages, we need to implement GetEnumerator(). (By doing so, we are essentially implementing IEnumerable.) Here's the implementation of this method from FriendArray.cpp:

```
IEnumerator* MyFriends::GetEnumerator()
{
    Console::WriteLine(S"Inside C++ : GetEnumerator()");
    m_iPos = -1;
    return this;
}
```

This method simply returns the this pointer, since we implement IEnumerator in the same class. We also set m_iPos to -1, because a 'for each' will call MoveNext() first, and then access the Current property. On a first call, we want that to be the first item in the list.

Here's the MoveNext() code.

```
bool MyFriends::MoveNext()
{
    Console::WriteLine(S"Inside C++ : MoveNext()");
    m_iPos++;

    return m_iPos < Count;
}
```

Here, we increment the m_iPos integer variable, which is checked against the count of our ArrayList object, m_ptrALNames. If m_iPos isn't less than the count, the loop should be terminated. If this method returns true, the 'for each' loop will continue its execution; if it returns false, the loop will terminate.

The following code snippet shows the implementation of get_Current():

```
Object* MyFriends::get_Current()
{
    Console::WriteLine(S"Inside C++ : get_Current()");
    if(m_iPos == -1)
    {
        Console::WriteLine(S"Invalid Operation\n");
        return S"Error : Invalid Operation";
    }

    return GetValue(m_iPos);
}
```

After the initial validation of m_iPos, the element pointed to by this index is obtained using GetValue() and returned to the caller. That leaves us with just one more method to implement: Reset(). This function doesn't take any arguments, as it simply resets the index. We just set the index, m_iPos, to -1:

```
void MyFriends::Reset()
{
    Console::WriteLine(S"Inside C++: Reset()");
    m_iPos = -1;
    return;
}
```

So far, then, we've developed the MyFriends C++ class that implements the IEnumerator interface. Let's now look at a C# client that accesses this class.

Building a client

Add a new C# console application called TestClient to our existing solution. Before writing any code, we need to add a reference to the MyFriends class to the project. You can do this by right-clicking on the project node in Solution Explorer and selecting **Add Reference** – you should be able to see FriendArray under the **References** node of the TestClient. Now we're all set to write the code that tests the C++ class. Open the Class1.cs C# file, and add the following code to the Main() function, not forgetting also to add a using directive for the FriendArray namespace at the top of the file:

```
static void Main(string[] args)
{
    Console.WriteLine("Output from C# program: Beginning of C# TestClient");

    // Create MyFriends class
    MyFriends l_objFriends = new MyFriends();

    // Add elements to it
    l_objFriends.Value ="Jack";
    l_objFriends.Value ="Prabhu";
    l_objFriends.Value ="Aparna";

    // Print all elements
    Console.WriteLine("C# program: Before foreach()");
    foreach(string str in l_objFriends)
    {
        // Print the element
        Console.WriteLine("C# program: {0}", str);
    }
    Console.WriteLine("C# program: End of foreach()");
    Console.WriteLine("C# program: End of C# TestClient");
}
```

First, we create a MyFriends instance called l_objFriends and add three names to the list. Then we use a foreach loop to iterate through the list and print out all the elements. The output of the entire program is shown below:

```
Output from C# program: Beginning of C# TestClient
C# program: Before foreach()
Inside C++: GetEnumerator()
Inside C++: MoveNext()
Inside C++: get_Current()
C# program: Jack
```

```
Inside C++: MoveNext()
Inside C++: get_Current()
C# program: Prabhu
Inside C++: MoveNext()
Inside C++: get_Current()
C# program: Aparna
Inside C++: MoveNext()
C# program: End of foreach()
C# program: End of C# TestClient
```

From the above output, it's clear that `foreach` uses `GetEnumerator()`, `MoveNext()`, and `get_Current()` in order to iterate through the elements of a list. You could also watch the execution sequence by placing breakpoints in the `FriendArray.cpp` file and executing the program in debug mode.

Threading

The rest of this chapter will focus on the threading model exposed by .NET. We'll show how you can take advantage of it in your Managed C++ applications, using a set of useful classes defined in the `System::Threading` namespace. We'll look in particular at the `Thread` and `ThreadPool` classes, thread synchronization objects, the `Monitor` class, and the `ReaderWriterLock` class. Along the way, we'll examine various other details that pertain to threading in .NET, such as exceptions.

In the .NET execution model, applications are organized into one or more **application domains** (often abbreviated to **AppDomains**). An application domain can be thought of as a logical process, whereas traditional Win32 processes can be thought of as physical processes; a single Win32 process may actually house more than one application domain. Each application domain is considered to be a 'hard' boundary, and code executing in one application domain cannot access code executing in another one directly. This too is similar to Win32 processes, where each process runs in its own virtual address space, (for the most part) independently from other processes.

An application domain may contain one or more logical groupings of execution requirements called **contexts**, and these form another kind of execution boundary. The objects executing in a given context cannot access code in a different context directly, since the execution requirements might be different (and even incompatible).

Inside both application domains and contexts, threads of execution operate. When more than one thread is operating, an application is said to be multithreaded. Let's begin our exploration by looking at how to create a thread in a managed application using the .NET Framework's threading model.

Threading types

The `System::Threading::Thread` class provides methods and properties for individual thread management (such as creating them and destroying them), while `System::Threading::ThreadPool` allows an application to use a system-provided thread in order to perform work.

Thread class

To create a thread of execution within the managed environment, we can create a `Thread` instance. The .NET Framework threading model nicely separates the actual creation and control of a thread from its entry point by means of a delegate called `ThreadStart`.

To create a `Thread` instance, you must pass a `ThreadStart` delegate to the `Thread` constructor. The delegate can target any function that returns `void` and takes no parameters, implying that we can't pass state information to the target of the `ThreadStart` delegate directly. Instead, we make the target of the `ThreadStart` delegate a method of a class that can expose state information to be accessed by the thread function when it runs. Let's see how all this works in an example:

```
using namespace System;
using namespace System::Threading;

__gc class gcSimple
{
private :
    String* strToday;
public:
    // Public constructor
    gcSimple()
    {
        strToday = DateTime::Now.ToShortDateString();
    }

    void ThreadFunc1()
    {
        Console::WriteLine(S"Today is {0}", strToday);
        for(int i = 0; i < 10; i++)
        {
            Console::WriteLine(S"Thread ID = {0}, i = {1}",
                    AppDomain::GetCurrentThreadId().ToString(), i.ToString());
            for(int j = 0; j < 10000000; j++)
            {
                int jj = j * j;
            }
        }
    }
};
```

First, we define a managed class called `gcSimple` that has a method called `ThreadFunc1()`. This will later act as a target for the `ThreadStart` delegate instance that we'll pass to the `Thread` constructor. `ThreadFunc1()` contains a simple `for` loop that displays the thread ID and the loop index. It spins in a nested `for` loop for a while, keeping the thread running (as opposed to sleeping). This allows us to see the thread in its 'running' state. Our thread class contains a `String*` member, `strToday`, which is initialized to the current date in the public constructor and accessed in the thread function. This is a different approach from Win32 or MFC threading, where we have to pass values to a thread function as `void*`. In .NET, the entire object is passed to the `ThreadStart` delegate.

```
int _tmain(void)
{
    gcSimple* st = new gcSimple;
    Thread* t1 = new Thread(new ThreadStart(st, gcSimple::ThreadFunc1));
    Console::WriteLine(S"t1 is in the {0} state", __box(t1->ThreadState));
```

We start by creating an instance of the gcSimple class. Then we create a new Thread instance, passing to it a new ThreadStart instance whose target is the ThreadFunc1() method. At this point, the thread is *not* executing. The Thread class exposes a number of properties, and one of these is ThreadState, which indicates the state the thread is currently in. After creating the thread instance, we display its state to the console:

```
t1 is in the Unstarted state
```

Next, the thread is started by calling the Start() method on t1:

```
Console::WriteLine(S"starting t1");
t1->Start();
Thread::Sleep(0);
Console::WriteLine(S"t1 is in the {0} state", __box(t1->ThreadState));
```

After the main thread starts the t1 thread, it calls Thread::Sleep(0), forcing a thread context switch to occur. When I executed this program, the thread ID was 1728; based on the output below, it had enough time to display one line of output before a context switch occurred, transferring control back to the main thread, which reported that thread t1 was in the 'running' state:

```
starting t1
Today is 1/30/02
Thread ID = 1728, i = 1
t1 is in the Running state
```

Note that the output here and in the examples below will depend on factors such as your processor speed, CPU utilization, the number of other processes running, and so on. Furthermore, you can alter the way the application behaves by the way you call Sleep(). For example, if you were to pass 1000 as the parameter, you'd see more output from the thread function before main() resumed execution.

> *Throughout the samples in this chapter, we'll make judicious use of the* Thread::Sleep() *method to force thread context switches to occur at the most inopportune times. This helps to uncover any synchronization bugs.*

Next, the main thread suspends t1 by calling the Suspend() method:

```
Console::WriteLine(S"suspending t1");
t1->Suspend();

Thread::Sleep(0);
Console::WriteLine(S"t1 is in the {0} state", __box(t1->ThreadState));
```

Execution of the above code yields the following output:

```
suspending t1
t1 is in the Suspended state
```

After the main thread suspends the t1 thread, it again calls Sleep(0). A context switch then occurs back to the main thread, which reports that t1 is now in the 'suspended' state. Next, the thread is resumed by calling the Resume() method on t1:

```
    Console::WriteLine(S"resuming t1");
    t1->Resume();
    Thread::Sleep(0);
    Console::WriteLine(S"t1 is in the {0} state", __box(t1->ThreadState));
```

Execution of the above code yields the following output:

```
resuming t1
Thread ID = 1728, i = 2
t1 is in the Running state
```

Once resumed, the t1 thread is able to start processing again. It displays a single line of output prior to a thread context switch granting control back to the main thread, which indicates that the t1 thread is now 'running' again.

Lastly, we can wait until the t1 thread finishes by calling the Join() method on t1:

```
    Console::WriteLine(S"joining t1");
    t1->Join();
    Console::WriteLine(S"t1 has finished");
    return 0;
}
```

Execution of the above code yields the following output:

```
joining t1
Thread ID = 1728, i = 5
Thread ID = 1728, i = 6
Thread ID = 1728, i = 7
Thread ID = 1728, i = 8
Thread ID = 1728, i = 9
t1 has finished
```

The Join() method causes the calling thread to block until the t1 thread's ThreadStart delegate target method returns, at which point Join() returns and the main thread is allowed to continue executing, reporting that t1 has finished. The output above shows the execution of the program once t1 is joined to the main function.

Slight changes to this code can make our program work very differently. If we were to comment out all the Thread::Sleep(0) calls in the main function, we'd see different output. After 'starting' the child thread t1, the main thread would never yield time to t1, instead executing all the statements until it reached the Join() call. The t1 thread would remain in the 'unstarted' state until then.

ThreadPool class

In many application designs, a thread spends the majority of its time in a waiting or suspended state. For example, consider an application that uses a single thread to handle socket I/O for each connected client (known as the "thread-per-connection" model). Most of the time, each thread is suspended while it waits for data to be sent or received.

A common alternative to this is the notion of a **thread pool** – a group of threads that are kept waiting and then farmed out to do work when requested. In the case of the socket I/O threads, a thread pool could be used to reduce the number of threads required, while still allowing the servicing of the same number of connections (if not more). In effect, each thread performs work for several connections at once and therefore stays busier. Let's see how the problem of spawning multiple threads to do a job simultaneously can be solved in .NET

The .NET Framework provides the `ThreadPool` class, which can be used to queue work items for execution by threads in the pool. All the members of `ThreadPool` are static. The CLR takes care of managing the threads in the pool, increasing and decreasing their number as needed, based on an internal algorithm that takes into account the number of CPUs on the machine, how many work items are in the pool, and various other details. Using the thread pool is also a quick and easy way of performing asynchronous function calls.

Let's take a look at a simple example. First of all, we need to define a class that has a method we can execute on a `ThreadPool` thread:

```
__gc class MyThreadContext
{
public:
    // Simple pool usage
    void SimpleThreadFunc(Object* obj)
    {
        // Display the passed parameter
        Console::Write(S"Today is {0}:", obj);
        Console::WriteLine(S"Thread ID {0} in SimpleThreadFunc()",
                        AppDomain::GetCurrentThreadId().ToString());
        int nWorkerThreads;
        int nIOThreads;

        // Get the available thread count
        ThreadPool::GetAvailableThreads(&nWorkerThreads, &nIOThreads);
        Console::WriteLine(S"Available Worker threads: {0}",
                        nWorkerThreads.ToString());
        Thread::Sleep(1000);
    }
};
```

`MyThreadContext` defines a method called `SimpleThreadFunc()` that takes a single parameter of type `Object*`. This method will be used as a target of a `WaitCallback` delegate, which we'll look at shortly. In operation, it first displays the passed `Object` and then the thread ID to the console. We obtain this latter value using the static method `AppDomain::GetCurrentThreadID()`, which returns the identifier of the current thread. Next, the number of available threads in the thread pool is determined using the static `ThreadPool::GetAvailableThreads()` method, which takes two `Int32*` arguments and sets them to the number of available worker and I/O threads. After outputting the former, the function then sleeps for a second, allowing other threads to do work.

Now we can use the `ThreadPool` class to invoke the `SimpleThreadFunc()` method we just defined. Here's a snippet of code that does this:

```
// Declare the string
String* strToday = DateTime::Today.ToShortDateString();
MyThreadContext* tc = new MyThreadContext;

// Use the process-wide ThreadPool thread(s) to call the ThreadFunc() method
for(int i = 0; i < 5; i++)
{
    ThreadPool::QueueUserWorkItem(
            new WaitCallback(tc, MyThreadContext::SimpleThreadFunc), strToday);
}

// Give enough time for the work items to finish
Thread::Sleep(10000);
```

This code creates an instance of the MyThreadContext class and then enters a for loop that calls
ThreadPool::QueueUserWorkItem(). This method takes a first parameter of type WaitCallback,
which is a delegate that we instantiate by pointing it to the MyThreadContext instance's
SimpleThreadFunc() method, defined above. Notice the difference between the ThreadStart
delegate and the WaitCallback delegate: here we're passing any additional arguments to
QueueUserWorkItem() (in this case, strToday) through to the thread function. The example places
five work items in the queue for the ThreadPool and then sleeps for ten seconds to allow the
ThreadPool to process them. Executing this code results in output something like the following:

```
Today is 2/1/02:Thread ID 285 in SimpleThreadFunc()
Available Worker threads 24
Today is 2/1/02:Thread ID 271 in SimpleThreadFunc()
Available Worker threads 23
Today is 2/1/02:Thread ID 285 in SimpleThreadFunc()
Available Worker threads 23
Today is 2/1/02:Thread ID 271 in SimpleThreadFunc()
Available Worker threads 23
Today is 2/1/02:Thread ID 285 in SimpleThreadFunc()
Available Worker threads 23
```

SimpleThreadFunc() is invoked five times; on my test machine, this caused the ThreadPool to use
two threads to perform the work, as can be seen from the number of distinct thread IDs (285 and 271).
On your machine, you may see different results – it's even possible that only one thread will be used to
handle all the work items.

Notice the relationship between the number of threads used and the number of available worker
threads. By default, there are 25 available worker threads. When the first thread with ID 285 was used,
the available count fell to 24. Later on, it fell to 23... but no further. We can conclude that ThreadPool
only uses a new thread when it is necessary; otherwise, it tries to complete the task with an existing one.
It frees the programmer from the burden of creating and destroying threads.

A problem with this example is that the main thread of execution relies on timing to ensure that the work
items finish – it sleeps for ten seconds before exiting. If the work items do not finish within that time, some of
them won't get processed – it's the programmer's responsibility to ensure programmatically that every work
item is processed before the main thread exits. Thread synchronization events are a better way of handling
this, and we'll be looking at those later in the chapter.

Thread synchronization types

When writing multithreaded applications, we need to ensure that access to shared resources is synchronized, and .NET provides several types that can be used to synchronize threads. Each synchronization class in the .NET Framework class library provides a different category or style of synchronization, and is therefore suitable for a different synchronization problem. Let's look at each one in turn.

Interlocked

The most fundamental form of synchronization is achieved by using the `Interlocked` class from the `System::Threading` namespace, which provides four methods to increment, decrement, assign, or compare and assign a value atomically. All the members of this class are static and overloaded – versions of the `Increment()` and `Decrement()` methods take pointers to `int` or `__int64` values, while the `Exchange()` and `CompareExchange()` functions take `int*`, `Object**`, or `float*` arguments.

Interlocked::Increment and Interlocked::Decrement

The `Increment()` method provides a way to increment a variable atomically and returns the incremented value – you pass either an `int*` or a `long*`. It protects against the potential danger of a thread context switch taking place during an operation such as n++, where n is a variable that's shared between threads. It's not hard to use – you just have to remember that if you're writing multithreaded code, you should avoid writing code like this:

```
n++;
```

and use this instead:

```
Interlocked::Increment(&n);
```

The `Interlocked::Decrement()` method works in the same way, except that (as the name suggests) it decrements a variable atomically and returns the decremented value.

Interlocked::Exchange

The `Exchange()` method to allows us to read and assign a value to a variable atomically – it provides overloaded forms for `int`, `float`, and `Object*` values. The method assigns a specified value to a specified location and then returns the value that the location held prior to the assignment.

The following example attempts to implement a simple spin-lock mechanism, first using non-interlocked code in order to demonstrate the problems that arise:

```
// Wait on the spin lock
while(1 == n)
{
    Console::WriteLine(S"Thread ID {0} waiting for spin lock to open",
            AppDomain::GetCurrentThreadId().ToString());
    Thread::Sleep(100);
}

Thread::Sleep(100);
```

```
// Take the spin lock
n = 1;

// Do some work
Console::WriteLine(S"Thread ID {0} has the spin lock",
            AppDomain::GetCurrentThreadId().ToString());

Thread::Sleep(100);

Console::WriteLine(S"Thread ID {0} releasing the spin lock",
            AppDomain::GetCurrentThreadId().ToString());

// Release the spin lock
n = 0;
```

First, this code waits on the spin lock that's implemented by the variable n. While the value of n is 1, it stays in the while loop, sleeping for 100 milliseconds on each iteration. When the code detects that n is not 1, it exits the while loop and sleeps for another 100 milliseconds, before taking the spin lock by setting n to 1. At this point, it 'owns' the lock, and other threads will be waiting in their while loops. After doing some work (displaying some thread ID information to the console), it releases the spin lock by setting n to 0.

The basic flow of this code is correct, but due to the thread context switches, it's not 'thread-safe'. Look at the following output, which results from its execution by three concurrent threads:

```
Thread ID = 1796 has the spin lock
Thread ID = 1820 has the spin lock
Thread ID = 1808 has the spin lock
Thread ID = 1796 releasing the spin lock
Thread ID = 1820 releasing the spin lock
Thread ID = 1808 releasing the spin lock
```

Obviously, the code is not working correctly – all three threads think they own the spin lock! The problem arises because a thread context switch occurs between the time when the value of n is read to see if it is equal to 1, and the time when the thread takes the spin lock by assigning 1 to n.

To correct this code, we need to use the Exchange() method to test the value and assign 1 in a single, atomic operation:

```
while(1 == Interlocked::Exchange(&n, 1))
{
    Console::WriteLine(S"Thread ID {0} waiting for spin lock to open",
            AppDomain::GetCurrentThreadId().ToString());
    Thread::Sleep(100);
}

Thread::Sleep(100);

// Do some work
Console::WriteLine(S"Thread ID {0} has the spin lock",
            AppDomain::GetCurrentThreadId().ToString());
Thread::Sleep(100);
```

```
Console::WriteLine(S"Thread ID {0} releasing the spin lock",
                AppDomain::GetCurrentThreadId().ToString());

// Release the spin lock
Interlocked::Exchange(&n, 0);
```

n starts at 0, because no threads actually own the lock yet. The while loop tests the return value of the Exchange() method and, as long as it is 1, spins. The first thread to execute this code will set the value of n to 1, thereby taking the lock. All other threads will spin in the while loop until the owning thread releases the lock. Execution of this code on my machine by three concurrent threads results in the following output:

```
Thread ID 1812 has the spin lock
Thread ID 384 waiting for spin lock to open
Thread ID 1480 waiting for spin lock to open
Thread ID 1812 releasing the spin lock
Thread ID 384 has the spin lock
Thread ID 1480 waiting for spin lock to open
Thread ID 384 releasing the spin lock
Thread ID 1480 has the spin lock
Thread ID 1480 releasing the spin lock
```

Now, only one thread owns the spin lock at any one time. The other threads are waiting for the spin lock to be released.

Interlocked::CompareExchange

The CompareExchange() method atomically compares a variable to some value and, if equal, assigns a value to it. Once again, it is overloaded in three forms for the types int, float, and Object*.

The code below compares the value of an integer variable (n) to 0. If the result of the comparison is true, a value of 1 is assigned to n. The intent is to use the variable n as a switch that only allows execution of the code block following the if when n equals 0:

```
if(n == 0)
{
    Thread::Sleep(100);
    n = 1;
    Console::WriteLine(S"Thread ID {0} set n = 1",
                    AppDomain::GetCurrentThreadId().ToString());
}
else
{
    Thread::Sleep(100);
    Console::WriteLine(S"Thread ID {0}, n != 0",
                    AppDomain::GetCurrentThreadId().ToString());
}
```

If n is 0, the code assigns it 1, causing any subsequent comparisons of n with 0 to evaluate to false, thereby preventing further execution of the code block following the if conditional. Once again, however, we have a problem if multiple threads are executing this code. In this case, it's possible that more than one thread will execute the code block following the if conditional, as the following output from executing this code with three concurrent threads shows:

```
Thread ID = 1716, set n = 1
Thread ID = 1420, set n = 1
Thread ID = 1740, set n = 1
```

Each thread evaluates (n == 0) as true, because a thread context switch occurs before any thread can assign a value of 1 to n. To fix this, we can use Interlocked::CompareExchange():

```
if(Interlocked::CompareExchange(&n, 1, 0) == 0)
{
    Thread::Sleep(100);
    Console::WriteLine(S"Thread ID 0} set n = 1",
                        AppDomain::GetCurrentThreadId().ToString());
}
else
{
    Thread::Sleep(100);
    Console::WriteLine(S"Thread ID {0}, n != 0",
                        AppDomain::GetCurrentThreadId().ToString());
}
```

Executing the above code with three concurrent threads produces the following output.

```
Thread ID = 1816, set n = 1
Thread ID = 1844, n != 0
Thread ID = 1644, n != 0
```

In this case, all three threads attempt the same CompareExchange() method, but the value of n is not zero for two of them. The function does not perform the assignment and returns the current value of n: 1.

WaitHandle

The System::Threading::WaitHandle class provides methods that allow a thread to wait for a variable length of time on a synchronization object. This class encapsulates objects that wait for exclusive access to shared resources. While the WaitHandle class is declared as abstract, there are currently three classes in the .NET Framework class library that derive from it: Mutex, AutoResetEvent, and ManualResetEvent. In this section, we'll examine these classes in detail.

Mutex

A **mutex** is a synchronization object that allows just one thread to 'own' it at any given time. When a thread attempts to acquire a mutex that's owned (locked) by another thread, the former will block until either a timeout period elapses or the mutex is released. The following code demonstrates using a named WroxMutex instance to synchronize three threads:

```
Mutex* m = new Mutex(false, S"WroxMutex");

for(int i = 0; i < 2; i++)
{
    Console::WriteLine(S"Thread ID {0} waiting to claim the mutex",
                        AppDomain::GetCurrentThreadId().ToString());
```

185

```
    if(m->WaitOne(1000, false))
    {
        Console::WriteLine(S"Thread ID {0} owns the mutex",
                            AppDomain::GetCurrentThreadId().ToString());
        Thread::Sleep(100);
        Console::WriteLine(S"Thread ID {0} releasing the mutex",
                            AppDomain::GetCurrentThreadId().ToString());
        m->ReleaseMutex();
    }
    else
    {
        Console::WriteLine("Thread ID {0} failed to claim the mutex",
                            AppDomain::GetCurrentThreadId().ToString());
    }
}
```

First, we instantiate a `Mutex` instance, passing the constructor a value of `false`, to indicate that the `Mutex` is initially 'unowned' (passing `true` would give ownership to the calling thread), and a string that will be used as the name of this `Mutex` instance.

The `Mutex::WaitOne()` method waits for the given amount of time (in milliseconds), until the current thread receives a signal when the time interval expires. When `ReleaseMutex()` is called for the first thread, the next thread will issue `WaitOne()`, and other threads wait until the second thread calls `ReleaseMutex()`. In our sample, this process occurs twice per thread, in a `for` loop.

Named mutexes are accessible across processes, and therefore they support synchronization of threads in different processes, as well as threads within the same process. In this example, however, all the threads are running in the same process. The following output results from concurrent execution of this code by three threads:

```
Thread ID = 217 waiting to claim the mutex
Thread ID = 217 owns the mutex
Thread ID = 60 waiting to claim the mutex
Thread ID = 177 waiting to claim the mutex
Thread ID = 217 releasing the mutex
Thread ID = 60 owns the mutex
Thread ID = 217 waiting to claim the mutex
Thread ID = 60 releasing the mutex
Thread ID = 60 waiting to claim the mutex
Thread ID = 177 owns the mutex
Thread ID = 177 releasing the mutex
Thread ID = 177 waiting to claim the mutex
Thread ID = 217 owns the mutex
Thread ID = 217 releasing the mutex
Thread ID = 60 owns the mutex
Thread ID = 60 releasing the mutex
Thread ID = 177 owns the mutex
Thread ID = 177 releasing the mutex
```

As the output shows, only one thread owns the mutex at any given time – it looks similar to the spin lock example we implemented in the previous section on the `Interlocked` class. The difference is that in the spin lock case, the thread is in a busy loop, sleeping periodically but for the most part just spinning in the loop. When a thread is waiting for the mutex to be released by another thread, it is in a suspended state, which is a much more efficient use of system resources.

Synchronization events

Events are a form of synchronization object that allow a thread to 'signal' other threads that might be waiting for some condition to occur. There are two synchronization event types defined in the System::Threading namespace:

- ❑ AutoResetEvent
- ❑ ManualResetEvent

Both of these types expose a Set() method that's used to place the synchronization object in a 'signaled' state (allowing one or more threads to unblock), and a Reset() method that's used to place the synchronization object in a 'non-signaled' state (causing any threads that wait on the event to block). Threads wishing to wait for an event to become signaled can use the WaitOne() method that's inherited from WaitHandle – calling this method will block the thread if the event is in the non-signaled state.

The differences between the two types relate to how the waiting threads are unblocked when the event is signaled. The AutoResetEvent allows *a single* thread to be unblocked when the event is placed in the signaled state by a call to the Set() method. After unblocking a single thread, the system automatically places the event back in the non-signaled state. The ManualResetEvent allows *all* blocking threads to be unblocked when the event is placed in the signaled state by a call to the Set() method. The event must be placed in the non-signaled state manually, by a thread calling the Reset() method.

The following example is a simulation of a 50-yard dash, and it uses the ManualResetEvent to start a group of threads running. The threads 'run' a race using a for loop that goes from 1 to 10:

```
__gc class Runner
{
public:
    Runner()
    {
        m_start = new ManualResetEvent(false);
        m_finished = 0;
    }

    void Race()
    {
        // Wait for the starting signal
        m_start->WaitOne();

        // Run the race
        for(int i = 1; i <= 10; i++)
        {
            Console::WriteLine(S"Runner {0} at track position {1}",
                                Thread::CurrentThread->Name, i.ToString());
            Thread::Sleep(AppDomain::GetCurrentThreadId());
        }

        m_position = Interlocked::Increment(&m_finished);
    }

    static ManualResetEvent* m_start;
    int m_position;
```

```
private:
    static int m_finished;
};
```

The Runner class contains a static ManualResetEvent* member, which is used to make sure that all the threads start the race at the same time. It also defines another static member called m_finished, which is incremented by each thread as it finishes. The original value of m_finished is stored in the m_position instance member, in order to store the position in which the thread finished.

The constructor creates a new instance of a ManualResetEvent (initially in the non-signaled state) and sets m_finished to 0.

The Race() method simulates the running of the race, starting with a call to WaitOne() on the m_start event, causing the thread to block until the event is signaled by the main thread (which we'll see shortly). After WaitOne() returns, the thread enters a for loop that will display progress information for the current thread, and then sleep for an amount of time that depends on the thread's ID. When the loop exits, the thread looks to see where it finished the race.

The following code instantiates some runners, assigns new Thread instances to each Runner instance's Race() method, and starts the race:

```
Runner* r1 = new Runner;
Thread* t1 = new Thread(new ThreadStart(r1, Runner::Race));
t1->Name = S"W";

Runner* r2 = new Runner;
Thread* t2 = new Thread(new ThreadStart(r2, Runner::Race));
t2->Name = S"R";

Runner* r3 = new Runner;
Thread* t3 = new Thread(new ThreadStart(r3, Runner::Race));
t3->Name = S"O";

Runner* r4 = new Runner;
Thread* t4 = new Thread(new ThreadStart(r4, Runner::Race));
t4->Name = S"X";

t1->Start();
t2->Start();
t3->Start();
t4->Start();
```

At this point, even though the threads have started, they're all waiting for the start event to be signaled:

```
Console::WriteLine(S"Runners ready!");
Thread::Sleep(1000);

Console::WriteLine(S"Bang!");

// Start the race
Runner::m_start->Set();
```

Upon calling the Set() method of the Runner::m_start event, all waiting threads will be signaled, at which point they unblock and start executing. The output will look something like this:

```
Runners ready!
Bang!
Runner W at track position 1
Runner R at track position 1
Runner O at track position 1
Runner X at track position 1
Runner X at track position 2
Runner O at track position 2
Runner R at track position 2
Runner W at track position 2
```

Now the main thread just waits for all threads to finish and then displays how each 'runner' fared:

```
// Wait for all runners to finish
t1->Join();
t2->Join();
t3->Join();
t4->Join();

// See how they did...
Console::WriteLine(S"Runner {0} finished {1}",
                        t1->Name, r1->m_position.ToString());
    Console::WriteLine(S"Runner {0} finished {1}",
                        t2->Name, r2->m_position.ToString());
    Console::WriteLine(S"Runner {0} finished {1}",
                        t3->Name, r3->m_position.ToString());
    Console::WriteLine(S"Runner {0} finished {1}",
                        t4->Name, r4->m_position.ToString());
```

To save paper, here are just the last few yards of the race:

```
Runner W at track position 10
Runner O at track position 10
Runner X at track position 8
Runner R at track position 9
Runner X at track position 9
Runner R at track position 10
Runner X at track position 10
Runner W finished 1
Runner R finished 3
Runner O finished 2
Runner X finished 4
```

Monitor

Until now, we've just been synchronizing access to some shared variable or resource. Often, though, it's necessary to ensure that a whole region of code is executed in an atomic manner. These regions are often called **critical sections**. Only a single thread is allowed to execute the code in a critical section at any one time, and other threads block until the current thread exits.

.NET provides for critical section synchronization via the `System::Threading::Monitor` class, which provides the static methods `Enter()`, `TryEnter()`, and `Exit()` to support critical section functionality. When using the `Monitor`, we don't create an instance of a `Monitor` proper – rather, we pass a pointer to an object on which we wish to enforce monitor semantics to one of the `Monitor`'s methods.

In this section, we'll develop an application that accesses an `ArrayList` object using multiple threads. In our application, we'll have two threads: one thread to add elements to `ArrayList` and another one to retrieve them. Here's a code snippet that shows how we might use the `Monitor` class to ensure that only one thread executes a region of code at any given time on a given object instance:

```
__gc class gcMonitor
{
private:
    ArrayList*m_ptrList;

    // Number of elements
    int m_iCount;

public:
    // Public constructor
    gcMonitor(int l_iCount)
    {
        m_ptrList = new ArrayList;
        m_iCount = l_iCount;
    }

    // Function to add elements to array
    void Put()
    {
        Monitor::Enter(this);

        // Add elements to your array

        Monitor::Exit(this);
    }

    // Rest of code to follow

};
```

`Put()` uses a `Monitor` to guarantee that only a single thread will ever execute code between the `Enter()` and `Exit()` method calls for a given instance of `Monitor`. When multiple threads issue `Enter()` on the same object, the threads will block until the object is released by an `Exit()` call (by the same thread that already issued `Enter()`).

The `Monitor::TryEnter()` method is similar to `Enter()`, except that it allows a timeout value to be specified (or to not wait at all) if the `Monitor` is currently occupied. This function will return `true` if the blocked object is released before the timeout period or `false` otherwise.

The code extract on the next page shows the implementation of the `Put()` function that adds elements to the `m_ptrList`.

```
void Put()
{
    for(int i = 0; i < m_iCount; i++)
    {
        // Lock the m_ptrList
        Monitor::Enter(m_ptrList);
        String* l_strText = String::Format(S"Index = {0}", i.ToString());

        // Do operations of m_ptrList
        m_ptrList->Add(l_strText);
        Console::WriteLine(S"Inside Put() = '{0}'", l_strText);

        // Simulate a lengthy operation
        Thread::Sleep(500);

        // Release the lock
        Monitor::Exit(m_ptrList);
    }
}
```

This function is fairly self-explanatory. In a loop, we lock m_ptrList using Enter() and then add an element to the list. The wait of 500 ms is just to simulate a lengthy operation. Finally, we release the lock by calling Exit().

Now let's look at the implementation of the corresponding Get() method, which can retrieve elements from m_ptrList in a loop:

```
void Get()
{
    for(int i = 0; i < m_iCount; i++)
    {
        // Lock the m_ptrList
        Monitor::Enter(m_ptrList);

        // Do operations on m_ptrList
        String* l_strText = dynamic_cast<String*>(m_ptrList->Item[i]);
        Console::WriteLine(S"Inside Get = {0}", l_strText);

        // Simulate a lengthy operation
        Thread::Sleep(100);

        // Release the Lock
        Monitor::Exit(m_ptrList);
    }
}
```

This function is similar to Put(), except that we're using the ArrayList::Item property to retrieve the value. Here also we have called Sleep(100) to simulate a lengthy process.

In the main function, we create a single instance of gcMonitor and pass the same reference to two threads, A and B. Thread A will be calling Put() to add values to the gcMonitor::m_ptrList, and thread B will call Get() to extract and print the values:

191

```
int _tmain(void)
{
    // Create one gcMonitor object
    // Pass number of elements as 5
    gcMonitor* l_ptrMonitor = new gcMonitor(5);

    // Create thread A
    Thread* ptrThreadA =
                new Thread(new ThreadStart(l_ptrMonitor, gcMonitor::Put));

    // Create thread B
    Thread* ptrThreadB =
                new Thread(new ThreadStart(l_ptrMonitor, gcMonitor::Get));

    // Start the threads
    ptrThreadA->Start();
    Thread::Sleep(100);          // Start thread B a little later
    ptrThreadB->Start();

    // Join them to main
    ptrThreadA->Join();
    ptrThreadB->Join();

    return 0;
}
```

When we create thread A, the method gcMonitor::Put() is passed. For thread B, gcMonitor::Get() is passed. In between the two calls to start the threads, Sleep(100) is issued to make sure that thread B always starts after thread A.

When thread A is processing, thread B will have already issued a call to Enter() and will be waiting for the m_ptrList to be released. When it is released, thread B immediately locks the m_ptrList and retrieves the first element. Thread B then prints the value and waits, by which time thread A would have issued a call to Enter() (on its second iteration in the for loop) on the list, and will be waiting for thread B to release it. This process carries on five times, since this was passed as an argument to the gcMonitor constructor. The following list shows the output of the program:

```
Inside Put() = 'Index = 0'
Inside Get = Index = 0
Inside Put() = 'Index = 1'
Inside Get = Index = 1
Inside Put() = 'Index = 2'
Inside Get = Index = 2
Inside Put() = 'Index = 3'
Inside Get = Index = 3
Inside Put() = 'Index = 4'
Inside Get = Index = 4
```

Even though thread A takes more time in every iteration than thread B, B never overtakes A because the Enter() and Exit() calls control the actions of the threads. If we were to comment out these calls and execute the program, thread B would try to retrieve elements from the list that have not yet been added, causing an exception to be thrown.

Apart from the methods we've seen in this section, the Monitor class exposes a number of others, including Pulse(), PulseAll(), and Wait(). Pulse() is used to notify a waiting thread when there's a change in the state of the locked object and PulseAll() will notify all waiting threads. Wait(), on the other hand, will release the lock on the current object, block the current thread, and wait until the current thread regains the object. All these functions must be called from within a synchronized block of code or a SynchronizedLockException will be raised.

ReaderWriterLock

The ReaderWriterLock class maintains two locks: one for synchronizing reads and one for synchronizing writes. Multiple threads may hold the *read* lock concurrently, while only one thread may hold the *write* lock at any given time – and only then if no thread currently holds the read lock. The class implements what is commonly called 'single writer, multiple reader' semantics.

This class is very helpful in situations where many threads access a common resource, with some threads performing read-only (non-mutating) operations and other threads performing write-only (mutating) operations. Consider, for example, a shared data structure with many members. If multiple threads were accessing this, we wouldn't want a thread to modify the state of the structure while we were in the middle of reading it elsewhere – that could lead to inconsistent values. We can use ReaderWriterLock to ensure that reading doesn't occur until there are no other threads currently in the middle of modifying the state information. The list below summarizes the behavior of ReaderWriterLock:

- ❑   If any thread is writing, no other thread can read. The read will block until writing is complete.

- ❑   If any thread is writing, no other thread can write. The write will block until the first thread completes writing.

- ❑   If any thread is reading, no other thread can write. The write will block until all readers have completed.

- ❑   While a thread is reading, other threads can also read.

The following example uses a ReaderWriterLock instance to protect an ArrayList during iteration. One thread acts as a reader and simply iterates over the array, adding each value it contains and displaying the sum. A second thread acts as a writer, updating each value in the array to a new random value. Let's look at the reader class first.

```
__gc class MyReader
{
public:
    static ArrayList* m_pList;
    ReaderWriterLock* m_pLock;

    MyReader(ArrayList* pList, ReaderWriterLock* pLock)
    {
        m_pList = pList;
        m_pLock = pLock;
    }
```

```
    void ThreadFunc()
    {
        for(int i = 0; i < 3; i++)
        {
            Work();
        }
    }

    void Work()
    {
        Console::WriteLine(S"ThreadID {0} acquiring Reader lock...",
                    AppDomain::GetCurrentThreadId().ToString());

        // Acquire the read lock and read the string
        m_pLock->AcquireReaderLock(Timeout::Infinite);

        Console::WriteLine(S"ThreadID {0}, Reader lock acquired... reading data",
                    AppDomain::GetCurrentThreadId().ToString());
        Thread::Sleep(1000);

        int sum = 0;
        for(int i = 0; i < m_pList->Count; i++)
        {
            int value = *(dynamic_cast<__box int*>(m_pList->Item[i]));
            sum += value;
        }

        Console::WriteLine(S"ThreadID {0}, sum of data = {1}",
                    AppDomain::GetCurrentThreadId().ToString(), sum.ToString());

        Console::WriteLine(S"ThreadID {0} releasing Reader lock...",
                    AppDomain::GetCurrentThreadId().ToString());

        m_pLock->ReleaseReaderLock();

        Console::WriteLine(S"ThreadID {0}, Reader lock released",
                    AppDomain::GetCurrentThreadId().ToString());
    }
};
```

MyReader has a method called ThreadFunc() that will be used as the target of a ThreadStart delegate. This method calls the Work() method three times in a for loop; the latter waits until it acquires the reader lock by calling the AcquireReaderLock() method, passing an infinite timeout value. When AcquireReaderLock() returns, the thread adds up the values in the list and displays the result. It then releases the reader lock by calling the ReleaseReaderLock() method.

Here's the writer class:

```
__gc class MyWriter
{
public:
    static ArrayList* m_pList;
    ReaderWriterLock* m_pLock;
```

```
MyWriter(ArrayList* pList, ReaderWriterLock* pLock)
{
    m_pList = pList;
    m_pLock = pLock;
}

void ThreadFunc()
{
    for(int i = 0; i < 3; i++)
    {
        Work();
    }
}

void Work()
{
    Console::WriteLine(S"ThreadID {0} acquiring Writer lock...",
                AppDomain::GetCurrentThreadId().ToString());

    // Acquire the writer lock and write some data
    m_pLock->AcquireWriterLock(Timeout::Infinite);

    Console::WriteLine(S"ThreadID {0}, Writer lock acquired, modifying data",
                AppDomain::GetCurrentThreadId().ToString());
    Thread::Sleep(1000);

    for(int i = 0; i < m_pList->Count; i++)
    {
        int value = (new Random(i))->Next(1000);
        int oldval = *(dynamic_cast<__box int*>(m_pList->Item[i]));
        int newval = oldval + value;
        m_pList->Item[i] = __box(newval);
    }

    Console::WriteLine(S"ThreadID {0} releasing Writer lock...",
                AppDomain::GetCurrentThreadId().ToString());

    m_pLock->ReleaseWriterLock();

    Console::WriteLine(S"ThreadID {0}, Writer lock released",
                AppDomain::GetCurrentThreadId().ToString());
}
};
```

Like MyReader, MyWriter defines a ThreadFunc() method that will be used as the target of a ThreadStart delegate. This method calls the Work() method three times in a for loop. The Work() method waits until it acquires the writer lock by calling the AcquireWriterLock() method, passing it an infinite timeout value. Once AcquireWriterLock() returns, the code iterates over the vector, modifying each value. It then releases the writer lock by calling the ReleaseWriterLock() method.

Finally, bringing it all together, we can write code that starts up the reader and writer threads:

```
int _tmain(void)
{
    ArrayList* myList = new ArrayList;
    for(int i = 0; i < 10; i++)
    {
        int value = (new Random(i))->Next(1000);
        myList->Add(__box(value));
    }

    ReaderWriterLock* pLock = new ReaderWriterLock;

    MyReader* r = new MyReader(myList, pLock);
    MyWriter* w = new MyWriter(myList, pLock);

    Thread* t1 = new Thread(new ThreadStart(r, MyReader::ThreadFunc));
    Thread* t2 = new Thread(new ThreadStart(r, MyReader::ThreadFunc));
    Thread* t3 = new Thread(new ThreadStart(w, MyWriter::ThreadFunc));
    Thread* t4 = new Thread(new ThreadStart(w, MyWriter::ThreadFunc));

    t1->Start();
    t2->Start();
    t3->Start();
    t4->Start();

    t1->Join();
    t2->Join();
    t3->Join();
    t4->Join();

    return 0;
}
```

This code creates two reader threads and two writer threads. Executing it produces a great deal of output, of which just a sample is shown below. Notice that the readers are allowed to hold a lock concurrently, but the writers are not:

```
ThreadID = 1756, Acquiring Reader lock...
ThreadID = 1756, Reader lock acquired...reading data
ThreadID = 600, Acquiring Reader lock...
ThreadID = 600, Reader lock acquired...reading data
ThreadID = 1572, Acquiring Writer lock...
ThreadID = 1564, Acquiring Writer lock...
ThreadID = 1756, sum of data = 497
ThreadID = 1756, Releasing Reader lock...
ThreadID = 1756, Reader lock released
ThreadID = 1756, Acquiring Reader lock...
ThreadID = 600, sum of data = 497
ThreadID = 600, Releasing Reader lock...
ThreadID = 1572, Writer lock acquired...modifying data
ThreadID = 600, Reader lock released
ThreadID = 600, Acquiring Reader lock...
ThreadID = 1572, Releasing Writer lock...
```

```
ThreadID = 1572, Writer lock released
ThreadID = 1572, Acquiring Writer lock...
ThreadID = 1756, Reader lock acquired...reading data
ThreadID = 600, Reader lock acquired...reading data
ThreadID = 1756, sum of data = 4994

<< Rest of the output is intentionally removed >>
```

A final thing to note about the `ReaderWriterLock` class is that queued calls are always dealt with in sequence. For example: imagine an application with three threads, in which thread 1 acquires a reader lock and does some processing for quite a long time. Meanwhile, thread 2 issues a request for a write lock and waits for the reader lock. If a third thread comes along and requests a read lock, it is made to wait not only for thread 1 to finish reading, but also for thread 2 to finish writing, before it can start reading.

Thread exceptions

The .NET Framework defines several classes for dealing with the exceptions that can occur when you're using the classes in the `System::Threading` namespace. (Note, however, that exceptions cannot be thrown across thread boundaries.) This section looks at each type of exception in detail and shows some example code that causes specific exceptions to be thrown. The sample code in this section makes use of the following class:

```
__gc class MyThreadContext
{
public:
    static void ThreadFunc()
    {
        Console::WriteLine(S"In ThreadFunc()...");
        try
        {
            DoWork();
        }
        catch(Threading::ThreadAbortException*)
        {
            Console::WriteLine(S"In ThreadFunc(): Thread Aborted!");
        }
        catch(Threading::ThreadInterruptedException*)
        {
            Console::WriteLine(S"In ThreadFunc(): Thread Interrupted!");
        }
        __finally
        {
            Console::WriteLine(S"In ThreadFunc(): __finally clause");
        }
    }

    static void DoWork()
    {
        Console::WriteLine(S"In DoWork()...");
        try
        {
            Thread::Sleep(100000);
        }
```

```
      catch(Threading::ThreadAbortException*)
      {
         Console::WriteLine(S"In DoWork(): Thread Aborted!");
      }
      __finally
      {
         Console::WriteLine(S"In DoWork(): __finally clause");
      }
   }
};
```

There's nothing fancy here. The MyThreadContext managed class defines two methods:

❑   ThreadFunc() will be used as the target of a ThreadStart delegate by the example code later in this section. It sets up a try-catch-__finally block, and catches the various threading exceptions that might be thrown during the call to DoWork().

❑   DoWork() is called by the ThreadFunc() method, and does basically the same thing except that it sleeps for a really long time (100 seconds). This gives our sample code a chance to do something that causes an exception.

SynchronizationLockException

Earlier, we discussed the Monitor class. If we'd tried to call Pulse(), PulseAll(), or Wait() without first entering the Monitor, a SynchronizationLockException would have been thrown.

```
Thread* t = new Thread(new ThreadStart(0, MyThreadContext::ThreadFunc));

try
{
   Console::WriteLine(S"Calling Monitor::Pulse()...");
   Monitor::Pulse(t);

   // Calling PulseAll and Wait will cause the
   // SynchronizationLockException exception to be thrown
   // Monitor::PulseAll(t);
   // Monitor::Wait(t);
}
catch(Threading::SynchronizationLockException*)
{
   Console::WriteLine(S"SynchronizationLockException caught...");
}

try
{
   Console::WriteLine(S"Calling Monitor::Exit()...");
   Monitor::Exit(t);
}
catch(Threading::SynchronizationLockException*)
{
   // Interesting... Exit() does not throw...
   Console::WriteLine(S"SynchronizationLockException caught...");
}
```

Executing this code results in the following output:

```
Calling Monitor::Pulse()...
SynchronizationLockException caught...
Calling Monitor::Exit()...
```

ThreadAbortException

Exceptions of type ThreadAbortException occur when the Thread::Abort() method is called on a thread. It's a special kind of exception in that when caught, it's automatically re-thrown by the system, causing *all* catch handlers for this exception in the call stack to fire. The following code demonstrates this exception:

```
Thread* t = new Thread(new ThreadStart(0, MyThreadContext::ThreadFunc));

Console::WriteLine(S"Starting thread...");
t->Start();

Thread::Sleep(1000);

Console::WriteLine(S"Aborting thread...");
t->Abort();
```

Executing the above code results in the following output:

```
Starting thread...
In ThreadFunc()...
In DoWork()...
Aborting thread...
In DoWork(): Thread Aborted!
In DoWork() : __finally clause
In ThreadFunc() : Thread Aborted!
In ThreadFunc() : __finally clause
```

Notice that the exception is caught in both the DoWork() and the ThreadFunc() methods. In our sample, for illustration purposes, we've handled exceptions in both functions. A more standard practice is to handle exceptions in called functions and return the execution status to the caller.

ThreadInterruptedException

The .NET Framework threading model allows a thread to be interrupted while it is blocked (that is, suspended or waiting). The Thread::Interrupt() method can be used to interrupt a thread.

```
Thread* t = new Thread(new ThreadStart(0, MyThreadContext::ThreadFunc));

Console::WriteLine(S"Starting thread...");
t->Start();

Thread::Sleep(1000);

Console::WriteLine(S"Interrupting thread...");
t->Interrupt();
```

Executing the above code yields the following output:

```
Starting thread...
In ThreadFunc()...
In DoWork()...
Interrupting thread...
In DoWork() : __finally clause
In ThreadFunc() : Thread Interrupted!
In ThreadFunc() : __finally clause
```

ThreadStateException

Finally, some `Thread` class member functions may only be called when a thread is in a specific state. An exception of type `ThreadStateException` is thrown when a method is invoked while the `Thread` instance is in an illegal state for that particular call. The following code demonstrates this by calling the `Resume()` method on a thread that has not yet been started, let alone suspended.

```
Thread* t = new Thread(new ThreadStart(0, MyThreadContext::ThreadFunc));

try
{
    Console::WriteLine(S"Resuming thread...");
    t->Resume();
}
catch(Threading::ThreadStateException*)
{
    Console::WriteLine(S"ThreadStateException caught...");
}
```

Executing this code results in the following output:

```
Resuming thread...
ThreadStateException caught...
```

Summary

The .NET Framework class library makes a huge range of classes available to the developer, whatever language they are working in. If you're developing for the .NET platform, it's a good idea to become familiar with this library, since the types that it defines are tightly integrated with the CLR. The wide variety of classes available makes it impossible for us to cover all of them in one chapter, so here we've chosen to focus on a selection of utility classes that you will encounter time and again in your code. Many of these will be straightforward replacements for the classes from the C++ Standard Library, and many of them offer considerably more functionality.

We started this chapter by examining the `StringBuilder` class, and saw that if you're working with text that needs to be modified frequently, it's a good idea to choose `StringBuilder` over `String`. Next, we moved on to look at the classes in the `System::Text::RegularExpressions` namespace and got a flavor for how these classes can simplify the job of pattern matching and string manipulation.

Next, we focused on the classes and methods available to us for working with files, in particular `File`, `FileStream`, `StreamReader`, and `StreamWriter`. These classes are all part of the `System::File` namespace and provide methods for opening and closing files, reading from and writing to files, and so on.

After that, we moved on to a quick tour of the set of collection classes available in .NET. We looked at an example illustrating the use of `ArrayList` and saw the advantages that this gives us above an ordinary `Array`. We also saw how to provide custom implementations for the `IComparer` and `IEnumerator` interfaces, providing clients with the ability to sort classes and iterate through collections respectively.

Finally, we took a more in-depth look at the classes from the `System::Threading` namespace that give us the facilities for writing thread-safe multithreaded applications. We saw how the `ThreadPool` class with its set of static methods really takes the burden off the developer for creating and managing multiple threads. We looked at issues of thread safety, and we saw how to manage them using monitors, mutexes, events, and locks, and how to handle threading exceptions.

6

Windows Forms

In the last chapter, we saw some of the utility classes that the .NET Framework class library provides. Other parts of the library deal with data access, security, XML, and so on. In this chapter, we're going to take a look at the **Windows Forms** classes, a rich subset of the class library that supports the development of Windows GUI applications.

It's worth stating from the outset that managed C++ code is not a natural fit with the creation of Windows applications. While there are tools in Visual Studio .NET that allow Visual Basic and C# programmers to assemble their applications graphically (in much the same way as you'd create a GUI application with MFC), there is no such support for Visual C++ .NET. Still, managed C++ is a perfectly good .NET citizen, and there's nothing to stop us from doing the footwork ourselves. It also provides the opportunity to get a feel for the general principles behind programming with the .NET Framework and working with managed C++.

This chapter will provide an overview of Windows Forms and a brief comparison with MFC (Microsoft Foundation Classes). Later on, we'll examine how to create a form in managed C++, setting various properties, and adding events. We will also look at how to use some of the .NET controls in a managed C++ Windows Forms application. Next, we will look at displaying modal and modeless dialog boxes, and at the development of MDI applications in managed C++. Finally, we'll see how drag-and-drop is handled.

Windows Forms and MFC

As you're aware, the execution of an MFC-based application starts with the `InitInstance()` method of a `CWinApp`-derived class, where we create a window or thread, process Windows messages, and continue with execution. In managed C++, on the other hand (in fact, for all .NET languages), `main()` is *always* the first function to be called, and from there we use the `System::Windows::Forms::Application` class's static `Run()` method to create a window and process its messages. The Windows message loop runs in the thread from which the `Run()` method was called.

In MFC, `CWnd` is the base class for all windows and child controls; in Windows Forms, it's `System::Windows::Forms::Form`. Another important difference is that in MFC, dialogs are stored in resource files, where their layout and content are described using a separate language; in Windows Forms, dialogs and their child controls are embedded in your source file as C++ statements, which makes it easier to modify them programmatically.

As well as these architectural changes, Windows Forms introduce many new controls that you would have had to implement yourself in MFC. The `LinkLabel` control, for example, is capable of displaying a hyperlink. Other new controls in Windows Forms include `CheckedListBox`, `Splitter`, `ImageList`, `HelpProvider`, `ToolTip`, `ContextMenu`, `ToolBar`, `StatusBar`, `NotifyIcon`, and all the common open dialog boxes. None of these is available in MFC as a control that you can simply drag-and-drop into an application using the resource editor design time controls. You need to instantiate them dynamically, or to subclass the appropriate base class, to achieve similar functionality.

In MFC, we can develop SDI, MDI, or dialog based applications, and the classes we use for MDI or SDI and dialog based applications are different. On the other hand, in .NET all these classifications are removed and there is only one `Form` class. Various properties of the `Form` class will make it behave as an MDI parent or MDI child or SDI form or dialog box, and so on. We'll see how to do this later on in the chapter.

A Windows application in managed C++

So far, we've discussed the very basics of Windows Forms and looked at a brief comparison with MFC. In this section, we'll develop a form in managed C++. As mentioned above, Visual Studio .NET's form designer is only available for C# and Visual Basic projects, so in our example we will design, create, and add events to the form through code alone.

Open Visual Studio .NET and create a new **Managed C++ Application** called `FirstApp`. Add the following code to the `FirstApp.cpp` file, which creates a form with the caption **My First Managed C++ Windows Form**:

```
#include "stdafx.h"
#using <mscorlib.dll>
#using <System.dll>
#using <System.Windows.Forms.dll>
#include <tchar.h>

using namespace System;
using namespace System::Windows::Forms;
```

```
__gc class FirstApp : public Form
{
public :
   FirstApp()
   {
      Text = S"My First Managed C++ Windows Form";
   }
};

int _tmain(void)
{
   Application::Run(new FirstApp);
   return 0;
}
```

We've imported two assemblies that this application needs in order to function correctly: System.dll and System.Windows.Forms.dll. Next, we add a using statement for the System::Windows::Forms namespace to simplify the remainder of the code. (For every .NET class, the MSDN documentation lists the assembly to be imported and the namespace to be used.) Our main() function calls the static method, Application::Run(), passing in a pointer to a new instance of our FirstApp form class as a parameter. This creates a new Windows message loop in the current thread. The FirstApp class itself is very simple; it just assigns a string to the Text property of the Form class in the constructor. This will add a caption to our form. You can see that this works by compiling and running the application:

Note that running this application from the IDE brings up the console window first, before the form is launched.

The form contains a default icon (at the top left), along with maximize, minimize, and resize buttons. Furthermore, it is always given the same initial size. The height and width are set to 300 pixels by default, but it is resizable. You might also have noticed that when you run this application, Windows positions it so that it avoids any previous windows on the desktop. In the next section, we'll throw some light on how to change this default behavior.

Customizing forms and adding events

In this section, we'll focus on how to change the properties of a form and on handling form events. To begin, create a new managed C++ application called CustomizedForm. We'll change some the form's properties in the constructor, and add a couple of event handlers to the form for mouse events:

```
__gc class CustomizedForm : public Form
{
public:
    CustomizedForm()
    {
        Text = S"Customized Form";

        // Set WindowState property
        WindowState = FormWindowState::Maximized;

        // Add a handler for the MouseDown event
        MouseDown += new MouseEventHandler(this, OnMouseDown);

        // Add a handler for the MouseMove event
        MouseMove += new MouseEventHandler(this, OnMouseMove);
    }

private:
    void OnMouseDown(Object* ptrSender, MouseEventArgs* ptrMouse)
    {
        static_cast<Form*>(ptrSender)->Text = String::Concat(
                S"Customized Form, Mouse down at X = ", ptrMouse->X.ToString(),
                                            S", Y = ", ptrMouse->Y.ToString());
    }

    void OnMouseMove(Object* ptrSender, MouseEventArgs* ptrMouse)
    {
        static_cast<Form*>(ptrSender)->Text = String::Concat(
                S"Customized Form, Mouse move at X = ", ptrMouse->X.ToString(),
                                            S", Y = ", ptrMouse->Y.ToString());
    }
};
```

We can maximize the size of the window using the WindowState property. The other possible values for this are Minimized or Normal (the default). The interesting part of this application is the event-handling code, which you should find familiar from Chapter 2. In MFC, dealing with things like mouse movement involves calling up the Class Wizard to add a macro to a message map that associates the event with a method of your window class. In .NET, on the other hand, we use delegates:

```
        // Add a handler for the MouseDown event
        MouseDown += new MouseEventHandler(this, OnMouseDown);

        // Add a handler for the MouseMove event
        MouseMove += new MouseEventHandler(this, OnMouseMove);
```

To handle the MouseDown and MouseMove events, we just need to create two instances of the MouseEventHandler delegate, and then 'add' them to the list of delegates that each event holds. The MouseEventHandler constructor takes two parameters: a pointer to the object that contains the method you'll use to handle the event, and the name of that function. As a result of these two lines, when the form's MouseDown event is fired, the OnMouseDown() handler is called, and when the MouseMove event is fired, the OnMouseMove() handler is called.

The MouseDown and MouseMove events are defined in System::Windows::Forms::Control (from which Form is derived), in terms of a delegate called MouseEventHandler:

```
__event MouseEventHandler* MouseDown;
__event MouseEventHandler* MouseMove;
```

There are lots of other events defined in a Form class that you will find useful. Some broad categories of events are summarized below, but for a complete list, you should consult the documentation:

- ❑ Form appearance events, such as Activated, Closed, FontChanged, Resize, and Invalidated
- ❑ Keyboard events, such as KeyDown, KeyPress, KeyUp, and TextChanged
- ❑ Mouse events, such as MouseOver, MouseDown, MouseUp, and MouseEnter
- ❑ Drag-and-drop events, such as DragOver, DragEnter, DragLeave, and DragDrop

Having set up the event-handling mechanism, the next step is to write the event-handling methods themselves. The implementation is very straightforward; they simply update the form's caption with a string that contains the *X* and *Y* coordinates of the pointer, relative to the top-left corner of the form. (These numbers are stored in the X and Y properties of the MouseEventArgs object.) On this occasion, the casting of the Object* to a Form* is not essential, since all these methods and properties are members of the same object, but there's no harm in saying exactly what we mean!

Adding child controls

Since we've covered the basics, we'll now concentrate on adding **controls** to Windows Forms to perform actions such as accepting input and displaying results. In Windows Forms, controls can be broadly classified into the following types:

- ❑ Controls that display text, such as TextBox, Label, and RichTextBox
- ❑ Controls that display and/or manipulate pictures, such as PictureBox
- ❑ Controls that perform actions, such as Button
- ❑ Controls that display options, such as CheckBox, RadioButton, ListBox, ComboBox, MainMenu, and ContextMenu
- ❑ Advanced controls, such as TreeView, ListView, and TabControl
- ❑ ActiveX controls

All of these controls live in the System::Windows::Forms namespace and are derived from the Control class. The inheritance hierarchy is illustrated in the diagram overleaf:

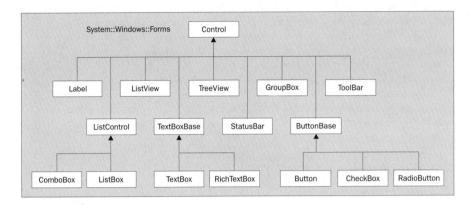

Note that this figure does not illustrate the complete hierarchy, but includes the controls discussed in this chapter.

In this section, we'll look first at how to add a Button to our form, and then at how to handle the events that it can fire. Later, we'll explore some of the other controls, including ImageList, TreeView, ListView, and StatusBar.

Working with button controls

In this example, we'll add a button that closes the form. At the same time, we'll add some code to ensure that our button remains at the center of the form, regardless of any resizing that may take place. We can keep track of the size of the form using the Resize event. In a handler for this event, we'll determine the center point of the form and move our button to that position.

Because our code is beginning to get a little more complex, we'll separate out some of the initialization code called from the constructor. We'll also include a member variable for our button control, which will be initialized in the CreateChildControls() method:

```
__gc class ButtonSample : public Form
{
public:
    ButtonSample()
    {
        InitForm();
        AddFormEvents();
        CreateChildControls();
    }

private:
    // rest of code

    Button* m_ptrbnButton;
};
```

The InitForm() method simply sets the caption and the start position of the form, while the AddFormEvents() method does exactly what its name suggests – it adds the event handler for the Resize event:

```
void InitForm()
{
    Text = S"Managed C++ - Button Sample";
    StartPosition = FormStartPosition::CenterScreen;
}

void AddFormEvents()
{
    // Add a handler for the Resize event
    Resize += new EventHandler(this, OnFormResize);
}
```

After creating our form, we need to create the child button control:

```
void CreateChildControls()
{
    int l_iButtonWidth = 100;
    int l_iButtonHeight = 25;

    // Determine center point of the window
    int l_iNewX = ClientSize.Width / 2 - l_iButtonWidth / 2;
    int l_iNewY = ClientSize.Height / 2 - l_iButtonHeight / 2;
    Point l_ptStart(l_iNewX,l_iNewY);

    // Create Button and set properties here
    m_ptrbnButton = new Button;
    m_ptrbnButton->Name = S"m_bnButton1";
    m_ptrbnButton->Width = l_iButtonWidth;
    m_ptrbnButton->Height = l_iButtonHeight;
    m_ptrbnButton->Text = S"&Click here";
    m_ptrbnButton->Location = l_ptStart;

    // Add handler for the button's click event
    m_ptrbnButton->Click += new EventHandler(this, OnButtonClick);

    // Add the button to the form
    Controls->Add(m_ptrbnButton);
}
```

In order to place the button in the center of the form, we need to know the size of the client area of our form (recall that this excludes the area occupied by the title bar, menu, toolbar, status bar, and so on). The client area is represented by the Form object's ClientSize property (a Size object), which itself has properties of Width and Height. We use these to calculate the coordinates of the center point of the form, which we then pass to a Point object. Note that by default the dimensions are specified in pixels.

The Size and Point classes are available in the System.Drawing.dll assembly, so at the beginning of our program, we need to add a directives to import the assembly and use the System::Drawing namespace.

Next, we create a new Button instance and set a few of its properties, using the point object that we've just created for the Location. We add a handler for the button's Click event, and finally, we add our new child control to the form by calling the Add() method of the form's built-in Controls collection. Add() takes the pointer of the control to be added as its single argument.

Let's now look at the two event handlers, beginning with OnFormResize(), in which we need to recalculate the center of the form and then relocate the control:

```
void OnFormResize(Object* l_ptrSender, EventArgs* l_ptrEventArgs)
{
    // Calculate center point
    int l_iNewX = ClientSize.Width / 2 - m_ptrbnButton->Width / 2;
    int l_iNewY = ClientSize.Height / 2 - m_ptrbnButton->Height / 2;
    Point l_ptNew(l_iNewX, l_iNewY);

    // Move the button to center of window
    m_ptrbnButton->Location = l_ptNew;
    m_ptrbnButton->Refresh();
}
```

Once we have the new coordinates for the center of the form, we simply assign a new Point object to the Location property of the button; compare that with having to call CWnd::MoveWindow() in an MFC-based application! Finally, Refresh() is called on the Button object, forcing the control to repaint itself.

The final step of our application is to handle the button's Click event:

```
void OnButtonClick(Object* l_ptrSender, EventArgs* l_ptrEventArgs)
{
    if(MessageBox::Show(S"Close this application ?", S"Button Sample",
        MessageBoxButtons::YesNo, MessageBoxIcon::Stop) == DialogResult::Yes)
    {
        Application::Exit();
    }
}
```

To prompt the user, we call System::Windows::Forms::MessageBox::Show(), a static method. Note that although we created the button at the beginning of the program, we haven't bothered to destroy it; the garbage collector does the work for us. The application looks like this:

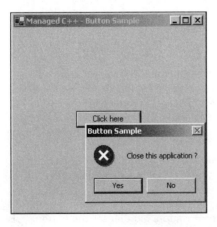

Working with text controls

In this section, we're going to look at `Label`, `LinkLabel`, and `TextBox` controls, which display static text, add a hyperlink, and enable a user to enter text respectively. The `LinkLabel` control is not available in earlier versions of MFC; to obtain the same functionality, one would have to subclass `CStatic`. However, with Windows XP and later versions of Windows, Microsoft has introduced a new class called `CLinkCtrl` in MFC.

To discover more about these controls, we'll develop a new Windows Forms application, `TextSample`, whose single form contains two `Label` controls, one `TextBox`, and one `LinkLabel`. The `TextBox` will accept a URL, and the `LinkLabel` will be updated dynamically with the URL:

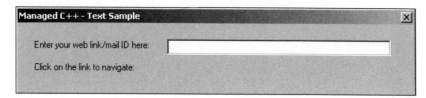

We'll start by creating a form and adding members for the various controls:

```
__gc class TextSample : public Form
{
private:
    Label* m_ptrLabel1;
    Label* m_ptrLabel2;
    TextBox* m_ptrTBWebLink;
    LinkLabel* m_ptrLLWebLink;

public:
    // Add public methods

};
```

When we initialize the form, we'll display it as a dialog box without maximize and minimize buttons. To do this, we'll set the `FormBorderStyle` property to the `FixedDialog` enumerated value, and the `MaximizeBox` and `MinimizeBox` properties to `false`:

```
void InitForm()
{
    Text = S"Managed C++ - Text Sample";
    FormBorderStyle = FormBorderStyle::FixedDialog;
    WindowState = FormWindowState::Normal;
    StartPosition = FormStartPosition::CenterScreen;
    MaximizeBox = false;
    MinimizeBox = false;
}
```

The following code fragment creates the controls and sets their properties:

```
void CreateChildControls()
{
    // Create Label1 control
    m_ptrLabel1 = new Label;
    Point l_pt(20, 20);
    m_ptrLabel1->Location = l_pt;
    m_ptrLabel1->Name = S"Label1";

    System::Drawing::Size l_sizeLabel1(175, 15);
    m_ptrLabel1->Size = l_sizeLabel1;
    m_ptrLabel1->Text = S"Enter your web link/mail ID here: ";
    m_ptrLabel1->TextAlign = System::Drawing::ContentAlignment::MiddleLeft;

    // Create Label2 control
    m_ptrLabel2 = new Label;
    l_pt.X = 20;
    l_pt.Y = 50;
    m_ptrLabel2->Location = l_pt;
    m_ptrLabel2->Name = S"Label2";

    System::Drawing::Size l_sizeLabel2(175, 15);
    m_ptrLabel2->Size = l_sizeLabel2;
    m_ptrLabel2->Text = S"Click on the link to navigate: ";
    m_ptrLabel1->TextAlign = System::Drawing::ContentAlignment::MiddleLeft;

    // Create TextBox control
    m_ptrTBWebLink = new TextBox;
    l_pt.X = 200;
    l_pt.Y = 20;
    m_ptrTBWebLink->Location = l_pt;
    m_ptrTBWebLink->Name = S"m_TBWebLink";

    System::Drawing::Size l_sizeTB(300, 20);
    m_ptrTBWebLink->Size = l_sizeTB;

    // Create LinkLabel control
    m_ptrLLWebLink = new LinkLabel;
    l_pt.X = 200;
    l_pt.Y = 50;
    m_ptrLLWebLink->Location = l_pt;
    m_ptrLLWebLink->Name = S"m_LLWebLink";

    System::Drawing::Size l_sizeLL(300, 15);
    m_ptrLLWebLink->Size = l_sizeLL;

    // rest of code to follow
}
```

We use the Size property with all of the controls to specify their size (height and width) in pixels, and we initialize this property using a Size object. When we create a Size object, we need to qualify it with the System::Drawing namespace, in order to resolve the ambiguity with the Size property of the Form object itself.

As with the button from the previous example, we add all these controls to the form using the `Add()` method of the form's `Controls` property.

Now we'll add events for the `TextBox` and `LinkLabel` controls. When the user enters the URL in the text box, we can simultaneously update the `LinkLabel` control, using the `TextBox`'s `TextChanged` event:

```
m_ptrTBWebLink->TextChanged += new EventHandler(this, OnTextChanged);
```

This adds the event handler `OnTextChanged()` to the `TextChanged` event. The implementation of the handler is very simple. When the event is fired, the `Text` property of the `TextBox` is simply assigned to the `Text` property of the `LinkLabel`:

```
void OnTextChanged(Object* l_ptrSender, EventArgs* l_ptrArgs)
{
    m_ptrLLWebLink->Text = m_ptrTBWebLink->Text;
}
```

When the user clicks the `LinkLabel`, the `LinkClicked` event is fired; this is how we handle it:

```
m_ptrLLWebLink->LinkClicked += new LinkLabelLinkClickedEventHandler(this,
                                                        OnLinkClicked);
```

This event requires a new delegate type, `LinkLabelLinkClickedEventHandler`. In the implementation of the handler function, we call `System::Diagnostics::Process::Start()` in order to navigate to a web link:

```
void OnLinkClicked(Object* l_ptrSender,
                   LinkLabelLinkClickedEventArgs* l_ptrArgs)
{
    String* l_ptrURL = m_ptrLLWebLink->Text;
    l_ptrURL->Trim();

    if(l_ptrURL->Length == 0)
    {
      MessageBox::Show(S"URL cannot be empty !", S"Managed C++ - Text Sample",
                       MessageBoxButtons::OK, MessageBoxIcon::Information);
      return;
    }

    // Open the URL
    System::Diagnostics::Process::Start(m_ptrLLWebLink->Text);
}
```

In the above sample, the default mail client can be opened when you use the `mailto` protocol. For example, typing `mailto:KNiranja@chn.cognizant.com` will open your mail client with the address KNiranja@chn.cognizant.com in the "To" list.

In the above example, we've seen the use of the `LinkLabel` control serving one hyperlink, but it is also possible to add multiple links to a single control. In the example, we embed one string in a single `LinkLabel` control and use two hyperlinks within it.

```
m_ptrLLWebLink->Text =
    S"For more information, visit us at www.cognizant.com or contact N. Kumar";

// Add links
m_ptrLLWebLink->Links->Add(34,17,S"www.cognizant.com");
m_ptrLLWebLink->Links->Add(63,14,S"mailto:KNiranja@chn.cognizant.com");
```

The `Add()` statements add the HTTP link `www.cognizant.com` and the `mailto:` link to the appropriate parts of the text. When the user clicks on either of the links, the `LinkClicked` event handler argument `LinkLabelLinkClickedEventArgs` should be used, which contains the link where the click event has occurred. Remember that earlier in our sample we simply used the `Text` property of the `LinkLabel` control, since it was a single URL. Here, however, we have multiple URLs in a single control, so we need to get the link using the `LinkData` property of the `LinkLabelLinkClickedEventArgs` argument. The code to get the clicked link and navigate to the URL is left for reader's exploration.

Selection controls

In this section, we'll develop an application, `SelectionControls`, which allows a user to input some personal information, and as each piece of data is entered, displays a formatted result. A `TextBox` control will be used to accept the name, a `RadioButton` will receive the gender of the user, a `ComboBox` will display a list of professions, and a `CheckedListBox` control will be used to accept hobbies. Tips about each control will be shown using a `ToolTip`. Here's the form:

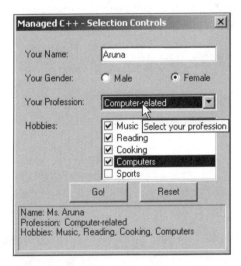

In the above screenshot, the label control at the bottom displays the data that's been entered by the user when the Go! button is pressed. Since we've already looked at the creation of forms and some controls, we'll just focus on code that's new.

As before, we have a `CreateChildControls()` method where we create and initialize all the controls. We start by creating the text box, and add a handler for its `LostFocus` event:

```
m_ptrTBName->LostFocus += new EventHandler(this, OnLostFocus);
```

To accept the user's gender, we display two `RadioButton` controls. When the option represented by the `RadioButtons` is changed, the `CheckedChanged` event will be fired. The following code also specifies a handler for this event, `OnCheckChangedRBMale()`:

```
m_ptrRBMale = new RadioButton;
l_pt.X = 110;
l_pt.Y = 50;
m_ptrRBMale->Location = l_pt;
m_ptrRBMale->Name = S"m_rbMale";

System::Drawing::Size l_sizeRBMale(50, 20);
m_ptrRBMale->Size = l_sizeRBMale;
m_ptrRBMale->Text = S"Male";
m_ptrRBMale->CheckedChanged +=
                    new EventHandler(this, OnCheckChangedRBMale);
m_ptrRBMale->TabIndex = 2;
```

We have similar code for the female radio button, except that we don't need to add an event handler to it. Since we only have two radio buttons, we only need to implement one handler; if the female radio button is clicked, then the male one automatically becomes unchecked, and so the `OnCheckChangedRBMale` event is fired.

The default behavior of `ComboBox` is to accept input in its text area so that new items can be added to the list it contains. To prevent this, we need to configure the combo box as a drop-down list by setting the `DropDownStyle` property to `DropDownList` (the other possible values being `Simple` and `DropDown`). When the option in the combo box is changed, the `SelectedIndexChanged` event will be fired; we're going to handle it with a function called `OnSelectedIndexChanged()`:

```
m_ptrCBProfession = new ComboBox;
l_pt.X = 110;
l_pt.Y = 80;
m_ptrCBProfession->Location = l_pt;

System::Drawing::Size l_sizeCBProfession(150, 20);
m_ptrCBProfession->Size = l_sizeCBProfession;
m_ptrCBProfession->DropDownWidth = 100;
m_ptrCBProfession->DropDownStyle = ComboBoxStyle::DropDownList;
m_ptrCBProfession->TabIndex = 4;
m_ptrCBProfession->SelectedIndexChanged +=
                    new EventHandler(this, OnSelectedIndexChanged);
```

Now we'll look at how to create the `CheckedListBox` control, for which we're not going to handle any events. The following code fragment shows how to create and place the control in the form:

```
m_ptrCLBHobbies = new CheckedListBox;
l_pt.X = 110;
l_pt.Y = 110;
m_ptrCLBHobbies->Location = l_pt;

System::Drawing::Size l_sizeCLBHobbies(150, 80);
m_ptrCLBHobbies->Size = l_sizeCLBHobbies;
m_ptrCLBHobbies->TabIndex = 5;
```

The next step is to create the two buttons with captions Go! and Reset, and a Label control that displays our output. We've already seen examples similar to this, so the full code is not listed here.

Finally a ToolTip control is created to display tool tip messages. After creating this control, we set messages for all the child controls by using the SetToolTip() method of the ToolTip class. The following code fragment illustrates this process in action:

```
m_ptrTTip = new ToolTip;
m_ptrTTip->SetToolTip(m_ptrTBName, S"Enter your name");
m_ptrTTip->SetToolTip(m_ptrCBProfession, S"Select your profession");
m_ptrTTip->SetToolTip(m_ptrCLBHobbies, S"Select your hobbies");
m_ptrTTip->SetToolTip(m_ptrbnGO, S"Click here to display the output");
m_ptrTTip->SetToolTip(m_ptrbnReset, S"Clear all input");
m_ptrTTip->SetToolTip(m_ptrLabelOutput, S"Displays the output");
```

After creating all the child controls and associating tool tip text with them, we call Controls->Add() on each in turn to add them to our form.

With that complete, the next step is to add some default options to the ComboBox and CheckedListBox controls that will appear when they are first displayed. Take a look at the SetDefaultValues() method, which adds default options to these controls:

```
void SetDefaultValues()
{
    // Add Items to ComboBox
    m_ptrCBProfession->Items->Add(S"None");
    m_ptrCBProfession->Items->Add(S"Student");
    m_ptrCBProfession->Items->Add(S"Computer related");
    m_ptrCBProfession->Items->Add(S"Government");
    m_ptrCBProfession->Items->Add(S"Private");
    m_ptrCBProfession->Items->Add(S"Self employed");
    m_ptrCBProfession->Items->Add(S"Retired");
    // Make "None" as default Profession option
    m_ptrCBProfession->SelectedIndex = 0;

    // Add Items to Hobbies
    m_ptrCLBHobbies->Items->Add(S"Music", false);
    m_ptrCLBHobbies->Items->Add(S"Reading books", false);
    m_ptrCLBHobbies->Items->Add(S"Cooking", false);
    m_ptrCLBHobbies->Items->Add(S"Computers", false);
    m_ptrCLBHobbies->Items->Add(S"Sports", false);
}
```

m_ptrCBProfession->Items returns a pointer to an object of type ObjectCollection. The Add() method of this type adds the string it is passed to the ComboBox object. Similarly, the first parameter to the m_ptrCLBHobbies->Items->Add() method adds a string to the CheckedListBox control, and the second (Boolean) parameter governs whether the option will be checked or (as here) unchecked.

Our last step is to implement the event handlers for all of our events. To help, we'll write a general function that looks at the current state of all inputs, generates the output string, and displays it in the output Label control:

```
    void DisplayOutput()
    {
        String* l_strName;
        String* l_strGender;

        // Get user name
        l_strName = m_ptrTBName->Text;

        // Get gender
        if(m_bMaleFlag)
            l_strGender = S"Name: Mr. ";
        else
            l_strGender = S"Name: Ms. ";

        // Determine the checked hobbies
        String* l_strTemp = S"";
        CheckedListBox::CheckedItemCollection* l_ptrHobbiesCollection =
                                            m_ptrCLBHobbies->CheckedItems;
        int nSelectedCount = l_ptrHobbiesCollection->Count();
        for(int nCount = 0; nCount < nSelectedCount; nCount++)
        {
            String* l_strItem = l_ptrHobbiesCollection->Item[nCount]->ToString();
            if(l_strTemp->Length == 0)
                l_strTemp = String::Concat(S"Hobbies: ", l_strItem);
            else
                l_strTemp = String::Concat(l_strTemp, S", ", l_strItem);
        }

        m_strHobbies = l_strTemp;

        // Form the output string
        String* l_strOutput;
        l_strOutput = String::Concat(l_strGender, l_strName);
        l_strOutput = String::Concat(l_strOutput, S"\n");
        l_strOutput = String::Concat(l_strOutput, m_strProfession);
        l_strOutput = String::Concat(l_strOutput, S"\n");
        l_strOutput = String::Concat(l_strOutput, m_strHobbies);

        m_ptrLabelOutput->Text = l_strOutput;

    }
```

The most interesting part of this method comes when we determine the list of hobbies checked by the user. The CheckedItems property of the CheckedListBox returns a pointer to a CheckedItemCollection, which represents the list of items that are checked in the control. Having discovered the size of this collection through its Count property, we use a for loop to iterate through every checked item and get its text using the ToString() method. The list of hobbies is then finally stored in the form's m_strHobbies member variable, which is the last thing to be added to the Label control before it's output.

We'll now take a quick look at the event handling methods. These mainly consist of ascertaining the values in the different selection controls and calling DisplayOut() to update the label.

We haven't set the m_bMaleFlag variable anywhere else, so we do it in the OnCheckChangedRBMale handler. The Checked property of the RadioButton control will return true if the RadioButton is checked and false if not:

```
void OnCheckChangedRBMale(Object* l_ptrSender, EventArgs* l_ptrArgs)
{
    m_bMaleFlag = m_ptrRBMale->Checked;
    DisplayOutput();
    m_ptrCBProfession->Focus();
}
```

The profession is stored using the m_strProfession variable, the value of which is set in the OnSelectedIndexChanged() event handler:

```
void OnSelectedIndexChanged(Object* l_ptrSender, EventArgs* l_args)
{
    m_strProfession =
            String::Concat(S"Profession: ", m_ptrCBProfession->SelectedItem);
    DisplayOutput();
}
```

After entering a name in the text control and tabbing out of that control, the output is refreshed with the new name, and the focus is set. This is achieved by implementing OnLostFocus() to call DisplayOutput() and set the focus to the **Male** radio button:

```
void OnLostFocus(Object* l_ptrSender, EventArgs* l_ptrArgs)
{
    DisplayOutput();
    m_ptrRBMale->Focus();
}
```

The handler for the Click event of the **Go!** button is similar to the one above:

```
void OnClickGOButton(Object* l_ptrSender, EventArgs* l_ptrArgs)
{
    DisplayOutput();
}
```

The last event left to deal with is the Click event of the **Reset** button. The implementation for this handler needs to clear the TextBox and the output Label control, and uncheck all checked hobbies. One thing to be aware of is that in the CheckedListBox control, "selecting" an item just means highlighting it, while "checking" an item actually places a mark in the check box. We need to clear both things in this handler, before setting the focus to the **Name** text box with the TextBox::Focus() function:

```
void OnClickResetButton(Object* l_ptrSender, EventArgs* l_ptrArgs)
{
    // Clear Name TextBox
    m_ptrTBName->Text = S"";
```

```
    // Make "None" the default Profession option
    m_ptrCBProfession->SelectedIndex = 0;

    // Uncheck all checked items
    m_ptrCLBHobbies->ClearSelected();
    int nTotalCount = m_ptrCLBHobbies->Items->Count;
    for(int nCount = 0; nCount < nTotalCount; nCount++)
    {
        if(m_ptrCLBHobbies->GetItemChecked(nCount))
        {
            m_ptrCLBHobbies->SetItemChecked(nCount, false);
        }
    }

    // Clear Output Label control
    m_ptrLabelOutput->Text = S"";

    // Set the Focus to Name control
    m_ptrTBName->Focus();
}
```

More child controls

Often in Windows programming, when a background process is running for quite a long time, we will see a progress bar being displayed that shows the status. Another common scenario is when the user has to select a value and is offered a range that they can scroll through (like adjusting the volume in a volume control). In this section, we'll deal with some more .NET controls, including NumericUpDown, TrackBar, ProgressBar, and Timer. The first of these addresses the situation where we need the user to enter one of a fixed range of values; it acts like a combination of MFC's CSpinButtonCtrl and CEdit classes. TrackBar and ProgressBar, meanwhile, are direct relations of CSliderCtrl and CProgressCtrl respectively.

The NumericUpDown control uses Minimum and Maximum properties to represent a range of values, and Value to represent the current value (which is always between Minimum and Maximum). When the arrow buttons are clicked, the Value is incremented or decremented depending upon the Increment property. When Value is set to be less than Minimum or greater than Maximum, an exception of type ArgumentException will be raised.

Although quite different in appearance from NumericUpDown, TrackBar and ProgressBar possess similar properties, and their functionality is also similar – it's still a matter of coping with a value in a given range. As such, they also have Minimum, Maximum, and Value properties; the latter affects the needle position of TrackBar and the state of ProgressBar.

Generally, timers are used to assist in the performance of any regular background processes that the system may require – for example, periodic refreshing of the folders and files in Windows Explorer. In our example, we'll create a Timer object, set its Interval property, and call its Start() and Stop() methods. Notice how this differs from MFC, which implements timers using the SetTimer() and KillTimer() methods of the CWnd class.

Take a look at the form below, which contains all the controls we just discussed. (The code for this form can be found in the MoreControls project.) The maximum values for the TrackBar and ProgressBar controls are set to 50 (as specified by the first NumericUpDown control), while the second NumericUpDown control sets the Interval value for the timer object, which is 100 (milliseconds) in our case. The Start button will start the timer, which increments the Value properties of the TrackBar and ProgressBar controls till they reach their Maximum values. The Reset button will reset both TrackBar and ProgressBar to their initial state. Note that both buttons are disabled while the timer is running:

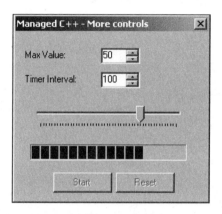

The following code fragment shows how to create the first NumericUpDown control and set its properties. The Minimum, Maximum, Value, and Increment properties are set to 1, 100, 100, and 1 respectively. When the control is first shown, its value will be 100:

```
// Create NumericUpDown control for the range
m_ptrNUDMaxValue = new NumericUpDown;
l_pt.X = 110;
l_pt.Y = 20;
m_ptrNUDMaxValue->Location = l_pt;
m_ptrNUDMaxValue->Name = S"m_NumericUpDown1";

System::Drawing::Size l_sizeNUD1(50, 20);
m_ptrNUDMaxValue->Size = l_sizeNUD1;
m_ptrNUDMaxValue->TabIndex = 1;
m_ptrNUDMaxValue->Minimum = 1;
m_ptrNUDMaxValue->Maximum = 100;
m_ptrNUDMaxValue->Value = 100;
m_ptrNUDMaxValue->Increment = 1;
```

The second NumericUpDown control will control the timer. This time, Minimum and Value are set to 100, Maximum to 1000, and Increment to 100:

```
m_ptrNUDTimer = new NumericUpDown;
l_pt.X = 110;
l_pt.Y = 50;
m_ptrNUDTimer->Location = l_pt;
m_ptrNUDTimer->Name = S"m_NumericUpDown2";
```

```
System::Drawing::Size l_sizeNUD2(50, 20);
m_ptrNUDTimer->Size = l_sizeNUD2;
m_ptrNUDTimer->TabIndex = 2;
m_ptrNUDTimer->Minimum = 100;
m_ptrNUDTimer->Maximum = 1000;
m_ptrNUDTimer->Value = 100;
m_ptrNUDTimer->Increment = 100;
```

The creation of the TrackBar and ProgressBar is very similar to NumericUpDown, except for the setting we give to the Value property:

```
// Create TrackBar control
m_ptrTrackBar = new TrackBar;
l_pt.X = 20;
l_pt.Y = 90;
m_ptrTrackBar->Location = l_pt;

System::Drawing::Size l_sizeTrackBar(200, 20);
m_ptrTrackBar->Size = l_sizeTrackBar;
m_ptrTrackBar->TabIndex = 0;
m_ptrTrackBar->Minimum = 1;
m_ptrTrackBar->Maximum = 100;
m_ptrTrackBar->Value = 1;

// Create ProgressBar control
m_ptrProgressBar = new ProgressBar;
l_pt.X = 20;
l_pt.Y = 140;
m_ptrProgressBar->Location = l_pt;

System::Drawing::Size l_sizeProgressBar(200, 20);
m_ptrProgressBar->Size = l_sizeProgressBar;
m_ptrProgressBar->TabIndex = 0;
m_ptrProgressBar->Minimum = 1;
m_ptrProgressBar->Maximum = 100;
m_ptrProgressBar->Value = 1;
```

Next, we create a Timer object and add a handler for the Tick event that will be fired every time the interval elapses:

```
m_ptrTimer = new Timer;
m_ptrTimer->Tick += new EventHandler(this, OnTimerTick);
```

Note that the timer's interval will be set elsewhere, but before Start() is called – if we don't do that, the event will never fire.

After creation of the timer control, the two buttons are created, and all the controls are added to the form. All, that is, except the timer object, because it doesn't have any visual appearance. When a control is not visible, we don't need to add it to the form; the Timer, DataSet, and OleDbConnection are examples of invisible controls.

Our next step is to get hold of the values from the NumericUpDown controls, and start the timer. In the Start button's Click event handler, we begin by reading the properties of the first NumericUpDown control and storing them in members of our MoreControls class. The properties of TrackBar and ProgressBar are then set using these values, while the Interval property of the timer object is set from the Value property of the second NumericUpDown control. Lastly, the Start() method of the timer object is called, and the button controls are disabled to prevent the user from clicking them while the timer is running:

```
void OnClickStartButton(Object* l_ptrSender, EventArgs* l_ptrArgs)
{
    // Get the values from the UpDown controls
    m_nCurrMaxValue = static_cast<int>(m_ptrNUDMaxValue->Value);
    m_nMinValue = static_cast<int>(m_ptrNUDMaxValue->Minimum);
    m_nMaxValue = static_cast<int>(m_ptrNUDMaxValue->Maximum);
    m_nIncValue = static_cast<int>(m_ptrNUDMaxValue->Increment);
    m_nCurrentValue = m_nStartValue = m_nMinValue;

    // Set Range for TrackBar control
    m_ptrTrackBar->Minimum = m_nMinValue;
    m_ptrTrackBar->Maximum = m_nCurrMaxValue;
    m_ptrTrackBar->Value = m_nMinValue;

    // Set Range for ProgressBar control
    m_ptrProgressBar->Minimum = m_nMinValue;
    m_ptrProgressBar->Maximum = m_nCurrMaxValue;
    m_ptrProgressBar->Value = m_nMinValue;

    // Set the timer interval
    m_ptrTimer->Interval = static_cast<int>(m_ptrNUDTimer->Value);

    // Start the timer
    m_ptrTimer->Start();

    // Disable both the buttons
    m_ptrbnStart->Enabled = false;
    m_ptrbnReset->Enabled = false;
}
```

Inside the event handler for the timer's Tick event, we increment the value of m_nCurrentValue by the increment value, m_nIncValue. Then, m_nCurrentValue is checked against the maximum value; if it hasn't reached it, we set the Value properties of the TrackBar and ProgressBar controls – this is the statement that makes the controls' appearance change after we call Refresh() in order to have them repainted. If m_nCurrentValue is greater than the maximum value, the timer is stopped and the Reset button is enabled:

```
void OnTimerTick(Object* l_ptrSender, EventArgs* l_ptrArgs)
{
    try
    {
        m_nCurrentValue += m_nIncValue;
```

```
      if(m_nCurrentValue > m_nCurrMaxValue)
      {
         m_ptrTimer->Stop();

         /* Enable the Reset Button */
         m_ptrbnReset->Enabled = true;
         return;
      }

      // Set current values for the controls
      m_ptrProgressBar->Value = m_nCurrentValue;
      m_ptrTrackBar->Value = m_nCurrentValue;

      // Refresh the controls manually
      m_ptrProgressBar->Refresh();
      m_ptrTrackBar->Refresh();
   }
   catch (ArgumentException *e)
   {
      // Stop the timer
      m_ptrTimer->Stop();
      // Disable both the buttons
      m_ptrbnStart->Enabled = true;
      m_ptrbnReset->Enabled = true;
      MessageBox::Show(e->Message,S"Managed C++ - More controls",
                       MessageBoxButtons::OK, MessageBoxIcon::Stop);
   }
}
```

The catch block handles the ArgumentException exception, which is raised if the ProgressBar's or TrackBar's Value is out of range.

When the Reset button is clicked, the TrackBar and ProgressBar controls are reinitialized, and the Start button is enabled:

```
   void OnClickResetButton(Object* l_ptrSender, EventArgs* l_ptrArgs)
   {
      m_nStartValue = m_nMinValue;
      m_ptrProgressBar->Value = m_nStartValue;
      m_ptrTrackBar->Value = m_nStartValue;

      // Enable the Start button
      m_ptrbnStart->Enabled = true;
   }
```

Multiple document interface forms and menus

GUI application development can be broadly classified into three types: dialog-based applications, single document interface (SDI) applications, and multiple document interface (MDI) applications. So far in this chapter, we have seen both SDI and dialog-based applications. This behavior has been set by the value of the FormBorderStyle property – Sizable (the default value) for SDI applications and FixedDialog for dialogs.

MDI applications allow you to work with multiple forms simultaneously. In Windows Forms, creating an MDI application is pretty simple. The Form class has a property called IsMdiContainer; when this is set to true, the form behaves as an MDI container and allows multiple forms to be opened inside it. In any child form, the MdiParent property needs to be set to point to the container.

In MFC, developing MDI applications requires five classes, and even though the Class Wizard generates them, it's quite tricky to understand and then master the architecture. With Windows Forms, it's simply a matter of setting a few properties. The screenshot below shows four forms, with the outer one containing the other three:

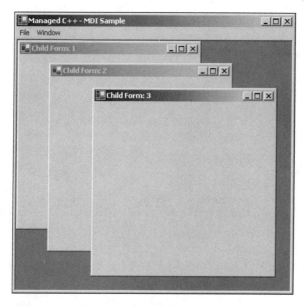

In this section, we'll also be seeing how to create menus on our forms. In the screenshot above, you can see File and Window as main menu items. Under the File option, the options are New Form and Close, while under Window, we will have Cascade, Tile Horizontal, and Tile Vertical menu options. In Windows Forms, menus are created using the MainMenu class, which is responsible for the main menu bar. The submenu items are created using the MenuItem class.

Our applications so far have been coded in single .cpp files, with member functions written inline. For this example, we'll start to place definitions in header files.

In the following MDIForm class declaration, we declare our menus and menu items, and add event handlers for individual menu items:

```
__gc class MDIForm : public Form
{
private:
    // Main menu item
    MainMenu* m_ptrMainMenu;
```

```
    // File and Window Menu items
    MenuItem* m_ptrFileMenu;
    MenuItem* m_ptrWindowMenu;

    // Subitems of File menu item
    MenuItem* m_ptrNewFormMenu;
    MenuItem* m_ptrCloseMenu;

    // Subitems of Window menu item
    MenuItem* m_ptrCascadeMenu;
    MenuItem* m_ptrHorizontalMenu;
    MenuItem* m_ptrVerticalMenu;

    void InitForm();
    void CreateMenu();

    // Click event handler of File->Close
    void OnFileClose(Object* l_ptrSender, EventArgs* l_ptrArgs);

    // Click event handler of File->New Form
    void OnFileNewForm(Object* l_ptrSender, EventArgs* l_ptrArgs);

    // Event handler for all Window options
    void OnArrangeWindows(Object* l_ptrSender, EventArgs* l_ptrArgs);

    // Child Form count
    int m_nFormCount;

public :
    // Public constructor
    MDIForm();
};
```

The `InitForm()` method will initialize the form, while `CreateMenu()` will create the menu items. We call these from the constructor:

```
// MDIForm constructor
MDIForm::MDIForm()
{
    InitForm();
    CreateMenu();
}
```

`InitForm()` sets the `IsMdiContainer` property to `true`, turning this form into an MDI container:

```
void MDIForm::InitForm()
{
    Text = S"Managed C++ - MDI Sample";
    WindowState = FormWindowState::Maximized;
    StartPosition = FormStartPosition::CenterScreen;
    IsMdiContainer = true;
    m_nFormCount = 0;
}
```

Our next task is to create menus and attach them to our MDI container. First, we create a `MainMenu` object, and then we create submenu items that are represented using `MenuItem` objects:

```
void MDIForm::CreateMenu()
{
   // Create main menu item
   m_ptrMainMenu = new MainMenu;

   // Create menu items for main menu
   m_ptrFileMenu = new MenuItem(S"&File");
   m_ptrWindowMenu = new MenuItem(S"&Window");
```

The argument passed to the `MenuItem` constructor is the caption for this menu. Next, the child menu items for the File menu need to be created. These `MenuItem` constructors are passed two arguments, the second of which specifies the functions that will handle the event that's fired when these menu items are selected:

```
   // Create child menu items for the File menu
   m_ptrNewFormMenu = new MenuItem(S"&New Form",
                          new EventHandler(this, OnFileNewForm));
   m_ptrCloseMenu = new MenuItem(S"&Close",
                          new EventHandler(this, OnFileClose));
```

Next, we add the child menu items to the File menu, and the File menu to the main menu, using the `Add()` method of the `MenuItem` object's `MenuItems` collection object:

```
   // Add child menus to the File menu
   m_ptrFileMenu->MenuItems->Add(0, m_ptrNewFormMenu);
   m_ptrFileMenu->MenuItems->Add(1, m_ptrCloseMenu);

   // Add the File menu item to main menu
   m_ptrMainMenu->MenuItems->Add(0, m_ptrFileMenu);
```

The child menu items for the Window menu are added and associated with event handlers in a similar fashion, as you can see. Note that all the three menu items are associated with the single handler `OnArrangeWindows()`:

```
   // Create child menu items for the Window menu
   m_ptrCascadeMenu = new MenuItem(S"&Cascade",
          new EventHandler(this, OnArrangeWindows));
   m_ptrHorizontalMenu = new MenuItem(S"Tile &Horizontal",
          new EventHandler(this, OnArrangeWindows));
   m_ptrVerticalMenu = new MenuItem(S"Tile &Vertical",
          new EventHandler(this, OnArrangeWindows));

   // Add child menus to the Window menu
   m_ptrWindowMenu->MenuItems->Add(0, m_ptrCascadeMenu);
   m_ptrWindowMenu->MenuItems->Add(1, m_ptrHorizontalMenu);
   m_ptrWindowMenu->MenuItems->Add(2, m_ptrVerticalMenu);

   // Add the Window menu item to main menu
   m_ptrMainMenu->MenuItems->Add(1, m_ptrWindowMenu);
```

Finally, the `MainMenu` object is attached to the MDI container:

```
    // Attach the menu to Form
    Menu = m_ptrMainMenu;
}
```

All that remains is to implement handlers for the various menu items and the `ChildForm` class. When **File | New Form** is selected, a new child form needs to be created and shown:

```
// Event handler for the File | New Form menu item
void MDIForm::OnFileNewForm(Object* l_ptrSender, EventArgs* l_ptrArgs)
{
    ChildForm* l_ptrChildForm = new ChildForm(this, ++m_nFormCount);
    l_ptrChildForm->Show();
}
```

We'll see the implementation of `ChildForm` shortly. Note that its constructor takes a pointer to the parent container and an integer that the container uses to keep track of the child forms.

When the user chooses **File | Close**, they are prompted with a message. Upon confirmation, the application is closed by calling the `Close()` method of the parent form:

```
// Event handler for the File | Close menu item
void MDIForm::OnFileClose(Object* l_ptrSender, EventArgs* l_ptrArgs)
{
    if(MessageBox::Show(
            "Do you wish to close this application?", "Managed C++ - MDI Sample",
            MessageBoxButtons::YesNo, MessageBoxIcon::Stop) == DialogResult::Yes)
    {
        Close();
    }
}
```

Almost all MDI applications allow their users to arrange the forms they contain, and we've already added items to the **Window** menu with this functionality in mind. The `Form::LayoutMdi()` method makes it very easy by taking one of three enumerated parameters – `Cascade`, `TileHorizontal`, or `TileVertical` – and arranging things accordingly. These parameters correspond to the available options on the **Window** menu. `OnArrangeWindows()` is called when the user selects any of these options, so we need to call it with a parameter that specifies which `MenuItem` object raised the event. This is determined via its `Index` property:

```
// Event handler for all Window options
void MDIForm::OnArrangeWindows(Object* l_ptrSender,EventArgs* l_ptrArgs)
{
    MenuItem* l_ptrCurrItem = dynamic_cast<MenuItem*>(l_ptrSender);

    // Determine the index and arrange accordingly
    switch(l_ptrCurrItem->Index)
    {
        case 0:
            LayoutMdi(MdiLayout::Cascade);
            break;
```

```
        case 1:
            LayoutMdi(MdiLayout::TileHorizontal);
            break;
        case 2 :
            LayoutMdi(MdiLayout::TileVertical);
            break;
        default:
            break;
    }
}
```

All that's left is the implementation of the ChildForm class:

```
__gc class ChildForm : public Form
{
public:
    // Public constructor
    ChildForm(Form* ptrParent, int l_nCount);
};

// ChildForm constructor
ChildForm::ChildForm(Form* ptrParent, int l_nCount)
{
    Text = String::Concat(S"Child Form: ", l_nCount.ToString());
    WindowState = FormWindowState::Normal;
    MdiParent = ptrParent;
}
```

The ChildForm instance is numbered, and this value is passed into the constructor. More importantly, we set the MdiParent property to be a pointer to the parent container, which is passed in the first parameter. If this property is not set, the child form will not be created within the MDI window boundary, and cannot be arranged within its parent form. When the parent form is closed, the child forms will be closed automatically.

Modal and modeless forms

A modal child form will not allow focus to pass back to its parent until it is closed and can be displayed in Windows Forms using the ShowDialog() method:

```
l_ptrChildForm = new ChildForm(S"Child Form - Modal");
l_ptrChildForm->ShowDialog()
```

To show a modeless form, you just need to use the Show() method instead, as we saw in the example above:

```
l_ptrChildForm = new ChildForm(S"Child Form - Modeless");
l_ptrChildForm->Show();
```

In MFC, a modal dialog is shown using the CWnd::DoModal() method. To display a modeless dialog, we have to allocate memory for the dialog object dynamically, create it by calling CWnd::Create(), and call its CWnd::ShowWindow() method to display it.

Advanced controls in Windows Forms

So far in this chapter, we've discussed several of the controls available in Windows Forms. In this section, we'll look at a final handful of more advanced controls that you haven't seen so far: `TreeView`, `ListView`, `StatusBar`, and `ImageList`. Later on, we'll go through how to implement drag-and-drop among Windows Forms.

Developing Windows Explorer

We'll develop an application called `Explorer` that simulates the behavior of Windows Explorer: it will display system drives, folders, and files. To implement it, we'll add drives and folders to a `TreeView` control and files to a `ListView` control. On selecting a folder or a drive in the `TreeView`, the `ListView` will be refreshed with files. We'll also allow the user to copy a file by dragging it from the `ListView` and dropping it on a folder in the `TreeView`. The application looks like this:

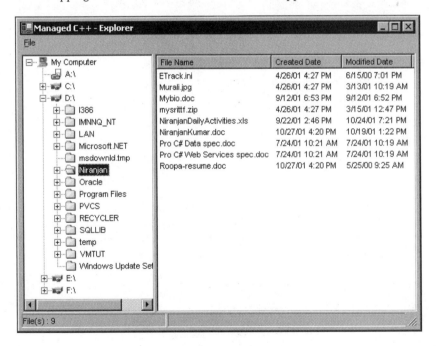

The nodes in the `TreeView` control are displayed with images, while the `ListView` control displays filenames, created dates, and modified dates. The `StatusBar` control is used to display the number of files and a status message, and there are two menu items: File | Refresh and File | Close. The complete code for this application is available for download, so we'll only focus on the interesting aspects here.

First, we need to define our `ExplorerForm` class and declare the pointer variables for all the controls we'll use. Among others, we need to create pointers of type `TreeView` (for the tree view control), `ListView` (for the list view control), `ImageList` (to associate an image with a `TreeView` node), `StatusBar`, two `StatusBarPanel` objects, and the menu items.

```
__gc class ExplorerForm : public Form
{
private :
    // Child Controls
    TreeView* m_ptrTVFolders;
    ListView* m_ptrLVFiles;
    ToolTip* m_ptrToolTip;
    ImageList* m_ptrImageList;
    StatusBar* m_ptrStatusBar;
    StatusBarPanel* m_ptrSBPanel1;
    StatusBarPanel* m_ptrSBPanel2;

    // Menus
    MainMenu* m_ptrMainMenu;
    MenuItem* m_ptrFileMenu;
    MenuItem* m_ptrRefreshMenu;
    MenuItem* m_ptrCloseMenu;
```

The steps involved in creating the form are initialization, menu creation, child control creation, and then population of the TreeView. This sequence is reflected in the implementation of the ExplorerForm class's constructor.

```
ExplorerForm::ExplorerForm()
{
    InitForm();
    CreateMenu();
    CreateChildControls();
    PopulateDrives();
}
```

Since we've already dealt with form initialization and menu creation, we'll focus here on the creation of the advanced controls. In the CreateChildControls() method, all of the controls and their associated event handlers are added to the form. The following code fragment illustrates the creation of the TreeView and ListView controls:

```
    // Create TreeView control
    m_ptrTVFolders = new TreeView;
    m_ptrTVFolders->AllowDrop = true;

    // TreeView events
    m_ptrTVFolders->AfterSelect +=
                    new TreeViewEventHandler(this, OnAfterSelectTVFolders);
    m_ptrTVFolders->DragEnter +=
                    new DragEventHandler(this, OnDragEnterTVFolders);
    m_ptrTVFolders->DragOver +=
                    new DragEventHandler(this, OnDragOverTVFolders);
    m_ptrTVFolders->DragLeave +=
                    new EventHandler(this, OnDragLeaveTVFolders);
    m_ptrTVFolders->DragDrop +=
                    new DragEventHandler(this, OnDragDropTVFolders);
```

```
// Create ListView control
m_ptrLVFiles = new ListView;
m_ptrLVFiles->MultiSelect = false;
m_ptrLVFiles->View = View::Details;
m_ptrLVFiles->FullRowSelect = true;
m_ptrLVFiles->Columns->Add(
                S"File Name", 325, HorizontalAlignment::Left);
m_ptrLVFiles->Columns->Add(
                S"Created Date", 100, HorizontalAlignment::Left);
m_ptrLVFiles->Columns->Add(
                S"Modified Date", 100, HorizontalAlignment::Left);


// ItemDrag event
m_ptrLVFiles->ItemDrag +=
                new ItemDragEventHandler(this, OnItemDragLVFiles);
```

To allow the dropping of dragged items onto a TreeView control, the AllowDrop property needs to be set to true. We'll be adding the code that implements this functionality later on.

Moving on to the events, AfterSelect will be fired immediately after a node in a TreeView control is selected. We're handling the event because this is the time when we need to display the files in a folder. The DragEnter, DragOver, DragLeave, and DragDrop events are all involved in adding drag-and-drop functionality, as you'd probably already guessed.

The MultiSelect property of a ListView control allows the control to contain several selected items at once; to keep things simple in this example, we're setting it to false here so that the user can select only one item at a time. The View property represents the style of the ListView – setting it to View::Details means that the items can be displayed with sub-items.

Setting the FullRowSelect property to true will highlight the entire row when an item from the ListView is selected. (The default behavior is for only the first item to be highlighted.) The ListView is then given three columns, with captions **File Name**, **Created Date**, and **Modified Date**. The ItemDrag event will be fired when an item is dragged from the ListView, so we'll handle this event too.

Note that we *haven't* set the Location and Size properties for TreeView or ListView. These will actually be set depending upon the size and width of the form as passed to the Resize event handler, which we'll see shortly.

The code extract below shows the creation of a StatusBar control with panels:

```
// Create Status Bar control
m_ptrStatusBar = new StatusBar;
m_ptrStatusBar->ShowPanels = true;

// To display file count
m_ptrSBPanel1 = new StatusBarPanel;
m_ptrSBPanel1->Text = S"";
m_ptrSBPanel1->Width = 200;
m_ptrSBPanel1->BorderStyle = StatusBarPanelBorderStyle::Sunken;
m_ptrStatusBar->Panels->Add(m_ptrSBPanel1);
```

```
// To display messages
m_ptrSBPanel2 = new StatusBarPanel;
m_ptrSBPanel2->Text = S"";
m_ptrSBPanel2->BorderStyle = StatusBarPanelBorderStyle::Sunken;
m_ptrSBPanel2->AutoSize = StatusBarPanelAutoSize::Spring;
m_ptrStatusBar->Panels->Add(m_ptrSBPanel2);
```

The StatusBar is divided into two panels. Rather than set the Width property of the second panel, we set its AutoSize property to the enumerated value Spring, which means it will automatically be resized to fill the whole status bar area whenever the form is resized.

The next section of code shows the creation of the ImageList, and the process of adding images to it and adding it to our TreeView control:

```
// Create ImageList control
m_ptrImageList = new ImageList;
m_ptrImageList->TransparentColor = Color::Transparent;
m_ptrImageList->ColorDepth = ColorDepth::Depth32Bit;

// Add images to it
m_ptrImageList->Images->Add(Image::FromFile(S"MyComputer.bmp"));
m_ptrImageList->Images->Add(Image::FromFile(S"FloppyDrive.bmp"));
m_ptrImageList->Images->Add(Image::FromFile(S"Drive.bmp"));
m_ptrImageList->Images->Add(Image::FromFile(S"FolderClose.bmp"));
m_ptrImageList->Images->Add(Image::FromFile(S"FolderOpen.bmp"));
m_ptrTVFolders->ImageList = m_ptrImageList;
```

We're now almost done with CreateChildControls(); all that remains is to set up the tool tips (which you've seen before), set the positions of the various controls, and finally add them to the parent form. The second of these steps is handled by our ArrangeControls() method, which is also called whenever the user changes the size of the form.

In ArrangeControls(), the Width of the TreeView control is set to one third of the client area's width, while the remaining two thirds are occupied by the ListView control. Also, the height of the TreeView and the ListView are both reduced by 26 pixels, in order to display the StatusBar at the bottom. To improve the appearance of the GUI, we introduce a gap between the TreeView and ListView controls, by adding five pixels to the TreeView's X position:

```
// Function to arrange the controls when the form is resized
void ExplorerForm::ArrangeControls()
{
   Point l_pt(2, 6);

   int l_nHeight = ClientSize.Height;
   int l_nWidth = ClientSize.Width;

   // Make the tree control's width 1/3 of form's width
   int l_nTreeViewWidth = l_nWidth / 3;

   // Create TreeView control
   m_ptrTVFolders->Location = l_pt;
   System::Drawing::Size l_sizeTreeView(l_nTreeViewWidth, l_nHeight - 26);
   m_ptrTVFolders->Size = l_sizeTreeView;
```

```
    l_pt.X = l_nTreeViewWidth + 5;
    l_pt.Y = 6;

    // Create ListView control
    m_ptrLVFiles->Location = l_pt;
    System::Drawing::Size l_sizeListView(
                        l_nWidth - (l_nTreeViewWidth + 5), l_nHeight - 26);
    m_ptrLVFiles->Size = l_sizeListView;

    return;
}
```

The final method to be called by the `ExplorerForm` is `PopulateDrives()`, which adds all the drives on the current machine to the `TreeView`. If there are any nodes already in the control, these are cleared before a root node is created using the `TreeNode` class. In our application, the `TreeView` control will have a root node labeled as **My Computer**, and all the drives will be added as child nodes of this one.

The `TreeNode` constructor takes the label of the node, an image index, and a selected image index. The first of these is the index of the image to be displayed when the node is in normal state, while the second is the index of the image to show when the node is in selected mode. Note that the indexes are zero-based.

To add child nodes to the root node, we need to get hold of a `TreeNodeCollection*` for it, and call `Add()` on this object. In our code, this is `l_ptrCollection`, which is initialized immediately after the root node is added to the `TreeView`. The function then continues to add drives to the control (under the root node) in a `for()` loop, using `Environment::GetLogicalDrives()`, which returns a list of drives in a `String*` array. For every node in the `TreeView`, a new `TreeNode` object needs to be created:

```
void ExplorerForm::PopulateDrives()
{
    try
    {
        // Clear if there are any items already present
        if(m_ptrTVFolders->Nodes->Count > 0)
        {
            m_ptrTVFolders->Nodes->Clear();
        }
        m_ptrRootNode = new TreeNode(S"My Computer", 0, 0);
        m_ptrTVFolders->Nodes->Add(m_ptrRootNode);
        TreeNodeCollection* l_ptrCollection = m_ptrRootNode->Nodes;

        // Display drives
        String* l_ptrDrives[] = Environment::GetLogicalDrives();
        for(int l_nCount = 0; l_nCount < l_ptrDrives->Length; l_nCount++)
        {
            String* l_strDrive = l_ptrDrives[l_nCount];
            if(String::Equals(l_strDrive, S"A:\\"))
            {
                TreeNode* l_ptrCurrNode = new TreeNode(l_strDrive, 1, 1);
                l_ptrCollection->Add(l_ptrCurrNode);
                continue;
            }
```

```
            // Add child node
            TreeNode* l_ptrCurrNode = new TreeNode(l_strDrive, 2, 2);
            l_ptrCollection->Add(l_ptrCurrNode);
        }
    }
    catch(Exception* l_ptrException)
    {
        MessageBox::Show(l_ptrException->Message);
    }
    return;
}
```

In the above code, the **My Computer** node takes 0 for both the image index and the selected image index. Then, the A: drive takes an index value of 1, while the rest of the drives use 2, which represents the Drive.bmp bitmap. In the case of any runtime errors, an exception will be raised that we'll handle by passing its Message property to MessageBox::Show().

With that, we've finished displaying drives in the TreeView control. The next steps are to populate folders *under* the current drive in the TreeView, and to display the corresponding files in the ListView when a node in the TreeView is clicked. We'll use the AfterSelect event to achieve this.

In the AfterSelect handler, we need to do some initial validation. If the user has clicked on the root node, there's no need to display any files in the ListView, and we should clear any files that are there at present. If the user has clicked on a drive, we need to populate folders recursively under this drive in the Treeview, and present all the files on the selected drive in the ListView. If the user has clicked on a folder, we just need to display the files under the selected folder in the ListView:

```
void ExplorerForm::OnAfterSelectTVFolders( Object* l_ptrSender,
                                    TreeViewEventArgs* l_ptrEventArgs)
{
    try
    {
        TreeNode* l_ptrCurrNode = l_ptrEventArgs->Node;
        if(l_ptrCurrNode == m_ptrRootNode)
        {
            // Clear all ListView items if root node is selected
            m_ptrLVFiles->Items->Clear();
            return;
        }

        Cursor = Cursors::WaitCursor;

        // If there are no child nodes, populate the folder.
        // Refresh folders only for the drive nodes.
        if( l_ptrCurrNode->Nodes->Count == 0 &&
            (l_ptrCurrNode->ImageIndex == 1 || l_ptrCurrNode->ImageIndex == 2 ) )
        {
            m_ptrSBPanel2->Text = String::Concat(
                S"Refreshing Drive '", l_ptrCurrNode->Text, S"'. Please wait...");
            PopulateFolders(l_ptrCurrNode->Text, l_ptrCurrNode->Nodes);
        }
```

```
        // Populate Files for the selected folder
        int l_iFileCount = PopulateFiles(l_ptrCurrNode->FullPath);
        String* l_strText = String::Concat(S"File(s): ", l_iFileCount.ToString());

        Cursor = Cursors::Arrow;
        m_ptrSBPanel1->Text = l_strText;
        m_ptrSBPanel2->Text = S"";

        // Store the current node
        m_ptrSourceNode = l_ptrCurrNode;
    }
    catch(Exception* l_ptrException)
    {
        Cursor = Cursors::Arrow;
        String* l_strError = String::Concat(
            S"Error occurred while refreshing files: ", l_ptrException->Message);
        MessageBox::Show(l_strError, S"Managed C++ - Explorer",
                    MessageBoxButtons::OK, MessageBoxIcon::Error);
        l_ptrException->Finalize();
    }
    return;
}
```

If the clicked node is the root node, the ListView items are cleared and the function ends. The second if condition determines whether the clicked node is a drive by using the ImageIndex property. If it *is* a drive, the PopulateFolders() method is called:

```
void ExplorerForm::PopulateFolders(
            String* l_strCurrDir, TreeNodeCollection* l_ptrCollection)
{
    try
    {
        String* l_strFolders[] = Directory::GetDirectories(l_strCurrDir);
        for(int l_nCount = 0; l_nCount < l_strFolders->Length; l_nCount++)
        {
            String* l_strFilePath = l_strFolders->Item[l_nCount]->ToString();
            String* l_strFileName = GetFileNameFromPath(l_strFilePath);
            TreeNode* l_ptrTreeNode = new TreeNode(l_strFileName, 3, 4);
            l_ptrCollection->Add(l_ptrTreeNode);
            PopulateFolders(l_strFilePath, l_ptrTreeNode->Nodes);
        }
    }
    catch(Exception* l_ptrException)
    {
        String* l_strError = String::Concat(
            S"Error occurred while refreshing folder: ", l_ptrException->Message);
        MessageBox::Show(l_strError, S"Managed C++ - Explorer",
            MessageBoxButtons::OK, MessageBoxIcon::Error);
        l_ptrException->Finalize();
    }
    return;
}
```

The `Directory::GetDirectories()` static method takes a directory path and will return an array of `String` pointers, each element containing a directory name. In the `for` loop, these directories are added to the current node by passing the directory name and the values 3 and 4 as the image and selected indexes respectively. `PopulateFolders()` is then called recursively, by passing the child directory's path and `TreeNodeCollection*` as arguments. This process continues till all the directories are added to the `TreeView` control.

`GetFileNameFromPath()` takes a full path and returns the final part of the string, as delimited by a backslash character. For example, if `C:\Niranjan\Sairam.exe` were passed, this function would return `Sairam.exe`. The delimiting character is specified by the `PathSeparator` property of the `TreeView` class, the default value of which is a backslash.

Getting back to our `AfterSelect` handler, when the user selects a *folder* in the `TreeView`, the second `if` condition will fail and `PopulateFiles()` will be called. This method takes the full path of the current node and displays the files it contains in the `ListView` control. It also returns the number of files it finds, which is displayed in the first panel of the `StatusBar` control. Later on, in `PopulateFiles()`, the member pointer m_ptrSourceNode is initialized to the current node; this will later be used in the `TreeView`'s `DragDrop` event handler.

Listing files in a `ListView` control is straightforward. The `Directory::GetFiles()` static method takes a directory name and returns a list of files as a `String*` array; we employ a `for` loop to iterate through each element, adding the files' names, creation dates, and modified dates to the `ListView`. This last operation requires the `ListViewItem` object, whose constructor takes a `String*` array that represents the various sub-items. After creation, the `ListViewItem` is passed to the `Add()` method of the `ListView`'s `Items` collection, which adds the item to the control:

```
int ExplorerForm::PopulateFiles(String* l_strCurrDir)
{
    int l_nFileCount = 0;

    try
    {
        String* l_strSubItems[] = {S"", S"", S"", S""};
        String* l_strCreationTime = S"";
        DateTime l_dtCreatedTime;
        DateTime l_dtModifiedTime;
        String* l_strModifiedTime = S"";

        m_ptrLVFiles->Items->Clear();
// Remove the "My Computer" string from the current path
        String* l_strCurPath = l_strCurrDir->Remove(0, 12);
        String* l_strFiles[] = Directory::GetFiles(l_strCurPath);

        for(; l_nFileCount < l_strFiles->Length; l_nFileCount++)
        {
            l_strSubItems[0] = GetFileNameFromPath(l_strFiles[l_nFileCount]);
            l_dtCreatedTime = File::GetCreationTime(l_strFiles[l_nFileCount]);
            l_dtModifiedTime = File::GetLastWriteTime(l_strFiles[l_nFileCount]);

            l_strSubItems[1] = String::Concat(l_dtCreatedTime.ToShortDateString(),
                    S" ", l_dtCreatedTime.ToShortTimeString());
```

```
              l_strSubItems[2] = String::Concat(l_dtModifiedTime.ToShortDateString(),
                    S" ", l_dtModifiedTime.ToShortTimeString());
              ListViewItem* l_ptrLVItem = new ListViewItem(l_strSubItems);
              m_ptrLVFiles->Items->Add(l_ptrLVItem);
          }
       }
       catch(Exception* l_ptrException)
       {
          Cursor = Cursors::Arrow;
          String* l_strError = String::Concat(
              S"Error occurred while refreshing files: " ,l_ptrException->Message);
          MessageBox::Show(l_strError, S"Managed C++ - Explorer",
              MessageBoxButtons::OK, MessageBoxIcon::Error);
          l_ptrException->Finalize();
       }
       return l_nFileCount;
   }
```

Note that before calling `Directory::GetFiles()`, the `String::Remove()` method is called to remove the first 12 characters (which is nothing but the string "My Computer\") from the current node.

Implementing drag-and-drop in Windows Forms

Last of all, we'll discuss the basics of drag-and-drop and its implementation in Windows Forms through the `TreeView` and `ListView` controls. We can think of `ListView` as the source control, from which we drag files, and `TreeView` as the target control, into which we drop files. We've already put in place some of the foundations of the drag-and-drop mechanism, by setting the `AllowDrop` property of the `TreeView` control to `true` and adding handlers for all of the relevant events. Now we need to implement the handlers for these events. The steps involved in implementing drag-and-drop behavior are summarized below:

1. Set the `AllowDrop` property of the target control to `true`.

2. Handle the `ItemDrag` event of the source control to enable dragging an item from it.

3. Call `DoDragDrop()`, and set the drag effects that will appear when an item is dragged over the target control and fires the `ItemDrag` event.

4. Handle the `DragEnter`, `DragOver`, `DragLeave`, and `DragDrop` events in the target control.

Listed below is the sequence of events fired if the user drags an item from the source control and drops over the target control:

1. `ItemDrag` in source control – when the item is dragged from the source control.

2. `DragEnter` in the target control – when the dragged item enters into the target control.

3. `DragOver` in the target control – when the cursor moves over the target dragging the item.

4. `DragDrop` in the target control – when the item is dropped on the target control.

If the user drags the item over the target event, but moves the cursor out again without dropping the item, then the DragLeave event is fired.

Having seen the basics of drag-and-drop operation, let us move on to the code section. In our sample application, we first have to handle the ItemDrag event of ListView. Going back to our discussion of the ExplorerForm::CreateChildControls() method, you may recall the following line of code.

```
m_ptrLVFiles->ItemDrag += new ItemDragEventHandler(this, OnItemDragLVFiles);
```

The first argument passed to the handler is a pointer to the object that fired the event, while the second is a pointer to an object of type ItemDragEventArgs. The Item property of ItemDragEventArgs returns a pointer to the item being dragged. We cast this to a ListViewItem* and store it in a member variable called m_ptrDragLVItem. Finally, we call DoDragDrop(), passing the ListViewItem pointer and DragDropEffects::Copy as parameters:

```
// ListView -> ItemDrag event handler
void ExplorerForm::OnItemDragLVFiles(
                       Object* l_ptrSender, ItemDragEventArgs* l_ptrArgs)
{
    m_ptrDragLVItem = static_cast<ListViewItem*>(l_ptrArgs->Item);
    DoDragDrop(m_ptrDragLVItem, DragDropEffects::Copy);
    return;
}
```

The above code will enable us to drag an item *from* the ListView control. Next, we need to handle the drag events, which, if you recall, we've already added to the TreeView control:

❑   In OnDragEnterTVFolders(), we need to set the dragging effect in the mouse cursor.

❑   In OnDragOverTVFolders(), we need to highlight the current node with different background and foreground colors.

❑   In OnDragLeaveTVFolders(), the control should be reset to its normal state.

❑   In OnDragDropTVFolders(), the dragged item is identified, the node dropped on is determined, and the file is copied to the destination folder.

The implementation of OnDragEnterTVFolders() is pretty simple. We simply set the Effect property of the DragEventArgs object appropriately, which results in the mouse pointer being changed. Note that we should use the same DragDropEffects value across all functions, otherwise the drag-and-drop operation will not work:

```
// TreeView -> DragEnter event handler
void ExplorerForm::OnDragEnterTVFolders(
                       Object* l_ptrSender, DragEventArgs* l_ptrArgs)
{
    l_ptrArgs->Effect = DragDropEffects::Copy;
}
```

When an item is dragged over the TreeView control, the DragOver event will be fired; the second parameter to this event's handler is also of type DragEventArgs*. Here we need to highlight the current node as and when the user moves over the TreeView control, which is a rather protracted process.

From the `DragEventArgs` object, we can determine the current coordinates of the mouse cursor. These are then passed to a helper function called `FindTreeNode()`, which returns a pointer to current node. If the coordinates don't correspond to any node, the function returns a null pointer. When `FindTreeNode()` returns a valid node other than the root node, the `BackColor` and `ForeColor` are changed to `DarkBlue` and `White` respectively. At the same time, the previously selected node's pointer is stored in `m_ptrOldNode`, and its `BackColor` and `ForeColor` properties are restored to their original values:

```
void ExplorerForm::OnDragOverTVFolders(Object* l_ptrSender,
                                       DragEventArgs* l_ptrArgs)
{
    // Get the current node
    TreeNode* l_ptrCurrNode = FindTreeNode(l_ptrArgs->X, l_ptrArgs->Y);
    if(l_ptrCurrNode)
    {
        // If a valid node
        if(l_ptrCurrNode->ImageIndex > 0)
        {
            // If not root node
            l_ptrCurrNode->BackColor = Color::DarkBlue;
            l_ptrCurrNode->ForeColor = Color::White;
            if(m_ptrOldNode && (m_ptrOldNode != l_ptrCurrNode))
            {
                // Restore the color of previous node
                m_ptrOldNode->BackColor = m_ptrRootNode->BackColor;
                m_ptrOldNode->ForeColor = m_ptrRootNode->ForeColor;
            }
            m_ptrOldNode = l_ptrCurrNode;
        }
    }
}
```

The implementation of `FindTreeNode()` takes the coordinates of the mouse cursor and returns a node pointer. In this function, the `TreeNode::Bounds::Contains()` method takes a `Point` object and returns `true` if the point falls inside a node. In a `while` loop, `FindTreeNode()` searches from the root node to the last visible node. It returns a `TreeNode*` if successful and a null pointer if not:

```
TreeNode* ExplorerForm::FindTreeNode(int l_iXPos, int l_iYPos)
{
    TreeNode* l_ptrCurrNode = m_ptrRootNode;
    Point l_pt(l_iXPos, l_iYPos);
    l_pt = PointToClient(l_pt);
    while(l_ptrCurrNode)
    {
        if(l_ptrCurrNode->Bounds.Contains(l_pt))
        {
            // If the node is found, return it
            return l_ptrCurrNode;
        }
        l_ptrCurrNode = l_ptrCurrNode->NextVisibleNode;
    }
```

```
        // Return a null pointer if the node is not found
        return 0;
    }
```

When the mouse cursor leaves the `TreeView` control without dropping the item on it, we need to restore the `BackColor` and `ForeColor` of the last changed node; this is done in response to the `DragLeave` event, as is the setting of `m_ptrOldNode` to a null pointer:

```
void ExplorerForm::OnDragLeaveTVFolders(Object* l_ptrSender,
                                        EventArgs* l_ptrArgs)
{
    if(m_ptrOldNode)
    {
        if(m_ptrOldNode->ImageIndex > 0)
        {
            m_ptrOldNode->BackColor = m_ptrRootNode->BackColor;
            m_ptrOldNode->ForeColor = m_ptrRootNode->ForeColor;
        }
        m_ptrOldNode = 0;
    }
}
```

The last event to be handled is `DragDrop`, and here we can again make use of our `FindTreeNode()` helper. If the node dropped upon is valid and is not the root node, the item's `FullPath` is determined, giving the destination folder. (The source folder is available in `m_ptrSourceNode`, which was initialized in the `TreeView` control's `AfterSelect` event handler, and the source file name is retrieved from the `m_ptrDragLVItem->Text` property.) The full paths to the source and destination are then formed, and `File::Copy()` is called to copy the file. Finally, the current node (where the dragged item was dropped) is selected using the `SelectedNode` property, and the focus is set to the `TreeView` control:

```
void ExplorerForm::OnDragDropTVFolders(Object* l_ptrSender,
                                       DragEventArgs* l_ptrArgs)
{
    try
    {
        // Find the current node where the item is dropped
        TreeNode* l_ptrCurrNode = FindTreeNode(l_ptrArgs->X, l_ptrArgs->Y);
        if(l_ptrCurrNode)
        {
            // Change the color of the current node
            if(l_ptrCurrNode->ImageIndex > 0)
            {
                l_ptrCurrNode->BackColor = m_ptrRootNode->BackColor;
                l_ptrCurrNode->ForeColor = m_ptrRootNode->ForeColor;
            }
            m_ptrOldNode = 0;
        }
        else
        {
            // If null, return
            return;
        }
```

```
      // If dropped over root node
      if(l_ptrCurrNode == m_ptrRootNode)
      {
         m_ptrTVFolders->SelectedNode = m_ptrRootNode;
         m_ptrTVFolders->Focus();
         m_ptrDragLVItem = 0;
         MessageBox::Show(S"Cannot copy the dragged item to 'My Computer' node",
                     S"Managed C++ - Explorer", MessageBoxButtons::OK,
                     MessageBoxIcon::Information);
         return;
      }

      // Copy the dragged file to the dropped location
      Cursor = Cursors::WaitCursor;
      String* l_strTargetDir = l_ptrCurrNode->FullPath;
      String* l_strSourceFullPath = String::Concat(
                  m_ptrSourceNode->FullPath, S"\\", m_ptrDragLVItem->Text);

      l_strTargetDir = l_strTargetDir->Remove(0, 12);
      l_strSourceFullPath = l_strSourceFullPath->Remove(0, 12);

      String* l_strSourceFile = GetFileNameFromPath(l_strSourceFullPath);
      String* l_strTargetFullPath = String::Concat(
                  l_strTargetDir, S"\\", l_strSourceFile);

      // Copy the file
      File::Copy(l_strSourceFullPath, l_strTargetFullPath);

      // Change to destination folder
      m_ptrTVFolders->SelectedNode = l_ptrCurrNode;
      m_ptrTVFolders->Focus();

      // Reset m_ptrDragLVItem to a null pointer
      m_ptrDragLVItem = 0;
      Cursor = Cursors::Arrow;
   }
   catch(Exception* l_ptrException)
   {
      Cursor = Cursors::Arrow;
      String* l_strError = String::Concat(
                  S"Error occurred while copying file: ", l_ptrException->Message);
      MessageBox::Show(l_strError, S"Managed C++ - Explorer",
                  MessageBoxButtons::OK, MessageBoxIcon::Error);
      l_ptrException->Finalize();
   }
}
```

Last but not least, we need to create the form in the application's `main()` function. Since drag-and-drop is OLE functionality, we need to call the `Application::OleRequired()` static method to enable it – this initializes OLE on the current thread. Alternatively, the current thread can be set to STA type by calling `Thread::set_ApartmentState()`:

```
int _tmain(void)
{
   try
   {
      Application::OleRequired();
      Application::Run(new ExplorerForm);
   }
   catch(Exception* l_ptrException)
   {
      String* l_strText = String::Concat(
                     S"Error in creating form: ", l_ptrException->Message);
      MessageBox::Show(l_strText, S"Managed C++ - Explorer",
                     MessageBoxButtons::OK, MessageBoxIcon::Stop);
   }
   return 0;
}
```

This completes our Explorer application, which is capable of exploring your local hard disk. You should now be able to copy files by dragging from `ListView` and dropping over the `TreeView` control. For simplicity, this application implements only file copy functionality, but you could easily extend this to implement move and delete operations, opening files (when the user double-clicks an item in `ListView`), and so on.

Summary

In this chapter, we have taken a quick tour of Windows Forms in .NET and how to use them in managed C++. We have looked at using a lot of controls, some of which will be new to those familiar with coding Windows programs in MFC. We looked at event handling in Windows forms and saw how straightforward this is to implement in the .NET event model. Although there is no direct support in Visual C++ .NET for visual design of forms, the classes available in the .NET Framework class library make it relatively straightforward to do Windows Forms development in managed C++.

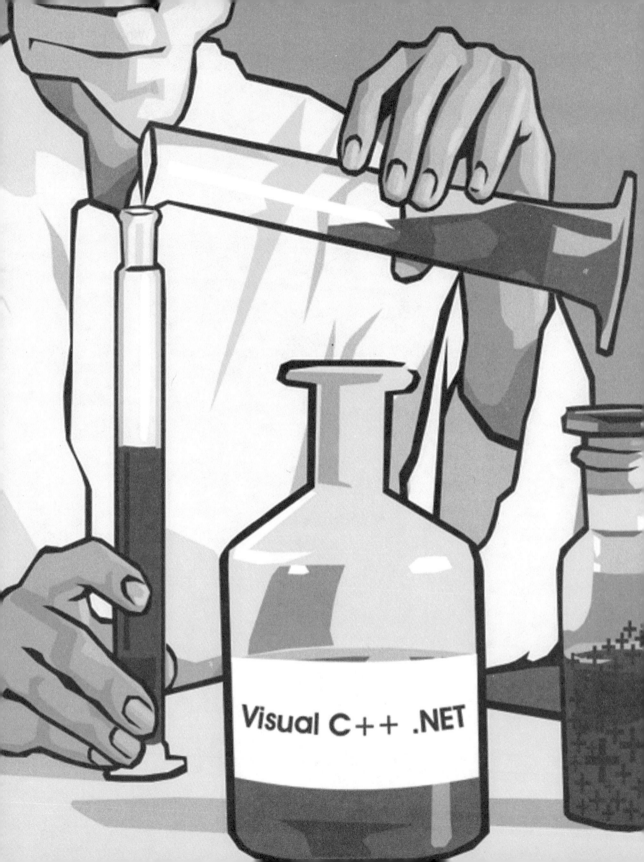

7

Managed and unmanaged code

In some ways, it would be nice if we could just forget about the millions of lines of C++ code that were written before anyone had ever heard of .NET, but this 'unmanaged' code is present in everything from desktop applications to operating systems. You'll almost certainly have code in C++ source files, static libraries, and DLLs that has been debugged and works quite well, thank you very much. When considering the .NET platform, a key decision facing many C++ programmers is whether existing code should be brought into the managed world, left unmanaged... or a mixture of both.

As you'd expect it to, Microsoft has developed interoperability features that allow you to bridge these two worlds – after all, the Windows operating system itself, its system DLLs, and the Win32 APIs are all in native code, and this is unlikely to change in the near future. C++ programmers are in a unique position, because C++ is currently the only .NET language capable of producing both managed and unmanaged code and data. In this chapter, we will see:

❑ How to mix managed and unmanaged code. We'll look at compiling your unmanaged C++ code with the /clr flag and Microsoft's "It Just Works" (IJW) mechanism, and at how to use some new pragmas to control how different sections of your source code are compiled.

❑ How to create a proxy (or wrapper) class around existing, unmanaged C++ code, so that it can be accessed from managed code. We'll examine how to deal with specific issues such as constructors, destructors, member functions, and overloaded operators.

❑ How the transition from the managed to the unmanaged world works. We'll discuss the use of marshaling between managed and unmanaged code, and when it needs to take place. We will look at the System::Runtime::InteropServices::Marshal class and its use. We'll also examine Platform Invocation Services (PInvoke) in detail: what it is and when to use it.

After reading this chapter, you should have a full understanding of what managed and unmanaged code are, their differences, how to mix them, and how to build bridges between them for use in your applications.

Note that we won't be looking at the special features that Microsoft has developed for COM interoperability here, as that will be the focus of the next chapter.

Mixing managed and unmanaged code

Any decision to start the move from unmanaged to managed code is not one that should be made lightly. Because of the additional features provided by the CLR, managed code can have reduced performance and flexibility, and may not be right for all scenarios. Before we begin to look at the conversion process, it's only right that we should explore the reasons why you might *not* want to write managed code.

❑ Unmanaged code is almost always faster than managed code, because it doesn't have any of the overheads associated with CLR services such as garbage collection and reference tracking. There are many kinds of applications where this may not matter (UI applications, for example), but there are others (system utilities, tools, games, and so on) where it's very important indeed.

❑ Unmanaged code can call directly into the Win32 API functions, as well as existing C++, without incurring the cost of the transition from managed to unmanaged code.

❑ Unmanaged code is more 'deterministic' than managed code. Precisely when the garbage collector will run is unpredictable, and this has the potential to cause problems with unmanaged resources such as database connections, file handles, and communications ports. If you need to be certain about when things happen, that's a good reason for keeping your application unmanaged.

Furthermore, there are several specific limitations of managed classes that you need to consider. A managed class:

❑ Can only be derived from other managed types. Equally, a class that's derived from a managed type is always managed, by implication.

❑ Can only support single implementation inheritance (although .NET does support inheritance from multiple interfaces). If you have code that utilizes a lot of multiple inheritance and want to keep it that way, you need to stay with unmanaged code.

❑ Cannot have friend functions or classes.

❑ Cannot have an overridden new or delete operator.

❑ Cannot be used with the sizeof() and offsetof() operators.

❑ Cannot be a template. .NET has no support for generic programming or templates in the first release (although it's rumored to be coming in version 2). If you want to do template-based programming, you need to stay with unmanaged C++.

❑ Can contain references to other managed types, but if you want to contain complete instances of *un*managed types, the restrictions can be quite significant – they must be very simple. You can only use the types that are identified in the C++ standard as POD (Plain Old Data) types.

The /clr flag and It Just Works (IJW)

Now, let's say that after considering all of the above, you've decided that in order to get access to the features of .NET, you want to begin writing Managed C++ code. That decision doesn't prevent you from keeping parts of the existing codebase unmanaged for now. Done carefully, this technique can save you from having to rewrite large parts of your existing applications.

The simplest way to start the transition to managed code is to do what we did in Chapter 2, and recompile your unmanaged code with the /clr flag – Microsoft says, "**It Just Works**" (**IJW**). Officially, the /clr flag "is to enable Managed Extensions and make your code managed", but this rather vague description tells us little about what's happening, or why this flag is so important in migrating to managed code. In fact, the IJW feature is an impressive feat of engineering by the Visual C++ .NET team: you can take an MFC C++ application, add some templates, some STL containers, some multiple inheritance... and then recompile with /clr, and it just works!

The main thing to understand about this process is that the /clr switch does not magically convert all of your unmanaged code into managed code – the problems we listed in the previous section can't be surmounted so easily. What it does is to change the compilation target: when you use the native compiler, you generate native assembly language code; when you compile with the /clr flag, you generate MSIL in an assembly. Once you've made the change, all the services of the CLR (such as .NET security) will be available to your functions, and POD types will be converted to managed __value types – but that's as far as it goes.

Limitations of IJW

Without making alterations to your code, any objects being allocated on the heap will come from the *unmanaged* heap – to the CLR, they will just be opaque blobs of data. Only those types that you subsequently mark with the __gc or __value specifiers will become managed data, and this is the direct cause of several of the items in the following list of the limitations of IJW:

- ❑ You can't just recompile all your class libraries and then inherit from them in the managed world.

- ❑ You can't easily pass managed code pointers to your functions and classes.

- ❑ Inline assembly language is problematic. If it assumes knowledge of the native stack layout, calling conventions outside of the current function, or some other low-level information about the computer, it may fail if that knowledge is applied to the stack frame for a managed function. Functions containing inline assembly code are generated as unmanaged functions.

- ❑ The vprintf() functions cannot be called from a program compiled with /clr.

- ❑ The use of the dllexport or dllimport attributes on classes is not permitted under /clr.

- ❑ The use of functions that are not fully prototyped is not permitted under /clr.

Some of these issues, such as inline assembly code, are beyond the scope of this book; but we *can* take a look at some of the more common problems. IJW will allow us to take existing C-style code and pass pointers around quite happily, as long as we stay unmanaged. However, we get into immediate difficulty if we attempt to pass a managed type to an unmanaged function. Take a look at the following code:

```
#include "stdio.h"

#using <mscorlib.dll>
using namespace System;
```

```
// Here, we will create a managed data type: a structure
__gc struct ManagedStruct
{
    int x;
    int y;
};

void swap1(int* px, int* py)
{
    int temp;
    temp = *px;
    *px = *py;
    *py = temp;
}

int main()
{
    ManagedStruct* ps = new ManagedStruct;
    ps->x = 2;
    ps->y = 4;

    swap1(&ps->x, &ps->y);
    printf("x = %d y = %d\n", ps->x, ps->y);
    return 0;
}
```

This will not compile. We receive the following error message:

```
error C2664: 'swap1' :
cannot convert parameter 1 from 'int __gc *__w64 ' to 'int *'
```

We're trying to pass managed pointers – the addresses of the structure members – to a function whose parameters are unmanaged pointer types, and the compiler will simply not allow this to happen. Even if we could get it by the compiler, this code would not be safe. The garbage collector's heap compaction process will move objects around the managed heap, so memory references will change.

If we want to solve this problem without rewriting our unmanaged swap1() function, we need to use the __pin keyword, which we'll discuss shortly.

The managed and unmanaged pragmas

We've seen that compiling without the /clr flag generates unmanaged, native code, and that compiling with it generates MSIL. We can therefore determine what happens on a per-module basis. Sometimes, however, we need a finer degree of control over the IJW mechanism, and to this end there are a new pair of #pragma directives that allow you to mix managed and unmanaged code explicitly in a single module. They look like this:

```
// mixed.cpp

// ...managed code by default...
```

```
#pragma unmanaged

// ...unmanaged code...

#pragma managed

// ...managed code...
```

These pragmas are most useful in the process of migrating native C++ code to managed code – they allow you to port your code incrementally, without incurring the costs of porting whole applications at once. For example, this author found them extremely useful in a task that involved taking a large body of STL-based C++ and converting portions of it to work in the managed world.

Note that without the /clr flag, these #pragmas will be completely ignored – unmanaged code will be generated by default.

The __pin keyword

In managed code, the __pin keyword declares a pointer to an object (or to an embedded object of a managed class) and prevents that object from being moved during garbage collection. This is useful when passing the address of a managed type to an unmanaged function, because it means that the address will not change unexpectedly during resolution of the unmanaged function call.

The following code extract declares a pinning pointer, named pinnedObject, to a __gc object:

```
CLivesOnManagedHeap __pin* pinnedObject = pManagedHeapObject;
```

Beware that pinning pointers come at a cost. A pinned object can severely affect the efficiency of managed heap compaction, and the rate of object allocation and garbage collection. For a heap with every fifth object pinned, object allocation and cleanup is about 25 times slower than for the non-pinned case.

> **The garbage collector is designed to maintain a non-fragmented heap, and pinning pointers decrease its performance massively. It is important to limit the amount of time that you keep pointers pinned as much as you can.**

When we no longer need an object to remain pinned, we can 'unpin' it by either setting the pinning pointer to zero or allowing it to go out of scope:

```
pinnedObject = 0;
```

Let's revisit our simple example, and pin the managed pointers before we pass them to the unmanaged function, to make sure they will stay 'fixed' in memory. The main() function now looks like this:

```
int main()
{
    ManagedStruct* ps = new ManagedStruct;
    ps->x = 2;
    ps->y = 4;
```

```
    int __pin* pinnedX = &ps->x;
    int __pin* pinnedY = &ps->y;

    swap1(pinnedX, pinnedY);
    printf("x = %d y = %d\n", ps->x, ps->y);
    return 0;
}
```

With this change in place, the code behaves as we want it to – and we didn't need to change our 'old', unmanaged function at all.

Using managed types from unmanaged code

In the last section, we looked at a way to solve some of the problems of calling unmanaged functions from managed code. Here, we're going to take a look at things from the other side. When mixing managed and unmanaged code, you'll soon come across the problem that unmanaged C++ code can't access managed types directly. The following code demonstrates the kind of thing we cannot do:

```
#using <mscorlib.dll>
#include <tchar.h>

using namespace System;

__gc class Foo
{
public:
    void ShowSomeFoo(int number)
    {
        Console::WriteLine(number.ToString());
    }
};

#pragma unmanaged
void UseFoo(Foo* pFoo)
{
    pFoo->ShowSomeFoo(2);
}

#pragma managed
int _tmain(void)
{
    Foo* pFoo = new Foo;
    UseFoo(pFoo);
    return 1;
}
```

Without the pragmas, this code would compile and run quite happily (provided that the /clr flag was set). However, as a result of the #pragma unmanaged directive, we're attempting to use an unmanaged function, UseFoo(), to call into a managed method. We're also trying to manipulate a managed data type from an unmanaged function. The compiler soon lets us know that it is not happy:

```
error C3821: 'pFoo':
managed type cannot be used in an unmanaged function

error C3175: 'Foo::ShowSomeFoo' :
cannot call a method of a managed type from unmanaged function 'UseFoo'
```

What we need here is a mechanism that lets us put the managed type somewhere that we *can* access it from unmanaged code, and lets the CLR know that we're holding an unmanaged reference to the managed object. The solution is to use the __value type System::Runtime::InteropServices::GCHandle, which allows you to create a managed type on the managed heap, but to hold the pointer to it as a __value type. The technique for using it is quite simple: we call GCHandle::Alloc() to generate a handle, and then GCHandle::Free() to free it. Thus, using this type, we have the following:

```
#using <mscorlib.dll>
#include <tchar.h>

using namespace System;
using namespace System::Runtime::InteropServices;

__gc class Foo
{
public:
    void ShowSomeFoo(int number)
    {
        Console::WriteLine(number.ToString());
    }
};

__nogc class FooWrapper
{
private:
    void* handle;

public:
    FooWrapper()
    {
        handle = GCHandle::op_Explicit(GCHandle::Alloc(new Foo)).ToPointer();
    }

    ~FooWrapper()
    {
        (GCHandle::op_Explicit(handle)).Free();
    }

    void ShowSomeFoo(int number)
    {
        Foo* pFoo = static_cast<Foo*>(GCHandle::op_Explicit(handle).Target);
        pFoo->ShowSomeFoo(number);
    }
};
```

```
#pragma unmanaged
void UseFoo(FooWrapper* pFooWrapper)
{
    pFooWrapper->ShowSomeFoo(2);
}

#pragma managed
int _tmain()
{
    FooWrapper* pFooWrapper = new FooWrapper;
    UseFoo(pFooWrapper);
    return 1;
}
```

This example uses a basic wrapper class, a technique that we'll cover in great detail in the next section. In the wrapper, we declare a void* data member. Then, in the constructor, we call two methods of GCHandle (Alloc() and op_Explicit()) to obtain an integer (actually a System::IntPtr), and use the latter's ToPointer() method to convert this integer to a pointer. In the destructor, we use GCHandle::op_explicit() and GCHandle::Free().

The FooWrapper::ShowSomeFoo() method uses the GCHandle::Target property to set the object that the handle represents. Since the Target property returns a System::Object*, we simply cast it to a pointer to the Foo object. After rewriting main() and UseFoo() to use the wrapper class, but without changing the latter's unmanaged status, we can use the managed Foo class without having to alter it in any way.

Now, you're probably thinking that although this works, it's kind of clumsy – and of course you'd be right. It turns out that Microsoft provides a template called gcroot<> to simplify this process – it's a smart pointer around GCHandle. Let's try using that, and see what we get.

```
#include <gcroot.h>

#using <mscorlib.dll>
#include <tchar.h>

using namespace System;
using namespace System::Runtime::InteropServices;

// Code omitted for brevity

__nogc class FooWrapper
{
private:
    gcroot<Foo*> m_pFoo;

public:
    FooWrapper()
    {
        m_pFoo = new Foo;
    }
```

```
    ~FooWrapper()
    {
    }

    void ShowSomeFoo(int number)
    {
        m_pFoo->ShowSomeFoo(number);
    }
};

    ...
```

I'll think you'll agree that this is a much easier, cleaner solution. It's also a good induction into the more general subject of writing wrapper classes, which will be occupying our minds in the next section.

Writing managed proxy classes

The last example we wrote successfully used a managed class from unmanaged code, but for the most part, interoperability between managed and unmanaged code means doing the opposite. After our early successes with IJW, though, what else is there to cover? In fact, there are a number of reasons for seeking other solutions, not least of which is that IJW is a *C++* mechanism that allows unmanaged *C++* code to work with Managed *C++* code (most of the time). What if you want to expose your unmanaged C++ functionality to C#, or to Visual Basic .NET, or to one of the other .NET languages?

However one looks at the politics, much managed .NET development will be done in either C# or Visual Basic .NET, because of all the benefits they offer. If you're convinced that the managed world of .NET offers significant benefits to you as a developer, you will most likely want to port your code such that *all* managed clients can access it. It therefore makes complete sense to look at the area of writing managed proxy classes to allow complete managed access to our unmanaged C++ classes.

The proxy design pattern

The concept of using wrappers is a well-known and recurring solution to a common problem in software design. In their seminal work *Design Patterns: Elements of Object-Oriented Software*, the four authors (commonly known as the "Gang of Four", or just "GOF") began to refer to such solutions as software design "patterns", and one of the patterns they identified was the **proxy**. Essentially, when you create a wrapper class, you're implementing the proxy design pattern.

The proxy pattern "provide[s] a surrogate or placeholder for another object to control access to it" (GOF, page 207). That is exactly what we wish our managed wrapper to do to the unmanaged code that's being accessed. "Proxy is applicable whenever there is a need for a more versatile or sophisticated reference to an object than a simple pointer" (GOF, page 208). In UML, the proxy pattern looks like the diagram overleaf.

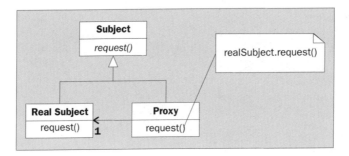

Basic wrapping steps

Microsoft has outlined a set of steps that you should follow in order to create a managed wrapper for an unmanaged C++ class:

1. Create a managed class and declare a single member that points to the unmanaged class.

2. For each constructor of the unmanaged class, define a corresponding constructor for the managed class, which creates an instance of the unmanaged class via the unmanaged new operator, calling the original constructor.

3. If the managed class holds the only reference to the unmanaged class, define a destructor that calls the `delete` operator on the member pointer to the unmanaged class.

4. Deal with overloaded operators

5. For each remaining method in the unmanaged class, declare an identical method that simply delegates the call to the unmanaged version, performing any parameter marshaling that's required.

There are further issues you must consider, however. For example, just what exactly do you wrap? At first, you may think that you need to wrap every single member function and data member of your C++ class, but this might not make sense. One of the opportunities afforded to you when you wrap a class is the ability to **refactor** the public interface. During the act of constructing managed wrappers, you'll often find places where the original design and implementation of the C++ class could be improved and/or exposed differently. Alternatively, you may realize that some public methods would make no sense to a managed client. Another consideration is that you shouldn't expose any more to managed code than was originally exposed to unmanaged C++. This last point leads to two guidelines:

❑ If you have a private member, it was designed not to be accessible to unmanaged classes. Following that logic, it shouldn't be accessible to managed classes either.

❑ Helper functions in the class are internal functions and should not be wrapped.

Let's see how these steps work in practice by looking at an example. For the purposes of demonstration we'll use a linked list, as this will illustrate enough of the issues without being overwhelming. First, we'll take a quick look at the unmanaged class definition, and then we'll wrap it with a managed class. We can then test our code by calling into the original unmanaged C++ from C#, via the managed proxy.

An unmanaged linked list

The complete implementation of this example, IntList, is available for download from www.wrox.com along with the rest of the code for this book. Here, we'll just take a look at the class definitions, which are in IntList.h:

```cpp
#pragma once

#pragma unmanaged

#include <iostream>

// The class representing the actual items in the list
class Item
{
public:
    Item(int value, Item* ItemToLinkTo = 0);

    int value() const
    { return m_value; }

    void next(Item* link)
    { m_next = link; }

    Item* next()
    { return m_next; }

private:
    int m_value;
    Item* m_next;
};

inline Item::Item(int value, Item* item) : m_value(value)
{
    if(!item)
        m_next = 0;
    else
    {
        m_next = item->m_next;
        item->m_next = this;
    }
}

// Here is the actual integer linked list
class IntList
{
public:
    // Constructors, operator, and destructor
    IntList() : m_front(0), m_end(0), m_current(0), m_size(0)
    { }

    IntList(const IntList &rhs) : m_front(0), m_end(0), m_current(0)
    { insert_all(rhs); }
```

```
    IntList& operator=(const IntList &rhs)
        {
            remove_all();
            insert_all(rhs);
            return *this;
        }

    ~IntList()
        { remove_all(); }

    // Accessors
    Item* front() const
        { return m_front; }

    int size()
        { return m_size; }

    // Member insert methods
    void insert(Item* ptr, int value);
    void insert_all(const IntList &rhs);
    void insert_end(int value);
    void insert_front(int value);

    // Member remove methods
    int remove(Item* ptr);
    int remove(int value);
    void remove_front();
    void remove_all();

    // Member find and iterate methods
    Item* find(int value);
    Item* next_iter();

    Item* init_iter()
        { return m_current = m_front; }

    // Member concat and reverse methods
    void concat(const IntList&);
    void reverse();
    IntList concat_copy(const IntList&) const;
    IntList reverse_copy() const;

    // Display the list
    void display();

private:
    // Helper functions
    void bump_up()
        { ++m_size; }

    void bump_down()
        { --m_size; }
```

```
    Item* m_front;
    Item* m_end;
    Item* m_current;
    int m_size;
};
```

Wrapper construction

We'll start by building the managed class that will wrap our linked list. First, create a new **Managed C++ Class Library** called `ManagedList`, and then copy the files `IntList.h` and `IntList.cpp` (the unmanaged linked list implementation) into the project folder, before adding them to the project itself.

Step 1: Create a member pointer to the unmanaged class

Next, we define a managed class called `MList`, and declare a data member whose type is a pointer to the class being wrapped – that is, an `IntList*`. Here's the code so far, from `ManagedList.h`:

```
// Managed wrapper class for the IntList sample

#pragma once
#include "IntList.h"

#pragma managed
#using <mscorlib.dll>

using namespace System;

namespace ManagedList
{
   public __gc class MList
   {
   public:

   private:
      IntList __nogc* m_pIntList;
   };
}
```

Step 2: Wrapping constructors

When creating your wrapper, it won't always make sense to have a wrapping constructor to match every constructor in the unmanaged class. There are two questions you need to ask yourself before you start:

- ❑ Does this constructor make sense, and is it needed?

- ❑ Will this constructor make sense in the managed environment?

In the first case, you may very well discover that you created some constructors in your original unmanaged class that are no longer needed. Remember: you now have the chance to refactor your class.

In the second case, the constructor might involve initializing types that you no longer use in a managed environment. Suppose, for example, that you have a class that performs transparent audio compression and decompression, using some of the Windows multimedia services (version 1 of the .NET Framework class library has no support for multimedia). Such a class might look something like this:

```
public class MyAudio
{
    MyAudio(LPCSTSR fileName);
    MyAudio(WAVEFORMATEX format, LPCTSTR fileName);
}
```

Managed clients will never be passing around a WAVEFORMATEX structure, so you'll neither want nor need to expose the second constructor to them.

These kinds of decisions must be made on an application-by-application basis – if your managed client won't use a particular data structure or feature exposed by a constructor, then don't wrap it. Moving back to the example in hand, *our* unmanaged class has the following constructors:

```
IntList() : m_front(0), m_end(0), m_current(0), m_size(0)
{ }

IntList(const IntList &rhs) : m_front(0), m_end(0), m_current(0)
{ insert_all(rhs); }
```

Default constructor

Let's address the default constructor first, as this is quite straightforward. The implementation of the default constructor in the wrapper class simply consists of instantiating the class we are wrapping, as follows:

```
MList::MList()
{
    m_pIntList = new IntList;
}
```

Copy constructor

The copy constructor, on the other hand, brings up an interesting set of issues. In traditional C++, we often find it necessary to have a user-defined copy constructor and a copy assignment operator to prevent member-wise copying. To accomplish the equivalent action in Managed C++, we need to implement the ICloneable interface in our MList class:

```
public __gc class MList : public ICloneable
{
public:
    MList();

    virtual Object* Clone()
    {
        // Create an instance of the managed list
        MList* ml = new MList;
        *(ml->m_pIntList) = *m_pIntList;        // Calls IntList copy constructor
```

```
      // Deep copy other members from this->... to ml->...

      return ml;
   }
```

The code shows the implementation of the `Clone()` method, in which we create an `MList` instance and call the copy constructor of the unmanaged class, `IntList`, through the managed pointer. In this case, we don't have any additional data members – if we did, we would 'deep copy' each of them to the new managed class too.

Step 3: Wrapping destructors

Compared with constructors, destructors are straightforward. Basically, the technique is to have a destructor in the managed wrapper that calls the destructor in the unmanaged class. Applying that to our example, we have:

```
~MList() { m_pIntList->~IntList(); }
```

Now, it may have crossed your mind to wonder why we need to use a destructor here – hasn't everyone been shouting about the fact that you don't have to call `delete` with .NET? What you have to remember is that the automatic garbage collection of managed objects applies to the freeing of managed objects, but *nothing else*. If you have resources such as database connections in your class, you still need to close those. Here we have a pointer to an unmanaged object, and you *must* call the destructor in the unmanaged class explicitly, so that the underlying unmanaged object is destroyed.

Step 4: Dealing with overloaded operators

Like a copy constructor, an overloaded `operator=()` is not allowed in Managed C++. However, we *can* define a method called `Assign()` and call it explicitly:

```
   // Assignment operator
   virtual MList* Assign(MList* other)
   {
      if(this != other)
      {
         *m_pIntList = *(other->m_pIntList);

         // Deep copy other members from this-> to other->...
      }
      return this;
   }
```

For the various other operators, the .NET Framework makes a provision for overloading using the `op_XXXX()` syntax, and Managed Extensions for C++ allows you to implement all of them.

Step 5: Wrapping member functions

Often, member functions can be wrapped simply by delegating the implementation of the function to the unmanaged class. Here are the functions declared in the header:

```
// Member insert methods
void insert(Item* ptr, int value);
void InsertEnd(int value);
void InsertFront(int value);
void InsertAll(const IntList& rhs);

// Member remove methods
int remove(int value);
void RemoveFront();
void RemoveAll();

// Member find and iterate methods
Item* find(int value);

void display();
```

Then, in the implementation, we simply call the corresponding function in the unmanaged class:

```
// Member insert methods
void MList::insert( Item *ptr, int value )
{
    m_pIntList->insert(ptr, value);
}

void MList::InsertEnd(int value)
{
    m_pIntList->insert_end(value);
}

void MList::InsertFront(int value)
{
    m_pIntList->insert_front(value);
}

void MList::InsertAll(const IntList& rhs)
{
    m_pIntList->insert_all(rhs);
}

// Member remove methods
int MList::remove(int value)
{
    return(m_pIntList->remove(value));
}

void MList::RemoveFront()
{
    m_pIntList->remove_front();
}
```

```
void MList::RemoveAll()
{
    m_pIntList->remove_all();
}

// Member find and iterate methods
Item * MList::find(int value)
{
    return(m_pIntList->find(value));
}

// Display the list
void MList::display()
{
    m_pIntList->display();
}
```

However, not all member functions can be dealt with in such a straightforward way. There are three major issues that you need to look at:

❑   Accessor functions

❑   Functions with default arguments

❑   Functions with a variable number of arguments

Only the first of these applies to our linked list, so let's take a look at that first, and we'll talk about how to deal with the other two cases later on.

Accessor functions

Traditional C++ uses the idiom of defining member accessor functions to access private member variables. Managed C++ has full support for properties and formalizes the notion of accessors through them.

In Chapter 2, we saw that properties are really just methods that are accessed by clients as if they were member variables. When the client code specifies the property, a method is called depending on how the property is being accessed, allowing the client code to interact with the object in well-defined and syntactically simplified ways.

Let's take a look at our IntList sample class again. We have two accessor methods currently defined, both of which are 'get' methods:

```
Item* front() const
{ return m_front; }

int size()
{ return m_size; }
```

The front() accessor method gets the value of the front-most member (the 'head') of the IntList. Note that this is a read-only member variable, as indicated by the lack of a 'set' method. The size() method is similar in nature.

Both of these accessor methods are great candidates to become properties in our managed wrapper. In the header file, we declare the properties:

```
__property Item* get_Front();
__property int get_Size();
```

And in the .cpp file, you can find the implementation:

```
Item* MList::get_Front()
{
    return(m_pIntList->front());
}

int MList::get_Size()
{
    return(m_pIntList->size());
}
```

With that, our unmanaged list class is well and truly wrapped, and we can turn our attention to testing it.

Testing the managed wrapper with a C# client

Use Visual Studio .NET to create a new Visual C# **Console Application**, and name it ManagedListTest. You may leave the class so created with its default name of Class1, since it doesn't much matter. Right-click on **References** in the Solution Explorer, and choose **Add Reference**:

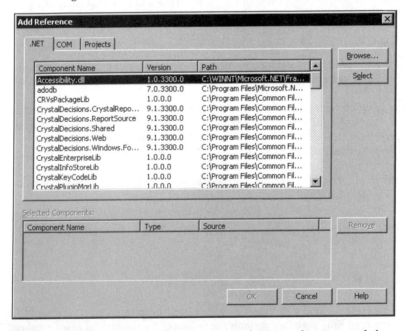

Under the **Projects** tab, Browse to the ManagedList project's Debug directory, and choose ManagedList.dll. After the ManagedList has been added as a reference, you'll need to tell the C# compiler that we'll be making use of the namespace within it. Add the following line of code to Class1.cs:

```
using ManagedList;
```

Now we're ready to call methods and test our managed wrapper. In the `Main()` method, let's first instantiate a new instance of the managed list:

```
MList sharpList = new MList();
```

Next, we'll call the methods to insert values at the front and back of the list, and to display the list:

```
for(int ix = 0; ix < 10; ++ix)
{
    sharpList.InsertFront(ix);
    sharpList.InsertEnd(ix);
}
sharpList.display();
```

Let's now use the two properties. We've defined `Size` as a property in the Managed C++, so we simply access it by using the property name:

```
int size = sharpList.Size;
Console.WriteLine("Size of the managed list is {0} items", size.ToString());
```

Now we want to verify the all-important functionality of the `Clone()` method, which serves the function of C++'s copy constructor. Add the following code to `Class1.cs`:

```
MList newList = (MList)sharpList.Clone();
size = newList.Size;
Console.WriteLine("Size of the clone is {0} items", size.ToString());
Console.WriteLine("And the members are...");
newList.display();
```

Finally, let's test the assignment operator.

```
newList.InsertFront(100);
newList.InsertFront(1000);
size = newList.Size;
Console.WriteLine("Size of the clone is NOW {0} items", size.ToString());
Console.WriteLine("And the members are...");
newList.display();

// Now assign to the original to test the "assignment operator"
sharpList.Assign(newList);
size = sharpList.Size;
Console.WriteLine("Size of the original is NOW {0} items", size.ToString());
Console.WriteLine("And the members are...");
sharpList.display();
```

Here's the output that you get when you build and run the application:

```
20 )( 9 8 7 6 5 4 3 2 1 0 0 1 2 3 4 5 6 7 8 9 )
Size of the managed list is 20 items
Size of the clone is 20 items
And the members are...

20 )( 9 8 7 6 5 4 3 2 1 0 0 1 2 3 4 5 6 7 8 9 )
Size of the clone is NOW 22 items
And the members are...

22 )( 1000 100 9 8 7 6 5 4 3 2 1 0 0 1 2 3 4 5 6 7 8 9 )
Size of the original is NOW 22 items
And the members are...

22 )( 1000 100 9 8 7 6 5 4 3 2 1 0 0 1 2 3 4 5 6 7 8 9 )
```

As you can see, everything is working as expected. We can now use the functionality of our unmanaged C++ class from *any* .NET language.

Other wrapping issues

We mentioned earlier that there are two situations in which you need to be particularly careful about wrapping member functions and constructors, but which we haven't yet covered with our linked list class. These are:

❑   Functions with a variable number of parameters

❑   Functions with default parameters

Variable numbers of parameters

Managed C++ does not do what you'd expect it to do with functions that have a variable number of parameters. The compiler will automatically compile any such function to *unmanaged* code. In general, this is not what we want, and there is no way to wrap these functions directly. We need to look for alternatives.

One solution is to use overloading, although clearly the number of overloads you'll need to use will depend on the application in question – it could be very high! Microsoft recommends that you provide overloads that accept one, two, and three arguments, as well as an overload that takes an array of type `Object*`.

Handling default arguments

Managed C++ does not allow functions with default arguments, since this feature of C++ is not compliant with the Common Language Specification. This means that we cannot delegate the implementation of such members directly. The solution is to rewrite the member function as two functions – one that takes two arguments, and one that takes only one but then calls the two-argument function with the desired value.

If you're dealing with constructors defined with default arguments, then the situation is a little more complicated, because C++ does not allow us to call a constructor from within another constructor. To get around this problem, we have to use a helper function with the same number of parameters as the original constructor. This can be called by a group of overloaded constructors that invoke the helper and pass hard-wired values for the arguments that they themselves were not given.

Marshaling between managed and unmanaged code

So far, our efforts to bridge the gap between managed and unmanaged code have centered largely on finding ways around the various problems presented by pointers. However, we've yet to address the very real possibility that the unmanaged data being pointed to will simply be incompatible with managed code. To help us go further along this road, we need to comprehend fully the significant differences between managed and unmanaged code.

In order for managed and unmanaged code to coexist, some mechanism is needed to allow code executing inside (and therefore under the control of) the CLR to interoperate with code executing outside of the runtime. When interoperation takes place between managed and unmanaged code, one of three types of **interoperability transition** takes place:

❑   An internal call via a function pointer

❑   "It Just Works" (IJW)

❑   Platform Invoke (PInvoke)

We discussed IJW as a porting technique earlier in the chapter, but here we'll discuss it in the context of interoperability. In this section, we'll look under the hood at what happens during a managed-to-unmanaged transition. We'll look at the three kinds of transition and see when **marshaling** is involved. This will lead us into a detailed discussion of the `System::Runtime::InteropServices::Marshal` class and how it pertains to allocating managed memory, copying unmanaged memory blocks, and converting managed types to unmanaged types.

The managed-to-unmanaged transition

At the boundary between managed and unmanaged code, the following differences can apply. Some of these you're already familiar with; others we have yet to cover.

❑   Data types differ in representation

❑   Structures differ in layout

❑   Calling conventions differ

❑   Managed code doesn't count references on objects like COM does

❑   Managed code does not release allocated memory

❑   Managed code locates dynamically loaded code in private or shared assemblies

❑   Managed code is garbage collected – object references can be moved

If you're at all familiar with COM+, this is probably starting to look similar to the differences between runtime contexts and what the interceptor does to 'fix' the differences. The CLR runtime provides a 'transition thunk' (a piece of code that the compiler inserts between the two contexts) that suppresses garbage collection for the duration of a function call, sets up exception handling propagation, and provides marshaling (to/from unmanaged code) if needed.

Internal call transitions

The first of the transition types we listed above is the **internal call** mechanism. Internal call methods are generated by the runtime to be used in situations that are internal to the runtime – for example, by managed types to pass control inside the CLR itself. This transition is accomplished via a function pointer, and while no marshaling is involved, there are some stringent restrictions on the code being called: it must be IJW-compatible and under 100 instructions in length. Although this transition type is of little concern to Visual C++ .NET programmers, we mention it here for completeness. Examples of things that cause internal calls include the methods of the `System::GC` class and `System::Object::GetHashCode()`.

IJW transitions

As we saw earlier, IJW transitions occur as a result of Visual C++ .NET compiler tools, not the programmer. The linker resolves references, and the CLR's class loader creates transition thunks, to bridge the gap between managed and unmanaged code. The transition thunks set up exception-handling propagation and garbage collection, and provide some basic marshaling if it's needed. However, if you pass data that lives on the garbage-collected heap to unmanaged code, you will have to provide marshaling yourself.

Platform Invoke (PInvoke) transitions

PInvoke is a technology for transitioning from managed code to the unmanaged code that's implemented in platform-specific libraries, such as the DLLs in the Win32 API. It is worthy of note that PInvoke does not necessarily mean, "Make a Win32 call," but rather, "Make a platform-specific call." The current Microsoft implementation *does* make a Win32 call, but that doesn't have to be the case.

With PInvoke, the .NET runtime takes care of marshaling all the arguments to the function in the unmanaged DLL, and of unmarshaling the return values and `out` parameters when the function call returns. Though most operating system services are accessible through the .NET Framework class library, there might be occasions when you need to call Win32 API functions directly, and PInvoke can be used in those cases. Internally, many of the methods in the class library use PInvoke to perform their task!

There are actually two distinct kinds of PInvoke services: the basic services (which are usually referred to as PInvoke) and the COM services (usually called COM interop). There are two separate layers because COM has more complex requirements than simple function calls, such as ensuring that reference counting happens and that `QueryInterface()` is called correctly.

> *We'll have more to say about PInvoke later on, and we'll see more on COM interoperability in the next chapter.*

When do we need to marshal?

Under most circumstances, when a call is made from managed code to unmanaged code, the arguments of the call must be marshaled. Given that fact, there are two questions to be asked:

- ❑ How simple or extensive the does the marshaling need to be?
- ❑ Who is responsible for the marshaling – the runtime or you?

This area can get quite overwhelming, but understanding a few key concepts will unlock much of the mystery of interoperability and marshaling. We've already seen that there is a boundary between unmanaged code and managed code. The next thing to grasp is that when we call out of (or into) managed code, arguments are passed on a call stack. So far, so good. Now comes a crucial concept: this call stack contains parameters that are instances of types that have some meaning to *both* worlds: managed and unmanaged. The 'value' in the stack actually has two types: a managed type and an unmanaged type. *At its most basic level, we can think of interoperability marshaling as a set of rules for mapping types on one side to types on the other.*

The next notion is that of **isomorphic types**, which, though it sounds tricky, is simply an indication of whether a conversion is needed. When a managed type contains only isomorphic data types and has its layout specified, then the representation of the type is identical in the managed and unmanaged worlds, and no conversion is necessary. In any case other than having isomorphic data, some conversion (marshaling) is required in order to get the managed type to be 'understood' by unmanaged code. A copy of the managed data is created and passed to the unmanaged code; when it comes back, the copy is converted back into managed form and overwrites the original.

> Note that Microsoft sometimes uses the terms "blittable" and "non-blittable" in place of "isomorphic" and "non-isomorphic".

Just like COM+ interception, the two sides must match exactly. If even one parameter is a non-isomorphic type, then the stack frame must be marshaled into a format that the unmanaged world understands – and conversion may also have to occur in the other direction, for values passed back. These requirements lead us naturally into a discussion of the `System::Runtime::InteropServices::Marshal` class.

The InteropServices::Marshal class

`System::Runtime::InteropServices::Marshal` contains a bunch of neat utility methods to help with interoperability tasks. Except for the ones inherited from `System::Object`, its methods are static, which means that you'll almost certainly never instantiate it directly. The Microsoft documentation says that the `Marshal` class "provides a collection of methods pertaining to allocating unmanaged memory, copying unmanaged memory blocks, and converting managed to unmanaged types". Many of the capabilities of this class pertain to COM interop, which is not the focus of this chapter, but we can still make good use of it here.

Marshaling strings

One of the most useful things we can do with the `Marshal` class is to convert a managed string (a non-isomorphic type) to an unmanaged string, so that we can use it in a call to a traditional Win32 API function. The following snippet of a Microsoft table shows the string mappings used by the marshaler:

`wtypes.h`	C++	**Managed Extensions**	**Common language runtime**
CHAR	char	Char	Char
LPSTR	char*	String* [in], StringBuilder* [in, out]	String [in], StringBuilder [in, out]
LPCSTR	const char*	String*	String
LPWSTR	wchar_t*	String* [in], StringBuilder* [in, out]	String [in], StringBuilder [in, out]
LPCWSTR	const wchar_t*	String*	String

Let's look at an example. The types in the table – CHAR, LPSTR, LPCSTR, LPWSTR, and LPCWSTR – occur quite often in Windows C++ code, and if you call a function that takes one as a parameter, you'll need to perform some marshaling. We're going to create a managed string containing the name of the machine by using the managed System::Environment class, and then use the services of the Marshal class to pass it to the Win32 MessageBoxW() function.

As we'll see later, it would also be possible to call the API function using PInvoke, but for the purposes of this example we'll use IJW.

```
#using <mscorlib.dll>
#include <tchar.h>
#include <windows.h>

using namespace System;
using namespace System::Runtime::InteropServices;

// Libraries that we want to use
#pragma comment(lib, "user32.lib")

int _tmain(void)
{
    Text::StringBuilder* buildMeAString = new Text::StringBuilder;
    buildMeAString->Append(S"The name of your machine is ");
    buildMeAString->Append(System::Environment::MachineName);

    // Convert that managed string to an LPCWSTR
    IntPtr aString;
    aString = Marshal::StringToHGlobalAuto(buildMeAString->ToString());
    MessageBoxW(0, static_cast<LPCWSTR>(aString.ToPointer()),
                                    L"Look Ma! I marshaled!", MB_OK);

    // Free the string...
    Marshal::FreeHGlobal(aString);

    return 0;
}
```

Compile this code with the /clr switch, and IJW handles everything but the marshaling. The pragma lets the compiler know that we'll be using a function in the user32.dll library, and we then proceed to build a string consisting of some text and the name of the machine. To understand what happens next, the first thing you need to know is that the prototype of the Win32 MessageBoxW() function looks like this:

```
int MessageBoxW(HWND hWnd, LPCWSTR lpText, LPCWSTR lpCaption, UINT uType);
```

The problem is that LPCWSTR is not a managed type and therefore isn't compliant with the CLS. If we want to call this function from .NET, we must marshal between the LPCWSTR type and the managed String type.

Marshal's static `StringToXXXX()` methods return values of type `System::IntPtr`, a managed type that inherits from `System::ValueType`. We use the `StringToHGlobalAuto()` method to copy the contents of a managed `String` into the Windows global heap, converting it to ANSI format if needed, before using `IntPtr::ToPointer()` to convert the value of this instance to a pointer to an unspecified type – in other words, to a `void*`. This can then be cast to the appropriate type for the function, before we call `Marshal::FreeHGlobal()` to free the `IntPtr` before the application shuts down. The results on my machine are:

An alternative to the `Marshal::StringToXXXX()` methods is to use the `PtrToStringChars()` function. This is defined in `vcclr.h`, and it gives direct access to the characters in a `String` object, allowing high-performance calls to unmanaged functions that take `wchar_t*` strings. The technique is not without its drawbacks, though, not least of which is that it returns a `__gc` pointer that you'll need to pin in order to call a Win32 function.

```
const System::Char* PtrToStringChars(const System::String* s)
```

Another problem is that the pointer returned is an *interior* `__gc` pointer – it points to the first character of the string in a `System::String` object. Interior pointers are expensive, because they require special handling by the garbage collector and therefore more processing; they may be incremented and decremented directly. Finally, `PtrToStringChars()` returns a Unicode string that you may have to convert to an ANSI one in some circumstances.

Despite all of this, the `PtrToStringChars()` function does offer some performance benefits over `Marshal::StringToHGlobalAuto()` on this occasion. It allows us to replace these lines of code:

```
IntPtr aString;
aString = Marshal::StringToHGlobalAuto(buildMeAString->ToString());
MessageBoxW(0, static_cast<LPCWSTR>(aString.ToPointer()),
                                     L"Look Ma! I marshaled!", MB_OK);
Marshal::FreeHGlobal(aString);
```

With these:

```
const wchar_t __pin* aString = PtrToStringChars(buildMeAString->ToString());
MessageBoxW(0, aString, L"Look Ma! I marshaled!", MB_OK);
```

PInvoke: calling unmanaged functions from managed code

At last, we come to a topic that we seem to have been previewing for some time. Essentially, PInvoke is a means for transitioning from managed to unmanaged code, combined with a mapping mechanism that maps a static method entry point to a Windows DLL file entry point and a DLL loader. We've already said a little about how PInvoke effects the managed-unmanaged transition, so we'll be focusing mainly on its other two elements in this section.

To understand PInvoke's entry point mapping mechanism, it's useful to review the structure of a DLL and its representation in a Windows PE format file. Recall that DLLs contain exported functions, and that in Visual C++ there are two possible ways to export DLL functions: with the `__declspec` modifier or with a `.def` file. When the compiler finds either of these, it puts some extra information in the resulting `.obj` file; when the linker comes into play, it detects the embedded information about the exported variable, function, or class, and automatically produces a `.lib` file that contains a table of the symbols exported by the DLL and their relative addresses.

There are two ways to call a method in a DLL. If you use load-time dynamic linking (explicit linking), you link your code with the import library for the DLL and make explicit calls to the functions. If you use run-time dynamic linking (implicit linking), you use `LoadLibrary()` to load the DLL into your address space at runtime, and then `GetProcAddress()` to get the addresses of the DLL's exported functions. The functions are indirectly referenced by the function pointers returned by `GetProcAddress()`.

PInvoke does its job by mapping a static method declaration in your managed code to an entry point in a DLL that can be resolved via `LoadLibrary()` and `GetProcAddress()`. The stack frame is encoded in a managed method declaration, but the method body is not there! It is provided by the external, native DLL. Worthy of note here is that PInvoke uses **delay loading**, which means that there is no call to `LoadLibrary()`, and therefore no drain on resources, until the first invocation of a method.

To mark a method as being in an external, native DLL, you must provide information about how to call that DLL. This is done with the `System::Runtime::InteropServices::DllImport` attribute, which provides information about the function endpoint, the calling convention, the character set representation (Unicode or ANSI), and (in the case of COM interop) possible signature manipulation. We can handle Unicode/ANSI attributes explicitly through this attribute, or we can allow the platform to handle it through the defaults (which are quite reasonable in most cases).

The other thing that PInvoke does, and therefore needs to know how to do, is to marshal the parameters. We use the `System::Runtime::InteropServices::MarshalAs` attribute to supply this information. In the next few sections, we'll look at some examples to see how all this works.

Using PInvoke to call exported functions in unmanaged DLLs

We'll begin our journey with PInvoke by picking on a Win32 API function and examining how that API can be called from managed code. Let's use the `sndPlaySound()` API function from `winmm.dll` as our guinea pig. The first thing that you need to do is to provide a managed definition for the unmanaged function, and then use the `DllImport` attribute to indicate that this function will be called using PInvoke. The first argument to this attribute indicates the name of the unmanaged DLL that exports the function. Besides this one, there are other, named arguments that allow you to specify the character set, aliases, calling convention, and so on.

The Win32 `sndPlaySound()` API function in `winmm.dll` has the following signature:

```
BOOL sndPlaySound(LPCSTR lpszSound, UINT fuSound);
```

The first parameter of sndPlaySound() specifies the path to a WAV file or represents a registered Windows system sound. The second parameter specifies a flag that controls how the sound will be played. To import this function into a Managed C++ application, you have two choices. You *could* simply include the header file, link with the import library, and use IJW (rather as we did earlier with MessageBoxW()) –this is a quick solution, but its disadvantage is that you have to specify the marshaling explicitly in code (rather than by using attributes), with all the additional complexity that implies. The other choice is to use PInvoke, for which you'll need to provide a managed definition (either static or extern) for sndPlaySound() and then tag this definition with the DllImport attribute.

```
__gc class MyWin32Bridge
{
public:
    [DllImport(S"winmm.dll", CharSet = CharSet::Auto)]
    static bool sndPlaySound(String* pstrWaveFile, int nSoundFlag);
};
```

It's always nice to pack these functions as static methods of a managed class, but there's nothing preventing you from providing managed definitions for these functions at global scope. To do that, you'd just have to prefix the managed definition with the extern keyword rather than the static keyword, as shown below:

```
[DllImport(S"winmm.dll", CharSet = CharSet::Auto)]
extern bool sndPlaySound(String* pstrWaveFile, int nSoundFlag);
```

Note that we've replaced the unmanaged data types – the BOOL return type, and the LPCSTR and UINT parameters – with their managed counterparts: bool, String*, and int. The DllImport attribute's first parameter indicates that sndPlaySound() is exported from winmm.dll, while the Charset named parameter specifies the character set to be used for marshaling string parameters. It can take one of the following Charset enumeration values:

Charset enumeration	Description
Ansi	Marshal as ANSI strings only
Unicode	Marshal as Unicode strings only
Auto	Marshal automatically, based on the operating system character set (Windows NT/2000/XP vs. Windows 9x/ME)

To invoke sndPlaySound() in winmm.dll using PInvoke, you just need to call the managed function definition by passing the appropriate arguments:

```
int _tmain(void)
{
    MyWin32Bridge::sndPlaySound(S"C:\\winnt\\Media\\ringin.wav", 0);
    return 0;
}
```

You can even assign an alias for the unmanaged function in your managed definition. The EntryPoint named parameter to the DllImport attribute can be used to specify the actual name of the unmanaged function. Once that's done, you're at liberty to provide any other function name of your choice in your managed definition:

```
__gc class MyWin32Bridge
{
public:
    [DllImport(S"winmm.dll", CharSet=CharSet::Auto, EntryPoint=S"sndPlaySound")]
    static bool PlayMyWaveFile(String* pstrWaveFile, int nSoundFlag);
};
```

You can now call `sndPlaySound()` using its `PlayMyWaveFile()` alias, like this:

```
MyWin32Bridge::PlayMyWaveFile("C:\\winnt\\Media\\ringin.wav", 0);
```

Receiving callback notifications in a Managed C++ application using PInvoke

Callbacks provide a mechanism by which a function can repeatedly call into a handler function that you've registered with it. The function can invoke that callback handler whenever it wants to notify it or pass it some data. Callbacks are often used in Win32 APIs – especially enumeration-based APIs that will invoke a callback handler to pass information about an element in a collection that it's enumerating.

Using PInvoke, you can register a *managed* callback handler function and pass it to an *unmanaged* function that supports callbacks. In this section, we'll take a look at an example of how this can be accomplished by invoking the `EnumWindows()` API function from a Managed C++ application and registering a managed callback handler function with it. The handler function will be notified as the currently open windows get enumerated by `EnumWindows()`. Take a look at the signature of the `EnumWindows` API function:

```
BOOL EnumWindows(WNDENUMPROC lpEnumFunc, LPARAM lParam);
```

The first parameter, which is of type `WNDENUMPROC`, is a pointer to a callback function that has the following function signature:

```
BOOL CALLBACK EnumWindowsProc(HWND hwnd, LPARAM lParam);
```

The `EnumWindows()` function will repeatedly invoke the callback handler, passing it the window handles of the top-level windows that are currently open. To register a managed callback handler with `EnumWindows()` using PInvoke, you first need to declare a delegate that's based on the `EnumWindowsProc()` callback handler. That would look something like this:

```
__delegate bool EnumWindowsProcCallBack(long hWnd, long lParam);
```

The next order of business is to define a managed function that will represent the callback handler. This managed function definition will be pointed to by the `EnumWindowsProcCallBack` delegate and, therefore, will need to have the same signature. We'll use this callback handler to display the title of the window, which we can obtain from the window handle that's passed to it by `EnumWindows()`:

```
static bool DisplayWindowTitle(long hWnd, long lParam)
{
    // Use the window handle to display the window's title
}
```

As always, you'll have to provide a managed function definition for the EnumWindows() API function, and use the DllImport attribute to specify the DLL that exports EnumWindows():

```
[DllImport(S"user32.dll")]
static bool EnumWindows(EnumWindowsProcCallBack* pfnCallback, long lParam);
```

Before invoking EnumWindows(), you'll have to create an instance of the EnumWindowsProcCallBack delegate by passing it the address of the DisplayWindowTitle() callback handler function:

```
EnumWindowsProcCallBack* pfnCallback =
        new EnumWindowsProcCallBack(0, &MyWin32Bridge::DisplayWindowTitle);
```

The above example assumes that the DisplayWindowTitle() callback handler is a static method of the MyWin32Bridge managed class. Finally, you'll have to pass this delegate instance as a parameter to the EnumWindows() call via PInvoke:

```
MyWin32Bridge::EnumWindows(pfnCallback, 0);
```

The above call will result in EnumWindows() repeatedly calling the DisplayWindowsTitle() callback handler, once for every top-level window that it finds. Here's the compete code that demonstrates what you've seen in this section:

```
using namespace System;
using namespace System::Text;
using namespace System::Runtime::InteropServices;

// Declare a delegate for the WNDENUMPROC callback function
__delegate bool EnumWindowsProcCallBack(long hWnd, long lParam);

// Constant for maximum length of the window's title
#define MAX_TITLE_CHARS 512

__gc class MyWin32Bridge
{
public:
  // Managed definition for the EnumWindows API (USER32.DLL)
  [DllImport(S"user32.dll")]
  static bool EnumWindows(EnumWindowsProcCallBack* pfnCallback, long lParam);

  // Managed definition for the GetWindowText API (USER32.DLL)
  [DllImport(S"user32.dll")]
  static int GetWindowText(long hWnd, StringBuilder* lpstrTitle, int nMaxCount);

  // Callback handler representing the EnumWindowsProcCallBack delegate
  // EnumWindows sends its callback notifications to this handler
  static bool DisplayWindowTitle(long hWnd, long lParam)
  {
    // Create a new StringBuilder
    StringBuilder* lpstrTitle = new StringBuilder(MAX_TITLE_CHARS);
```

```
      // Get the window's title
      GetWindowText(hWnd,lpstrTitle, MAX_TITLE_CHARS);

      // Check if this window has a title
      if(!lpstrTitle->ToString()->Equals(S""))
      {
        // Display the title
        Console::WriteLine(lpstrTitle);
      }
      return true;
    }
};

int _tmain(void)
{
    // Create an instance of the EnumWindowsProcCallBack delegate, passing
    // to it the address of the appropriate callback handler function
    EnumWindowsProcCallBack* pfnCallback =
            new EnumWindowsProcCallBack(0, &MyWin32Bridge::DisplayWindowTitle);

    // Call the EnumWindows API in user32.dll
    MyWin32Bridge::EnumWindows(pfnCallback, 0);
    return 0;
}
```

Using PInvoke to pass structures to functions in unmanaged DLLs

There may be times when your managed code needs to call an unmanaged function that requires you to pass an unmanaged structure or a user-defined data type as an argument. On such occasions, you need to set up a managed class or structure that conforms to the same physical layout and byte order as the unmanaged structure, and can therefore be passed to the unmanaged function in lieu of the unmanaged structure. You can gain additional control over how a managed class or structure is physically laid out by using the StructLayout attribute (see Chapter 4.)

Before we go any further, let's put together an unmanaged Win32 DLL that exports a function called GetDepartmentDetails(). This function populates a structure called DEPARTMENT_DETAILS, which will ultimately be passed in from a Managed C++ application. Here's the code for the GetDepartmentDetails() function, exported from a DLL called DepartmentDetails.dll:

```
#include "stdafx.h"
#include <tchar.h>

BOOL APIENTRY DllMain(HANDLE hModule, DWORD ul_reason, LPVOID lpReserved)
{
    return TRUE;
}

typedef struct tagDEPARTMENT_DETAILS
{
    DWORD m_dwEmployeeID;
    BOOL m_bIsEmployeeManager;
    CHAR m_chEmployeeSection;
    INT m_nDepartmentNumber;
```

```
    WORD m_wDivisionNumber;
    DWORD m_dwReportingManagerID;
} DEPARTMENT_DETAILS;

extern "C" __declspec(dllexport) void __stdcall
GetDepartmentDetails(int nEmployeeID, DEPARTMENT_DETAILS* pDetails)
{
    pDetails->m_dwEmployeeID = 10236;
    pDetails->m_bIsEmployeeManager = TRUE;
    pDetails->m_chEmployeeSection = 'A';
    pDetails->m_nDepartmentNumber = 3;
    pDetails->m_wDivisionNumber = 726;
    pDetails->m_dwReportingManagerID = 34752;
}
```

To keep the GetEmployeeDetails() function as simple as possible, we do nothing more than populate the DEPARTMENT_DETAILS structure with a set of values that are always the same, paying no attention to the employee ID (specified in the first parameter) for which the department details need to be retrieved.

Let's now create a Managed C++ application that calls this function using PInvoke. The first thing that we need to do is to recreate the DEPLOYMENT_DETAILS structure with exactly the same physical layout. The following definition is for a managed class called DepartmentDetails; its members are organized to have the same layout as the DEPARTMENT_DETAILS unmanaged structure:

```
[StructLayout(LayoutKind::Sequential)]
__gc class DepartmentDetails
{
public:
    unsigned long m_lEmployeeID;
    bool m_bIsEmployeeManager;
    char m_chEmployeeSection;
    int m_nDepartmentNumber;
    unsigned short m_wDivisionNumber;
    unsigned long m_lReportingManagerID;
};
```

Using managed data types for the members in the managed class that correspond to the unmanaged data types of the unmanaged structure's members will ensure that the byte alignment and layout are identical. With all that spadework done, let's provide the managed definition for the GetDepartmentDetails() function that's exported by DepartmentDetails.dll:

```
_gc class DepartmentDetailsBridge
{
public:
    [DllImport(S"DepartmentDetails.dll")]
    static void GetDepartmentDetails(int nEmployeeID,
                                      DepartmentDetails* pDetails);
};
```

You can invoke the `GetDepartmentDetails()` function by passing it a pointer to the `DepartmentDetails` managed class instead of the `DEPARTMENT_DETAILS` unmanaged structure:

```
DepartmentDetails* pObjDetails = new DepartmentDetails;
DepartmentDetailsBridge::GetDepartmentDetails(1011, pObjDetails);
```

Here's the complete source code for the Managed C++ application that invokes an unmanaged function expecting an unmanaged structure for its parameter:

```
#using <mscorlib.dll>
#include <tchar.h>

using namespace System;
using namespace System::Text;
using namespace System::Runtime::InteropServices;

// Define a __gc class laid out like the DEPARTMENT_DETAILS structure
[StructLayout(LayoutKind::Sequential)]
__gc class DepartmentDetails
{
public:
    unsigned long m_lEmployeeID;
    bool m_bIsEmployeeManager;
    char m_chEmployeeSection;
    int m_nDepartmentNumber;
    unsigned short m_wDivisionNumber;
    unsigned long m_lReportingManagerID;
};

__gc class DepartmentDetailsBridge
{
public:
    [DllImport(S"DepartmentDetails.dll")]
    static void GetDepartmentDetails(int nEmployeeID,
                                     DepartmentDetails* pDetails);
};

int _tmain(void)
{
    // Create an instance of the DepartmentDetails object
    DepartmentDetails* pObjDetails = new DepartmentDetails;

    // Call the unmanaged function to get the department details
    DepartmentDetailsBridge::GetDepartmentDetails(1011, pObjDetails);

    // Display the results
    Console::WriteLine(S"Employee ID: {0}",
                    pObjDetails->m_lEmployeeID.ToString());
    Console::WriteLine(S"Is Manager: {0}",
                    pObjDetails->m_bIsEmployeeManager ? S"YES" : S"NO");
    Console::WriteLine(S"Belongs to: {0}",
        pObjDetails->m_chEmployeeSection == 'A' ? S"Section A" : S"Section B");
    Console::WriteLine(S"Dept. Number: {0}",
                    pObjDetails->m_nDepartmentNumber.ToString());
```

```
    Console::WriteLine(S"Division Number: {0}",
                       pObjDetails->m_wDivisionNumber.ToString());
    Console::WriteLine(S"Reporting Manager ID: {0}",
                       pObjDetails->m_lReportingManagerID.ToString());

    return 0;
}
```

And just to prove that everything works as described above, here's the output that you get when you build and run the application:

```
Employee ID: 10236
Is Manager: YES
Belongs to: Section A
Dept. Number: 3
Division Number: 726
Reporting Manager ID: 34752
```

Explicit marshaling for non-blittable data types

As we saw earlier, blittable data types have the same representations in both managed and unmanaged memory. In other words, they don't necessitate any explicit conversions when marshaling them between managed and unmanaged code. If you're passing a structure containing only blittable data types to unmanaged code, then the whole structure is blittable. The same holds true for an array whose elements are blittable data types. Here's a list of some of the common data types that are blittable:

- ❑ ELEMENT_TYPE_I1 (char)

- ❑ ELEMENT_TYPE_UI1 (unsigned char)

- ❑ ELEMENT_TYPE_I2 (short)

- ❑ ELEMENT_TYPE_UI2 (unsigned short)

- ❑ ELEMENT_TYPE_I4 (int, long)

- ❑ ELEMENT_TYPE_UI4 (unsigned int, unsigned long)

- ❑ ELEMENT_TYPE_R4 (float)

- ❑ ELEMENT_TYPE_I8 (__int64)

- ❑ ELEMENT_TYPE_U8 (unsigned __int64)

- ❑ ELEMENT_TYPE_R8 (double)

- ❑ ELEMENT_TYPE_PTR (void)

On the other hand, non-blittable data types have multiple representations in unmanaged memory for a given managed type. For example, a data type such as a managed String could represent an ANSI string (LPSTR), a Unicode string (LPWSTR), or a BSTR in unmanaged memory. Here are some of the non-blittable data types and their *possible* data type representations in unmanaged memory:

277

Non-blittable type	Possible conversion scenarios
ELEMENT_TYPE_BOOLEAN	BOOL (4 bytes), VARIANT_BOOL (2 bytes)
ELEMENT_TYPE_CHAR	ANSI character, Unicode character
ELEMENT_TYPE_STRING	ANSI String (LPSTR), Unicode String (LPWSTR), BSTR
ELEMENT_TYPE_VALUETYPE	struct (fixed layout UDT)
ELEMENT_TYPE_CLASS	class, interface
ELEMENT_TYPE_OBJECT	interface, VARIANT
ELEMENT_TYPE_ARRAY	interface, SAFEARRAY
ELEMENT_TYPE_SZARRAY	interface, SAFEARRAY

You can use the MarshalAs attribute to specify how you want a non-blittable type to be marshaled to unmanaged memory. As an example, let's assume that you need to call the _wcsrev() C run-time library function to reverse a string. Take a look at the signature for the _wcsrev() function:

```
wchar_t* _wcsrev(wchar_t* string);
```

The function accepts a Unicode string as its parameter and returns the reversed Unicode string. If you were to call this function from a Managed C++ application via PInvoke, you could instruct the marshaler to marshal the managed string as a Unicode-based LPWSTR to the unmanaged function, and then to marshal it back again as a Unicode-based string. Here's how you would provide the managed definition for the _wcsrev() function in a Managed C++ application:

```
public __gc class MyPInvokeBridge
{
public:
    [DllImport(S"msvcrt.dll"), MarshalAs(UnmanagedType::LPWStr)]
    static String* _wcsrev([MarshalAs(UnmanagedType::LPWStr)]String*);
};
```

To begin with, you need to use the DllImport attribute to specify that msvcrt.dll exports the _wcsrev() function. Then, you can use the MarshalAs attribute to specify that the function parameter and the return type need to be marshaled specifically as Unicode based LPWSTR strings. Here's how you would invoke the above function:

```
int main(void)
{
    String* pstrReversed = MyPInvokeBridge::_wcsrev(S"Hello there!");
    Console::WriteLine(pstrReversed);
    return 0;
}
```

However, note that (as ever) there is a degree of performance overhead associated with passing non-blittable data types to unmanaged functions, because of the conversions that need to be done by the marshaler.

Performance considerations

One of the questions that has been raised repeatedly during this chapter is, "How much is this going to cost?" Microsoft claims in its documentation that PInvoke "has an overhead of between 10 and 30 x86 instructions per call." The author has determined that the performance overhead is extremely dependent on how much and what kind of marshaling needs to take place.

Microsoft states in the Partition II Metadata spec 14.5.6.3: "Transitions from managed to unmanaged code require a small amount of overhead to allow exceptions and garbage collection to correctly determine the execution context. On an x86 processor, under the best circumstances, these transitions take approximately 5 instructions per call/return from managed to unmanaged code. In addition, any method that includes calls with transitions incurs an 8 instruction overhead spread across the calling method's prologue and epilogue." The "best circumstances" Microsoft is referring to are when there is no marshaling involved.

To increase performance, a general guideline is to have fewer PInvoke calls with more data, rather than more calls with less data. Also, it's important to note that even when marshaling is taken into account, the PInvoke and C++ wrapper performance costs are less than with COM interop, because one less layer is involved. COM interop must wrap the C++ class as well as generating the RCW wrapper (see the next chapter).

Summary

In this chapter, we've covered quite a bit of ground on how traditional C++ and Managed C++ code can coexist and interoperate with each other seamlessly. In the first part of the chapter, we reviewed managed code and data, noted some of the limitations of managed classes, and looked at some scenarios that require code to stay unmanaged. We took a whirlwind look at the /clr flag and the IJW mechanism as a first method of converting code from unmanaged to managed. We saw that as impressive as this technology is, there are limitations and cases where other techniques are appropriate. We examined the need for the __pin keyword to keep pointers fixed in memory when passing a managed pointer to an unmanaged function.

In the second part of the chapter, we looked at the idea of using wrappers around unmanaged code and at all the issues that come up when trying to apply them to an unmanaged C++ class. We learned about specific techniques that apply to the wrapping of the important areas of a C++ class: constructors, destructors, member functions, and overloaded operators.

In the third part of the chapter, we took a journey through the types of transition between managed and unmanaged code. We peered 'under the covers' in an attempt to understand what was happening, and then looked at interop marshaling in detail, focusing on marshaling strings with the help of the System::Runtime::InteropServices::Marshal class.

Finally, we examined the PInvoke mechanism, which allows managed code to call functions exported from unmanaged DLLs. We saw how a managed callback handler function could receive callback notifications sent from unmanaged code, and looked at ways of passing managed classes instead of unmanaged structures as parameters to unmanaged functions. Finally, we discussed how you could instruct the interop marshaler to marshal a non-blittable managed data type to a specific data type in unmanaged memory.

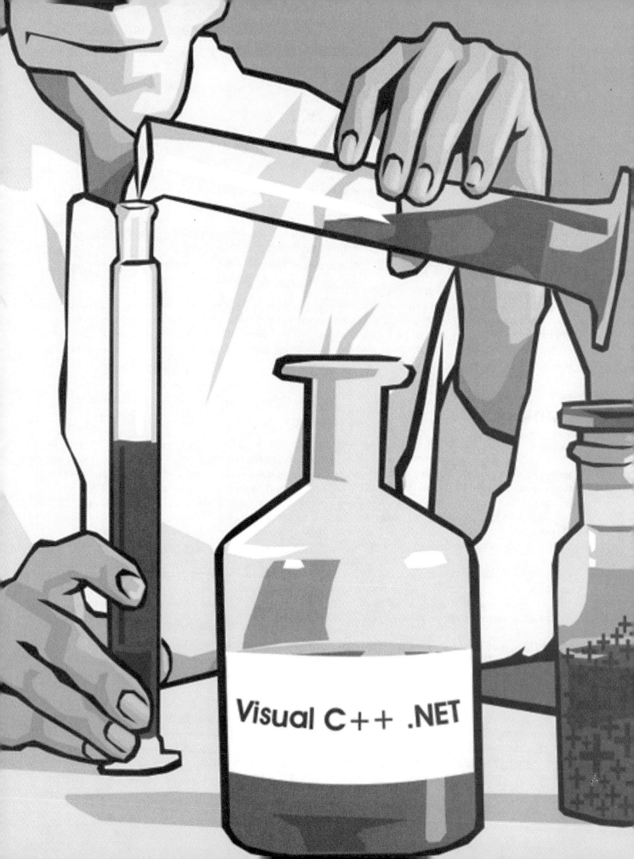

8

COM interoperability

Component software facilitates reusability, modularity, interoperability, and a whole gamut of other compelling benefits that have led many companies to adopt component frameworks such as COM or CORBA for their software development needs. Componentization has also been fueled by the support from development tools that generate a major part of the boilerplate code for the plumbing required by the object model, helping developers to concentrate on business logic rather than the nitty-gritty of the workings. There is a huge market for software components, with companies investing heavily in software componentization and keeping it as a key business imperative to remain at the competitive edge of software development.

If you've ever developed software using Microsoft technologies, you will have used COM in one way or another. Until the advent of .NET, COM was the heart and soul of Microsoft's component software development initiative, forming the foundation for the core services offered by the Windows platform. Now, developers have begun to wonder whether .NET has put the extinguisher on COM. Questions abound about what role COM will play in the grand scheme of things offered by the .NET Framework.

In this chapter, we'll try to answer these questions. In the first half, we'll focus on ways in which you can reuse COM components from Managed C++ applications, and after that we'll look at the other side of things, and examine how you can use Managed C++ components from unmanaged C++ COM-aware clients.

From COM to .NET

COM embodies an extremely elegant object model, and it has gained widespread acceptance from corporations for developing reusable software components. There exists a huge investment made by companies the world over in applications and components based on COM.

With the advent of the .NET Framework, the new avatar of component-oriented development, programming has become simpler, allowing developers to produce components more quickly. Companies who have been riding the COM wave all along need to understand that as a technology, COM is not moving forward into .NET. While .NET does support the interface-based programming model that COM has made us familiar with, its component development paradigm does away with COM-related idiosyncrasies such as registry entries, issues with component versioning, having to deal with the enigmatic IUnknown and IDispatch interfaces, etc.

To take advantage of the benefits provided by the .NET programming model and the CLR, developers can use any one of the .NET development languages to write their components. Microsoft's forthcoming products and future direction will also be closely tied to the .NET platform, providing all the more reason for companies to rethink their component development strategies carefully, and to plan an effective migration path to port their existing components to .NET.

The need for interoperation

Some of the core services required by .NET business components and enterprise applications, such as automatic transaction management, object pooling, and JIT activation, are still only provided through COM+ services. Furthermore, though all trace of the COM programming model has disappeared from .NET, it's very much still present in the bowels of the CLR. Companies who have invested heavily in COM development are not likely to ditch all of their components overnight and jump onto the .NET bandwagon just because it offers a richer, simplified programming model. Porting all of their existing components over to .NET is likely to be a Herculean task.

Microsoft realized that this would be the case, and saw that it would need to provide some kind of interoperability mechanism to allow COM and .NET to interoperate. In the first half of this chapter, we'll be focusing on how you can use this interoperability mechanism to expose your legacy COM components to Managed C++ applications.

Similarly, companies don't want to be locked out of the benefits that .NET will offer. Let's assume that your company decides to follow the rising star, and starts building components using .NET – probably using a .NET-friendly language such as C# or Visual Basic .NET. You'll definitely want these managed components to be accessible from legacy applications – unmanaged code. Again, the interoperability infrastructure makes this happen seamlessly. In the second half of this chapter, we'll examine in detail how you can get .NET components to masquerade as COM components in the eyes of COM-aware unmanaged clients.

Using COM components from Managed C++

A managed application cannot consume a COM component directly, because it's clueless about COM-specific interfaces such as IUnknown and IDispatch. Fortunately, the .NET Framework makes it extremely easy to expose a COM component to a .NET application as if it were a managed component. The .NET application is fooled into believing that it is talking to one of its own breed. Before we see in detail how this magic happens, take a look at this diagram below that explains the interaction between the managed client and a COM component:

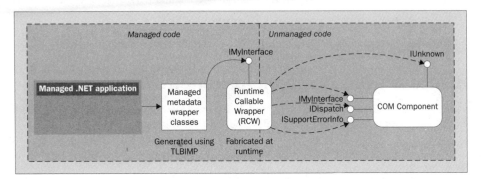

The .NET application talks to the COM component *only* through managed wrapper classes that contain metadata about the classes, interfaces, methods, properties, and events associated with the COM component. You have to generate these wrappers by using a utility called the **type library importer** (tlbimp.exe), which is available as a part of the .NET Framework. Once you've done that, you can create and invoke methods on the COM component by creating and invoking the corresponding methods in these classes, in a way that looks as though you're only making method calls on a managed component.

So, how do these managed wrappers interact with the COM component? When you create a COM component through a wrapper, an intermediate substrate known as the **runtime callable wrapper** (**RCW**) is fabricated at runtime by the CLR. The RCW acts as the client of the COM component, while the target of the method calls made by the managed client is not the COM component itself, but the RCW. The RCW knows how to translate a managed call into a COM-specific invocation request by consuming the required COM interfaces, so that the .NET application thinks that it's interacting with a managed .NET component, while the COM component thinks that it's being invoked by a COM-aware unmanaged client. The CLR creates one RCW for each instance of the COM component.

The RCW handles the marshaling of managed types to COM-specific data types, and also unmarshals return types from COM back into managed data types. Similarly, it takes care of transforming HRESULT-based error codes returned by the COM component into .NET exceptions. The RCW manages the lifetime of the COM component through reference counting. When the managed client no longer needs the managed metadata wrapper objects, the RCW is marked for garbage collection as well. The RCW is eventually garbage collected by the CLR, during which process it releases its references on the COM component, freeing the latter from unmanaged memory.

Let's see how all of this works in practice by going through a series of scenarios illustrating interoperability between COM and .NET. In this section, we'll look at:

❑   How to use both early binding and late binding to consume a COM component from Managed C++

❑   How a Managed C++ application can be used to sink events sourced from a COM component

❑   How a COM collection class can be used from Managed C++

❑   Reusing ActiveX controls by hosting them in .NET containers such as Windows Forms

❑   Reuse models for COM components from managed code

❑   How managed threads declare their COM apartment preferences

Calling into a COM component from .NET

In this section, we'll kick off by building a simple, classic COM component called MyTimeKeeper using ATL 3.0. The component maintains a daily timesheet for the number of work hours that an employee has put in. Then, we'll see how to generate a metadata wrapper assembly from the component's type library. Finally, we'll see how we can use a Managed C++ application to consume the MyTimeKeeper COM component.

Building a COM component

Let's begin by creating the MyTimeKeeper component using ATL. Bring up the ATL COM AppWizard in your Visual C++ 6.0 IDE, choose the Dynamic Link Library (DLL) option (which is the default) in the Wizard, and click on the Finish button. Add a new COM object to this project using the familiar Insert I New ATL Object... menu option, choose a Simple Object type, and name the object MyTimeKeeper. To keep the component as simple as possible, choose the following attributes:

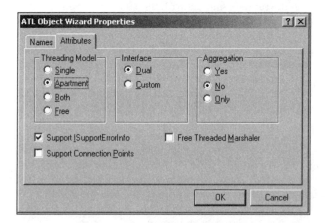

The MyTimeKeeper component supports two interfaces: IMyTimeKeeper and ITimeTeller. The Wizard will have generated the former for you automatically, but you'll have to add ITimeTeller to the IDL file by hand, and also modify the class definition for the CMyTimeKeeper class appropriately. We'll take a look at the class definition in a minute; here's what the changes and the coclass definition in the IDL file look like:

```
[
    object,
    uuid(E5A89168-4E1F-41BE-8017-92D5D8C69845),
    dual,
    nonextensible,
    helpstring("IMyTimeKeeper Interface"),
    pointer_default(unique)
]
interface IMyTimeKeeper : IDispatch
{
    [id(1), helpstring("method GetEmployeeWorkHours")]
    HRESULT GetEmployeeWorkHours([in] long lEmpCode, [out,retval] float* pVal);
};


[
    object,
    uuid(B38660BD-D898-4d59-90E8-0E6E952D8551),
    dual,
    helpstring("ITimeTeller Interface"),
    pointer_default(unique)
]
interface ITimeTeller : IDispatch
{
    [propget, id(1), helpstring("property CurrentTime")]
    HRESULT CurrentTime([out, retval] BSTR *pVal);
};


[
    uuid(A353FD49-E94E-42CE-A599-8FB1218D79D0),
    version(1.0),
    helpstring("MyTimeKeeper 1.0 Type Library")
]
library MyTimeKeeperLib
{
    importlib("stdole2.tlb");
    [
        uuid(50CEDB6E-475E-4D29-B314-ABDDF27A31CA),
        helpstring("MyTimeKeeper Class")
    ]
    coclass MyTimeKeeper
    {
        [default] interface IMyTimeKeeper;
        interface ITimeTeller;
    };
};
```

The IMyTimeKeeper interface contains a method called GetEmployeeWorkHours() that looks up the number of work hours that an employee has put in, based on the specified employee code. The ITimeTeller interface contains a read-only property called CurrentTime, which returns the current time.

Here's the class definition for the `MyTimeKeeper` class:

```
// Define a map that will store the employee code
// along with the corresponding number of hours worked today
typedef map<long, float> EmployeeWorkHoursMap;

class ATL_NO_VTABLE CMyTimeKeeper :
  public CComObjectRootEx<CComSingleThreadModel>,
  public CComCoClass<CMyTimeKeeper, &CLSID_MyTimeKeeper>,
  public ISupportErrorInfo,
  public IDispatchImpl<IMyTimeKeeper, &IID_IMyTimeKeeper, &LIBID_TIMEKEEPERLib>,
  public IDispatchImpl<ITimeTeller, &IID_ITimeTeller, &LIBID_TIMEKEEPERLib>
{
public:
    CMyTimeKeeper() {}
    HRESULT FinalConstruct();

    // Wizard-generated macros go in here. Omitted for brevity.

    BEGIN_COM_MAP(CMyTimeKeeper)
        COM_INTERFACE_ENTRY(IMyTimeKeeper)
        COM_INTERFACE_ENTRY2(IDispatch, IMyTimeKeeper)
        COM_INTERFACE_ENTRY(ISupportErrorInfo)
        COM_INTERFACE_ENTRY(ITimeTeller)
    END_COM_MAP()

private:
    EmployeeWorkHoursMap m_mapEmployeeWorkHours;

public:
    // ISupportsErrorInfo
    STDMETHOD(InterfaceSupportsErrorInfo)(REFIID riid);

    // IMyTimeKeeper methods
    STDMETHOD(GetEmployeeWorkHours)(/*[in]*/ long lEmpCode,
                                    /*[out, retval]*/ float* pVal);
    // ITimeTeller methods
    STDMETHOD(get_CurrentTime)(/*[out, retval]*/ BSTR *pVal);
};
```

We'll override the `FinalConstruct()` method to perform all our initialization. Let's populate the `EmployeeWorkHoursMap` instance with a set of employee codes and the work hours put in by each employee.

```
HRESULT CMyTimeKeeper::FinalConstruct()
{
    // Populate a map with employee codes and the corresponding hours worked
    m_mapEmployeeWorkHours[1001] = 8.0;
    m_mapEmployeeWorkHours[1002] = 8.5;
    m_mapEmployeeWorkHours[1003] = 7.5;
    m_mapEmployeeWorkHours[1004] = 6.0;

    // Add some more employees' work hours here
    return S_OK;
}
```

The implementation of the `IMyTimeKeeper::GetEmployeeWorkHours()` method examines a pre-populated map to check whether the specified employee code exists. If it does, the number of work hours put in by that employee is returned. If the employee code is not found, it raises an exception with the `TK_E_EMPLOYEE_CODE_NOT_FOUND` error code and an appropriate description with the help of the `AtlReportError()` function.

`AtlReportError()` sets up rich error information through an error information object that implements the `ICreateErrorInfo` and `IErrorInfo` interfaces. It uses the `ICreateErrorInfo` interface to populate the error information in the error object, and allows clients to retrieve this error information through the `IErrorInfo` interface. Here's the code for the `GetEmployeeWorkHours()` method:

```
STDMETHODIMP CMyTimeKeeper::GetEmployeeWorkHours(long lEmpCode,
                                              float* pWorkedHours)
{
    // Check if the pointer is valid
    if(NULL == pWorkedHours)
       return E_POINTER;

    // Declare an Iterator for the map containing the employee details
    EmployeeWorkHoursMap::iterator pos;

    // Try to locate the employee using the specified employee code
    pos = m_mapEmployeeWorkHours.find(lEmpCode);

    // Did we find a match?
    if(pos != m_mapEmployeeWorkHours.end())
    {
       // Set the return value with the number of hours
       // that this employee has worked
       *pWorkedHours = pos->second;
    }
    else
    {
       // Oops! We did not find an employee for the specified employee code
       return AtlReportError(__uuidof(MyTimeKeeper),
                        OLESTR("Specified employee code does not exist"),
                        __uuidof(IMyTimeKeeper),TK_E_EMPLOYEE_CODE_NOT_FOUND);
    }

    // Return the status
    return S_OK;
}
```

Make sure that you define a value for the `TK_E_EMPLOYEE_CODE_NOT_FOUND` error code by adding the following to your IDL file. This ensures that the error code is exported to the MIDL-generated header file.

```
cpp_quote("#define TK_E_EMPLOYEE_CODE_NOT_FOUND 0x80040001L")
```

The implementation of the `CurrentTime` property of the `ITimeTeller` interface is again fairly trivial, doing nothing more than returning the current time:

```
STDMETHODIMP CMyTimeKeeper::get_CurrentTime(BSTR* pbstrCurrTime)
{
    // Check if the pointer is valid
    if(NULL == pbstrCurrTime)
        return E_POINTER;

    // Get the local time
    SYSTEMTIME sysTime;
    ::GetLocalTime(&sysTime);

    // Format the current time
    TCHAR strCurrentTime[255] = {0};
    _stprintf(strCurrentTime, "%d-%d-%dT%d:%d:%d",
            sysTime.wYear, sysTime.wMonth, sysTime.wDay,
            sysTime.wHour, sysTime.wMinute, sysTime.wSecond);

    // Set the return value with the current time
    CComBSTR bstrCurrentTime(strCurrentTime);
    *pbstrCurrTime = bstrCurrentTime.Detach();

    // Return the status
    return S_OK;
}
```

And that's all there is to do! Go ahead and build the project; we'll soon see how we can get a Managed C++ application to talk to this COM component. As you'd expect you'll also find the code for this project in the downloadable files for this book.

The type library importer (TLBIMP) utility

If we want to use our COM component from .NET, the first thing we need to do is to generate a managed metadata wrapper assembly from the type information in the component's type library. As mentioned earlier, the .NET Framework SDK ships with a tool that does this job for you: the type library importer. Issue the following at the command line:

```
> tlbimp TimeKeeper.tlb /out:TimeKeeperMetadata.dll
```

The above command generates a metadata wrapper assembly called TimeKeeperMetadata.dll from the component's type library, TimeKeeper.tlb.

Let's use ILDasm to take a peek at the metadata wrapper classes in TimeKeeperMetadata.dll and see how the type library importer has transformed the information in the type library to .NET type information:

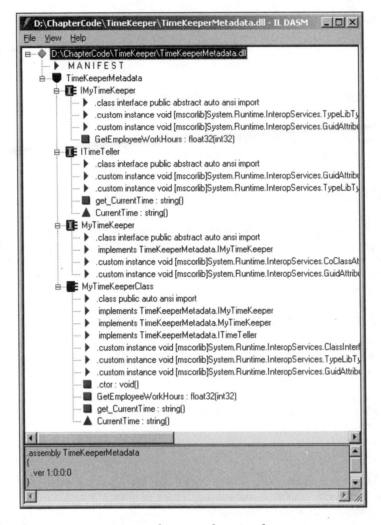

Looking at this, there are some important things to take note of:

❑ The type library importer has placed all generated types in the `TimeKeeperMetadata` namespace. By default, the namespace name is based on the name of the metadata wrapper assembly. However, you can generate a namespace of your choice by using the `/namespace` command-line option with `tlbimp`.

❑ The `IMyTimeKeeper` and `ITimeTeller` interfaces have been imported into the wrapper assembly as managed interfaces, and retain their original names.

❑ When the `coclass` is imported into the wrapper assembly, the type library importer generates *two* managed wrapper classes. They are:

❑ An abstract class associated with the same GUID as the COM `coclass`'s default interface. When the type library importer generates a name for this class, it uses the COM `coclass` name. (In our example, this class would be assigned the name `MyTimeKeeper`.) The class inherits from the default interface (`IMyTimeKeeper`), but does not provide an implementation for the interface's methods.

❑ A concrete class that derives from the abstract class and implements all the interfaces supported by the `coclass`. The implementations of the methods in this class call into the RCW, which acts like a proxy to the COM component. When the type library importer generates a name for this class, it appends *Class* to the coclass name. In our example, this class would be named `MyTimeKeeperClass`. To create the COM component from managed code, you'll need to create an instance of this class.

❑ The `GetEmployeeWorkHours()` method and the `CurrentTime` property are listed as `public` members of the `IMyTimeKeeper` and `ITimeTeller` interfaces respectively, which are both implemented by `MyTimeKeeperClass`. The type library importer converts the COM-specific parameter types used by these methods to their managed equivalents. For example, `GetEmployeeWorkHours()` expects a `long` data type to be passed; this has been transformed into an `Int32` managed type. You'll also notice that the `float` parameter that was marked `[out, retval]` in `GetEmployeeWorkHours()` has been transformed into the method's return value.

Early binding to a COM component from a Managed C++ application

Now that we've got hold of a managed metadata wrapper assembly from the COM type library, let's build a Managed C++ application that'll create and invoke methods on the COM component. You can start by creating a new **Managed C++ Application** called `TimeKeeperClient`.

Our first order of business is to import the type information in the metadata wrapper assembly into our Managed C++ application in the same way as we'd import any assembly: with the `#using` directive.

```
#using <mscorlib.dll>
#using "TimeKeeperMetadata.dll"
```

Next, we need two `using namespace` directives: one for the `TimeKeeperMetadata` namespace created by the type library importer, and another for the `System::Runtime::InteropServices` namespace, whose facilities we'll be using quite frequently.

```
using namespace System;
using namespace System::Runtime::InteropServices;
using namespace TimeKeeperMetadata;
```

To create an instance of the `MyTimeKeeper` COM component, you just need to create an instance of the `MyTimeKeeperClass` class that's defined in the metadata wrapper assembly. To invoke the methods and properties of the COM component, you simply call the corresponding methods and properties of the `MyTimeKeeperClass` object:

```
MyTimeKeeperClass* pTimeKeeper = new MyTimeKeeperClass;

int nEmployeeCode = 1002;
float sWorkHours = pTimeKeeper->GetEmployeeWorkHours(nEmployeeCode);
```

```
Console::WriteLine(S"Employee {0} has worked today for {1} hours",
                   nEmployeeCode.ToString(), sWorkHours.ToString());

Console::WriteLine(S"The Time teller says: {0}", pTimeKeeper->CurrentTime);
```

Since the MyTimeKeeperClass class implements both IMyTimeKeeper and ITimeTeller, you can call any method or property that either of these interfaces supports using the pointer to the MyTimeKeeperClass instance. It's just as if you were creating and invoking methods on a C++ object. Deep under the hood, the RCW is working hard to take care of reference counting on the COM object, querying for the interfaces supported by the COM object, handling the appropriate marshaling of data between the managed and unmanaged code, extracting rich error information from the COM object, and a whole bunch of other things as well, to make this interoperability magic happen.

IUnknown::QueryInterface semantics in the Managed C++ world

If you want to check whether a COM object supports a specific interface dynamically, as you could using COM's IUnknown::QueryInterface(), you can try using the dynamic_cast or the __try_cast operator to cast the object to the desired interface type. If the cast succeeds, it implies that the QueryInterface() call has also succeeded, indicating that the object does indeed support the desired interface. If the cast fails, it signifies that the QueryInterface() call has failed. Using the __try_cast operator to perform the cast results in a System::InvalidCastException exception being thrown if the cast fails, from which you can ascertain whether the QueryInterface() call has succeeded:

```
IArbitrary* pIArbitrary = 0;
try
{
    ITimeTeller* pITimeTeller = __try_cast<ITimeTeller*>(pTimeKeeper);
    Console::WriteLine(S"The Time teller says: {0}", pTimeKeeper->CurrentTime);

    pIArbitrary = __try_cast<IArbitrary*>(pTimeKeeper);
}
catch(InvalidCastException* pCastExcep)
{
    Console::WriteLine(S"Invalid cast exception message: {0}",
                       pCastExcep->Message);
}
```

The complete code for the MyTimeKeeperClient project, including more extensive exception-handling functionality, is available for download from the Wrox web site. Remember that before you run this Managed C++ application, you'll need to make sure that the TimeKeeperMetadata.dll assembly is present in the same folder as the executable.

Deterministic release of a COM component from Managed C++

We saw earlier that when a managed application creates a COM component, the CLR creates an RCW that acts like a managed proxy to the COM component, and that the RCW 's lifetime is controlled entirely by the CLR. However, since the RCW is the actual client of the COM component, it holds references to the COM component (using the classic COM reference counting mechanism) until the garbage collector runs the Finalize() method on the RCW. When the Finalize() method is invoked, the RCW calls IUnknown::Release() on the COM component, thereby freeing it from memory. The COM component's lifetime is therefore non-deterministic; it stays around in memory until the RCW is eventually garbage collected.

Now, there may be occasions when the COM component is holding onto precious resources such as file handles, database connections, and so on, that need to be freed in a deterministic and timely manner. In such cases, you can explicitly force the RCW to release its references on the COM component, so freeing the latter from memory. You can do this by calling the `ReleaseComObject()` static method of the `System::Runtime::InteropServices::Marshal` class.

For example, the following line of code in our Managed C++ client application would explicitly instruct the RCW to release its reference on the `MyTimeKeeper` COM component:

```
Marshal::ReleaseComObject(pTimeKeeper);
```

If your COM component interoperates with managed applications, try to free resources from your component when they are no longer needed, rather than relying on implicit release of these resources when the component is destroyed.

Late binding to a COM component from a Managed C++ application

In the previous section, we referenced the generated metadata wrapper from the Managed C++ application, resulting in early binding to the COM component. This kind of binding provides for compile-time type checking and better performance. However, there could be occasions when you don't have the type information that early binding requires, or you might be presented with a need to create a specific COM component on the fly. If you're accessing a COM component that supports only a pure dispinterface, then you're limited to using late binding to consume the COM component. In such cases, you can use .NET reflection to get the job done.

To begin with, you need to know the CLSID or the ProgID of the COM component. With this information, you can use the `GetTypeFromProgID()` or the `GetTypeFromCLSID()` static methods of the `System::Type` class to get managed type information from the COM component. Here's an example of how these methods can be used to get type information for the `MyTimeKeeper` COM component:

```
Type* pTypeTimeKeeper = Type::GetTypeFromProgID(S"TimeKeeper.MyTimeKeeper");

Type* pTypeTimeKeeper = Type::GetTypeFromCLSID(
                    System::Guid(S"{22077040-DBB2-43E5-A325-2A852C0DF143}"));
```

Once you have the type information, you can create an instance of the COM component using the `CreateInstance()` static method of the `System::Activator` class, as shown below:

```
Object* pObjTimeKeeper = Activator::CreateInstance(pTypeTimeKeeper);
```

To invoke a method or get/set the value of a property, use the `InvokeMember()` method of the `System::Type` object that you obtained earlier from the ProgID or the CLSID. Here's the function prototype for `InvokeMember()`:

```
Object* InvokeMember(String*, BindingFlags, Binder*, Object*, Object* []);
```

There are five parameters, which we'll take a look at in more detail. The first represents the name of the method or property, while the second parameter, a `System::Reflection::BindingFlags` enumeration, is used to indicate whether you're invoking a method or getting/setting the value of a property. Here are the most commonly used `BindingFlags` values:

Action	Binding flags to be used
Invoke a method	`BindingFlags::InvokeMethod`
Get the value of a property	`BindingFlags::GetProperty`
Set the value of a property	`BindingFlags::SetProperty`

The third parameter is a pointer to a `Binder` object instance that can be used for selecting between multiple overloaded functions, and for type coercions. This parameter is rarely used – usually, you can simply pass the default binder, identified by the `DefaultBinder` static property of the `System::Type` class.

The fourth parameter is a pointer to the `Object` that is the target of the member invocation. In other words, it represents the `Object` whose method or property you're going to invoke. For this parameter, you'd have to pass the `Object` pointer that you got back from the `Activator::CreateInstance()` call.

The fifth parameter is an array of `Object` pointers. The array contains the boxed values of the method's parameters (if you're invoking a method) or the boxed value of the property (if you're setting the value of a property).

Here's an example of how you might invoke the `GetEmployeeWorkHours()` method of the default `IMyTimeKeeper` interface in the `MyTimeKeeper` COM component:

```
int nEmployeeCode = 1002;
Object* pObjArgsArr[] = new Object*[1];
pObjArgsArr[0] = __box(nEmployeeCode);

Object* pRetVal = pTypeTimeKeeper->InvokeMember(S"GetEmployeeWorkHours",
                        BindingFlags::InvokeMethod, Type::DefaultBinder,
                        pObjTimeKeeper, pObjArgsArr);
```

The return value from the `InvokeMember()` method is a pointer to an `Object` that contains the boxed return value of the method call or the boxed value of the property. You will need to unbox the `Object` pointer to get back the actual value – you can use the `dynamic_cast` or the `__try_cast` operator to perform the unboxing operation. The return value of the `GetEmployeeWorkHours()` method is a `float data type`, so you need to unbox the `Object` pointer to get back a return value based on the managed `Single` data type:

```
float sEmpWorkHours = *dynamic_cast<Single*>(pRetVal);
Console::WriteLine(S"Employee {0} has worked today for {1} hours",
                nEmployeeCode.ToString(), sEmpWorkHours.ToString());
```

The complete code for this version of the client application is in the `MyTimeKeeperClientLate` folder of the downloadable source code.

Sinking COM component events in a .NET application

COM's interface-based programming paradigm lends itself to enabling bi-directional communication between a component and its consumer. It enables a component's consumer to register the interface pointer of its event sink with a component that sources events. The component can then use this interface pointer to call back into the consumer's event sink, which handles event notifications. When the consumer no longer wants to receive event notifications, it can revoke the registration of the event sink's interface pointer from the component. COM's **connection points** define a standard programming protocol for the registration and revocation of an event sink's callback interface.

In the .NET world, on the other hand, and as you saw in Chapters 2 and 6, event notifications are handled through **delegates**. In this section, we'll examine how a Managed C++ application can subscribe to and receive event notifications from an unmanaged COM component that sources events.

Building a COM component that sources events using ATL 3.0

As we did at the start of the last section, let's quickly put together a COM component that sources events. This time, our COM object will model a thermostat that will notify its subscribers whenever the temperature falls outside a predefined temperature range.

Using Visual Studio 6.0, create a new project called `ThermostatApp` with the ATL COM AppWizard, choosing the Executable option. Add a new, simple ATL COM object to this project, and name it `Thermostat`. (Later on, we'll see how to turn this into a singleton object, so that all clients can connect to the same instance.) Make sure that you check the Support Connection Points option, to make the Wizard add an outgoing interface to the `Thermostat` component:

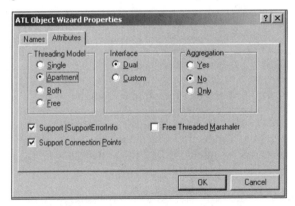

The `Thermostat` component implements an incoming interface called `IThermostat` and also sources events through its outgoing interface, `_IThermostatEvents`. The `IThermostat` interface supports two methods: `SetCurrentTemperature()` and `GetCurrentTemperature()`:

```
interface IThermostat : IDispatch
{
    [id(1), helpstring("method SetCurrentTemperature")]
    HRESULT SetCurrentTemperature([in] float fTemperature);

    [id(2), helpstring("method GetCurrentTemperature")]
    HRESULT GetCurrentTemperature([out, retval] float* pTemperature);
};
```

The outgoing interface, _IThermostatEvents, supports two types of notification: one when the temperature shoots up over the permissible upper limit, and the other when the temperature plummets down below the permissible lower limit. These are represented by the OnExceededUpperThreshold() and OnExceededLowerThreshold() event notification methods respectively:

```
dispinterface _IThermostatEvents
{
    properties:
    methods:
    [id(1), helpstring("method OnExceededUpperThreshold")]
    void OnExceededUpperThreshold([in] float fTemperature);

    [id(2), helpstring("method OnExceededLowerThreshold")]
    void OnExceededLowerThreshold([in] float fTemperature);
};
```

Take a look at the coclass definition in the IDL file. Notice that the _IThermostatEvents interface is tagged with the [source] attribute, indicating that it's an outgoing interface:

```
coclass Thermostat
{
    [default] interface IThermostat;
    [default, source] dispinterface _IThermostatEvents;
};
```

Go ahead and compile your project so that the type library gets generated. This will allow you to use the outgoing interface from the type library to generate the helper proxy class for event notifications, using the Implement Connection Point Wizard. Right-click on the CThermostat class in the ClassView pane, and choose the Implement Connection Point... option in the context menu that appears. Then, choose the _IThemostatEvents interface from the list, and click OK button to generate the helper proxy class. The CThermostat class derives from this class, so that it can call the corresponding Fire_EventHandler() helper methods to fire off events to its subscribers.

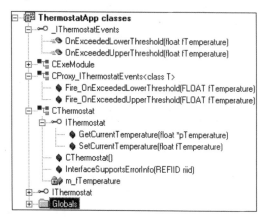

The implementation of the SetCurrentTemperature() method checks to see whether the temperature is within allowable limits. If these have been overstepped, it fires off an event to its subscribers using the Fire_EventHandler() helper methods generated by the Implement Connection Point Wizard:

295

```
// Define the threshold values for the temperature
#define MAXIMUM_TEMPERATURE_THRESHOLD 80.0
#define MINIMUM_TEMPERATURE_THRESHOLD 20.0

CThermostat::CThermostat()
{
   // Set the initial temperature
   m_fTemperature = 50.0;
}

STDMETHODIMP CThermostat::SetCurrentTemperature(float fTemperature)
{
   if(fTemperature > MAXIMUM_TEMPERATURE_THRESHOLD)
   {
      // Fire an event indicating that the temperature
      // has exceeded the upper thereshold
      Fire_OnExceededUpperThreshold(fTemperature);
   }
   else if(fTemperature < MINIMUM_TEMPERATURE_THRESHOLD)
   {
      // Fire an event indicating that the temperature
      // has plummeted below the lower threshold
      Fire_OnExceededLowerThreshold(fTemperature);
   }
   else
   {
      // We are within safe limits - No notifications required
      // Just set the temperature and bail out
      m_fTemperature = fTemperature;
   }

   // Return the status
   return S_OK;
}
```

The implementation of the GetCurrentTemperature() method does nothing more than return the current temperature maintained by the thermostat:

```
STDMETHODIMP CThermostat::GetCurrentTemperature(float* pfTemperature)
{
   // Check if the pointer is valid
   if(NULL == pfTemperature)
      return E_POINTER;

   // Return the current temperature
   *pfTemperature = m_fTemperature;

   return S_OK;
}
```

And finally, to make all clients use the same instance of the Thermostat COM component, we'll make it a singleton by adding the following ATL macro to the CThermostat class definition:

```
DECLARE_CLASSFACTORY_SINGLETON(CThermostat)
```

You can now go ahead and build the project. In the next section, we'll see how we can subscribe to event notifications from the Thermostat component using a Managed C++ application.

Using a Managed C++ application to sink events from a COM component

In this section, we'll create a Managed C++ application that subscribes to event notifications from the Thermostat COM component. Let's get rolling by creating a new Managed C++ Application called Thermostatwatcher.

Once again, the first thing you need to do is to use the type library importer to generate a metadata wrapper from the type library of the Thermostat component:

```
> tlbimp ThermostatApp.tlb /out:ThermostatMetadata.dll
```

Next, as before, you should open the wrapper assembly with ILDasm, where you'll see a rather more complicated set of types:

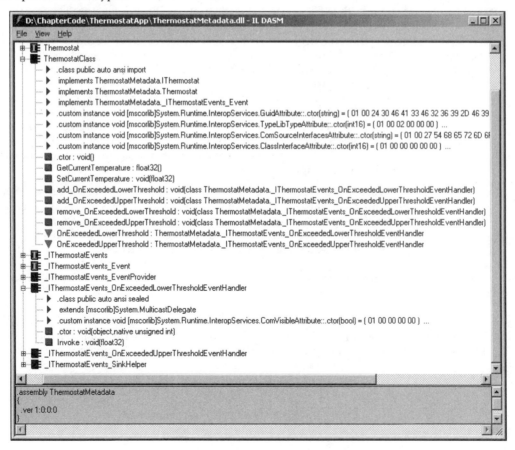

IThermostat (the incoming interface) and _IThermostatEvents (the outgoing interface) have been imported as managed interfaces, with the same names retained. Each of the methods in the _IThermostatEvents (outgoing) interface has been mapped to a corresponding multicast delegate class that's named according to the pattern *OutgoingInterfaceName_MethodName*EventHandler. In our example, the two delegate classes for the OnExceededLowerThreshold() and OnExceededUpperThreshold() methods in the outgoing interface are named _IThermostatEvents_OnExceededLowerThresholdEventHandler and _IThermostatEvents_OnExceededUpperThresholdEventHandler respectively. The method signatures in the outgoing interface also get transformed into Invoke() methods in the corresponding delegate classes, with matching signatures and unmanaged parameter types substituted with their managed counterparts. For example, the void OnExceededLowerThreshold([in] float fTemperature) method in the component's outgoing interface gets imported as void Invoke([in] float32 fTemperature) in the multicast delegate class.

A managed interface named _IThermostatEvents_Event is also generated; this interface contains event members representing each of the multicast delegate types mentioned above. The events are imported with the same name as the method name in the outgoing interface. In our example, the events are called OnExceededLowerThreshold and OnExceededUpperThreshold.

On top of all these, two helper classes are generated that provide the implementation for gluing COM's connection points mechanism with .NET's delegate-based event-handling mechanism. They are:

❑ A class generated with the name *OutgoingInterfaceName*_EventProvider, which in our example is _IThermostatEvents_EventProvider. This provides the implementations of the add_*XXX*() and remove_*XXX*() methods for adding and removing the delegates associated with these events. Its instance members based on the Runtime::InteropServices::UCOMIConnectionPointContainer and Runtime::InteropServices::UCOMIConnectionPoint classes are used to interact with the RCW to hook event notifications from the COM component to the delegate-based event handlers in managed code. This class also maintains an ArrayList of sink helper objects (which we'll see in the next bullet) to keep track of the event handlers that have subscribed to notifications from the COM component.

❑ A sink helper class named *OutgoingInterfaceName*_SinkHelper, which in our example is _IThermostatEvents_SinkHelper. Each sink helper instance caches the cookie returned by the RCW after a successful IConnectionPoint::Advise() call on the COM component. Instances of these classes (and hence the cookies) are stashed away in an ArrayList maintained by _IThermostatEvents_EventProvider.

As we saw earlier, the coclass is imported by tlbimp as two managed wrapper classes. On this occasion, they are:

❑ An abstract class named Thermostat that's associated with the same GUID as the coclass's default incoming interface (IThermostat). This abstract class inherits from both the incoming interface (IThermostat) and the outgoing interface (_IThermostatEvents).

❑ A concrete `ThermostatClass` class that implements the `Thermostat` abstract class and the `_IThermostatEvents_Event` interface. You'll need to instantiate this class to create an instance of the COM component. You can use the event members (inherited from `_IThermostatEvents_Event`) in this class to subscribe to event notifications. When we build a Managed C++ application that subscribes to events from the `Thermostat` COM component, we'll bind delegate instances referencing our event handler methods to the events supported by this class. When the `+=` or `-=` operators are used on the events to add or remove delegates bound to these events, the corresponding `add_XXX()` and `remove_XXX()` methods in the `_IThermostatEvents_EventProvider` class are used.

Now that we have a fairly good idea of the wrapper classes that the type library importer has generated for us, let's get on and use them to receive event notifications from the COM component in a Managed C++ application.

To subscribe to event notifications from the COM component, you'll have to create an instance of the delegate that represents your event notification method. The delegate will reference the method that will handle event notifications. To do this, you need to pass the function pointer of the event handler as an argument to the delegate's constructor. Finally, the delegate instance needs to be hooked to its event. Let's take a more detailed look at how we can accomplish these actions, step-by-step.

First, we'll add a reference to the `ThermostatMetadata` assembly with the `#using` directive:

```
#using "ThermostatMetadata.dll"
```

Next, we'll create a new Managed C++ class called `ThermostatNotificationHandler` that will host the event notification handler methods. This class consists of two static methods – `OnLowerThreshold()` and `OnUpperThreshold()` – both of which will serve as event notification handlers for events sourced by the `Thermostat` component:

```
__gc class ThermostatNotificationHandler
{
public:
    static void OnLowerThreshold(float fLowTemperature)
    {
        Console::WriteLine(S"Below lower threshold : {0}",
                           fLowTemperature.ToString());
    }
    static void OnUpperThreshold(float fHighTemperature)
    {
        Console::WriteLine(S"Above upper threshold : {0}",
                           fHighTemperature.ToString());
    }
};
```

To distance ourselves from the possibility of getting carpal tunnel syndrome – and from having to type annoyingly long names for the delegates that the type library importer has generated – we can `typedef` them to smaller names, as exemplified below:

```
typedef _IThermostatEvents_OnExceededLowerThresholdEventHandler
        LOW_TEMPERATURE_HANDLER;
typedef _IThermostatEvents_OnExceededUpperThresholdEventHandler
        HIGH_TEMPERATURE_HANDLER;
```

With that done, we create an instance of the LOW_TEMPERATURE_HANDLER delegate that references the event notification handler function. We can do so by passing a function pointer to the event handler as an argument to the delegate's constructor:

```
LOW_TEMPERATURE_HANDLER* pLowHandler = new LOW_TEMPERATURE_HANDLER(
                0, &ThermostatNotificationHandler::OnLowerThreshold);
```

The only thing that remains to be done is to wire this delegate to its event by adding it to the list of delegates bound to the event. This is how to bind the LOW_TEMPERATURE_HANDLER delegate to the OnExceededLowerThreshold event:

```
ThermostatClass* pThermostat = new ThermostatClass;
pThermostat->OnExceededLowerThreshold += pLowHandler;
```

The above statement will effectively wire OnExceededLowerThreshold notifications sent from the Thermostat COM component to the ThermostatNotificationHandler::OnLowerThreshold() handler method.

When you no longer desire to receive event notifications, you can use the -= operator to disengage the delegate from the event, like this:

```
pThermostat->OnExceededLowerThreshold -= pLowHandler;
```

Under the hood, the += operator calls the add_OnExceededLowerThreshold() method of the ThermostatClass object in the metadata wrapper assembly. This uses the Runtime::InteropServices::UCOMIConnectionPoint class's Advise() method to instruct the RCW to call IConnectionPoint::Advise() on the COM component, which returns a cookie identifying the subscriber. When the RCW passes this cookie back to the managed world, it's stashed away in the _IThermostatEvents_SinkHelper class's m_dwCookie member.

On a similar note, the -= operator calls the remove_OnExceededLowerThreshold() method of the ThermostatClass object in the metadata wrapper assembly. This uses the Runtime::InteropServices::UCOMIConnectionPoint class's Unadvise() method by passing it the cookie it had stashed away in the _IThermostatEvents_SinkHelper class's m_dwCookie member. This triggers the RCW to call IConnectionPoint::Unadvise() on the COM component, thus effectively disengaging the subscriber from event notifications.

As we can see from this example, the Managed C++ application uses delegates to subscribe to and receive event notifications, while the COM component uses connection points to source events. Both the .NET application and the COM component continue to use their own native event handling mechanisms, while the RCW provides the appropriate plumbing to bracket these two mechanisms together. As usual, you'll find the complete source code for this example on the Wrox web site: www.wrox.com.

Exposing a COM-based collection class to a .NET application

When developing any kind of non-trivial object model with COM, you'll usually need to represent a group of objects as a collection. Suppose that you wanted to allow a user to iterate through the books in a library – you could model the `Library` object as a collection containing `Book` objects, allowing the user to enumerate through the individual `Books`.

Commonly used object models, such as ADO, CDO, and so on, make heavy use of collections. In ADO, for example, the `Fields` and `Parameters` objects represent collections of `Field` and `Parameter` objects respectively. In terms of programmatic support, COM provides interfaces such as `IEnumVARIANT`, which allows you to enumerate through a collection of `VARIANT`s. Furthermore, libraries such as ATL allow you to develop COM collections more easily by providing helper classes that supply implementations of the methods needed to expose a collection.

In this section, we'll take a look at how you can expose a collection using COM, and then we'll see how easy it is to consume this collection from a Managed C++ application.

Building a COM component that exposes a collection using ATL 3.0

We'll build a COM component called `WroxBookCollection` that models a collection of books. Using Visual Studio 6.0, create a new ATL project using the **ATL COM AppWizard**, and choose the default **Dynamic Link Library (DLL)** option. Add a new, simple ATL COM object called `WroxBookCollection` to this project, giving it the same attributes as the `MyTimeKeeper` COM component that we built earlier.

As you know, a typical COM component that models a collection supports the following read-only properties:

❑   `Count` – returns the number of elements in the collection.

❑   `Item` – allows clients to retrieve the item at a specified index in the collection. This property is assigned a DISPID value of 0, represented by the `DISPID_VALUE` constant. Using this DISPID enables clients such as Visual Basic to use this as the default property, when the property name is not specified explicitly while making a method call.

❑   `_NewEnum` – returns the interface pointer to an object that supports the `IEnumVARIANT` interface, which allows the client to enumerate through the underlying collection. The underscore prefix prevents the property from being displayed in type library browsers. This property is assigned a DISPID value of −4, represented by the `DISPID_NEWENUM` constant. Using this DISPID enables Automation controllers like Visual Basic to use the `For-Each...Next` syntax to enumerate through the collection.

Open the IDL file and add the following methods to the `IWroxBookCollection` interface of the `WroxBookCollection` object:

```
interface IWroxBookCollection : IDispatch
{
    [propget, id(1), helpstring("property Count")]
    HRESULT Count([out, retval] long *pVal);
```

```
    [propget, id(DISPID_NEWENUM), helpstring("property _NewEnum"),restricted]
    HRESULT _NewEnum([out, retval] LPUNKNOWN* pVal);

    [propget, id(DISPID_VALUE), helpstring("property Item")]
    HRESULT Item([in] long lIndex, [out, retval] VARIANT* pVal);
};
```

The [restricted] *attribute on the _NewEnum property prevents this property from being directly exposed to clients.*

We won't provide an implementation for these three methods in our component; rather, we'll borrow the implementation from the ICollectionOnSTLImpl<> ATL helper class, and specialize it to our requirements. You'll have to provide ICollectionOnSTLImpl<> with a copy policy on how exactly you'd like the items in your collection to be passed back to the client when it requests a specific item in the collection. Since the WroxBookCollection will only hold the titles of the books, you just have to define a policy to ensure that the strings that represent these titles are copied into the VARIANT parameter passed through the copy() method.

We'll provide this copy policy through a class called DeepCopyBooks:

```
// Class that provides a policy on how the items in the collection get copied
class DeepCopyBooks
{
public:
    static HRESULT copy(VARIANT* pVarDest, BSTR* pbstrBookTitle)
    {
        // Assign to a CComVariant
        CComVariant varBookTitle(*pbstrBookTitle);

        // Copy the book title to the VARIANT
        return varBookTitle.Detach(pVarDest);
    }

    static void init(VARIANT* pVar)
    {
        ::VariantInit(pVar);
    }

    static void destroy(VARIANT* pVar)
    {
        ::VariantClear(pVar);
    }
};

// Define an STL vector to hold the collection of books
typedef vector<CComBSTR> WROXBOOKS_COLLECTION_VECTOR;

// Define a COM enumerator based on the vector
typedef CComEnumOnSTL<IEnumVARIANT, &IID_IEnumVARIANT, VARIANT,
    DeepCopyBooks, WROXBOOKS_COLLECTION_VECTOR> VarEnum;

// Collection class helper for STL based containers
typedef ICollectionOnSTLImpl<IWroxBookCollection, WROXBOOKS_COLLECTION_VECTOR,
    VARIANT, DeepCopyBooks, VarEnum> IWroxBookCollectionImpl;
```

All that remains to be done is to make the CWroxBookCollection class derive from the specialization of the ICollectionOnSTLImpl template class, which we've typedef'd as IWroxBookCollectionImpl:

```
class ATL_NO_VTABLE CWroxBookCollection :
    public CComObjectRootEx<CComSingleThreadModel>,
    public CComCoClass<CWroxBookCollection, &CLSID_WroxBookCollection>,
    public ISupportErrorInfo,
    public IDispatchImpl<IWroxBookCollectionImpl, &IID_IWroxBookCollection>
{
    HRESULT FinalConstruct();

    // Rest of the boilerplate code goes in here. Omitted for brevity.
}
```

Finally, we'll add some of our favorite Wrox books into the book collection. The m_coll member of ICollectionOnSTLImpl represents the container for the collection, which in our case is an instance of an STL vector containing CComBSTR strings (typedef'd as WROXBOOKS_COLLECTION_VECTOR):

```
HRESULT CWroxBookCollection::FinalConstruct()
{
    // Add some books to the collection
    m_coll.push_back(CComBSTR(_T("Professional C# programming")));
    m_coll.push_back(CComBSTR(_T("Professional Visual C++ .NET")));
    m_coll.push_back(CComBSTR(_T("Professional C# Web Services")));
    m_coll.push_back(CComBSTR(_T("Professional ASP.NET")));
    return S_OK;
}
```

We're finally done creating the WroxBookCollection COM component. Let's see how we can consume it from a Managed C++ application.

Using a Managed C++ application to consume a COM-based collection

After creating an assembly called WroxBookCollectionMetadata.dll using the type library importer, this is what you'll see in ILDasm:

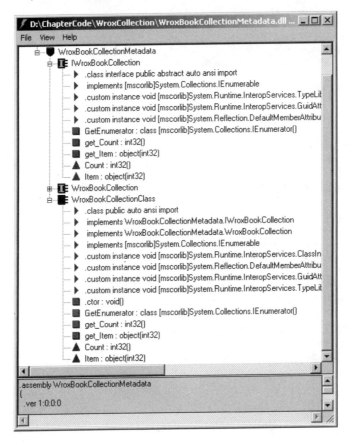

What do we have this time? Well, for a start, the IWroxBookCollection interface has been imported as a managed interface with the same name. The interface's collection-specific properties have also been imported; you'll notice that two of the three – Count and Item – have been preserved with no noticeable transformations (except for the substitution of unmanaged data types for their managed counterparts), while _NewEnum has been replaced with a method called GetEnumerator(), which returns a System::Collections::IEnumerator interface that represents an enumerator for the collection. IWroxBookCollection also implements the System::Collections::IEnumerable interface, which indicates that it allows clients to enumerate through its underlying collection.

> *IEnumerable and IEnumerator are the primary enablers for enumerating through collections in .NET. A client wanting to know whether an object supports enumeration can do so by checking whether the object supports IEnumerable. Once it gets hold of the IEnumerable interface, it can use the IEnumerable::GetEnumerator() method to obtain an enumerator that allows for iteration through the collection.*

As usual, the coclass for the WroxBookCollection component has been imported as two managed classes. First, we have an abstract class named WroxBookCollection that inherits from the default IWroxBookCollection interface. Second, there's a concrete class named WroxBookCollectionClass that implements the WroxBookCollection abstract class and provides the implementation for its methods. To create the WroxBookCollection COM component, you'll need to create an instance of the WroxBookCollectionClass class. All its methods internally call into the RCW, which in turn calls into the COM collection component.

The GetEnumerator() method of the WroxBookCollectionClass interacts with the RCW to expose the IEnumVARIANT-based COM collection as a .NET collection based on the IEnumerator interface. To get this mapping to work, it uses the System::Runtime::InteropServices:: CustomMarshalers::EnumeratorToEnumVariantMarshaler class.

To begin using our COM object, the first step is to create a new Managed C++ application called TechieBookWorm. Once you've referenced the assembly containing the metadata wrappers, you can start playing around with the collection. For starters, let's get the number of books by using the Count property of WroxBookCollectionClass:

```
WroxBookCollectionClass* pColl = new WroxBookCollectionClass;

void nNumberOfBooks = pColl->Count;
Console::WriteLine(S"Number of books: {0}", nNumberOfBooks.ToString());
```

To get an object at a specified position in the collection, you have to use the Item property, as shown below:

```
Console::WriteLine(S"The second book is: {0}", pColl->Item[2]);
```

Note that the index is *one-based*, rather than the zero-based indexes that we're used to. pColl->Item[1] gets the very first element in the collection.

We can get hold of the collection's enumerator using the GetEnumerator() method, as shown below:

```
IEnumerator* pEnum = pColl->GetEnumerator();
```

The enumerator initially positions itself *before* the first element in the collection, so you'll have to call MoveNext() before you can actually access it. Thereafter, you can call the MoveNext() method repeatedly until you hit the end of the collection, when it will return a Boolean false value. As you step through the collection, you can use the Current property to get the element being pointed to; the Current property returns a System::Object pointer that you can cast back to the underlying String pointer using dynamic_cast or __try_cast:

```
while(pEnum->MoveNext())
{
    Object* pObjBookTitle = pEnum->Current;
    String* pstrTitle = dynamic_cast<String*>(pObjBookTitle);
    Console::WriteLine(pstrTitle);
}
```

The complete source code for the Managed C++ TechieBookWorm sample is contained in the folder of the same name, in the source code for this book.

Using ActiveX controls from .NET applications

In this section, we'll see how easy it is to host an ActiveX control in a Windows Forms application. Rather than developing one of these heavyweights from scratch, for demonstration purposes we'll reuse one of the ActiveX controls that will be lying around on your machine: the Windows Media Player control. Provided that you have WMP installed, this can be found at *Windows Folder*\System32\msdxm.ocx.

At the time of writing, there is no direct support in the Visual Studio .NET IDE for generating Windows Forms-based applications using Managed C++. The assumption is that on the whole, developers will use C# or Visual Basic .NET for their Windows Forms development. That being the case, we'll use a C# based Windows Forms application to host the WMP ActiveX control. Let's start by creating a new Visual C# **Windows Application** named MyMediaPlayer:

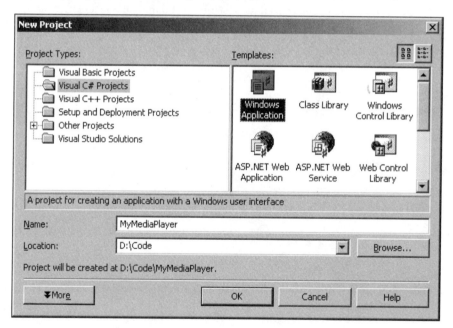

Next, use the Tools | Customize Toolbox... menu item to bring up the Customize Toolbox dialog. If the WMP ActiveX control is registered on your machine, it should appear in the list of controls under the COM Components tab. Check the Windows Media Player item in the list of controls, and then click OK:

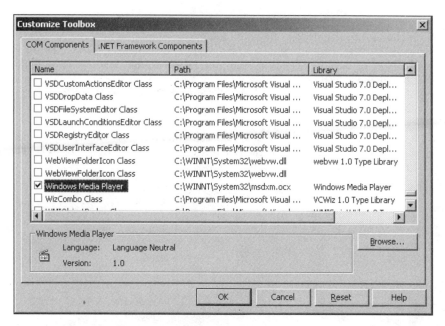

Now you can select the control from the toolbox and drag it over to the Windows Forms designer:

When you do this, Visual Studio .NET takes care of generating the appropriate metadata wrappers from the ActiveX control's type library, and of adding references to these wrapper assemblies in the project. It uses the ActiveX importer tool (aximp.exe) to generate two such wrappers:

❑ AxInterop.MediaPlayer.dll wraps up the ActiveX control to make it look like a .NET Windows Forms control. A Windows Form is only capable of hosting controls that inherit directly or indirectly from System::Windows::Forms::Control. Therefore, the ActiveX importer generates a managed wrapper class (AxMediaPlayer) that derives from System::Windows::Forms::AxHost, which itself derives from System::Windows::Forms::Control. The System::Windows::Forms::AxHost framework class performs the plumbing needed to present the ActiveX control to .NET as if it were a native Windows Forms control.

❑   `Interop.MediaPlayer.dll` contains managed wrapper classes containing managed type information for the properties, methods, and events supported by the WMP ActiveX control. This assembly is functionally similar to the wrapper assemblies generated by the type library importer that we used in the earlier examples. However, the Windows Form does not use this assembly directly – rather, it uses `AxInterop.MediaPlayer.dll`, which in turn uses this assembly to communicate with the ActiveX control's RCW. The RCW is created by the CLR at both design time and runtime, and calls into the ActiveX control to complete the circuit.

Take a look at the diagram below, and you'll see the roles that these two metadata wrapper assemblies play (along with the RCW) to masquerade the ActiveX control as a Windows Forms control when presenting it to the Windows Form:

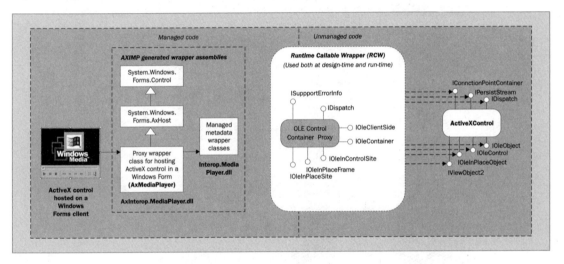

The methods and property accessors/modifiers in the `AxMediaPlayer` wrapper class call their counterparts in the `Interop.MediaPlayer.dll` assembly's `MediaPlayerClass` class, whose implementation routes the call to the RCW. The RCW invokes the corresponding method or gets/sets the value of a property in the ActiveX control. It also takes care of mapping the delegate-based event handling mechanism used by the Windows Form to the connection point event-handling mechanism used by the ActiveX control. The RCW implements all the interfaces that any ActiveX control container should implement, thus duping the ActiveX control into believing that it is indeed sitting on top of an ActiveX control container.

Design-time properties

You can modify design-time properties of the ActiveX control by using the Visual Studio .NET Properties window, which inspects the ActiveX control through the metadata wrapper classes and exposes properties for modification at design time. If you like, you can try changing the value of the control's `ShowControls` property by setting its value to `False`.

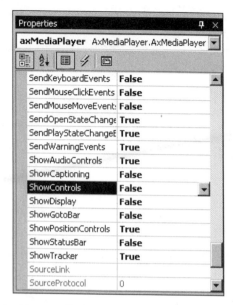

You should see that the ActiveX control's design-time appearance on the Windows Form is immediately updated to hide its media control bar. Furthermore, since the control supports persistence for this property, the changes made at design time will stay on at runtime.

Run-time properties and methods

Next, we'll see how to invoke methods and properties of the control at runtime. Let's add a Play button and a Stop button to the form, which call the WMP control's Play() and Stop() methods respectively. We'll use the control's FileName property to set the media clip that we'd like to play.

Here's the code for the event handler methods for the **Play** and **Stop** buttons' `Click` events:

```
private void buttonPlay_Click(object sender, System.EventArgs e)
{
    try
    {
        // Set the path of the media file that we'd like to play
        axMediaPlayer.FileName = textBoxFileName.Text;

        // Start playing the media
        axMediaPlayer.Play();
    }
    catch(Exception ex)
    {
        MessageBox.Show(ex.Message);
    }
}

private void buttonStop_Click(object sender, System.EventArgs e)
{
    try
    {
        // Stop playing the media
        axMediaPlayer.Stop();

        // Update the message in the status bar
        labelStatus.Text = "Last played media: " + m_strCurrentFile;
    }
    catch(Exception ex)
    {
        MessageBox.Show(ex.Message);
    }
}
```

As you can see, invoking the ActiveX control's methods or properties is fairly straightforward. The classes in the metadata wrapper assembly make it appear as though you're just calling methods or getting/setting properties on a managed class.

Event handling

Finally, let's see how we can receive event notifications from the WMP ActiveX control. We'll register event handlers for the `NewStream` and `EndOfStream` events; the former is raised when the control begins to load the media clip, while the latter is raised when the media clip has reached its end. To view all of the events sourced by the control in Visual Studio .NET, click on the icon that represents a lightning flash in the WMP control's **Properties** window.

Double-clicking on the NewStream event will make the Visual Studio .NET forms designer generate an event handler method called axMediaPlayer_NewStream() (following the naming convention *ControlName_EventName*). Repeat this for the EndStream event, and if you now take a look at the InitializeComponent() method in the form, you'll notice that the delegates that reference the event handler methods have been wired to their respective events.

```
this.axMediaPlayer.NewStream +=
        new System.EventHandler(this.axMediaPlayer_NewStream);

this.axMediaPlayer.EndOfStream +=
        new AxMediaPlayer._MediaPlayerEvents_EndOfStreamEventHandler(
                                    this.axMediaPlayer_EndOfStream);
```

A System::EventHandler delegate that references the axMediaPlayer_NewStream() event handler method is bound to the NewStream event, and a _MediaPlayerEvents_EndOfStreamEventHandler delegate that references the axMediaPlayer_EndOfStream() event handler method is hooked up to the EndOfStream event. When the NewStream event is received, we'll update the status message at the bottom of the form to display the current media clip being played. When the EndOfStream event is received, we'll update the status message to display the last media clip that was played. Take a look at the event handlers for both these events:

```
private void axMediaPlayer_NewStream(object sender, System.EventArgs e)
{
    labelStatus.Text = "Now playing: " + m_strCurrentFile;
}


private void axMediaPlayer_EndOfStream(object sender,
                    AxMediaPlayer._MediaPlayerEvents_EndOfStreamEvent e)
{
    labelStatus.Text = "Last played media: " + m_strCurrentFile;
}
```

We've added very little code by hand, but the ActiveX control is comfortably ensconced in a Windows Form, and behaves as if it's a managed Windows Forms control. The metadata wrapper classes and the RCW substrate handle all the plumbing to preserve the illusion that they are interacting with one of their own ilk. Companies can preserve their existing ActiveX controls by hosting them in .NET containers such as Windows Forms, while they plan a migration strategy to the more powerful cousins of ActiveX controls: .NET Windows Forms controls.

Reuse models for COM components from managed code

One of the primary goals of component software is the ability to reuse existing software components from within applications or from other components. In the COM world, one component can reuse the services of another through **containment** or **aggregation**.

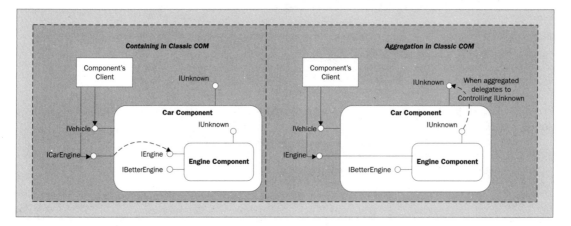

In the diagram above, the Car component reuses the Engine component's implementation using the 'containment' reuse model. In this model, the outer component (Car) does not expose the inner component's (Engine's) interfaces directly to the client. Instead, it just delegates calls to its contained instance of the Engine component.

In the 'aggregation' reuse model, the Car component exposes one or more interfaces of the Engine component directly to its client. The client can talk directly to the inner component. When it's aggregated, the inner component (Engine) delegates the reference counting and interface querying semantics to the outer component (Car).

You can reuse COM components from managed .NET components through inheritance or containment, but not through aggregation. In this section, we'll run through an example that illustrates both scenarios. We'll create two COM components, Vehicle and Engine. Then, we'll create a Managed C++ component called Car that reuses the Vehicle and Engine COM components through implementation inheritance and containment respectively:

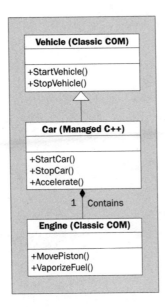

Using the Visual C++ 6.0 **ATL COM AppWizard**, create a new project called `Automotive` by choosing the default project options, and add two new COM objects called `Vehicle` and `Engine` to the project. The `Vehicle` COM component will expose two methods through its `IVehicle` interface: `StartVehicle()` and `StopVehicle()`:

```
[id(1), helpstring("method StartVehicle")]
HRESULT StartVehicle([out,retval] BSTR* pbstrStatus);
```

```
[id(2), helpstring("method StopVehicle")]
HRESULT StopVehicle([out,retval] BSTR* pbstrStatus);
```

```
STDMETHODIMP CVehicle::StartVehicle(BSTR* pbstrStatus)
{
    if(NULL == pbstrStatus) return E_POINTER;

    CComBSTR bstrStartMsg(_T("From Classic COM: Vehicle Start"));
    *pbstrStatus = bstrStartMsg.Detach();
    return S_OK;
}

STDMETHODIMP CVehicle::StopVehicle(BSTR* pbstrStatus)
{
    if(NULL == pbstrStatus) return E_POINTER;

    CComBSTR bstrStopMsg(_T("From Classic COM: Vehicle Stop"));
    *pbstrStatus = bstrStopMsg.Detach();
    return S_OK;
}
```

The `Engine` COM component exposes two methods through its `IEngine` interface: `MovePiston()` and `VaporizeFuel()`:

```
    [id(1), helpstring("method MovePiston")]
    HRESULT MovePiston([out,retval] BSTR* pbstrStatus);

    [id(2), helpstring("method VaporizeFuel")]
    HRESULT VaporizeFuel([out,retval] BSTR* pbstrStatus);
```

```
    STDMETHODIMP CEngine::MovePiston(BSTR* pbstrStatus)
    {
        if(NULL == pbstrStatus) return E_POINTER;

        CComBSTR bstrMovePistonMsg(_T("From Classic COM: Move Piston"));
        *pbstrStatus = bstrMovePistonMsg.Detach();
        return S_OK;
    }

    STDMETHODIMP CEngine::VaporizeFuel(BSTR* pbstrStatus)
    {
        if(NULL == pbstrStatus) return E_POINTER;

        CComBSTR bstrVaporizeMsg(_T("From Classic COM: Vaporize Fuel"));
        *pbstrStatus = bstrVaporizeMsg.Detach();
        return S_OK;
    }
```

Once again, we'll use the type library importer to generate a metadata wrapper assembly (called AutomotiveMetadata.dll) from the components' type library. Then, we'll start the process of putting together a Managed C++ application called ReuseManagedClient that will serve as our test bed for examining both reuse models.

The Managed C++ Car component inherits from the metadata wrapper class for the Vehicle COM component using the ubiquitous C++ inheritance syntax. For containment of the Engine component, the Car component caches a pointer to the Engine component's metadata wrapper class and then creates a new instance of the Engine component, either in its constructor or before the component's first use (lazy loading).

```
    __gc class Car : public VehicleClass
    {
    private:
        EngineClass* m_pEngine;
    public:
        Car()
        {
            m_pEngine = new EngineClass;
        }

        // Rest of the code goes in here
    };
```

Let's add a new method to the Car class to see how it could reuse the code available in the Engine and Vehicle COM components:

```
   void StartCar()
   {
      Console::WriteLine(StartVehicle());
      Console::WriteLine(m_pEngine->MovePiston());
      Console::WriteLine(m_pEngine->VaporizeFuel());
      Console::WriteLine(S"Managed C++: Started Car");
   }
```

The StartCar() method calls the StartVehicle() method, which results in calling the corresponding method implementation in the Vehicle COM component from which the Car class derives. After that, the Car object uses its contained instance of the Engine COM component's metadata wrapper to invoke that component's MovePiston() and VaporizeFuel() methods. The metadata wrappers and the RCW drive the managed-to-unmanaged transitions whenever a COM method invocation is required, allowing managed code to reuse classic COM code using inheritance and containment just as if it was reusing other Managed C++ classes.

> *If you haven't done so already, this would be a good point at which to open up the complete source code for the Automotive and ReuseManagedClient projects.*

Next, let's take a look at how we can override the Vehicle COM component's StartVehicle() and StopVehicle() methods in our Managed C++ Car class:

```
   __gc class Car : public VehicleClass
   {

   // The rest of the Car class's implementation goes here

   public:
      // Overrides base class COM implementation VehicleClass::StartVehicle
      String* StartVehicle()
      {
         // Explicitly call the implementation in the Vehicle COM component
         Console::WriteLine(VehicleClass::StartVehicle());
         return S"[Overridden] Managed C++: Vehicle Start";
      }

      // Overrides base class COM implementation VehicleClass::StopVehicle
      String* StopVehicle()
      {
         return S"[Overridden] Managed C++: Vehicle Stop";
      }
   };
```

With these two methods added to the Car class, any calls to StartVehicle() and StopVehicle() result in the invocation of the methods in the Managed C++ Car object, rather than those in the Vehicle COM component. The C++ scope resolution operator can be used on the VehicleClass metadata wrapper to call the Vehicle COM component's implementation explicitly, whenever required. The overridden implementation in Car can also provide additional implementation or processing before or after calling the base class's implementation.

Clearly, this is just the kind of behavior you'd expect, and you may be wondering why we're dwelling on this subject. The thing is, there's rather an important caveat: When overriding methods from a base class whose implementation is provided by a classic COM component, you *cannot* do so selectively. In other words, if you decide to override one method, you *must* override them all. Failure to do this won't result in compile-time errors, but you'll get a System::TypeLoadException exception at runtime.

You can test this by temporarily commenting out the StopVehicle() overridden method in the Car class and retaining only the overridden implementation for the StartVehicle() method. Make an attempt to run the application now, and you'll get this error:

```
System.TypeLoadException: Types extending from COM objects should override all
methods of an interface implemented by the base COM class.
```

Managed C++ applications can use ordinary C++ inheritance and containment syntax to reuse the code that's available in COM components. They can also use managed code wherever required in order to add more functionality and to use the features offered by the .NET Framework class library. Thus, in terms of code reuse, managed components can get the best of both the managed and unmanaged worlds.

Managed threads and COM apartments

In the COM world, an unmanaged thread calling into a COM component can enter either a single-threaded apartment (STA) or a multi-threaded apartment (MTA). A COM client in the unmanaged world uses one of the following calls to indicate to COM that its thread is entering an STA:

```
::CoInitialize(NULL);
::CoInitializeEx(0, COINIT_APARTMENTTHREADED);
```

Similarly, a COM client uses the following call to indicate that its thread is entering an MTA:

```
::CoInitializeEx(0, COINIT_MULTITHREADED);
```

The threads in managed applications can also declare their apartment preferences before calling into COM components. By default, a managed thread chooses to live in an MTA. However, you can use the System::Threading::Thread class's ApartmentState property to specify the type of COM apartment that you want the managed thread to enter. Here are the possible values for the ApartmentState enumeration:

ApartmentState value	Description
STA	Thread enters an STA.
MTA	Thread enters an MTA.
Unknown	ApartmentState has not been set. Default behavior is to enter an MTA.

Here's a trivial Managed C++ application that demonstrates how to set the ApartmentState property for a managed thread:

```
#using <mscorlib.dll>

using namespace System;
using namespace System::Threading;

int _tmain(void)
{
    // Get a pointer to the current thread
    Thread* pThread = Thread::CurrentThread;

    // Get the current apartment state
    ApartmentState enumState = pThread->ApartmentState;
    Object* pObject = __box(enumState);
    Console::WriteLine(S"Default apartment state: {0}", pObject->ToString());

    // Set the apartment state to STA
    pThread->ApartmentState = ApartmentState::STA;

    // Get the new apartment state
    enumState = pThread->ApartmentState;
    pObject = __box(enumState);
    Console::WriteLine(S"Current apartment state: {0}", pObject->ToString());

    // Create your COM components here...

    return 0;
}
```

For the ApartmentState property to take effect, you have to make sure that you set it *before* the managed thread creates the COM component. Taking advantage of this feature can be helpful when you want to do away with the additional proxy-stub baggage that's incurred in calls between two incompatible apartments.

Another way of forcing an application's primary thread to enter an STA is to tag its entry point with the STAThread attribute:

```
[STAThread]
int _tmain(void)
{
    // Thread has entered an STA
    // Create your COM components here...
    return 0;
}
```

However, there's a caveat here: you can use this attribute only if your application doesn't use the C runtime library (CRT). If you use the CRT, the attribute will be injected into the actual entry point of your application, which is inside the CRT – the attribute will therefore have no effect on your managed application's primary thread.

For more information on managing threads in .NET applications, see Chapter 5.

Using Managed C++ components from COM-aware C++

In the first half of this chapter, we looked at exposing COM components to Managed C++ applications. In this section, we'll turn things the other way around, and see how unmanaged, COM-aware clients can consume Managed C++ components.

Unmanaged COM clients cannot consume a managed component directly. You'll need to provide them with COM-specific type information such as they'd normally retrieve from a COM type library. You'll also need to publish binding details (such as the component's CLSID, ProgID, etc.) that will facilitate the unmanaged COM client binding to the managed component. The trouble is, a managed component is completely COM-agnostic, and isn't associated with any kind of COM-specific type or binding information. How then can an unmanaged COM-aware client consume a managed component?

Clearly, we're going to have to export our managed component's type information to a COM type library. In order for the COM runtime to locate this information, we'll also have to make sure that all the binding information goes into the registry. Thankfully, the .NET Framework provides two tools – the **type library exporter** (tlbexp.exe) and the **assembly registration utility** (regasm.exe) – to generate a COM type library from a managed component's type information and attributes. regasm.exe also adds entries to the registry so that the COM runtime can bind to the component.

We'll be discussing both of these tools in more detail later on; in the meantime, take a look at the diagram below to see how an unmanaged, COM-aware application interacts with a managed component:

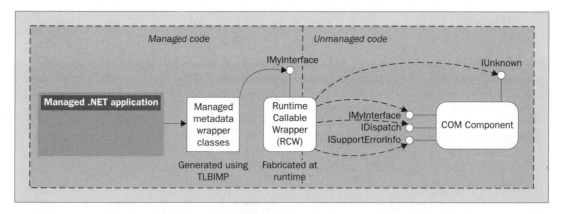

The unmanaged COM application can use the tlbexp/regasm-generated type library to create the managed component in the same way as it would go about creating a COM component. The registry entries direct the COM runtime to load mscoree.dll (the .NET CLR), which uses further information in the registry entries to load the assembly that hosts the managed component. The CLR also fabricates a **COM callable wrapper** (**CCW**) that embodies a COM proxy to the managed component – it presents the .NET component to the unmanaged client as if it were an ordinary COM component. There is one CCW created for each instance of the managed component that gets created.

The managed component lives by the rules of the CLR and is garbage-collected by the .NET runtime. All COM-based semantics that the unmanaged client uses (reference counting, querying for supported interfaces, late-bound calls using IDispatch, and so on) are serviced by the CCW. It also takes care of marshaling data between the unmanaged and managed memory. The CCW's lifetime is controlled by the unmanaged client, and it dies when its reference count drops down to zero, which happens when the client releases the last reference to it. At this point, the CCW also releases its hold on the managed component, leaving the .NET garbage collector to clean up.

In our journey through the rest of this chapter, we'll see how easy it is to consume Managed C++ components from unmanaged COM clients. We'll also examine how events sourced from a Managed C++ component using delegates can be consumed by an unmanaged C++ application using connection points. Finally, we'll discuss how attributes can be used to control the way a Managed C++ class or interface gets exposed to COM.

Building a .NET component using Managed C++

Let's get the ball rolling by creating a Managed C++ component that mimics a couple of the functions performed by the dashboard panel in a car. Create a new Managed C++ class library project called Dashboard; we'll begin by defining an interface called IDashboard that contains all the methods and properties that we want to expose from the Dashboard component. Our managed component's class will implement this interface:

```
namespace Dashboard
{
    public __gc __interface IDashboard
    {
        __property float get_Speed();
        __property void set_Speed(float value);

        __property float get_GallonsConsumed();
        __property void set_GallonsConsumed(float value);

        float computeMilesPerGallon(int nMiles);
    };
}
```

Although you could add the methods and properties directly to the component's class (without explicitly inheriting them from an interface) and still expose them to unmanaged COM clients, it's not recommended that you do so. It's a good design decision to factor out all your methods and properties into an interface and then make the managed class implement this interface. We'll see why later, in the section called *Controlling how a managed C++ class gets exported to a COM type library*.

As shown above, the IDashboard managed interface exposes two properties – Speed and GallonsConsumed – and a method named computeMilesPerGallon(). Let's define our managed component's class, which we'll call Dashboard, and make it implement the IDashboard interface:

```
[ClassInterface(ClassInterfaceType::None)]
public __gc class Dashboard : public IDashboard
{
```

319

```
    private:
        float m_sCurrentSpeed;
        float m_sGallonsConsumed;
        bool m_bFuelTankEmpty;

    public:
        Dashboard() : m_sCurrentSpeed(20),
                      m_sGallonsConsumed(2),
                      m_bFuelTankEmpty(false)
        {
        }

        // Rest of the methods and properties go here...
    };
```

The first thing you'll notice is that we've tagged the Dashboard class with the
System::Runtime::InteropServices::ClassInterface attribute, which you can use to provide
information to the tlbexp and regasm utilities on how you'd like the managed component's class to be
exposed to COM. The attribute affects how the coclass section in the IDL will be defined when the
managed class is exported to a COM type library. We'll take a detailed look at the various values that
you can use for the ClassInterface attribute, and compare the effects of each of them on the
generated type library, later on. For now, make sure that you pass a value of
ClassInterfaceType::None for the attribute's parameter.

Besides making the class public, you also need to make sure that your class has a default public
constructor. This is mandatory if your class needs to be cocreateable from COM.

Let's go ahead and implement the methods and properties inherited from the IDashboard interface in the
Dashboard class. We'll begin by adding the implementations for the Speed property's get/set methods:

```
__property float get_Speed()
{
    return m_sCurrentSpeed;
}

__property void set_Speed(float value)
{
    if(value < 0.0)
    {
        throw new DashboardException(S"Speed cannot be set to a negative value.");
    }
    if(value > 150.0)
    {
        throw new DashboardException(S"Oops! Your engine has gone kaput.");
    }
    if(m_bFuelTankEmpty)
    {
        throw new DashboardException(S"Your fuel tank is empty.");
    }

    m_sCurrentSpeed = value;

    // Check whether we have exceeded the speed limit
    checkSpeed();
```

```
    }

private:
    void checkSpeed()
    {
        if(m_sCurrentSpeed > 75.0)
        {
            // Notify the driver that the current speed is unsafe
            // More on this later, when we see how to raise events
        }
    }
```

The get_Speed() accessor method for the Speed property returns the current speed, which is buried away in the m_sCurrentSpeed member. The set_Speed() mutator method for the Speed property checks to see whether the input value provided is valid – if it is, it sets the m_sCurrentSpeed member with the value passed to the method. If the value of the Speed property provided is either negative or exceedingly high, it raises an exception using the System::ApplicationException class.

```
// Define an application-specific exception for the Dashboard component
public __gc class DashboardException : public ApplicationException
{
public:
    DashboardException(String* pstrExceptionMsg) :
                                    ApplicationException(pstrExceptionMsg)
    {
    }
};
```

The DashboardException class, which we inherit from System::ApplicationException, is used to raise application-specific exceptions that result from failed validations or business logic. You can throw a DashboardException exception with a description of the error message; the error code associated with such an application-defined exception is COR_E_APPLICATION (0x80131600).

Next, we'll put together the implementation for the get/set methods of the GallonsConsumed property.

```
__property float get_GallonsConsumed()
{
    return m_sGallonsConsumed;
}

__property void set_GallonsConsumed(float value)
{
    // Perform some validation checks here. Omitted for brevity...

    m_sGallonsConsumed = value;

    // Check if the vehicle has enough fuel
    checkLowFuel();
}
```

```
private:
   void checkLowFuel()
   {
      // Assuming the capacity of our fuel tank is 20 gallons,
      // warn the driver whenever we have 3 gallons or less remaining
      if(m_sGallonsConsumed >= 17.0)
      {
         // Notify the driver that we're running low on fuel
         // More on this later, when we see how to raise events
      }
   }
```

The get_GallonsConsumed() and set_GallonsConsumed() methods allow you to access and modify the value of the GallonsConsumed property respectively. The checkSpeed() and checkLowFuel() methods (which are private to the class) verify that the values of the Speed and GallonsConsumed properties are within permissible limits – if they're not, events are raised. We'll see how to send event notifications from the Dashboard component in the next section.

Finally, the implementation of the computeMilesPerGallon() method returns the fuel efficiency of the vehicle by computing the vehicle's mileage per gallon of fuel, as shown below:

```
float computeMilesPerGallon(int nMiles)
{
   // Perform some validation checks here. Omitted for brevity...
   return static_cast<float>(nMiles)/m_sGallonsConsumed;
}
```

At this point, we can stop adding functionality to the Dashboard component – we've got sufficient code to expose it to an unmanaged, COM-aware client application and see how it all works together. Just for a change, though, we're going to add this component to the GAC, so before you hit the Build button, go the command line and create a new key:

```
> sn -k keypair.snk
```

Then, head to the AssemblyInfo.cpp file, and make a change to the AssemblyKeyFile attribute:

```
[assembly:AssemblyKeyFileAttribute("keypair.snk")];
```

Finally, build the project to obtain the Dashboard.dll assembly, and issue the following command to place it in the GAC:

```
> gacutil -i Dashboard.dll
```

Exposing .NET components to unmanaged applications

As described earlier, to consume a managed component from an unmanaged, COM-aware application, the first thing that you need to do is export the assembly hosting the managed component into a COM type library, which an unmanaged, COM-aware client can comprehend.

The type library exporter and the assembly registration utility

The .NET Framework provides us with two utilities to generate a type library from a managed assembly:

❑   The **type library exporter** (tlbexp.exe), which generates a COM type library from a managed assembly. The generated type library contains COM-specific type information for the managed types in the assembly.

❑   The **assembly registration utility** (regasm.exe), which can generate a COM type library from a managed assembly *and* register the requisite managed types in the assembly by making the appropriate COM-specific registry entries.

You could generate a type library from the Dashboard.dll managed assembly by using the following command:

```
> tlbexp Dashboard.dll /out:Dashboard.tlb
```

However, it's much easier to use the assembly registration utility, since we can get both type library generation and COM registration done in one go. Enter the following at the command line:

```
> regasm Dashboard.dll /tlb:Dashboard.tlb
```

The command issued above does the following:

❑   Generates a type library named Dashboard.tlb containing COM-specific type information for the public managed types in Dashboard.dll.

❑   Registers the public managed types (such as classes and interfaces) in Dashboard.dll with COM by making the appropriate registry entries.

Let's take a look at the registry entries made by regasm in order to expose the managed component to COM. Open the Dashboard.tlb type library in the OLE/COM object viewer (oleview.exe), and make a note of the CLSID of the component by looking up the value of the uuid attribute in the coclass definition:

```
[
    uuid(F43C95A7-E455-3911-87C1-5E0BDC121F22),
    version(1.0),
    custom({0F21F359-AB84-41E8-9A78-36D110E6D2F9},
    "DashboardNS.Dashboard")
]
coclass Dashboard {
    interface _Object;
    [default] interface IDashboard;
};
```

Once you've obtained the component's CLSID, look it up in the registry – it'll be under the CLSID key in the HKEY_CLASSES_ROOT hive.

> *Note that a different CLSID will be generated for the component every time you run it through the type library exporter or the assembly registration utility. You'll find out how to force a specific GUID to be associated with your component's CLSID in a later section.*

The component category that the component supports, as advertised through its Implemented
Categories *key, is a category named* .NET Category. *You can look this up by navigating to
the* HKEY_CLASSES_ROOT\Component Categories\
{62C8FE65-4EBB-45e7-B440-6E39B2CDBF29} key.

Click on the InProcServer32 key under the component's CLSID to display some of the additional
entries that regasm has made in addition to the standard entries that typical COM servers would make
in the registry. You'll notice at once that Assembly, Class, and RuntimeVersion are not entries
made by typical COM servers. These entries are used to provide the additional information about the
managed assembly and the managed component's type name to mscoree.dll.

Name	Type	Data
(Default)	REG_SZ	C:\WINNT\System32\mscoree.dll
Assembly	REG_SZ	Dashboard, Version=1.0.765.29658, Culture=neutral, PublicKeyToken=null
Class	REG_SZ	Dashboard.Dashboard
RuntimeVersion	REG_SZ	v1.0.3705
ThreadingModel	REG_SZ	Both

When exposed to COM, managed components declare their threading model as 'both', as indicated by
the ThreadingModel entry. In COM, a 'both'-threaded component always moves into the caller's
apartment. In the truest sense, managed components are analogous to 'both'-threaded COM
components that aggregate the free-threaded marshaler.

*When a 'both'-threaded COM component aggregates the free-threaded marshaler, its interface
pointer can be passed over to other apartments in the same process without any explicit inter-
apartment marshaling. The receiving apartment gets a direct interface pointer to the component,
without any proxy indirection.*

For all managed components that are exposed to COM, the (Default) entry under InProcServer32
is set to the path of mscoree.dll. The COM runtime loads mscoree.dll and calls
DllGetClassObject() to get the class factory of the COM object. mscoree.dll then uses the
Assembly and Class keys in the registry to load the assembly and create the managed component. At
this point, it also fabricates the COM callable wrapper (CCW), which acts like a COM proxy to the
managed component. Finally, mscoree.dll returns the IClassFactory pointer of the CCW to the
COM runtime, and then bails out. From then on, the unmanaged client interacts directly with the CCW,
which in turn calls into the managed component.

Consuming a Managed C++ component

Let's create a Visual C++ 6.0 MFC dialog-based application to consume the Dashboard component.
Once generated, the first thing you need to do is to import the types in the COM type library using the
#import compiler directive. Since the Dashboard.tlb type library contains references to some of the
.NET-specific types, you also need to import the mscorlib.tlb type library, which is provided with
the Framework and contains the relevant type information for the core CLR types.

```
#import "mscorlib.tlb"
#import "Dashboard.tlb" rename_namespace("DashboardNS")
using namespace DashboardNS;
```

You might need to add the folder path for `mscorlib.tlb` *to your list of include directories. In our installation, it's housed in* `Windows Folder\Microsoft.NET\ Framework\v1.0.3705`.

Add an instance of the smart pointer wrapper for the `IDashboard` interface as a `private` member of the dialog's class. These smart pointer wrappers are generated by the `#import` directive:

```
class CDashboardClientDlg : public CDialog
{
    // MFC Dialog macros and message maps omitted for brevity

    private:
        IDashboardPtr m_spDashboard;
};
```

Make sure that you initialize COM by calling `AfxOleInit()` or `CoInitialize(NULL)` in your application's `InitInstance()` method:

```
BOOL CDashboardClientApp::InitInstance()
{
    AfxOleInit();

    // MFC Wizard generated initialization code omitted for brevity
}
```

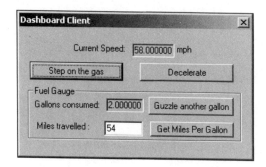

Next, add some buttons and text controls to your dialog (as shown above) so that we can interact with the `Dashboard` component. Create an instance of the `Dashboard` component in your dialog class's `OnInitDialog()` member function, and get the current values of the `Speed` and `GallonsConsumed` properties. We'll update the static text controls in the dialog with the current values of these two properties.

```
BOOL CDashboardClientDlg::OnInitDialog()
{
    CDialog::OnInitDialog();
```

```
// Dialog initialization code omitted for brevity

// Create an instance of the Dashboard component
HRESULT hr = m_spDashboard.CreateInstance(__uuidof(Dashboard));

// Did the creation succeed?
if(SUCCEEDED(hr))
{
    // Get the current speed and the fuel consumed
    float fSpeed = m_spDashboard->Speed;
    float fGallonsConsumed = m_spDashboard->GallonsConsumed;

    // Display the speed and the fuel consumed
    m_strSpeed.Format(_T("%f"),fSpeed);
    m_strGallonsConsumed.Format(_T("%f"),fGallonsConsumed);
    UpdateData(FALSE);
}
return TRUE;
}
```

The **Step on the gas** button increments the Speed property by 5 mph, while the **Decelerate** button decrements the Speed property by 5 mph. Here's the code for the ON_BN_CLICKED handler method for the former:

```
void CDashboardClientDlg::OnAccelerate()
{
    try
    {
        if(m_spDashboard != NULL)
        {
            // Step on the gas by 5 mph
            m_spDashboard->Speed = m_spDashboard->Speed + 5;

            // Display the speed in the dialog
            m_strSpeed.Format(_T("%f."),m_spDashboard->Speed);
            UpdateData(FALSE);
        }
    }
    catch(_com_error& e)
    {
        AfxMessageBox(e.Description());
    }
}
```

Keep clicking on the **Step on the gas** button to increment the Speed property. When you attempt to cross the 150 mph barrier, the Dashboard component throws back a DashboardException from its set_Speed() method. This is converted by the CCW into a failure HRESULT, which is then returned back to the COM client. The CCW creates an error information object that exposes rich error information to the COM client through its IErrorInfo interface.

The ON_BN_CLICKED handler for the **Guzzle another gallon** button increments the GallonsConsumed property by one gallon, as shown below:

```
void CDashboardClientDlg::OnGuzzleAnotherGallon()
{
    try
    {
        if(m_spDashboard != NULL)
        {
            // Make the Vehicle consume another gallon of fuel
            m_spDashboard->GallonsConsumed += 1;

            // Display the total number of gallons consumed
            m_strGallonsConsumed.Format(_T("%f"),m_spDashboard->GallonsConsumed);
            UpdateData(FALSE);
        }
    }
    catch(_com_error& e)
    {
        AfxMessageBox(e.Description());
    }
}
```

You can see how the GallonsConsumed property gets updated by clicking on the **Guzzle another gallon** button. Make an attempt to increase this property's value above 20 gallons, and you'll again get a DashboardException thrown from the Dashboard component, this time indicating that the vehicle's fuel tank is empty.

The ON_BN_CLICKED handler for the **Get Miles Per Gallon** button returns the fuel efficiency of the vehicle.

```
void CDashboardClientDlg::OnGetMilesPerGallon()
{
    try
    {
        if(m_spDashboard != NULL)
        {
            // Get the number of miles traveled
            UpdateData(TRUE);
            long lMilesTraveled = atoi((LPCTSTR)m_strMilesTraveled);

            // Calculate the car's fuel efficiency
            float fMilesPerGallon =
                        m_spDashboard->computeMilesPerGallon(lMilesTraveled);
```

```
CString strMilesPerGallon;
        strMilesPerGallon.Format(_T("Fuel efficiency is %f miles/gallon"),
                                                        fMilesPerGallon);


        AfxMessageBox(strMilesPerGallon);
    }
}
catch(_com_error& e)
{
    AfxMessageBox(e.Description());
}
}
```

It's extremely easy to consume managed components in unmanaged, COM-aware clients. All you need to do is generate a COM type library from the managed assembly, and then register the managed assembly using regasm. Once this is done, the unmanaged client uses the type library to create and invoke methods on the managed component as if it were a COM component. The CCW provides all the functionality that's required to entwine these two worlds together.

Sinking the events fired by a Managed C++ component

In this section, we'll return to our Managed C++ Dashboard component and get it to source some events. With that done, we'll take a look at how these events can be consumed by an unmanaged application.

The two events that we'll fire from the Dashboard component are OnSafeSpeedLimitExceeded, which will be raised when the speed overshoots the permissible speed limit of 75 mph, and OnLowFuelWarning, which will be raised when 3 gallons or less remain in the vehicle's 20-gallon fuel tank.

Adding events to the managed component

Let's start by defining an interface called IDashboardEvents that will represent the outgoing interface. To this, we'll add the methods that represent the OnSafeSpeedLimitExceeded and OnLowFuelWarning events to the outgoing interface. We'll make the IDashboardEvents interface a dispinterface, so that it can reach out to the broadest spectrum of clients. To do this, you'll have to tag it with the InterfaceType attribute, with a parameter set to ComInterfaceType::InterfaceIsIDispatch; note that this definition should be placed outside the Dashboard namespace that was created by Visual C++ .NET.

```
[InterfaceType(ComInterfaceType::InterfaceIsIDispatch)]
public __gc __interface IDashboardEvents
{
    void OnSafeSpeedLimitExceeded(float sCurrentSpeed);
    void OnLowFuelWarning();
};
```

We'll take a look at the other possible values that this attribute can take, and the effect of applying each to an interface, in the section called Controlling how a managed C++ interface gets exported to a COM type library.

For the `IDashboardEvents` managed interface definition shown above, the corresponding interface section in the IDL definition associated with the `tlbexp`/`regasm`-generated type library would look like this when viewed through the OLE/COM object viewer:

```
[
    uuid(2A02102C-FB9E-306F-9FF3-47232B5119D3),
    version(1.0),
    custom({0F21F359-AB84-41E8-9A78-36D110E6D2F9}, "IDashboardEvents")
]
dispinterface IDashboardEvents
{
    properties:
    methods:
        [id(0x60020000)] void OnSafeSpeedLimitExceeded([in] single sCurrentSpeed);
        [id(0x60020001)] void OnLowFuelWarning();
};
```

The next thing that you need to do is to declare a `delegate` for each of the methods in the outgoing interface. The delegates that correspond to the `OnSafeSpeedLimitExceeded()` and `OnLowFuelWarning()` event notification methods should look something like this:

```
__delegate void SpeedLimitDelegate(float sCurrentSpeed);
__delegate void LowFuelWarningDelegate();
```

Once the `delegates` have been declared, you need to declare `events` that represent those delegates as public members of the `Dashboard` component's class:

```
public __gc class Dashboard : public  IDashboard
{
public:
    __event SpeedLimitDelegate* OnSafeSpeedLimitExceeded;
    __event LowFuelWarningDelegate* OnLowFuelWarning;

    // Rest of the class implementation goes here
};
```

Things seem to be rather easy at the moment, so it's time for another of our caveats: *The event that you are declaring must have the same name as the method in the outgoing interface that its `delegate` type represents.* For example, the `event` representing the `SpeedLimitDelegate` delegate needs to have the same name as the method in the outgoing interface that the `SpeedLimitDelegate` represents, which happens to be `OnSafeSpeedLimitExceeded()`.

If you don't use the same name for the event and its corresponding method in the outgoing interface, you'll get a `DISP_E_UNKNOWNNAME` error from `mscorlib.dll` when the event is raised from the managed component. This is because internally, to obtain the DISPID of the method in the outgoing `dispinterface` that's implemented by the sink object (unmanaged code), the CCW proxy uses `IDispatch::GetIDsOfNames()` with the name of the event that's raised.

Finally, to indicate to the `Dashboard` class that `IDashboardEvents` will be its outgoing interface, you'll have to tag it with the `ComSourceInterfaces` attribute. The first parameter to this attribute contains the fully qualified type name of the interface that sources events. This will also provide appropriate metadata information to inform type library generation tools that the component supports an outgoing interface:

```
[
    ComSourceInterfaces(S"IDashboardEvents"),
    ClassInterface(ClassInterfaceType::None)
]
public __gc class Dashboard : public IDashboard
{
    // Rest of the class implementation goes here
}
```

For the above managed class definition, the `coclass` section in the IDL definition for the generated type library would look like this:

```
coclass Dashboard
{
    interface _Object;
    [default] interface IDashboard;
    [default, source] dispinterface IDashboardEvents;
};
```

In the IDL definition for the `tlbexp/regasm`-generated type library, the `IDashboardEvents` interface has been made the `Dashboard` component's default outgoing interface, as indicated by the `[default, source]` attributes.

Firing events from the managed component

Before you fire the event, you need to check whether there are any delegates bound to it, by making sure that the event member is non-null. To fire an event, you need to use the event member and invoke it as if it were a method. This results in invoking the delegates that have been bound to the event, which subsequently fires off the event to the event-handler sinks that have subscribed to notifications:

```
void checkSpeed()
{
    if(m_sCurrentSpeed > 75.0)
    {
        if(OnSafeSpeedLimitExceeded)
        {
            OnSafeSpeedLimitExceeded(m_sCurrentSpeed);
        }
    }
}
```

When the user sets the value of the `Speed` property, we'll call the `checkSpeed()` method to find out whether the speed limit has exceeded 75 mph. If so, we fire the `OnSafeSpeedLimitExceeded` event. Similarly, when the user sets the value of the `GallonsConsumed` property, the `checkLowFuel()` method is called to discover whether we have at least 3 gallons of fuel remaining in the vehicle's 20-gallon fuel tank. If not, we raise the `OnLowFuelWarning` event.

```
void checkLowFuel()
{
    if(m_sGallonsConsumed >= 17.0)
    {
        if(OnLowFuelWarning)
        {
            OnLowFuelWarning();
        }
    }
}
```

Since we've added event notification support to our `Dashboard` component, we'll have to register our updated `Dashboard.dll` component in the GAC. To modify the version number for your assembly, change the value of the `AssemblyVersionAttribute` in the `AssemblyInfo.cpp` file. We'll update the `Build` and `Revision` numbers to 1 in the version information, which is of the format *MajorVersion.MinorVersion.BuildNumber.RevisionNumber*, as shown below:

```
[assembly:AssemblyVersionAttribute("1.0.1.1")];
```

After you build the assembly, register it in the GAC using the same command that we used earlier:

```
> gacutil -i Dashboard.dll
```

Taking a quick peek at the GAC will confirm that both the versions of `Dashboard.dll` now exist side-by-side.

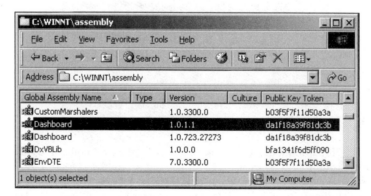

Finally, regenerate the type library containing updated type information from the assembly (since the outgoing interface has been added and the `coclass` definition has been modified), and re-register the types with COM. To do this, issue the following command from the DOS command line:

```
> regasm Dashboard.dll /tlb:Dashboard.tlb
```

Sinking Managed C++ events in an unmanaged C++ application

We'll add some code to our MFC client application so that we can subscribe to event notifications from the Dashboard Managed C++ component – the complete application, reflecting these changes, is to be found in the DashboardClient folder of the downloadable code archive.

First of all, we need to make a small change to the #import directive, which is to add the named_guids option. This is because you need the GUID of the Dashboard component's type library in order to set up the event sink in the client application. The named_guids option forces the compiler to generate GUID values for the type library, classes, and interfaces in the .tlh file.

```
#import "Dashboard.tlb" rename_namespace("DashboardNS") named_guids
```

At this stage, you should rebuild the MFC application so that the #import directive generates the updated wrappers for the new type library.

Next, we'll add a warning indicator panel to our earlier dialog, and throw in some static controls – including a couple of picture controls that will represent red warning lights. We'll make these two 'lights' visible whenever we receive an event notification from the Dashboard component to indicate that the driver has gone over the speed limit or that the vehicle is low on fuel.

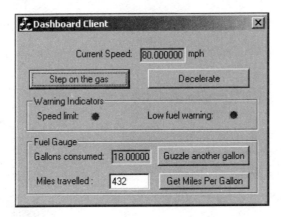

To set up a sink object that implements the IDashboardEvents outgoing interface, add an ATL COM object to the project with the ATL Object Wizard, naming it DashboardSink. ATL support will be added to our MFC project as a result of this action. We'll now have to make the DashboardSink object implement the IDashboardEvents interface, and then wire this event sink as a subscriber to event notifications from the Dashboard component. The steps involved in doing this are summarized below:

1. Derive the CDashboardSink class from an IDispEventImpl<> specialization for the IDashboardEvents dispinterface. The IDispEventImpl<> template class frees us from the hassle of having to provide an implementation for the IDispatch methods in the IDashboardEvents dispinterface:

```
#define IDC_DISPEVENT_ID 1

class ATL_NO_VTABLE CDashboardSink :
    public CComObjectRootEx<CComSingleThreadModel>,
```

```
public CComCoClass<CDashboardSink, &CLSID_DashboardSink>,
public ISupportErrorInfo,
public IDispatchImpl<IDashboardSink, &IID_IDashboardSink,
                     &LIBID_DashboardClientLib>,
public IDispEventImpl<IDC_DISPEVENT_ID, CDashboardSink,
                      &DIID_IDashboardEvents, &LIBID_DashboardNS, 1, 0>
{
    // The rest of the class definition goes here
}
```

2. Set up an event sink map that associates the DISPID of the event with a specific event handler method in the CDashboardSink class. For this, we'll need to know the DISPIDs of the OnSafeSpeedLimitExceeded() and OnLowFuelWarning() methods in the IDashboardEvents interface. If you take a look at the Dashboard.tlb type library through the OLE/COM object viewer, you'll notice that OnSafeSpeedLimitExceeded() and OnLowFuelWarning() have been assigned DISPID values of 0x60020000 and 0x60020001 respectively. The event sink that maps the DISPIDs of the events to their corresponding handler methods in the CDashboardSink class is shown below:

```
BEGIN_SINK_MAP(CDashboardSink)
    SINK_ENTRY_EX(IDC_DISPEVENT_ID, DIID_IDashboardEvents, 0x60020000,
                                                OnSafeSpeedLimitExceeded)
    SINK_ENTRY_EX(IDC_DISPEVENT_ID, DIID_IDashboardEvents, 0x60020001,
                                                OnLowFuelWarning)
END_SINK_MAP()
```

3. Add the event handlers for the OnLowFuelWarning and OnSafeSpeedLimitExceeded events to the CDashboardSink class. We'll use these event handlers to turn on the visibility of the dialog's static controls that display the red warning indicators. We'll have to make sure that the CDashboardSink class initially stashes away the window handles of these static controls, for which purpose we'll expose a method called SetWarningLights(). The MFC client application's dialog will need to call this method when it starts up, passing the window handles of the static controls that display these bitmaps. These handles are then stored away in member variables and used later when event notifications are received.

```
void __stdcall OnSafeSpeedLimitExceeded(float fCurrentSpeed)
{
    ::ShowWindow(m_hWndSpeedWarningLight, SW_SHOW);
}

void __stdcall OnLowFuelWarning()
{
    ::ShowWindow(m_hWndLowFuelWarningLight, SW_SHOW);
}

void SetWarningLights(HWND hWndSpeedWarningLight, HWND hWndLowFuelWarningLight)
{
    m_hWndSpeedWarningLight = hWndSpeedWarningLight;
    m_hWndLowFuelWarningLight = hWndLowFuelWarningLight;
}
```

The only thing remaining to be done now is to subscribe to event notifications from the `Dashboard` component. Here are the steps to wire the `DashboardSink` object to receive event notifications from the `Dashboard` component:

1. Add a member variable of type `CComObject<CDashboardSink>*` to the MFC dialog's class:

```
class CDashboardClientDlg : public CDialog
{
    // MFC Wizard-generated code. Omitted for brevity.

    private:
        // Smart pointer wrapper for the IDashboard interface
        IDashboardPtr m_spDashboard;

        // Dashboard sink object
        CComObject<CDashboardSink>* m_pDashboardSink;
};

CDashboardClientDlg::CDashboardClientDlg(CWnd* pParent /*=NULL*/) :
                            CDialog(CDashboardClientDlg::IDD, pParent)
{
    // MFC Wizard-generated code. Omitted for brevity.

    // Initialize the pointer
    m_pDashboardSink = NULL;
}
```

2. In the dialog's `OnInitDialog()` method, create an instance of the sink object, and call its `DispEventAdvise()` method by passing it a pointer to the `Dashboard` component that sources events. This will effectively call `IConnectionPoint::Advise()` on the `Dashboard` component's CCW, and wire event notifications from the `Dashboard` component to the `DashboardSink` object:

```
BOOL CDashboardClientDlg::OnInitDialog()
{
    // MFC wizard-generated dialog code. Omitted for brevity.

    // Initially hide the warning indicators. They will be made visible when
    // they receive the corresponding events from the Dashboard component.
    m_ctrlSpeedIndicator.ShowWindow(SW_HIDE);
    m_ctrlLowFuelIndicator.ShowWindow(SW_HIDE);

    // Create an instance of the Dashboard component
    HRESULT hr = m_spDashboard.CreateInstance(__uuidof(Dashboard));

    // Did the creation succeed?
    if(SUCCEEDED(hr))
    {
        // Create an instance of the sink object that will receive
        // event notifications from the Dashboard component
        hr = CComObject<CDashboardSink>::CreateInstance(&m_pDashboardSink);
        if(FAILED(hr)) AfxMessageBox(_T("Sink object creation failed"));
```

```
        if(m_pDashboardSink)
        {
            // Bump up the reference count
            m_pDashboardSink->AddRef();

            // Pass the dialog's static controls' window handles to the event
            // notification sink, so that it can display corresponding warning
            // indicators when it receives events from the Dashboard component
            m_pDashboardSink->SetWarningLights(m_ctrlSpeedIndicator.m_hWnd,
                                               m_ctrlLowFuelIndicator.m_hWnd);

            // Subscribe to event notifications from the Dashboard component
            hr = m_pDashboardSink->DispEventAdvise(m_spDashboard);
            if(FAILED(hr)) AfxMessageBox(_T("Failed in ICP::Advise"));
        }

        // Get the current speed and the fuel consumed
        float fSpeed = m_spDashboard->Speed;
        float fGallonsConsumed = m_spDashboard->GallonsConsumed;

        // Display the speed and the fuel consumed
        m_strSpeed.Format(_T("%f"),fSpeed);
        m_strGallonsConsumed.Format(_T("%f"),fGallonsConsumed);
        UpdateData(FALSE);
    }
    return TRUE;
}
```

3. In your dialog class's destructor, call the `DispEventUnadvise()` method on the `DashboardSink` object to disengage it from the `Dashboard` component that's sourcing events. This call wraps the call to `IConnectionPoint::Unadvise()` on the `Dashboard` component's CCW:

```
CDashboardClientDlg::~CDashboardClientDlg()
{
    if(m_pDashboardSink)
    {
        // Unwire the sink from the event source
        if(m_pDashboardSink->m_dwEventCookie != 0xFEFEFEFE)
        {
            m_pDashboardSink->DispEventUnadvise(m_spDashboard);
        }
        // Release the reference
        m_pDashboardSink->Release();
        m_pDashboardSink = NULL;
    }
}
```

As you've seen, it's fairly easy to consume events sourced from a Managed C++ component in an unmanaged client. (Or at least, it's not much more difficult than dealing with an unmanaged event source!) Under the hood, CCW synthesizes interfaces such as `IConnectionPointContainer` that are required by the connection point event-handling protocol. It also sets up the `IConnectionPoint` implementations for each of the outgoing interfaces, and allows these implementations to be discovered by the unmanaged client through `IConnectionPointContainer::FindConnectionPoint()`.

The `IConnectionPoint::Advise()` and `IConnectionPoint::Unadvise()` method implementations translate to adding and removing delegates referencing event handler stubs (set up by the CCW) to the corresponding events in the managed component. When the managed component fires an event, these event handler stubs in the CCW are invoked through the delegates bound to the event. These stubs relay the event to the unmanaged event sinks that have subscribed to event notifications. The diagram below gives you a bird's eye view of the interaction that happens between the unmanaged client and the managed component that sources events:

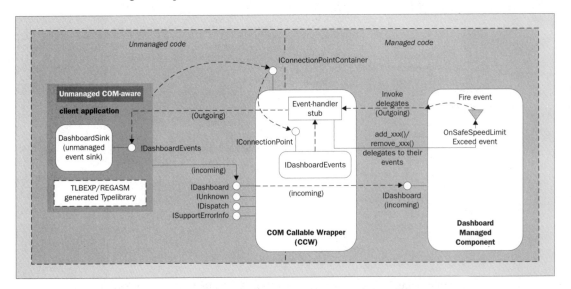

From the unmanaged client's perspective, there's nothing to suggest that it's sinking events from a Managed C++ component. The developer is thus freed from having to understand the intricacies involved in gluing together the delegate event mechanism in the .NET world and the connection point event mechanism in the COM world. The CCW does everything that's required to glue these two disparate event mechanisms together to facilitate interoperability between managed and unmanaged code.

Hosting Windows Forms controls in unmanaged containers

Earlier in this chapter, we saw how easy it was to host an unmanaged ActiveX control in a .NET Windows Form, and you might well wonder if the reverse is possible, too – that is, the ability to host Windows Forms controls in unmanaged control containers such as Visual Basic 6.0 forms, MFC dialogs, and so on. Unfortunately, Microsoft felt that although this was possible, it presented a lot of programming issues – and looking ahead, that few customers would need such a feature. As a result, Microsoft does not officially support Windows Forms control hosting in unmanaged containers.

At the time of writing, the only unmanaged container that you can use to host Windows Forms controls is Internet Explorer (IE) 5.x or higher. To do this, you simply use the `<object>` tag, just as you would do when hosting ActiveX controls in HTML pages:

```
<html>
<head>
<title>Hosting Windows Forms controls in IE 5.x</title>
</head>
```

```
<body>

<object id="ClockCtrl" classid="Clock.dll#ClockNS.ClockCtrl"
        width="500" height="100">
<param name="ClockCaption" value="Tick Tock">
</object>

</body>
</html>
```

The `classid` attribute in the `<object>` tag provides the assembly name and the fully qualified type name of the Windows Forms control, in the format *AssemblyURL#FullyQualifiedTypeNameOfControl*. The meanings of the `id`, `width`, and `height` attributes are unchanged from their normal use, and the `<param>` tag allows you to set the values of the properties exposed by the control, as you'd expect.

Should you be presented with a requirement for hosting Windows Forms controls in other unmanaged control containers, there exists an unofficial workaround. At the time of writing, Morgan Skinner provides information on how this can be done at www.codeproject.com/netcomponents/exposingdotnetcontrols.asp.

Controlling how a Managed C++ class is exported to a COM type library

In this section, we'll see how you can use attributes in a Managed C++ class to tailor the way it gets exposed to COM. The `ClassInterface` attribute allows you to control how the `coclass` definition is generated when a Managed C++ component is exported to a COM type library.

In the `Dashboard` component example, we defined an interface called `IDashboard` that contained the properties and methods we wanted to expose to COM, and used the `Dashboard` class to implement this interface. As we said at the time, we *could* have added the methods and properties directly to the `Dashboard` class instead of explicitly inheriting and implementing the `IDashboard` interface – after all, the methods and properties would still be available to unmanaged COM-aware clients. Let's take a moment now to see why this approach is taboo.

The ClassInterface attribute

Consider the following Managed C++ class:

```
[ClassInterface(ClassInterfaceType::AutoDual)]
public __gc class SportsCar
{
public:
    SportsCar() {}
    void GoVroom() {}
};
```

Notice that `SportsCar` doesn't explicitly inherit from any interface. It exposes a `public` method called `GoVroom()`. When this class is exported to a COM type library using `tlbexp` or `regasm`, you get a default interface called `_SportsCar` which has the same name as the managed class, prefixed with an underscore. This interface is known as the **class interface**. The class interface contains the methods of `System::Object` (from which the managed class inherits implicitly) in addition to the other `public` methods of the managed class, such as `GoVroom()`:

```
[
    odl,
    uuid(BFC2A389-5927-3097-AD19-810CE1693396),
    hidden,
    dual,
    nonextensible,
    oleautomation,
    custom({0F21F359-AB84-41E8-9A78-36D110E6D2F9},
    "RaceTrackNS.SportsCar")
]
interface _SportsCar : IDispatch
{
    [id(00000000), propget]
    HRESULT ToString([out, retval] BSTR* pRetVal);
    [id(0x60020001)]
    HRESULT Equals([in] VARIANT obj, [out, retval] VARIANT_BOOL* pRetVal);
    [id(0x60020002)]
    HRESULT GetHashCode([out, retval] long* pRetVal);
    [id(0x60020003)]
    HRESULT GetType([out, retval] _Type** pRetVal);
    [id(0x60020004)]
    HRESULT GoVroom();
};


[
    uuid(AB0BCF4B-7D3A-33B2-A3F3-D7E958139E46),
    version(1.0),
    custom({0F21F359-AB84-41E8-9A78-36D110E6D2F9},
    "RaceTrackNS.SportsCar")
]
coclass SportsCar
{
    [default] interface _SportsCar;
    interface _Object;
};
```

One of the disadvantages of this approach is that since the methods of the managed class are placed directly into the default interface, it would pose a whole slew of versioning problems to unmanaged clients. Think of what would happen if someone added another public method to the managed class, not suspecting that there are unmanaged clients using the component, too. When this new component is exposed to unmanaged clients through COM, the new method also becomes a part of the class interface (`_SportsCar`), breaking clients using the older component because of changes to the vtable. Even late-bound clients that use cached DISPIDs (obtained through the interface definition) would break, since these DISPIDs could get reshuffled or regenerated after new methods have been added to the class.

Late-bound clients using IDispatch::GetIDsOfNames() to obtain DISPIDs dynamically will continue to work, since they'll pick up the new DISPIDs. Clearly, managed clients will continue to work too. For safety's sake, though, exposing a managed component to COM through its class interface is generally not recommended, and it's prudent to avoid using the ClassInterface attribute with ClassInterfaceType::AutoDual. Here are the other possible values for this attribute:

ClassInterfaceType enumeration	The managed class is exposed to COM as...
AutoDual	A class whose default interface is the class interface, and which supports both early binding and late binding.
AutoDispatch	A class whose default interface is the class interface, and which supports only late binding. This is the default behavior exhibited by managed classes that are not tagged with the ClassInterface attribute, when exposed to COM.
None	A class whose default interface is the interface that it implements explicitly.

Our next experiment, then, is to tag our Managed C++ class's ClassInterface attribute with the value ClassInterfaceType::AutoDispatch, as shown below:

```
[ClassInterface(ClassInterfaceType::AutoDispatch)]
public __gc class SportsCar
{
public:
    SportsCar() {}
    void GoVroom() {}
};
```

Again, we don't explicitly inherit from a managed interface, and instead choose to expose the methods and properties from the managed class directly. When this managed class is exposed to COM, the coclass and interface sections in the IDL definition for the generated type library look something like this:

```
[
    uuid(713BE9EF-8A61-3A6D-90CA-1F203F56532E),
    version(1.0),
    custom({0F21F359-AB84-41E8-9A78-36D110E6D2F9}, "RaceTrackNS.SportsCar")
]
coclass SportsCar
{
    [default] interface _SportsCar;
    interface _Object;
};


[
    odl,
    uuid(F8DBBC03-868D-307C-86B4-36C23EB7E8D3),
    hidden,
    dual,
```

```
    oleautomation,
    custom({0F21F359-AB84-41E8-9A78-36D110E6D2F9},
    "RaceTrackNS.SportsCar")
]
interface _SportsCar : IDispatch
{
};
```

This time, the interface definition for the class interface (_SportsCar) doesn't list any of the methods in the IDL. This means that early binding is totally out of the question. The Managed C++ class can be consumed from COM-aware unmanaged clients only through late binding. The upside of this approach is that you no longer have the versioning issues associated with the class interface – new methods and properties can be added to the SportsCar class, and newer unmanaged clients can use these features. When older unmanaged clients use IDispatch::GetIDsOfNames() to obtain the DISPIDs, the updated DISPIDs will be returned and they can continue to use the older methods and properties.

Both of the above approaches have their share of woes. Ideally, you should factor out all the methods that you'd like to expose to unmanaged clients into an explicit interface, and get your Managed C++ class to inherit the interface and implement its methods. Then, turn off generation of the class interface by using the ClassInterfaceType::None value for the ClassInterface attribute's parameter. (This is exactly how we exposed the Dashboard component to COM earlier in this chapter.)

```
public __gc __interface IFastVehicle
{
    void GoVroom();
};

[ClassInterface(ClassInterfaceType::None)]
public __gc class SportsCar : public IFastVehicle
{
public:
    SportsCar() {}
    void GoVroom() {}
};
```

We've factored out the methods to be exposed to unmanaged clients into the IFastVehicle interface, and then we made the SportsCar class inherit from this interface. Finally, we turned off the generation of the class interface by tagging the SportsCar class with the ClassInterfaceType::None value for the ClassInterface attribute.

Let's take a look at the relevant IDL sections in the generated type library:

```
[
    odl,
    uuid(7F02B6D5-C469-3A36-85A3-E256E996F321),
    version(1.0),
    dual,
    oleautomation,
    custom({0F21F359-AB84-41E8-9A78-36D110E6D2F9},
    "RaceTrackNS.IFastVehicle")
]
```

```
interface IFastVehicle : IDispatch
{
    [id(0x60020000)] HRESULT GoVroom();
};

[
    uuid(2D9BAFB1-A19C-3374-A4F0-4751DEFC509E),
    version(1.0),
    custom({0F21F359-AB84-41E8-9A78-36D110E6D2F9},
    "RaceTrackNS.SportsCar")
]
coclass SportsCar
{
    interface _Object;
    [default] interface IFastVehicle;
};
```

The default interface of the SportsCar component is the IFastVehicle interface that allows you to use both early binding and late binding. Also, adding new methods and properties to the Dashboard class won't break any of the existing unmanaged COM-aware clients, as long as the IFastVehicle interface contract is preserved.

The ProgId and Guid attributes

As we've seen, the ClassInterface attribute can be very useful when you need to tune the way your managed class gets exposed to COM. In the final part of this section, we'll take a quick look at two other attributes that can be useful when you need to control the value of the ProgID for managed classes exposed to COM, and the values of the GUIDs for managed classes and interfaces exposed to COM.

By default, tlbexp and regasm assign the fully qualified type name of the class as the ProgID for a managed class that's registered with COM. However, you can *choose* a ProgID for your Managed C++ class by tagging it with the ProgId attribute:

```
[
    ClassInterface(ClassInterfaceType::None),
    ProgId("AcmeCompany.SportsCar")
]
public __gc class SportsCar : public IFastVehicle
{
    // Rest of the class definition
};
```

Similarly, tlbexp and regasm generate an arbitrary GUID for the component's CLSID every time a Managed C++ component is recompiled. For interfaces, however, the IID doesn't change across builds as long as the signatures of the methods in the interface haven't changed and no new methods have been added. If the interface definition changes, a fresh IID is generated. To preserve the same CLSID or IID across component rebuilds or interface definition changes, you have the option of specifying a value of your choice. You can do this by tagging your Managed C++ class or interface with the Guid attribute:

```
[
    ClassInterface(ClassInterfaceType::None),
    Guid("67881D41-FCFF-421b-9D47-699C5DFF5E3D")
]
public __gc class SportsCar : public IFastVehicle
{
    // Rest of the class definition
};
```

Controlling how a Managed C++ interface gets exported to a COM type library

Whenever a Managed C++ interface is exposed to COM, it's presented as a dual interface by default. However, it may be desirable to expose this interface either as a dispinterface or as a custom interface, and to help in this we have the `InterfaceType` attribute. This attribute takes one of the `ComInterfaceType` enumeration values shown below:

ComInterfaceType enumeration	Managed interface is exposed to COM as...
InterfaceIsDual	A dual interface
InterfaceIsIDispatch	A pure dispinterface
InterfaceIsIUnknown	A custom interface

Let's apply each of the above values to the `InterfaceType` attribute's parameter and see how the IDL definition differs in the generated type library:

1. Tagging a Managed C++ interface with an `InterfaceType` attribute whose parameter's value is `ComInterfaceType::InterfaceIsDual`:

```
[InterfaceType(ComInterfaceType::InterfaceIsDual)]
public __gc __interface IVehicle
{
};
```

When the Managed C++ interface shown above is exposed to COM, it's exported as a dual interface, indicated by the `[dual]` attribute in the interface's IDL definition, as shown below:

```
[
    odl,
    uuid(77E5CCF0-53BD-36DE-9346-E8C2BEC521F6),
    version(1.0),
    dual,
    oleautomation,
    custom({0F21F359-AB84-41E8-9A78-36D110E6D2F9},
    "VehicleNS.IVehicle")
]
interface IVehicle : IDispatch
{
};
```

If the `InterfaceType` attribute is not used on an interface, the type library exporter and the assembly registration utility expose the interface to COM as a dual interface.

2. Tagging a Managed C++ interface with an `InterfaceType` attribute whose parameter's value is `ComInterfaceType::InterfaceIsIDispatch`:

```
[InterfaceType(ComInterfaceType::InterfaceIsIDispatch)]
public __gc __interface IVehicle
{
};
```

When the Managed C++ interface shown above is exposed to COM, it's exported as a pure dispinterface, as seen in the interface's IDL definition shown below:

```
[
    uuid(77E5CCF0-53BD-36DE-9346-E8C2BEC521F6),
    version(1.0),
    custom({0F21F359-AB84-41E8-9A78-36D110E6D2F9},
    "VehicleNS.IVehicle")
]
dispinterface IVehicle
{
    properties:
    methods:
};
```

3. Tagging a Managed C++ interface with an `InterfaceType` attribute whose parameter's value is `ComInterfaceType::InterfaceIsIUnknown`:

```
[InterfaceType(ComInterfaceType::InterfaceIsIUnknown)]
public __gc __interface IVehicle
{
};
```

When the Managed C++ interface shown above is exposed to COM, it's exported as a custom `IUnknown` interface, as seen in the interface's IDL definition shown below:

```
[
    odl,
    uuid(77E5CCF0-53BD-36DE-9346-E8C2BEC521F6),
    version(1.0),
    oleautomation,
    custom({0F21F359-AB84-41E8-9A78-36D110E6D2F9},
    "VehicleNS.IVehicle")
]
interface IVehicle : IUnknown
{
};
```

As you can see, the `InterfaceType` attribute can be quite handy when you need to control how a Managed C++ interface gets exposed to COM.

Summary

We've covered a lot of ground in this chapter on how classic COM code and Managed C++ code can coexist and interoperate with each other seamlessly. We saw how easy it can be to consume COM components from Managed C++ applications, and how .NET managed components can be consumed from unmanaged C++ applications using plain COM invocation mechanisms.

The .NET Framework and its tools have made these tasks extremely easy for us. Under the hood, the RCW and CCW proxy wrappers that the CLR manufactures are laboring hard to latch the managed and unmanaged worlds together. The ability of Windows Forms to host ActiveX controls means that we can carry forward legacy controls into .NET applications, without having to rewrite these controls from scratch. Managed C++ components can use attributes to control how they get exposed to COM-aware clients.

Companies who have taken the .NET plunge can enjoy the rich and powerful features offered by the .NET programming model and its class library, and at the same time they can protect their existing investment by reusing COM components from managed code. Though there may be some performance overhead when interoperating with unmanaged COM components from managed code, the colossal benefits reaped from code reuse and investment protection often far outweigh it.

For all the diehard COM folks out there, it's important to understand that .NET components have not driven the nails into COM's coffin – there are thousands of legacy COM components that cannot be migrated overnight to .NET. Therefore, the COM interoperation infrastructure provided with .NET will remain an effective and viable solution to reuse existing COM components from .NET, at least until these components are fully ported to CLR managed code.

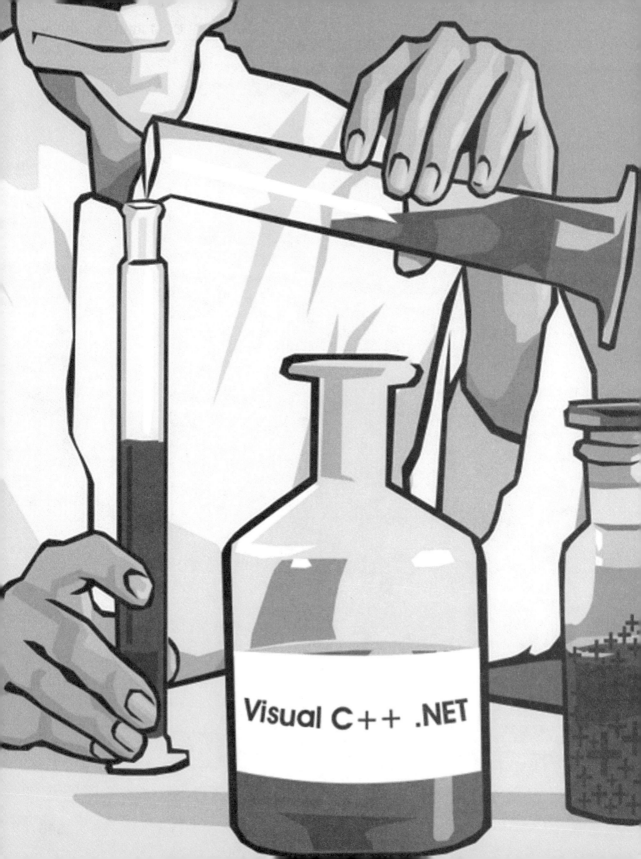

9

ATL COM programming

In this chapter, we're going to move right away from .NET programming and look at what's new for ATL and COM programmers in the new version of Visual C++. Aside from the huge interest (and loud noise) surrounding .NET and Managed Extensions, a lot of work has gone on to improve the existing facilities in 'unmanaged' C++ as well. ATL has undergone a complete revamp, with the introduction of ATL 7.0 bringing with it new C++ attributes designed to facilitate the creation of COM objects.

You may be wondering why, with the arrival of Managed C++ and .NET, there should be much interest in developing ATL further. In fact, there are two very good reasons:

❑   Supporting legacy applications

❑   Developing new COM components

Before .NET arrived, just about every application that Microsoft developed was based on COM. From using a common control in Visual Basic, to embedding Office documents in one another, to using the Outlook web interface, COM was – and still is – the glue binding everything together. A large number of the classes in the .NET Framework class library are in truth little more than wrappers around calls to Windows API functions or to COM components, which means that there is inevitably going to be a performance hit associated with using .NET. This hit may be small – and in time, .NET applications might actually run more quickly than native executables – but at present, if you want to write a component that is very small and lightweight, and has maximum efficiency, then you will still want to stick with COM and ATL. For some time into the future, these technologies will remain important.

We'll start off with a brief overview of the new features in ATL. Rather than going through all of them in detail, we'll develop a few short projects that should give you a feel for how things work in ATL 7.0. First, we'll generate a simple in-process server without using the new attributes, which will allow us to see what's changed in the Wizards and in the Wizard-generated code. Then we'll duplicate the process, but this time using attributes – and you'll see how much simpler it is to work with an attributed project. After that, we'll present a brief overview of some of the new utility classes in ATL, before finishing by developing a sample COM component that puts together some of the new stuff we've learned.

In this chapter, we assume that you are already familiar with ATL 3.0, and will focus on pointing out specifically what's new in ATL 7.0.

What's new in ATL?

The key new features of ATL 7.0 are summarized below:

❑   The introduction of **attributed programming for COM**. We first saw how attributes worked back in Chapter 4 – they simplify the code needed to write COM components enormously, by providing an extra level of preprocessing (one that is far more powerful than the C++ preprocessor). They can provide enough information to the C++ compiler about your components to obviate the need for a separate IDL file, and allow you better to separate the specifications of your objects from the code for their implementation.

❑   **ATL Server** has arrived, providing ATL support for writing ISAPI extensions and web services. ATL Server is not about writing COM components – it's a brand new library for the development of high-performance web applications.

❑   There is **better integration with MFC**. For example, some classes (such as CPoint and CSize) have been rewritten, and are now shared between ATL and MFC in a way that allows MFC to benefit from the lightweight approach of ATL. An important consequence of this is that it's now much easier to mix ATL and MFC in the same project.

❑   Some changes to the **ATL class structure**. You'll find, for example, that CComModule has gone and been replaced with more powerful classes such as CAtlDllModule and CAtlExeModule.

A glance at the documentation for ATL will reveal a large number of new **utility classes** concerned with areas such as file management, data conversion, and collections. Some windows classes that were previously available in the unsupported Windows Template Library (WTL) sample have found their way into ATL 7.0 proper. And developers who need to use strings will breathe a sigh of relief that with a new CAtlString class, ATL finally has the same powerful string manipulation facilities as MFC. (At the time of writing, the WTL sample hasn't been updated, but there are indications that Microsoft is working on a new, more powerful version of WTL to go with ATL 7.0.)

We won't be looking at ATL Server any further here, because that is the subject of the next chapter.

A simple ATL 7.0 project

We'll start off by creating a basic object in ATL. For the time being, we won't be using attributes, since there have been quite a few changes in the class structure of ATL, and these changes tend to be hidden by the attributes. Start up Visual Studio .NET, and create a new project of type **ATL Project**:

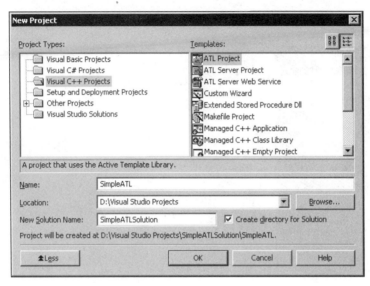

We'll call our project `SimpleATL` *and the solution* `SimpleATLSolution`. *We've created a separate directory for the solution so that we can create our client project in the same location.*

As with all the Wizards, the user interface in the dialog boxes used for ATL projects has had a complete overhaul in Visual Studio .NET. We get the following one, telling us that by default we have an in-process COM component that uses attributes:

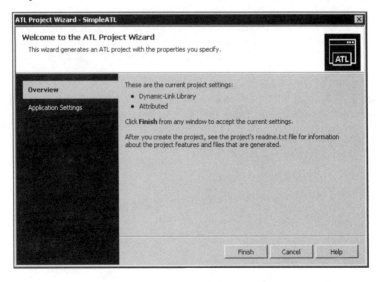

If an attributed DLL component is what you want, then you can just click on Finish straight away. In our case, however, we need to click on the Application Settings tab and deselect the Attributed checkbox therein:

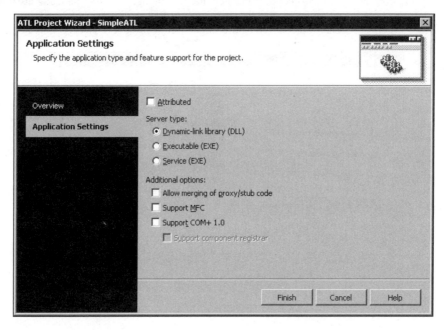

All of the familiar old project options from ATL 3.0 are still here. We can generate a DLL, an executable, or a service project. For a DLL project, we can opt to allow merging of proxy and stub code into the DLL (making redistribution simpler), and to support MFC. The old option to support MTS has been replaced by the equivalent option of supporting COM+ 1.0; if you do elect to support COM+, you can now also choose to support the component registrar. Just as for ATL 3.0, none of these additional options is available for executables or services.

> *Although we've already said that we're not going to use attributes here, in general you'll find life easier if you leave this box checked. You should note, however, that there is no attributed support for MFC or for merging of proxy/stub code. If you wish to do either of these, then you'll have to go for an old-style project.*

Let's see what we get when we click on Finish. An examination of the Solution Explorer quickly reveals that the files generated are apparently much the same as those in ATL 3.0:

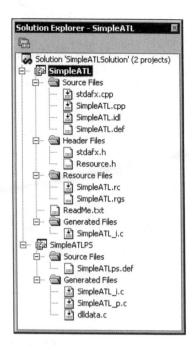

Visual Studio .NET has made things slightly easier for us by separating out the files that already exist and the files that will be generated on compilation (SimpleATL_i.c in the SimpleATL project, and SimpleATL_i.c, SimpleATL_p.c, and dlldata.c in the proxy/stub project, SimpleATLPS). In general, however, most of the files are indeed very similar to ATL 3.0 code. The main differences you'll find are:

❑ The stdafx.h file has been updated with a few new macros

❑ The file containing the main source code for the project, SimpleATL.cpp, uses some new ATL classes

Let's take a peek at the main file, SimpleATL.cpp. Recall that this is the file containing implementation code for the module as a whole, and is called (for example) when the DLL is loaded and unloaded:

```cpp
#include "stdafx.h"
#include "resource.h"
#include "SimpleATL.h"

class CSimpleATLModule : public CAtlDllModuleT<CSimpleATLModule>
{
public:
    DECLARE_LIBID(LIBID_SimpleATLLib)
    DECLARE_REGISTRY_APPID_RESOURCEID(
                    IDR_SIMPLEATL, "{98B48404-4E51-4057-A23E-56E99B58F738}")
};

CSimpleATLModule _AtlModule;
```

```
// DLL entry point
extern "C" BOOL WINAPI DllMain(
                    HINSTANCE hInstance, DWORD dwReason, LPVOID lpReserved)
{
    hInstance;
    return _AtlModule.DllMain(dwReason, lpReserved);
}

// Used to determine whether the DLL can be unloaded by OLE
STDAPI DllCanUnloadNow(void)
{
    return _AtlModule.DllCanUnloadNow();
}

// Returns a class factory to create an object of the requested type
STDAPI DllGetClassObject(REFCLSID rclsid, REFIID riid, LPVOID* ppv)
{
    return _AtlModule.DllGetClassObject(rclsid, riid, ppv);
}

// DllRegisterServer - Adds entries to the system registry
STDAPI DllRegisterServer(void)
{
    // Registers object, typelib, and all interfaces in typelib
    HRESULT hr = _AtlModule.DllRegisterServer();
    return hr;
}

// DllUnregisterServer - Removes entries from the system registry
STDAPI DllUnregisterServer(void)
{
    HRESULT hr = _AtlModule.DllUnregisterServer();
    return hr;
}
```

This defines a class called `CSimpleATLModule` that derives from a template class called `CAtlDllModuleT<>`, using the usual ATL trick of passing the derived class as a template parameter to a base class. `CAtlDllModuleT<>` is a new template that replaces the `CComModule<>` class of earlier ATL versions – and you can see that the familiar ATL 3.0 `DECLARE_LIBID` and `DECLARE_REGISTRY_APPID_RESOURCEID` macros for defining GUIDs have migrated into `CSimpleATLModule`.

You'll recall that `CComModule<>` implemented features to do with managing the set of components housed in a given DLL or EXE file. In ATL 3.0 projects, a global instance of this class was always defined in the main CPP file for the project:

```
// Code snippet from legacy ATL 3.0 project
CComModule _Module;
```

Now, we get similar features from a global instance of our new templated class:

```
CSimpleATLModule _AtlModule;
```

In fact, `CComModule<>` is now obsolete, having been replaced by a number of more specialized classes, one for each type of ATL project. The hierarchy looks like this:

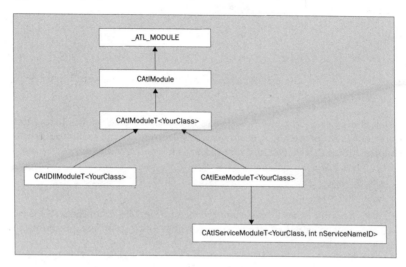

The reason for the change is really to do with structuring the background ATL code in a better, more object-oriented manner. We won't go into the details of the classes in the hierarchy, but you can see that there are three main templates geared to the three main kinds of COM components you can create: in-process, out-of-process, and service. There are other, similar classes (not shown) that are aimed at other types of ATL projects, such as Windows applications. The root type, _ATL_MODULE, is a simple C-style structure. The upshot of there being several specialized classes is that they can now handle some tasks that previously had to be explicitly coded up by the Wizard in your project.

We can start to see the benefits of this arrangement by examining the code for the DLL entry point in our `SimpleATL.cpp` file:

```
// DLL entry point
extern "C" BOOL WINAPI DllMain(
                HINSTANCE hInstance, DWORD dwReason, LPVOID lpReserved)
{
    hInstance;
    return _AtlModule.DllMain(dwReason, lpReserved);
}
```

The corresponding code in ATL 3.0 looked like this:

```
// This is legacy ATL 3.0 code!
extern "C" BOOL WINAPI DllMain(
                HINSTANCE hInstance, DWORD dwReason, LPVOID /*lpReserved*/)
{
    if(dwReason == DLL_PROCESS_ATTACH)
    {
        _Module.Init(ObjectMap, hInstance, &LIBID_ATLCLASSICDLLLib);
```

```
        DisableThreadLibraryCalls(hInstance);
    }
    else if(dwReason == DLL_PROCESS_DETACH)
        _Module.Term();
    return TRUE;      // ok
}
```

The benefits for the developer should be clear: your project has been simplified because code has been moved out of your C++ project and into the standard ATL files.

Next, take a look at the new `stdafx.h` file. We're not going to give the full listing here, because for the most part it just defines preprocessor symbols whose purposes are fairly obvious from the code, but there are a couple of lines that reflect key new features in ATL. At the end of the file, we find this:

```
using namespace ATL;
```

As of ATL 7.0, ATL definitions and classes are defined in the ATL namespace. This is in line with the increasing recognition that the use of namespaces for libraries is good programming practice because of the reduced risk of name clashes.

Earlier in the file, the preprocessor symbol _ATL_NO_AUTOMATIC_NAMESPACE is defined:

```
#define _ATL_NO_AUTOMATIC_NAMESPACE
```

This symbol is defined in connection with the following code sequence in the header file `atlbase.h`:

```
// From atlbase.h
#ifndef _ATL_NO_AUTOMATIC_NAMESPACE
using namespace ATL;
#endif //!_ATL_NO_AUTOMATIC_NAMESPACE
```

What's going on here is that by default, the ATL namespace will be included in `atlbase.h`. However, our own `stdafx.h` file defines a macro that prevents the namespace from being added there, so that the `using namespace` command appears instead in our own file – from which we can remove it if we wish. By defining the _ATL_NO_AUTOMATIC_NAMESPACE symbol in `SimpleATL.cpp`, we retain control of the use of the ATL namespace, and can remove the `using namespace` command if we encounter any name clashes. Admittedly it's a rather roundabout way of doing it, but it does the job.

Adding a component to the project

To add a component to the project, we right-click on the project in the Solution Explorer, and select **Add**, then **Add Class...** from the context menu. This gives us a dialog box asking us what kind of object we wish to add. It may be in a new style, but most of the options are the same as for the **Add ATL Object** dialog in Visual Studio 6.0:

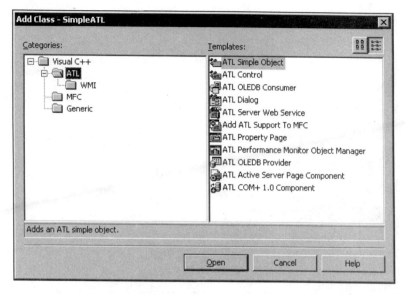

Compared to Visual Studio 6.0, the main additions are:

- ❑ Windows Management Instrumentation (WMI). If you need to write a WMI event provider or instance provider, there's built-in support that generates ATL code to get you started.

- ❑ ATL Performance Monitor Object Manager.

- ❑ ATL Server Web Service.

In this chapter, we're focusing on the changes to the structure of ATL, so we won't be covering these project types. Instead, just as you're used to, we'll select **Simple Object** in order to generate the code for a new COM class.

> *In case you're wondering, WMI is a technology that allows the querying and modification of hardware and local machine settings using industry-agreed standards. Using WMI, you can do things like load drivers or eject the CD or DVD without needing to use device-specific code. In some ways, it can be seen as the equivalent of Active Directory, but for the local machine and hardware instead of for a Windows domain.*

Having chosen our object type, we get presented with a dialog asking us to provide more information about it:

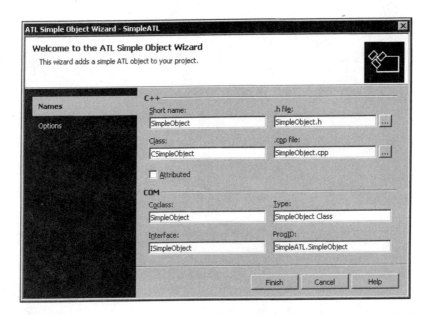

Things here are again quite similar to Visual Studio 6.0, in that the dialog has two tabs that allow us to choose the names and other options. We'll name the object `SimpleObject`. The most significant new feature on the Names tab is a check box allowing you to select an attributed object – even though we haven't used attributes for the project as a whole, we could still choose to simplify the code for this particular object if we wanted to. (It doesn't work the other way round, though: if you go for an attributed project, all your objects have to be attributed too.) At the moment, we're just trying to get a feel for the changes in ATL, so we'll leave the box unchecked.

The Options tab has a couple of additions too:

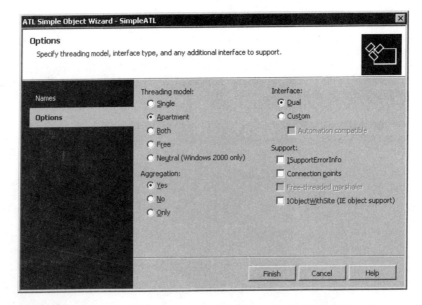

We can now choose the new neutral-threaded apartment model, provided that our object will be running on Windows 2000 or a later operating system (such as Windows XP). The neutral-threaded apartment is similar to a multi-threaded apartment, but it's a bit more flexible. If an object exists in a neutral-threaded apartment, then it can be accessed by only one thread at a time, but it is not attached to a particular thread. This means that after one call to the object has completed, it is acceptable for the next call to come in on a different thread. Neutral-threaded objects need not be thread-safe within a method call, but should not rely on successive calls coming on the same thread.

We can also elect to support an IE interface, `IObjectWithSite`.

For our object, we'll stick with apartment threading, and while this results in code that's similar to what you'd see generated by ATL 3.0, there's one big exception: the object map has gone. In detail, the code for the `SimpleObject.h` file looks like this:

```
#pragma once
#include "resource.h"        // main symbols

#include "SimpleATL.h"

// CSimpleObject

class ATL_NO_VTABLE CSimpleObject :
    public CComObjectRootEx<CComSingleThreadModel>,
    public CComCoClass<CSimpleObject, &CLSID_SimpleObject>,
    public IDispatchImpl<ISimpleObject, &IID_ISimpleObject,
                &LIBID_SimpleATLLib, /*wMajor =*/ 1, /*wMinor =*/ 0>
{
public:
    CSimpleObject()
    {
    }

DECLARE_REGISTRY_RESOURCEID(IDR_SIMPLEOBJECT)

BEGIN_COM_MAP(CSimpleObject)
    COM_INTERFACE_ENTRY(ISimpleObject)
    COM_INTERFACE_ENTRY(IDispatch)
END_COM_MAP()

    DECLARE_PROTECT_FINAL_CONSTRUCT()

    HRESULT FinalConstruct()
    {
        return S_OK;
    }

    void FinalRelease()
    {
    }
```

```
public:
};
```

```
OBJECT_ENTRY_AUTO(__uuidof(SimpleObject), CSimpleObject)
```

In the above code, the statements that are significantly different from ATL 3.0 are highlighted. Actually, the `FinalConstruct()` and `FinalRelease()` methods aren't really *new* – they were defined in ATL 3.0 as the recommended places in which you should put initialization and cleanup code – but in ATL 7.0, default do-nothing versions of these methods get added to your class automatically by the Wizard.

The `OBJECT_ENTRY_AUTO` macro is more interesting. It ensures that your class gets added to ATL's object map, which controls such things as registering the class and ensuring the class factory has all the information required to instantiate an object. In ATL 3.0, this aspect of the code was handled by the `OBJECT_ENTRY` macro, which was placed in the main `.cpp` file of the project:

```
// Legacy ATL 3.0 Wizard-generated code defining the object map for an
// object called CSimpleClassic
BEGIN_OBJECT_MAP(ObjectMap)
OBJECT_ENTRY(CLSID_SimpleClassic, CSimpleClassic)
END_OBJECT_MAP()
```

In ATL 7.0, `OBJECT_ENTRY` and its associated macros are deprecated – they'll work, but it's not recommended that you use them. `OBJECT_ENTRY_AUTO` supplies enough information for the object map to be constructed automatically. This doesn't really add any new features to your code, but it does simplify the Wizard-generated code for you, and leaves a bit less scope for bugs to be introduced when you start manually editing your code.

If you want your object not to be creatable using `CoCreateInstance()`, then you should replace `OBJECT_ENTRY_AUTO` with `OBJECT_ENTRY_NON_CREATEABLE_EX_AUTO`, like this:

```
OBJECT_ENTRY_NON_CREATEABLE_EX_AUTO(__uuidof(SimpleObject), CSimpleObject)
```

Adding methods

We'll finish off our simple object by adding some methods to the `ISimpleObject` interface of our new `SimpleObject` class. We'll go for one method and one read-only property, with the following declarations:

```
public:
    STDMETHOD(Square)(LONG value, LONG* result);
    STDMETHOD(get_ObjectString)(BSTR* pVal);
```

`Square()` will be implemented to produce the square of the integer that's passed in (passing in 4 will return 16), while `ObjectString()` is a read-only property that allows us to retrieve a string associated with the object. For our simple test object, this string will be hard-coded as, "This is a simple object".

There's little new to interest us here in terms of generated code, since there's no change from ATL 3.0, but the dialog box for adding new methods and properties has been dramatically improved. No longer do you need to type in the parameter list for a method manually. A set of check box, list box, and text box controls allows you to control the parameters precisely without having to worry about the exact syntax.

You can bring up this dialog box by clicking on the appropriate interface in the Class View and selecting either **Add Method** or **Add Property**, as appropriate. Note that you need to click on the *interface* (as shown in the screenshot), rather than the C++ class.

Selecting **Add Method...** gives us this dialog:

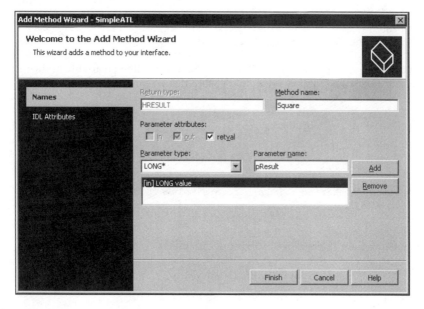

Here, we're adding the parameter [out, retval] LONG* pResult. The second tab of this dialog allows us to select various IDL attributes:

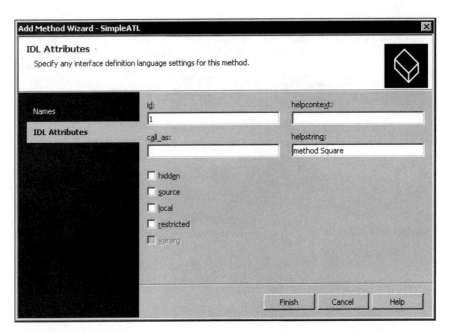

If we use the Wizard to add the property in the same way, we end up with the following function declarations:

```
public:
    STDMETHOD(Square)(LONG value, LONG* pResult);
    STDMETHOD(get_ObjectString)(BSTR* pVal);
```

Now we simply need to implement these functions. First, we define a variable in the CSimpleObject class to hold our hard-coded object string, and ensure that it's correctly initialized:

```
private:
    CComBSTR m_bstrObjectString;

public:
    HRESULT FinalConstruct()
    {
        m_bstrObjectString = L"This is a simple ATL object";
        return S_OK;
    }
```

The implementations are in the SimpleObject.cpp file:

```
STDMETHODIMP CSimpleObject::Square(LONG value, LONG* pResult)
{
    *pResult = value * value;
    return S_OK;
}
```

```
STDMETHODIMP CSimpleObject::get_ObjectString(BSTR* pVal)
{
    m_bstrObjectString.CopyTo(pVal);
    return S_OK;
}
```

The project is now ready to compile. Before we can test it, however, we'll need to put together a COM client to act as a test harness. We'll ask Visual Studio .NET to add a new project to the solution, choosing a C++ Win32 project to which we'll give the name Test Harness.

Before we finish creating this project, however, we'll modify the application settings to ensure that we generate a console application with ATL support:

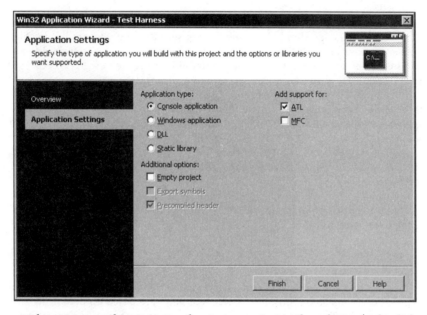

Once generated, we must set this project as the startup project in the solution (right-click on the project in the Solution Explorer, and select **Set As StartUp Project** from the context menu). Then, add the highlighted code to the new Test Harness.cpp file:

```
#include "stdafx.h"
#include <iostream>
#include "..\SimpleATL\SimpleATL.h"
#include "..\SimpleATL\SimpleATL_i.c"

using namespace std;

int _tmain(int argc, _TCHAR* argv[])
{
    CoInitialize(NULL);
    CComPtr<ISimpleObject> spObject;
    CoCreateInstance(CLSID_SimpleObject, NULL, CLSCTX_INPROC_SERVER,
                    IID_ISimpleObject, reinterpret_cast<void**>(&spObject));
```

```
    long value = 5;
    long result = 0;
    spObject->Square(value, &result);
    cout << value << " squared is " << result << endl;

    CComBSTR bstr;
    spObject->get_ObjectString(&bstr);
    CW2AEX<64> pszObjectString(bstr);
    cout << "object string is: " << static_cast<char*>(pszObjectString) << endl;

    spObject = NULL;
    CoUninitialize();
    return 0;
}
```

The first part of the added code simply involves making sure that the relevant header files are #included; we use iostream so that we can read from and write to the console. We also #include the header files containing the GUID and interface definitions for the new SimpleObject component, taken from the SimpleATL project.

The bulk of the code in the _tmain() function is standard ATL client code to instantiate a component and call methods on it. We call first Square() and then the ObjectString property, displaying the results of both operations.

For simplicity, we've not checked the returned HRESULTs, although obviously you'd need to do this in a real project.

One statement that might be unfamiliar is the conversion of the string from a Unicode BSTR to an ANSI string for redirecting to cout:

```
    CW2AEX<64> pszObjectString(bstr);
```

ATL 7.0 has introduced some new string conversion facilities that have rendered the familiar old macros (OLE2T, T2OLE, and so on) obsolete. These templates are based on new string conversion classes, and offer more flexibility and some performance improvements – in particular, there's no risk of stack overflow if you use them inside loops, which was a problem with the macros. The templates also have the benefit that they don't require the USES_CONVERSION macro (which is also obsolete) to be present in your code. The one we've chosen here, CW2AEX<n>, converts Unicode strings to ANSI, and is used when we can be confident that the string will not exceed n characters in length. (If we couldn't be certain of this, we'd use CW2A.) We'll cover some more of the new facilities later in the chapter.

The code is now ready to test and run, and shows that our object's methods are being called successfully.

Creating an attributed project

In Chapter 4, we looked at attributed programming, focusing on the new .NET attributes. We saw that the syntax for the new COM-related attributes is essentially identical to that for the .NET attributes, despite the fact that what's going on behind the scenes is very different. Some .NET attributes cause extra data to be added to the metadata in the emitted assembly, while others modify the compilation process itself (StructLayout, for example, changes the memory layout of a managed structure). COM- and ATL-related attributes, on the other hand, cause the C++ compiler to call up an **attribute provider**, which examines the attribute and then modifies the source code before it is passed to the compiler, based on that attribute.

> *We should stress here that the source file itself is not modified. Just as with preprocessor symbols,* you *don't see any changes to the source file, but the compiler does.*

Attributes are more powerful than the C++ preprocessor symbols they can be compared with. For one thing, the debugger recognizes them. For another, C++ preprocessor symbols can only be replaced in a fairly basic way, by simple textual substitution at the point in the file where the symbol occurs. An attribute provider, on the other hand, can examine the entire project and insert or modify whatever code is needed wherever it is needed, and can take account of parameters supplied to an attribute. For example, if you're writing a class that you intend to be a COM component instead of a plain C++ class, you simply mark the class with the coclass attribute. The attribute provider will recognize this, and modify the code in your project – including creating an associated IDL file if it doesn't exist already, or modifying its contents if it does – so that the class compiles to give the correct binary characteristics for a COM component.

The benefits to you are that you get simpler code to edit, and that maintenance is easier, because the attributes separate the description of what your code is intended to do from the code itself. If you were to decide that you didn't want your class to be a coclass after all, making the change is easy – you remove the coclass attribute from its definition! Without attributes, you'd have to remove all the associated ATL code and edit the IDL file manually. Indeed, perhaps the biggest benefit of attributes is that they do away with the need for you to maintain an IDL file by hand. Instead, your coclass and interface definitions all sit in the C++ file.

In this section, we're going to examine the effect on your code of using attributes, but we won't provide a complete guide to every attribute out there. For reference information about each new attribute and ATL class, you should consult the MSDN documentation. Here, we'll work through the development of a project with essentially the same COM class as the previous example, but this time using attributes. To start with, we'll ask Visual Studio .NET for a new C++ ATL project, giving it the name SimpleAttributedATL. When the relevant dialog box appears, we'll keep the default option: an attributed DLL project.

If you look at the SimpleAttributedATL.cpp file, you'll find some rather less familiar code:

```
#include "stdafx.h"
#include "resource.h"

// The module attribute causes DllMain, DllRegisterServer, and
// DllUnregisterServer to be automatically implemented for you
[ module(dll, uuid = "{B968C2A2-FC8F-45CF-BA18-8A550C532B4B}",
        name = "SimpleAttributedATL",
        helpstring = "Simple Attributed ATL 1.0 Type Library",
        resource_name = "IDR_SIMPLEATTRIBUTEDATL") ];
```

And that's it – the entire `SimpleAttributedATL.cpp` file! As (partly) commented in the code, the `module` attribute will be expanded to produce the basic `library` block of the IDL file and the whole of the code for implementing a DLL that's ready to host COM components. In other words, you get the definition of a class based on `CAtlModuleT<>`, the definition of a global instance of that class, as well as implementations of `DllMain()`, `DllCanUnloadNow()`, `DllGetClassObject()`, `DllRegisterServer()`, and `DllUnregisterServer()` – everything that we saw in the first project we generated.

As you can see, the `module` attribute takes several parameters. The first indicates the type of project, and can be `dll`, `exe`, or `service`. The next is a GUID (`uuid` parameter) – this will become the GUID of the associated type library. (If you omit this, a GUID will be automatically generated for you.) You will normally want to supply the name of the type library, and the Wizard-generated code also supplies a default `helpstring` and an identifier for the project resources. There are a large number of other possible parameters that you might choose to add manually, including the `lcid`, a `helpcontext`, and a `version` number. You'll notice that most of these attributes correspond directly to IDL attributes that have the same names and meanings.

Another important point to note is that if you check out the Solution Explorer for this project, you'll find that no IDL file is listed as having been created – it will be generated later, through the attributes. (It's not even listed as a generated file – the attribute provider, not Visual Studio .NET, generates it.)

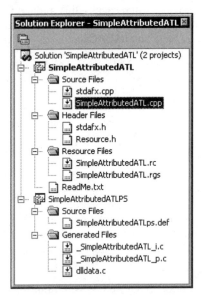

Let's carry on the sample by adding a COM component. As before, we'll work through the Wizards, selecting an attributed simple object and giving it the name `SimpleAttributedObject`. This causes the creation of a new header and (blank) source file containing the definition of a new `CSimpleAttributedObject` class. The following code gets placed in the header file:

```
#pragma once
#include "resource.h"        // main symbols
```

```
// ISimpleAttributedObject
[
    object,
    uuid("7E5CFDF6-39D7-46FD-8BD5-0C6B881B4A5B"),
    dual, helpstring("ISimpleAttributedObject Interface"),
    pointer_default(unique)
]
__interface ISimpleAttributedObject : IDispatch
{
};

// CSimpleAttributedObject

[
    coclass,
    threading("apartment"),
    vi_progid("SimpleAttributedATL.SimpleAttributedObj"),
    progid("SimpleAttributedATL.SimpleAttributed0.1"),
    version(1.0),
    uuid("5FFA75B6-EC61-4340-A06D-1918A56EE3C9"),
    helpstring("SimpleAttributedObject Class")
]
class ATL_NO_VTABLE CSimpleAttributedObject :
    public ISimpleAttributedObject
{
public:
    CSimpleAttributedObject()
    {
    }

    DECLARE_PROTECT_FINAL_CONSTRUCT()

    HRESULT FinalConstruct()
    {
        return S_OK;
    }

    void FinalRelease()
    {
    }

public:

};
```

This is very different from the equivalent code for the earlier non-attributed object, and we can clearly see the separation of the class and interface definitions. The class's ISimpleAttributedObject interface has been defined using a new keyword, __interface:

```
[
    object,
    uuid("7E5CFDF6-39D7-46FD-8BD5-0C6B881B4A5B"),
    dual, helpstring("ISimpleAttributedObject Interface"),
    pointer_default(unique)
]
```

```
__interface ISimpleAttributedObject : IDispatch
{
};
```

Declaring an __interface has the same effect as declaring a struct, but if you use the former, the compiler will enforce interface semantics. For example, all the methods in the interface will be interpreted as being pure virtual regardless of any "= 0" syntax you choose to apply, and the compiler will raise an error if you supply any implementation.

The interface definition has been decorated with several attributes that have been defined with the same meanings as their IDL equivalents. uuid indicates the GUID of the interface, while dual indicates that the interface is to be derived from IDispatch. object is somewhat misleading since, just as in IDL, it indicates that we're declaring a COM interface (as opposed to an old DCE interface). The presence of this attribute instructs the attribute provider to place an interface definition in the IDL file, creating the file if one doesn't already exist.

The definition of the class that represents the component is a lot simpler now. As you know, the functionality of COM classes in ATL is achieved by deriving the class from several ATL base template classes, including CComObjectRootEx<> and CComCoClass<>. In our code, however, the only thing the class has been explicitly derived from is the ISimpleAttributedObject interface:

```
[
    coclass,
    threading("apartment"),
    vi_progid("SimpleAttributedATL.SimpleAttributedObj"),
    progid("SimpleAttributedATL.SimpleAttributedO.1"),
    version(1.0),
    uuid("5FFA75B6-EC61-4340-A06D-1918A56EE3C9"),
    helpstring("SimpleAttributedObject Class")
]
class ATL_NO_VTABLE CSimpleAttributedObject :
    public ISimpleAttributedObject
{
```

The coclass attribute applied to the class definition instructs the attribute provider to modify the code for this class so that it represents a COM component with the parameters specified in the remaining attributes. The attribute provider will automatically add code to ensure that the class derives from the required ATL classes, as well as adding a COM map for the interfaces that the class implements. This is why the definition of the class doesn't explicitly contain a COM map, unlike the earlier non-attributed project. For the most part, the remaining attributes are similar to their IDL cousins; the only one that may not be clear is vi_progid, which specifies the version-independent ProgID.

Finally, we'll use the Wizards to add the same methods that we had in our previous sample. In this case, the code added to the class definition is identical to that for the earlier project:

```
public:
    STDMETHOD(Square)(LONG value, LONG* pResult);
    STDMETHOD(get_ObjectString)(BSTR* pVal);
```

Similarly, we'll manually add the same implementations of these methods. The only change is that we use a slightly different object string:

```
HRESULT FinalConstruct()
{
    m_bstrObjectString = L"This is a simple attributed ATL object";
    return S_OK;
}

private:
    CComBSTR m_bstrObjectString;
```

Note that when we add these methods, the Wizard automatically makes the appropriate modifications to the __interface definition:

```
[
    object,
    uuid("7E5CFDF6-39D7-46FD-8BD5-0C6B881B4A5B"),
    dual, helpstring("ISimpleAttributedObject Interface"),
    pointer_default(unique)
]
__interface ISimpleAttributedObject : IDispatch
{
    [id(1), helpstring("takes the square of a number")]
    HRESULT Square([in] LONG value, [out,retval] LONG* pResult);
    [propget, id(2), helpstring("property ObjectString")]
    HRESULT ObjectString([out, retval] BSTR* pVal);
};
```

This ensures that the correct interface definition is propagated through the generated IDL file to the type library and proxy/stub code.

Our project is now ready to compile. As before, we'll add a separate project containing test harness code. Apart from the different names of the interface and GUIDs, this is basically identical to the code presented earlier – the only other difference is a change in the way we convert the string. Since our new object string exceeds 64 bytes in length (when represented as a Unicode string), we can no longer use CW2AEX<64> to convert it to an ANSI string.

Now, it's true that we can specify whatever length we want to CW2AEX<> (CW2AEX<100> would do the trick here), but for the sake of demonstrating more ATL features, we'll instead use CW2A, which can cope with a string of arbitrary size at a slight performance cost:

```
CComBSTR bstr;
spObject->get_ObjectString(&bstr);
CW2A pszObjectString(bstr);
cout << "object string is: " << static_cast<char*>(pszObjectString) << endl;
```

As ever, you can find the full listing for this example, along with the rest of the source code for this chapter, in the archive that's downloadable from the Wrox web site.

Converting to an executable

In this section, we'll demonstrate the utility of attributes by converting the SimpleAttributedObject class of our last sample from a DLL server to an EXE server. Without attributes, this would require a considerable modification. With them, however, the only change we have to make to the C++ code in order to create an executable COM server is this:

```
// SimpleAttributedATL.cpp : Implementation of DLL Exports.

#include "stdafx.h"
#include "resource.h"

// The module attribute causes DllMain, DllRegisterServer, and
// DllUnregisterServer to be automatically implemented for you
[ module(exe, uuid = "{9DF208A2-F3BE-4F38-9C5C-54BBF95B8234}",
  name = "SimpleAttributedATL",
  helpstring = "SimpleAttributedATL 1.0 Type Library",
  resource_name = "IDR_SIMPLEATTRIBUTEDATL") ];
```

However, there are also a few changes that must be made to the compiler options. Bring up the Properties for the SimpleAttributedATL project, make sure that All Configurations is selected in the Configuration list box, and change the project type from Dynamic Library to Application:

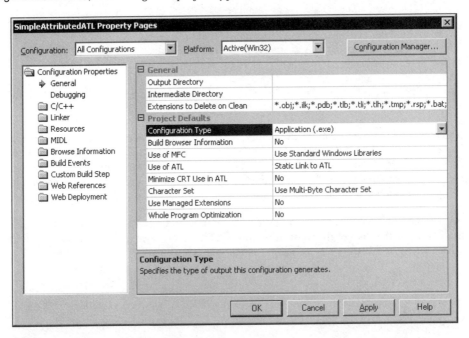

Secondly, we need to adjust the Linker settings so that the output file has the right name – that is, SimpleAttributedATL.exe rather than SimpleAttributedATL.dll:

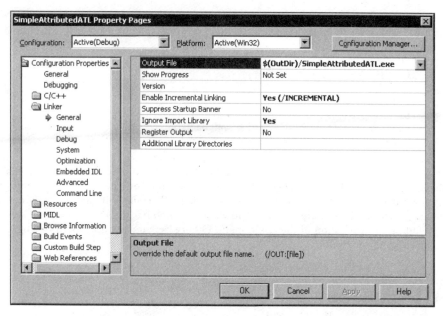

We also need to change the post-build step, in which the COM component is registered. For a DLL, this is done by running the `regsvr32` utility on the DLL, so the post-build step is `regsvr32 /s /c "$(TargetPath)"`. However, an executable registers itself by being run and passed the `regserver` flag, so we need to change the step to `"$(TargetPath)" /regserver`:

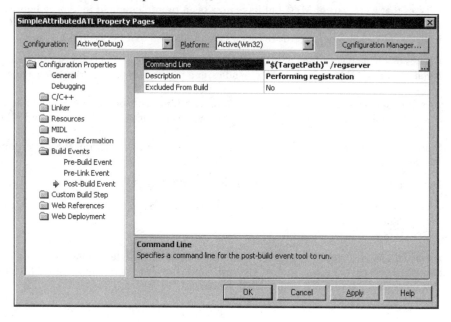

With these changes made, the component will compile and be registered successfully as an executable server. All that remains is to modify the code in the test harness to ensure that it calls up the appropriate type of component:

```
int _tmain(int argc, _TCHAR* argv[])
{
    CoInitialize(NULL);
    CComPtr<ISimpleAttributedObject> spObject;
    CoCreateInstance(CLSID_CSimpleAttributedObject, NULL, CLSCTX_LOCAL_SERVER,
            IID_ISimpleAttributedObject, reinterpret_cast<void**>(&spObject));
```

With these changes, the entire solution is ready to be compiled and run. Note, however, that because we didn't change any of the GUIDs between the two solutions, you won't be able to have both the DLL and EXE components registered at the same time – registering either one will automatically deregister the other. If you've just run the sample one way and want to switch back, you should make sure to do a full rebuild, including re-registration of the component. Otherwise, you run the risk of having incorrect registry entries for the component.

New ATL classes

We've now experienced a flavor of the new ATL attributes and seen some of the other changes to ATL. In this section, we'll take an overview of some of the new classes that are available to the ATL programmer, which really come from two sources:

- ❑ Classes that were part of MFC but have now been re-implemented in a more lightweight manner. They no longer rely on the MFC DLLs, and may therefore be used in MFC or ATL projects. Microsoft now regards these classes as being shared between ATL and MFC.

- ❑ Classes that have been added to ATL. These include dynamic array classes, wrappers around certain Windows objects (such as files, handles, and registry keys), and string conversion classes.

In both cases, the list of classes is extensive, and we'll restrict this discussion to some of the more significant additions. Looking at the first variety, the main classes that are now shared between ATL and MFC are:

- ❑ Simple classes such as CPoint, CSize, CRect, and so on, which wrap the corresponding Windows C structs

- ❑ Date-time manipulation classes such as CTime and CTimeSpan

- ❑ A string template, CStringT<>, and associated typedefs that provide extensive string-manipulation facilities

We'll illustrate CTime and CTimeSpan later in this chapter, when we develop a sample utilities component. We won't cover classes such as CPoint, since these are very simple indeed. Here, we'll look in a bit more detail at the new string handling classes.

New string classes

For a long time, MFC has had the CString class, which (depending on your compilation options) represents a Unicode or an ANSI string. It has a huge number of member functions for performing string manipulation, as well as operator overloads to make string concatenation syntactically easy. ATL, on the other hand, has had CComBSTR, which was designed specifically to wrap the BSTR that's used by the COM infrastructure to represent strings. Although CComBSTR makes such tasks as creating and destroying BSTRs a lot simpler, it doesn't expose many methods for general string manipulation. The other runner in this race is the STL string class – but from the point of view of ATL, this has the disadvantage that it requires linking to the CRT. It also has a slightly esoteric syntax that not all developers are comfortable with.

Now, to allow ATL the option of sophisticated string handling without having to link to a large library, Microsoft has completely rewritten the implementation of CString. Instead of being rooted in the MFC DLLs, CString is now based on a template called CStringT<>. (CStringT<> is defined in the atlstr.h header file, and implements all the functions that CString used to, but without any of the MFC baggage.) The template takes two parameters: the basic character type (char for ANSI, wchar_t for Unicode, or TCHAR to make the character dependent on your compilation options), and a class that indicates where resources are located and whether the CStringT<> object will use CRT support.

```
template<typename BaseType, class StringTraits>
class CStringT : public CSimpleStringT<BaseType>
```

Although CStringT<> gives us everything we need, it's unlikely that you'd enjoy declaring a template every time you wanted to use a string. Sympathetic to this, Microsoft has typedef'd two other classes based on CStringT<>. For projects using MFC, we have CString, just as before. For ATL users, we have CAtlString.

CAtlString sets up the CStringT<> parameters to support TCHAR characters and have no CRT dependency, as you'd expect from an ATL project. Although this sounds tricky, the result is that you can just declare a CAtlString variable in your code, and you get a string object with a rich set of methods to manipulate a string. It's worth pointing out that you're quite free to use either CAtlString or CString in an ATL project – you get the same methods, though the documentation hints that CString is preferred for projects that use MFC. In this chapter, we've gone for CAtlString.

To use CAtlString (or CString) in an ATL project, you'll need to #include the atlstr.h file. The facilities offered by this class include methods to perform concatenation, printf-style formatting, conversions, sub-string matching, and searching. We'll see a number of these operations taking place in the example that brings this chapter to a close.

String conversion classes

ATL has introduced six new template classes that are responsible for converting strings between the various different formats; these are CA2AEX<>, CA2CAEX<>, CA2WAEX<>, CW2AEX<>, CW2CWEX<>, and CW2WEX<>. In all cases, the template takes a single parameter that indicates the number of bytes to be used to store the string for the conversion. In general, however, you're more likely to use typedefs that are based on these classes, as we'll now demonstrate. Suppose that we have the following variables:

```
char* pszA = "Hello";
TCHAR* pszT = _T("Hello");
wchar_t* pszW = L"Hello";
```

Given these, we can declare new variables and perform conversions during the creation process, like this:

```
CW2A convertStrA(pszW);        // Convert wchar_t to char
CA2CT convertStrT(pszA);       // Convert char to const TCHAR
CT2W convertStrW(pszT);        // Convert TCHAR to wchar_t
```

Here, we're instantiating a variable of a type given by one of the conversion classes. In the first line, we declare a CW2A, and the result is an object that contains a buffer with the string "Hello" as a set of chars (ANSI characters). The object has been initialized through the passing of a string in wchar_t format. If we actually *need* a char*, we can extract the buffer using this technique:

```
char* pszRes = convertStrA;
```

Note that this sets pszRes to point to the buffer inside convertStrA – it doesn't copy the buffer. This kind of behavior is shared by the other conversions.

The above code demonstrates only a sample of the conversions that are possible, but it illustrates the way that you can work out the name of the typedef that's appropriate for the conversion you require. The first letter of the name is C. Then comes a letter that indicates what you are converting from (A, T, or W). Next is the character '2', followed by a letter indicating what you're converting to – again, A, T, or W. If the 'target' variable is constant, a C is inserted before the indicatory letter. Thus, CW2CT will convert a wchar_t string to a constant TCHAR string.

The beauty of this way of doing the conversion is that, because we're using class instances, the memory used to store the buffer will automatically be reclaimed when the instance goes out of scope.

```
{
    CA2CT convertStrT(pszA);                  // Convert char to TCHAR
    const TCHAR* pszResT = convertStrT;

    // convertStrT in scope here, so can use pszResT
}

// convertStrT no longer in scope. Memory will have been reclaimed. Shouldn't
// use pszResT any more either, as it may point to garbage.
```

What this means is that you can perform a conversion inside a loop, and you won't run the risk of a stack overflow. The classes use the stack for strings up to a certain length (128 bytes by default, which covers most cases), but will use malloc() to reserve space on the heap if the string is too long.

If you're not sure how long the strings you're dealing with will be, you should use the simple typedefs, as the above code does. If, however, you believe the string will fit into a buffer of a certain size, you can use a different typedef (or the actual class directly) in order to reduce the size of the buffer used. To do this, you add the string EX to the appropriate typedef, with a template parameter that indicates the number of bytes of memory to be used as a buffer. The following code performs the same conversions as our earlier samples, but with a buffer size of 64 in each case.

```
CW2AEX<64> convertStrA(pszW);     // Convert wchar_t to char
CA2CTEX<64> convertStrT(pszA);    // Convert char to TCHAR
CT2WEX<64> convertStrW(pszT);     // Convert TCHAR to wchar_t
```

There's a point that needs watching if you're used to working with the old ATL 3.0 macros. The following code is syntactically correct, so it will compile – it looks roughly like something you would have done in ATL 3.0. But you're strongly advised not to try it with the new typedefs:

```
char* pszResult = CW2A(L"Hello");
```

This code is misleading. It looks like you're doing a straight conversion and putting the result in pszResult, but in fact the result is placed in a temporary CW2A object that will have gone out of scope by the next line. pszResult will very soon point to garbage. The above code is completely equivalent to the following, which makes the scoping problem clearer:

```
char* pszResult;
{
    CW2A temp(L"Hello");
    pszResult = temp;
}
```

When using the new typedefs, you're better off using the syntax we presented initially. This makes it much more obvious that you're declaring a temporary object that performs the conversion and holds the converted string.

Example utilities project

In this final section of the chapter, we'll develop a short sample project that illustrates the use of attributes and some of the new ATL utility classes. We'll develop an executable COM component called UtilitiesComponent that's designed to perform certain utility tasks. This server will be able to:

❑   Work out the date of the next weekday after the current date, and return the result as a string. If the method is called on a Sunday, Monday, Tuesday, Wednesday, or Thursday, the result will simply be tomorrow's date. If it's invoked on a Friday or a Saturday, then the result will be the date of the following Monday.

❑   Remove all excess whitespace from a string, which means removing any leading or trailing whitespace, and replacing any set of consecutive whitespace characters inside the string with a single space character. For our purposes, whitespace is defined as space characters, tabs, or carriage returns.

This might seem a slightly odd combination of methods to put in the same component, but they nicely illustrate the use of the new CAtlString and CTime classes.

Our project will be called ATLUtilities, and we'll start off by creating it in Visual Studio .NET as an ATL Project, specifying that it should be an attributed DLL server. Then we use the usual Wizards to generate a component called UtilitiesComponent, and add methods to its IUtilitiesComponent interface that have the following signatures:

```
STDMETHOD(TrueTrim)(BSTR bstrInput, BSTR* pbstrResult);
STDMETHOD(get_NextWeekday)(BSTR* pVal);
```

Before we start modifying the Wizard-generated code, we'll make one change to the project. In ATL 3.0, Visual Studio 6.0 gave us a choice of configurations for ATL projects, including **Debug**, **Release**, **Unicode Debug**, and **Unicode Release**. If you wanted to use Unicode rather than the multi-byte character set (MBCS) in strings, then you would obviously choose the appropriate build.

Visual Studio .NET doesn't give us these choices – we just get plain **Debug** and **Release** configurations, which are set by default to use MBCS strings. If we wish to use Unicode, we need to change the project properties explicitly. Now, since we're going to be doing string manipulation, and COM BSTRs are always Unicode, it'll make things a lot easier to make this change. CAtlString works as either a Unicode or an MBCS class, depending on the project settings – but if we leave the project as MBCS, there'll be a performance hit due to the need to convert between formats when swapping strings between CAtlString and BSTR.

To set up our component to use Unicode strings throughout, we bring up the project properties dialog, locate the **General Configuration Properties**, ensure that **All Configurations** is selected in the **Configuration** list box, and change the **Character Set** to Unicode:

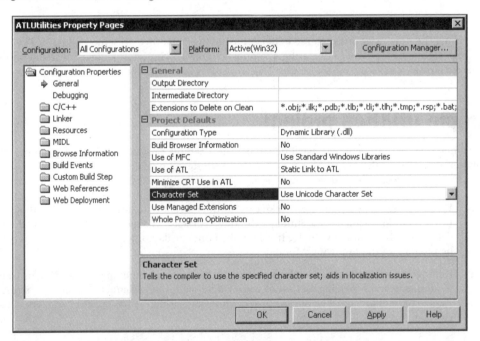

Now we're ready to start coding. Once we've created the component and used the Wizards to add the methods, we can add the following to the implementation of TrueTrim():

```
STDMETHODIMP CUtilitiesComponent::TrueTrim(BSTR bstrInput, BSTR* pbstrResult)
{
    const CAtlString csInput = bstrInput;
    CAtlString csResult;
```

```
      CAtlString csTemp;
      int pos = 0;

      while(!(csTemp = csInput.Tokenize(_T(" \n\t"), pos)).IsEmpty())
      {
         if(!csResult.IsEmpty())
            csResult += _T(" ");
         csResult += csTemp;
      }

      *pbstrResult = csResult.AllocSysString();
      return S_OK;
   }
```

This method illustrates just how easy string manipulation can be using CAtlString. The main benefits here lie in the use of the CAtlString::Tokenize() method to break up the string at whitespace characters, and the addition-assignment operator overload, CAtlString::operator+=(), to concatenate strings.

To understand what's going on in the while loop, we need to understand how Tokenize() works. This method takes two parameters:

❑   A string containing the set of characters indicating the tokens at which the string can be split

❑   The position at which we start searching through the CAtlString

Each time Tokenize() is called, it looks for a part of the string that's bounded by one or more of the token characters and splits this part off. This sub-string is returned by the method, while the second parameter is updated to reflect the new position at which to perform the next Tokenize() operation. The process is probably made clearer by an example.

If we have token characters of space, tab, and carriage return (as in the code above) and call Tokenize() against the string "   \t First   Second\nThird", then the method will return "First", while the position will be increased to 13, to point to the start of the word "Second". Calling Tokenize() again will update the starting point to 20 and return "Second". Calling it a third time will return "Third" and set the starting point to the end of the string. Calling it for the fourth time will return an empty string. Since this is the test we use for exiting the while loop, the code will exit.

In the body of the while loop, we construct a string that has no excess whitespace by concatenating the sub-strings that were extracted from the string. Finally, we copy the result back into the supplied BSTR and return.

Next, let's look at the second method, which implements the read-only NextWeekday property:

```
STDMETHODIMP CUtilitiesComponent::get_NextWeekday(BSTR* pVal)
{
   CTime currentTime = CTime::GetCurrentTime();
   int iDay = currentTime.GetDayOfWeek();
   int nDaysTillNextWeekday = 1;
   if(iDay == 6)
      nDaysTillNextWeekday = 2;
```

```
       else if(iDay == 5)
          nDaysTillNextWeekday = 3;

    CTimeSpan daysTillNextWeekday(nDaysTillNextWeekday, 0, 0, 0);
    currentTime += daysTillNextWeekday;
    CAtlString result = currentTime.Format(_T("%A, %d %B %Y"));
    (static_cast<CComBSTR>(result)).CopyTo(pVal);
    return S_OK;
}
```

This property illustrates the CTime and CTimeSpan classes that are shared between ATL and MFC. We start by obtaining the current time using the static CTime::GetCurrentTime() method, and then we identify what day of the week we are at by using CTime::GetDayOfWeek(). This returns an integer, where 1 is Sunday, 2 is Monday, and so on.

We use this integer to construct a CTimeSpan instance that represents the number of days we need to move forward from today to get to the next weekday: one day for Sunday thru Thursday, three days if it's a Friday, and two if it's a Saturday. Then we add this CTimeSpan to the current date and format the resulting CTime object as a string using CTime::Format(). This powerful method uses format specifiers to indicate exactly how you want the string formatted; we're using %A for the day of the week, %d for the day of the month, %B for the name of the month, and %Y for a four-digit year. (A complete list of specifiers can be found in the MSDN documentation.) Once we have the string, we simply convert and copy it back to a BSTR, and we can then return it to the client.

The only other change we need to make to the code for the component is to #include a couple of ATL header files that contain the definitions of the classes we use:

```
#include <atlstr.h>
#include <atltime.h>
```

The component is now ready for compilation, but we need a client to test it with. Choose to add a new project to the current solution, and create a new Win32 console application called UtilitiesTestHarness, remembering to add support for ATL as you do so. Then, just add the following code to the UtilitiesTestHarness.cpp file:

```
#include "stdafx.h"

#include "..\ATLUtilities\_ATLUtilities.h"
#include "..\ATLUtilities\_ATLUtilities_i.c"

int _tmain(int argc, _TCHAR* argv[])
{
   CoInitialize(NULL);
   CComPtr<IUtilitiesComponent> spObject;
   CoCreateInstance(CLSID_CUtilitiesComponent, NULL, CLSCTX_INPROC_SERVER,
             IID_IUtilitiesComponent, reinterpret_cast<void**>(&spObject));

   CComBSTR bstrNextWeekday;
   spObject->get_NextWeekday(&bstrNextWeekday);
   CW2A pszNextWeekday(bstrNextWeekday);
   cout << "Next weekday is " << static_cast<char*>(pszNextWeekday) << endl;
```

```
    CComBSTR bstrTestString = L"\thello  \n  there    ";
    CComBSTR bstrResult;
    spObject->TrueTrim(bstrTestString, &bstrResult);
    CW2A pszTestString(bstrTestString);
    cout << "Test string is >>" << static_cast<char*>(pszTestString);
    cout << "<<" << endl;

    CW2A pszResult(bstrResult);
    cout << "Result of TrueTrim is >>" << static_cast<char*>(pszResult);
    cout << "<<" << endl;

    spObject = 0;
    CoUninitialize();
    return 0;
}
```

Running the code gives the following (successful) result:

```
Next weekday is Monday, 14 January 2002
Test string is >>    hello
   there    <<
Result of TrueTrim is >>hello there<<
```

Summary

In this chapter, we've examined some of the new features in ATL 7.0 that make it easier than ever before to write COM components. The biggest single change is the introduction of attributes, which allow attribute providers to generate some ATL code automatically, based on your specific requirements. However, we have seen that attributes are not the only improvements to ATL. In particular, there are a number of new classes, changes to the ATL class hierarchy, and much better string handling facilities.

In the next two chapters, we'll continue to explore how ATL has been enhanced in Visual C++ .NET by examining a pair of related ATL technologies that have nothing to do with COM: ATL Server and ATL Server web services.

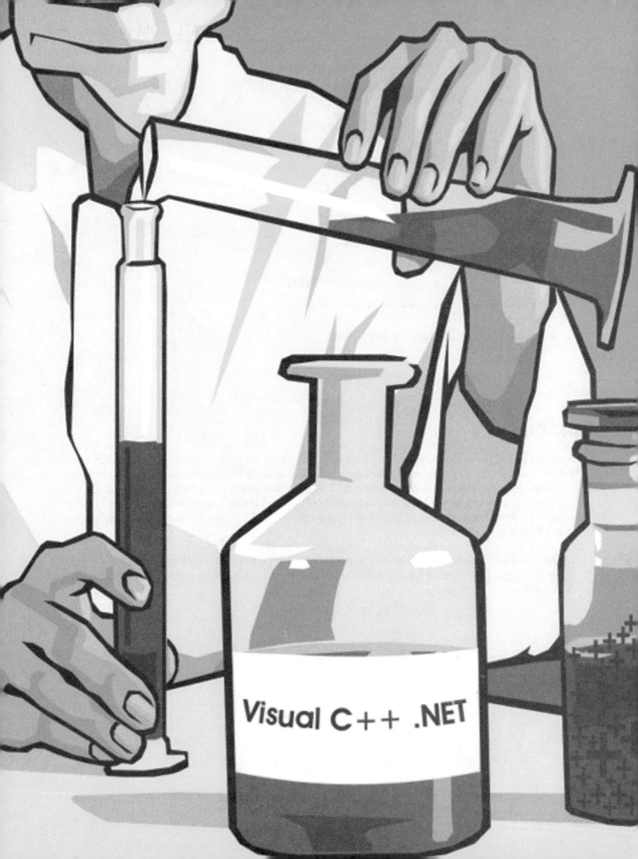

10

An introduction to ATL Server

ATL Server is a set of native C++ classes provided by Microsoft to facilitate the development of high performance web-based applications and web services. If you've been creating web applications by creating ISAPI extension DLLs, you'll find this technology a great boon – and as it's based on ATL, it makes development easy. ATL Server contains support for features such as message queuing, cryptography, SMTP mail, regular expressions, thread pooling, caching, and performance monitoring. Furthermore, it includes features that make debugging simple for even the most complex web applications.

In this chapter, we'll look at what ATL Server is, how it works, and how we can use it to build web applications. Along the way, we'll look at some examples that illustrate the features of ATL Server. Then, in the next chapter, we'll move on to focus specifically on its role in the creation of web services.

Architecture

The ATL Server programming model is based on user-created tags that are replaced at runtime by method invocations. The tags are placed in a **server response file** (**SRF**, also known as a **stencil**), while the methods are written in C++ and implemented in a **web application DLL**. By containing a mixture of static data and dynamic tags, the SRF file creates a very simple mechanism for designing templates and generating web content at runtime.

In essence, the way ATL Server works is not dissimilar to technologies like ASP: a request from a user for a 'web page' is the direct cause of some server-side processing whose result is customized HTML. ATL Server, though, uses C++ code that's compiled at development time before being deployed on the server, resulting in very high performance.

The ATL Server architecture runs on top of Internet Information Server (IIS); the components involved and a rough depiction of the way requests are handled are shown in the diagram below:

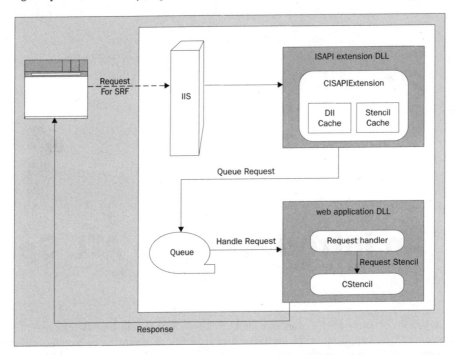

The architecture consists of one **ISAPI extension DLL** per IIS virtual directory, one or more web application DLLs, and one or more SRF files. This flexibility exists because you may decide to create several web application DLLs in your application, each implementing a logical piece of functionality. Similarly, you may create multiple SRFs to satisfy the user interface requirements of your application.

The procedure illustrated above begins when the client sends an HTTP request for an SRF (or, occasionally, a web application DLL) to the IIS server. The server will pass such requests to the ISAPI extension DLL, which in turn will either read the SRF file and make appropriate requests to handlers in the associated web application DLL, or check the query string for a handler parameter to be passed straight to the DLL. Either way, requests to the web application DLL are immediately queued, freeing the IIS threads to receive further client requests. Queued requests are dispatched to the appropriate handlers as and when they become available.

If you're familiar with writing ISAPI extensions in Visual C++, then you might have expected to define the functionality of the whole application in the ISAPI DLL itself. In ATL Server, however, the ISAPI DLL is used to receive requests from the client, and to return responses to the client. It passes the requests themselves to a request handler that's implemented in a web application DLL, and serves simply as a communication channel between IIS and the web application DLL.

Developing a simple ATL Server application

In this section, we'll start by looking at the ATL Server Wizard, using it to generate a simple web application for us. Later on, we'll add some of our own code, but for now let's stick to the default code and see what we can learn from it.

Creating the project

In Visual Studio .NET, create a new Visual C++ project with the ATL Server Project Wizard. (In the code that's available for download, this is called `FirstATLServerApplication`.) Once everything's settled down again, you'll find that the Project Settings section of the Wizard dialog looks like this:

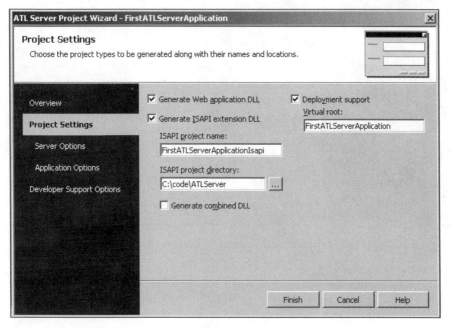

The default settings represented here specify that the ISAPI extension and the web application DLL will be created separately. The reason for allowing one or other of these options to be switched off is that, as suggested above, you can create multiple web DLLs within the same ATL Server application.

Now, although you'll usually create the web DLL and ISAPI DLL separately, it's possible to create a single DLL that includes the functionality of both. You might choose to do this in order to save loading time and reduce memory requirements, or simply to ease deployment; although you should also note that it has implications for your application's efficiency. Whatever the reason, if you choose to do this, you can select the Generate combined DLL option.

Deployment support is enabled by default, although it's also possible to switch it off here and add it later through the Web Deployment property page. Enabling this option means that the DLLs you create will be automatically registered on your machine during the project build operation. The Virtual root edit box allows you to specify the IIS virtual directory in which the project files will be installed. (Of course, this requires IIS to be installed on your machine.) If it doesn't already exist, the deployment tool automatically adds the virtual directory to IIS's public folder.

Beyond the project's basic settings, the generated ISAPI DLL can support many optional features that can be configured in the **Server Options** section. Though we won't need to go beyond the defaults provided by the Wizard in the applications that we'll develop in this chapter, it's worth taking a quick look at the kinds of things that are available.

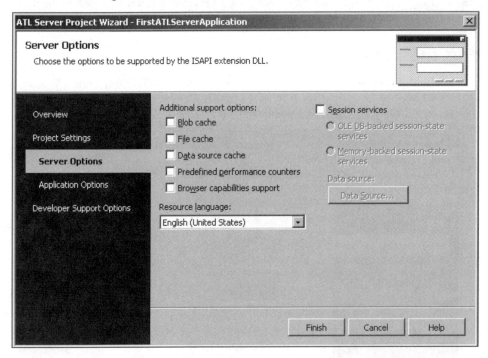

The features that can be added to the ISAPI extension DLL are summarized below:

❑   **Blob cache** enables efficient storage and retrieval of arbitrary binary data. If the request to and response from the web application DLL involve dealing with significant quantities of binary data, this option will help to improve the performance of the application, as such data will be cached by the system.

❑   **File cache** allows the efficient storage and retrieval of files and file data. If your application deals with `File` objects during the course of its conversations with its users, this option will help to improve the performance of the application by caching such operations.

❑   **Data source cache** allows OLE DB data source connections to be cached. If the application uses such a data source, then this option will once again result in improved application performance.

❑   **Predefined performance counters** are used to add performance-monitoring support to the ISAPI extension DLL.

❑   **Browser capabilities support** exposes a 'browser capabilities' service from the ISAPI extension DLL. Using this, the web server can detect what the browser is capable of – whether it supports Java, cookies, or scripting languages, for example.

Enabling Session services facilitates session-state management across multiple requests – client-specific data is stored in session variables. You may use memory or a database to store session information; when this check box is enabled, you get two options:

❑ With OLE DB-backed session-state services, session data is stored in an OLE DB data source and, naturally, if you select this option, you will need to specify the data source. Storing session data in a database will protect it from server crashes, and means that it can be kept for long periods – perhaps even until the next client session. (Think of shopping at Amazon, when your shopping cart is retained until you next log in.) However, storing session data in a database is likely to result in poor response times compared with the other option here.

❑ With Memory-backed session-state services, session data is persisted to memory. This can result in fast retrieval of session data, but there is no protection against server crashes.

Predictably, selecting the Application Options section presents us with a list of features that we can add to the web application DLL:

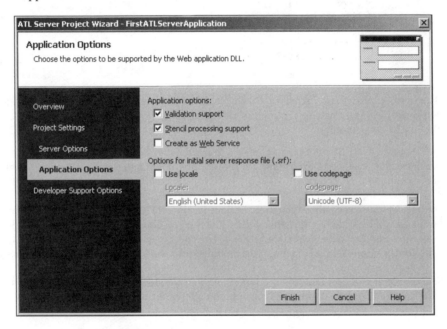

The various options here are summarized below:

❑ Validation support adds validation code for request parameters and form variables to the DLL. When you select this option, the Wizard adds the following definition to your code; the ValidateAndExchange() method is the first to be called in any communication sequence between the ISAPI extension DLL and the web application DLL:

```
HTTP_CODE ValidateAndExchange()
{
    // TODO: Put all initialization and validation code here
```

```
    // Set the content-type
    m_HttpResponse.SetContentType("text/html");

    return HTTP_SUCCESS;
}
```

In this method implementation, from which you have access to the request and response objects that are used for communication with the users of your application, you can perform any validation and initialization that you deem necessary.

❑ **Stencil processing support** results in the addition of a method to the source code that demonstrates the use of the `tag_name` attribute. When you select this option, the following block of code will be added:

```
protected:
    // An example of how to use a replacement tag with the stencil processor
    [tag_name(name = "Hello")]
    HTTP_CODE OnHello(void)
    {
        m_HttpResponse << "Hello World!";
        return HTTP_SUCCESS;
    }
```

The method provides a prototype for the replacement methods used by the stencil processor. For example, if you use `Hello` in your SRF file, the tag will be replaced at runtime by a call to the `OnHello()` method.

❑ If **Create as Web Service** is enabled, the Wizard generates the skeleton code for a web service; otherwise, code for a standard request handler is generated. We'll be looking at web services in the next chapter.

The final settings on this screen allow you to set options for the initial stencil. If you choose **Use locale**, the selected locale tag will be added to the generated SRF file. If you choose **Use codepage**, the selected codepage tag will be added to the generated SRF file. The codepage indicates the character set to be used; if your SRF file contains non-ANSI characters, you should specify the appropriate character set here.

Lastly, the **Developer Support Options** section allows you to add (or rather, to remove, since all of these are included by default) 'to do' comments, attributed code, and trace handling support:

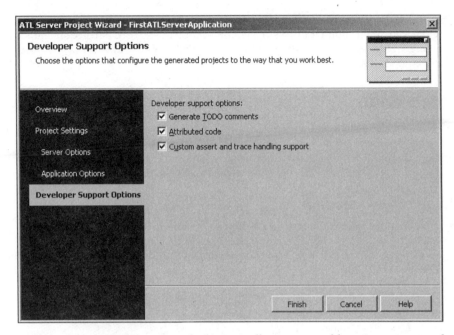

These options are fairly self-explanatory; the last one allows you to add tracing support and ASSERT statements that enable debugging using the WebDbg tool, which is available in the Tools folder of your Visual C++ installation. As stated earlier, we're going to stick with the default options in this project, so click Finish to generate the project files. The Solution Explorer will fill to contain the list of generated files shown here:

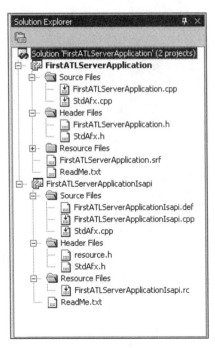

In amongst the usual Visual C++ files, FirstATLServerApplication.cpp and its corresponding .h file define the web application DLL; FirstATLServerApplicationIsapi.cpp and its corresponding .h file define the ISAPI extension DLL; and FirstATLServerApplication.srf is the service response file.

Generated code

Having examined the various configurable options, let's now spend a little time examining the code that the Wizard has generated for us, and learning more about what it does and how it does it. From our point of view, there are two files that are particularly important: FirstATLServerApplication.h and FirstATLServerApplication.srf. We'll start with the first of those two.

FirstATLServerApplication.h

This Wizard-generated header file is shown below; it contains the definition of the CFirstATLServerApplicationHandler class that will be used to process the stencil. The methods of this class can provide validation on input parameters and produce HTML output that will replace the tags in the SRF.

```
#pragma once

[request_handler("Default")]
class CFirstATLServerApplicationHandler
{
private:
    // Put private members here

protected:
    // Put protected members here

public:
    // Put public members here

    HTTP_CODE ValidateAndExchange()
    {
        // TODO: Put all initialization and validation code here

        // Set the content-type
        m_HttpResponse.SetContentType("text/html");

        return HTTP_SUCCESS;
    }

protected:
    // An example of how to use a replacement tag with the stencil processor
    [tag_name(name = "Hello")]
    HTTP_CODE OnHello(void)
    {
        m_HttpResponse << "Hello World!";
        return HTTP_SUCCESS;
    }
};
```

Applying the `request_handler` attribute to the `CFirstATLServerApplicationHandler` class exposes it as an ATL Server request handler class, enabling it to handle HTTP requests. It also results in the class being derived from `CRequestHandlerT<>`, an ATL class whose declaration is shown below:

```
template <class THandler,
          class ThreadModel = CComSingleThreadModel,
          class TagReplacerType = CHtmlTagReplacer<THandler> >
class CRequestHandlerT : public TagReplacerType,
                         public CComObjectRootEx<ThreadModel>,
                         public IRequestHandlerImpl<THandler>
```

This is the base class for all request handlers, and you can override its methods to provide additional initialization functionality. It also provides access to the server context, and references to the request and response objects through two vitally important member variables:

```
CHttpRequest m_HttpRequest;
CHttpResponse m_HttpResponse;
```

One of the methods that `CRequestHandlerT<>` defines is `ValidateAndExchange()`, which (as we've already discussed) gets overridden by default. You might decide to initialize class members in this method by assigning values to them from the m_HttpRequest object, or to perform some server-side validation. Another commonly overridden method is `CheckValidRequest()`, which has the following signature:

```
HTTP_CODE CheckValidRequest();
```

If you wish, you can implement this method to check the basic validity of a request; it will be called before the relatively expensive initialization of the request object takes place. This means that you can't use m_HttpRequest in your method code, although you are permitted to use the m_HttpResponse object to send a response to the client.

The parameter to the `request_handler` attribute ("Default" in this case) will be used in the stencil file to identify the handler class whose methods should be used to process the tags it contains. Since we chose to have stencil support in our project, the Wizard has added the `tag_name` attribute-decorated OnHello() method that we described earlier. In general, the methods that you define in this fashion have access to both m_HttpRequest and m_HttpResponse, and, in any real application, some additional processing would be likely – the method might extract data from the request object, perform some calculations on it, format the result, and *then* return it to the client.

Depending on the success of the operations performed in these methods, you may return a status code to the client – HTTP_SUCCESS predictably indicates success, HTTP_FAIL indicates failure, and there are a number of states in between that you should consult the documentation for if you're interested.

FirstATLServerApplication.srf

The other Wizard-generated file that we need to take a look at is the stencil file, whose very brief default contents are shown below:

```
{{// use MSDN's "ATL Server Response File Reference" to learn about SRF files.}}
{{handler FirstATLServerApplication.dll/Default}} This is a test: {{Hello}}
```

Interestingly, though, this is only one way of looking at the file! At the bottom left corner of the window in which this text is displayed are two buttons labeled **Design** and **HTML**. If you switch to the HTML view, you'll see something a little more familiar looking:

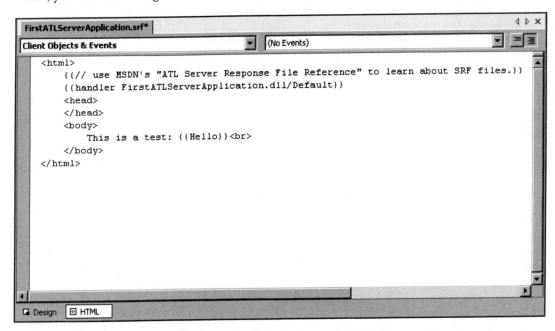

In this code, double braces ('{{' and '}}') mark the tags that will be processed by our web application DLL. There are three in the above listing, but the first of them is actually just a comment, as evidenced by the C++-style double forward slash. The second tag is rather more interesting, because it identifies the handler class that's associated with this file – in this case, the `CFirstATLServerApplicationHandler` class in `FirstATLServerApplication.dll` – by naming the DLL that contains it, and the attribute associated with the class.

When the client makes an HTTP request for the stencil, the static message `"This is a test: "` will be displayed in the client browser, followed by the content produced by the `Hello` tag – that is, the results of processing the `OnHello()` method. The tag invokes the handler method and executes the C++ code, which dynamically sets the content of the response object with the appropriate HTML.

In a more complex SRF file, you might have several tags:

```
{{handler aaa.dll/Default}} This is an example: {{TagA}} {{TagB}}
```

When this file is processed, it will replace `TagA` *and* `TagB` with HTML code generated by methods that are mapped to the tags using the `tag_name` attribute. Note that if a web page author specifies an invalid tag name by mistake, the tag name will be printed on the browser as is, since there is no replacement method available for the specified tag.

Stencil files allow the use of conditional expressions and program loops. The following code, for example, shows the use of an `if` condition. If the method linked to the `Available` tag returns a success code (that is, `HTTP_SUCCESS`), the static content defined in the `if` block will be displayed to the client; it's also possible to specify nested `if` conditions by using `else-elseif` constructs with similar syntax.

```
{{if Available}}
The resource is available
{{endif}}
```

The following code segment shows the use of `while` block. The handler loops until the method linked to by the `GetNextItem` tag returns a failure code (`HTTP_S_FALSE`). On each iteration, the `DisplayItem` tag is evaluated and the content it generates will be displayed in the client browser:

```
{{while GetNextItem}}
    {{DisplayItem}}
{{endwhile}}
```

For the simple example defined by the Wizard code, the HTML code that gets sent back to the client is therefore just this:

```
<html>
    <head>
    </head>
    <body>
        This is a test: Hello World!<br>
    </body>
</html>
```

Building, deploying, and running the application

When you build the solution in the Visual Studio .NET IDE, the three crucial files `FirstATLServerApplicationIsapi.dll`, `FirstATLServerApplication.srf`, and `FirstATLServerApplication.dll` are copied to an IIS virtual folder as the final stage in the process. As this copying takes place, the IIS service is stopped and then restarted.

With this done, you can run the application simply by typing the appropriate URL into your web browser. This opens the SRF file, which in turn causes the ISAPI extension DLL to be loaded. The latter loads up the web application DLL, invokes the appropriate command handler, and replaces the `Hello` tag in the SRF file with the HTML code it generates before returning it to the client. You should see the following output:

If you don't have IIS running on your machine, or an error occurs during the copying process, the project will not be deployed. Otherwise, through Visual Studio .NET, it's possible to modify the DLL code at any time, redeploy it, and test it without ever leaving the IDE. During the build process, the `.srf` and `.dll` files are registered with IIS, as you can see from the IIS manager:

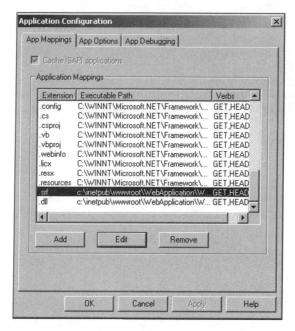

Once the application is fully tested, you may like to deploy it on a production server, something that's best achieved by creating a Visual Studio .NET Web Setup Project. For information about this and the other Wizards for creating setup and deployment projects, refer to the online documentation.

Modifying the code

In this section, we'll start to move beyond the basics and modify our ATL Server application so that it returns a table of tax rates for all the states in our database. Open the header file for the web application DLL (`FirstATLServerApplication.h`) and add the following declaration to the private section of the `CFirstATLServerApplicationHandler` class:

```
CAtlMap<LPSTR, double> map;
```

We use the `CAtlMap<>` template class here to create a map whose elements consist of a string pointer holding the state code and a floating-point value holding the tax rate. The map is then initialized in the class's generated `ValidateAndExchange()` method:

```
HTTP_CODE ValidateAndExchange()
{
    map.SetAt("IL", 6.5);
    map.SetAt("CA", 11.0);
    map.SetAt("FL", 12.0);
    map.SetAt("NY", 8.5);
    map.SetAt("DL", 7.5);
    map.SetAt("MA", 4.5);
    map.SetAt("OH", 12.5);
    map.SetAt("NJ", 5.5);
    map.SetAt("UT", 5.0);
    map.SetAt("CO", 14.0);
```

```
    // Set the content-type for response
    m_HttpResponse.SetContentType("text/html");

    return HTTP_SUCCESS;
}
```

Next, we create a new method called OnTaxRateTable(), and decorate it with the tag_name attribute as shown:

```
[tag_name(name = "TaxRateTable")]
HTTP_CODE OnTaxRateTable(void)
{
    LPSTR StateCode;
    double taxRate;

    // Display tax details
    m_HttpResponse << "<html>";
    m_HttpResponse << "<body bgcolor=#C0C0C0>";
    m_HttpResponse << "<p align=center><b><u>TAX DETAILS</u></b></p>";
    m_HttpResponse << "<table align= center border=1 width=53%>";
    m_HttpResponse << "<tr>";
    m_HttpResponse << "<td width=50% align=center><b>STATE CODE</b></td>";
    m_HttpResponse << "<td width=50% align=center><b>TAX RATE %</b></td>";
    m_HttpResponse << "</tr>";

    // To access the collection table
    POSITION pos = map.GetStartPosition();
    while(pos != NULL)
    {
        map.GetNextAssoc(pos, StateCode, taxRate);

        // Format Tax Rate for output
        CString strRate;
        strRate.Format(_T("%.2lf\n"), taxRate);

        m_HttpResponse << "<tr>";
        m_HttpResponse << "<td width=50% align=center>";
        m_HttpResponse << StateCode;
        m_HttpResponse << "</td>";
        m_HttpResponse << "<td width=50% align=right>";
        m_HttpResponse << strRate;
        m_HttpResponse << "</td>";
        m_HttpResponse << "</tr>";
    }

    m_HttpResponse << "</table>";
    m_HttpResponse << "</html>";

    return HTTP_SUCCESS;
}
```

The ISAPI extension DLL will call the `OnTaxRateTable()` method when it encounters the `TaxRateTable` tag in the SRF file. The method reads the contents of the map and creates an HTML table for display in the client. Obviously, then, the last thing that you need to do in order to make the application work is to modify the SRF file to include the `TaxRateTable` tag. Anything like the following will do the trick:

```
{{handler FirstATLServerApplication.dll/Default}} {{TaxRateTable}}
```

And if all has gone well, you ought to be presented with output that looks something like the following:

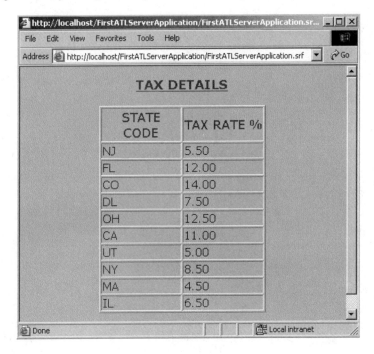

ATL Server guest book application

In this section, we'll develop a fully-fledged ATL Server application that uses many new features of the ATL library. This application can be used by any web site for gathering visitor information for marketing purposes. It uses an HTML-based form for users to enter information that's stored in a database after server-side validation. It also sends registration confirmation to the user by e-mail.

Create a new ATL Server Project in Visual Studio .NET, and name it `GuestBook`. Accept all of the default settings from the Wizard. This will generate two projects in your solution:

❑   `GuestBook`, containing the code for the web application DLL

❑   `GuestBookIsapi`, containing the code for the ISAPI extension DLL

The project also creates a sample SRF file that we'll modify in order to create the user interface.

Modifying the SRF

The full listing for this file is available for download along with the rest of the code for this chapter. As before, the SRF contains the HTML design of the form, so we need to add a `form` element with a 'submit' action that will re-request this same file:

```
<form id="Form1"
      action="http://localhost/GuestBook/GuestBook.srf" method="post">
...
</form>
```

Recall that when the client invokes the SRF file, the method defined in the handler class gets called. This method performs validation on the user input and prints any error messages on the same form. The first time the form is invoked, such validations should not be performed, as the form is empty. For this purpose, we create a hidden variable by adding the following HTML code to the SRF file; we'll see how this is used by the handler class a little later on.

```
<input type="hidden" name="bNotFirst" value="0" size="1">
```

We create the form by dragging and dropping controls from the toolbox. This is what the SRF looks like in the Design view:

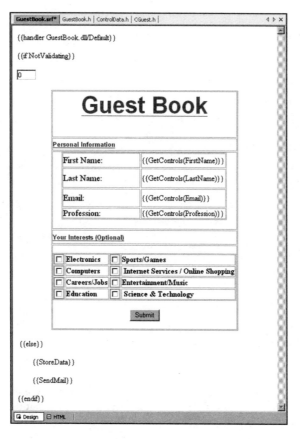

The `handler` tag at the start of the file specifies the name of the web application DLL and identifies the class that contains the request handlers. Our first action proper is to check the status returned by the `NotValidating` tag to see if validation on the input fields is required. The first time the SRF file is invoked, there is no user input, and the `NotValidating` tag returns `true` – the SRF file then displays a blank form to the user. After that, the form uses the `GetControls` tag with appropriate parameter values to display a user input control for each field.

In the `else` clause (that is, when the form is called for a second time, and contains input), we store the input fields to a database and send a confirmation message to the user. The `StoreData` tag performs the first of these actions, while `SendMail` deals with the second.

Implementing the handlers

Once the screen is created, we have to provide implementations for the various handlers in the `GuestBook.h` file. Modify the header file by adding the following private variable declarations:

```
private:
    CString Guest_Email;
    CString Guest_FName;
    CString Guest_LName;
    bool valid_input;
    CString errorMsg;
```

The GetControls tag

We'll now provide code for the methods associated with the tags used in the stencil, starting with `GetControls`:

```
[tag_name(name = "GetControls")]
HTTP_CODE OnGetControls(char* controlName)
{
    if(!strncmp(controlName, "Profession", 10))
    {
        m_HttpResponse << "<select name=\"Profession\">\n";
        for(int i = 0; i < (sizeof(professions) / sizeof(char*)); i++)
        {
            m_HttpResponse << "\t<option value=\""
                           << professions[i] << "\">"
                           << professions[i] << "</option>\n";
        }
        m_HttpResponse << "</select>";
        return HTTP_SUCCESS;
    }
    else
    {
        m_HttpResponse << "<input name=\"" << controlName << "\">";
        return HTTP_SUCCESS;
    }
}
```

In this method, we first check the input parameter, which designates the control name. Depending on the name, we create an appropriate HTML control for the user. Note that the `professions` array referred to in the above code is defined in an external file called `ControlData.h`.

The StoreData tag

The StoreData tag stores the input fields to a database. Here's the code:

```
[tag_name(name = "StoreData")]
HTTP_CODE OnStoreData(void)
{
    // Return true if and only if every form field was validated
    CDataSource ds;
    CCommand<CAccessor<CGuest> > cmd;
    CSession session;

    HRESULT hr = ds.OpenFromInitializationString(L"Provider=
        Microsoft.Jet.OLEDB.4.0;User ID=Admin;Data Source=C:\\GuestDB.mdb");

    if(SUCCEEDED(hr))
    {
        if(SUCCEEDED(session.Open(ds)))
        {
            CString FirstName(
                    CA2CT(m_HttpRequest.FormVars.Lookup("FirstName")));
            CString LastName(
                    CA2CT(m_HttpRequest.FormVars.Lookup("LastName")));
            CString Email(
                    CA2CT(m_HttpRequest.FormVars.Lookup("Email")));
            CString Profession(
                    CA2CT(m_HttpRequest.FormVars.Lookup("Profession")));

            char str[15];
            char buffer[3];
            char Item[30];
            char Interests[500];

            lstrcpy(Interests, "Interests: ");
            for(int i = 1; i < 9; i++)
            {
                lstrcpy(str, "chkInterest");
                _itoa(i, buffer, 10);
                lstrcat(str, buffer);
                lstrcpy(Item, "");
                lstrcpy(Item, m_HttpRequest.FormVars.Lookup(str));

                if(lstrcmp(Item, "") != 0)
                {
                    if(lstrcmpi(Interests, "Interests: ") != 0)
                    {
                        lstrcat(Interests, ",");
                    }
                    lstrcat(Interests,Item);
                }
            }

            CString SQLString("INSERT INTO Guest_Table VALUES('");
            SQLString += FirstName;
```

```
            SQLString += "','";
            SQLString += LastName;
            SQLString += "','";
            SQLString += Email;
            SQLString += "','";
            SQLString += Profession;
            SQLString += "',' ";
            SQLString += Interests;
            SQLString += "')";

            // Execute the query to insert records
            hr= cmd.Open(session, SQLString);
            m_HttpResponse << "<FONT color='#ff0033' size='6'>";
            m_HttpResponse << "Congratulations!"
            m_HttpResponse << "You have registered successfully.</FONT>";
            Guest_Email = CA2CT(m_HttpRequest.FormVars.Lookup("Email"));
            Guest_FName = CA2CT(m_HttpRequest.FormVars.Lookup("FirstName"));
            Guest_LName = CA2CT(m_HttpRequest.FormVars.Lookup("LastName"));
        }
        else
        {
            m_HttpResponse << "<FONT color='#ff0033'>Error at server.</FONT>";
        }
    }
    else
    {
        m_HttpResponse << "<FONT color='#ff0033'>Error at server.</FONT>";
    }

    return HTTP_SUCCESS;
}
```

First, we declare data source, command, and session variables, and then open the data source (you'll need to tailor the connection string appropriately for your system). The SQL string for updating the database is then built up by reading the form variable values, using the `FormVars` property of the `CHttpRequest` object. Then we run the query and send a confirmation message to the user.

The SendMail tag

The `SendMail` tag in the SRF is replaced at runtime by the output of the `OnSendMail()` method:

```
[tag_name(name = "SendMail")]
HTTP_CODE OnSendMail(void)
{
    CString Message("Congratulations!");
    Message += Guest_FName;
    Message += " ";
    Message += Guest_LName;
    Message += ", You have registered successfully.";

    CMimeMessage msg;
    msg.SetSender("abcom@vsnl.com");
    msg.SetSenderName(Guest_FName);
```

```
msg.AddRecipient(Guest_Email);
msg.AddCc("abcom@vsnl.com");
msg.SetSubject("Confirmation");
msg.AddText(Message);

CSMTPConnection connection;
if(!connection.Connect("202.54.1.1"))
{
    m_HttpResponse << "Could not connect to server!";
    return HTTP_SUCCESS_NO_PROCESS;
}
if(!connection.SendMessage(msg))
{
    m_HttpResponse << "Failed to send message!";
    return HTTP_SUCCESS_NO_PROCESS;
}

m_HttpRequest.DeleteFiles();
return HTTP_SUCCESS;
}
```

This method first composes a message for the user. Then, a `CMimeMessage` message object is created and its various properties are set. A connection to the mail server is obtained by calling the `Connect()` method on a `CSMTPConnection` object. (You'll need to use the appropriate URL for your mail server here.) Finally, the message itself is sent by calling the `SendMessage()` method on the `connection` object.

The NotValidating tag

The method for the `NotValidating` tag is shown below:

```
[tag_name(name = "NotValidating")]
HTTP_CODE OnNotValidating(void)
{
    // Return true if and only if every form field was validated
    if(!valid_input)
    {
        if(m_HttpRequest.FormVars.Lookup("bNotFirst"))
            m_HttpResponse << "<FONT color='#ff0033' size='3'>"
                           << errorMsg << "</FONT>";
        return HTTP_SUCCESS;
    }

    return HTTP_S_FALSE;
}
```

Here, we check the status of the `valid_input` flag that's set to `false` in the `ValidateAndExchange()` method if any of the input fields doesn't meet the specified criterion. Since we don't want to print an error message when the form is called the first time, we check for the presence of the hidden variable `bNotFirst` in the request object.

The ValidateAndExchange method

Finally, let's look at a section of the `ValidateAndExchange()` method, where each input field is validated using predefined rules. The code for the `FirstName` and `LastName` field validations is shown below:

```
m_HttpRequest.FormVars.Validate("FirstName", (LPCSTR*)NULL, 1, 20, &CValidate);
if(!CValidate.ParamsOK() || !atlRegExp.Match(
        CA2CT(m_HttpRequest.FormVars.Lookup("FirstName")), &atlRematchContext))
{
   valid_input = false;
   lstrcpy(errorMsg, "First name is required and may only contain letters
                     and spaces, and length should not exceed 20.");
   return HTTP_SUCCESS;
}

m_HttpRequest.FormVars.Validate("LastName", (LPCSTR*)NULL, 1, 20, &CValidate);
if(!CValidate.ParamsOK() || !atlRegExp.Match(
        CA2CT(m_HttpRequest.FormVars.Lookup("LastName")), &atlRematchContext))
{
   valid_input = false;
   lstrcpy(errorMsg, "Last Name is required and may only contain letters
                     and spaces, and length should not exceed 20.");
   return HTTP_SUCCESS;
}
```

The rest of the fields are validated in similar fashion – see the full listing for details.

Building and running the project

Once you've built the project, you can load it up in Internet Explorer, input some data on the displayed HTML form, and click on the Submit button. All the input fields will be validated by our web application DLL. On successful validation, the data is inserted into the database table and a confirmation e-mail message is sent to the client.

Other features of ATL Server

So far, we've examined the features of ATL Server that are purely concerned with the actual provision of dynamically generated HTML code. In addition to these, ATL Server provides classes for thread pooling, caching, and performance monitoring, and these will be the subjects of our discussion for the remainder of this chapter.

Thread pooling

The ATL Server library defines a class called `CThreadPool` for supporting pooling of worker threads. The functionality of this class is built on top of Windows NT's highly efficient IO completion ports; its declaration is shown below:

```
template <class Worker, class ThreadTraits = DefaultThreadTraits>
class CThreadPool : public IthreadPoolConfig
```

For each thread in a pool, an instance of a user-created Worker thread class will be created on the stack. The Initialize() method of this class will be called during object creation, and the Terminate() method is called during its destruction. The Execute() method implements the business functionality – the work you want to do.

The system creates a set of worker threads and maintains them in a pool. An independent thread monitors the status of all wait operations queued to the thread pool. When an event is signaled, one of the threads from the thread pool is assigned to execute a callback function. The result of this setup is an efficient use of resources – with a limited number of threads in the pool, the application will be able to service a large number of requests.

If your thread does not need to wait on an external event and is simply involved in dealing with business logic, it can still use a thread from a thread pool. For this, a method called QueueUserWorkItem() is provided in the CThreadPool class.

Caching

The ATL Server API allows the application programmer a significant degree of control over the caching that takes place with respect to network communications. Some of the classes that are used most frequently in this endeavor are listed below.

- ❑ CFileCache implements a cache where files are stored on disk, but their names are stored in a list in memory. When a file in the cache 'expires' according to the rules you define, the file is deleted.

- ❑ CStencilCache implements a stencil cache where preprocessed stencils can be stored in order to give faster response times.

- ❑ CBlobCache implements the functionality necessary for caching large binary objects. The data is added to the cache using the Add() method and removed using the RemoveEntry() method. The number of items currently stored in the cache can be retrieved by calling GetCurrentEntryCount().

- ❑ CMemoryCache is a generic cache that can be used for storing items of diverse types in memory.

Performance monitoring

You may monitor the performance of your ATL Server applications by using the Win32 performance monitoring API and ATL's performance monitoring support. The latter is a powerful tool for debugging and profiling, helping you to fine-tune your web applications; it requires the following two criteria to be satisfied:

- ❑ The application being monitored must define and expose performance values

- ❑ The application doing the monitoring must be able to locate and retrieve the data

For the second of these, you may use the Windows Performance Console, rather than having to create a separate performance-monitoring application. For the first, the following ATL entities may be used to expose performance data:

- ❑ The performance object manager
- ❑ The performance object
- ❑ The performance counter

The performance object manager exposes performance objects and counters to a monitoring application. It also controls access to these performance objects. The performance objects and counters use shared memory that the object manager is responsible for configuring.

The performance object may represent some or all of the performance data exposed by the application. A human-readable name is associated with each performance object. A monitoring application such as Windows Performance Console may use this name while creating a user interface. A single performance object may be shared between several application instances, or an application may create several instances to allow for more specific monitoring.

A performance counter represents an individual element of performance data, and a single performance object may contain several such counters, each of which has a human-readable name. The counter data exists in shared memory, and should be accessed only through thread-safe code.

Summary

The ATL library has been greatly enhanced by the incorporation of support for web applications. In this chapter, we took a quick tour of the ATL Server architecture and saw the capabilities of this framework. We saw how an ISAPI extension DLL, a web application DLL, and an SRF file can work together to respond to HTTP requests with dynamically generated content.

The ISAPI extension DLL receives a user request, parses it, and dispatches it to a queue for the appropriate web application DLL. This frees the IIS for the next incoming request, resulting in a big improvement in response times compared with the traditional ASP model. In the next chapter, we'll see how this architecture extends to the provision of web services.

11

ATL Server web services

The Internet is shifting towards a service-based infrastructure. People use computers to read e-mail, to get stock price information, to shop, to pay bills, or simply to locate the best Chinese restaurant in town. At different times, a user of such a service is likely to want to access it using devices such as a PDA, a mobile phone, a desktop computer, and so on. In technical terms, what they want is for traditional software to be converted to service-based software that can be accessed easily by a variety of client devices – and, indeed, by other services.

There are existing technologies, such as DCOM, CORBA, RMI, and RPC, that are capable of delivering services over the Web. However, applications that rely on these technologies center on the use of tightly coupled distributed components, and there is no standard for communication between the different technologies. This makes it extremely difficult for two different services to interoperate with each other.

A **web service** can be defined as a self-describing, modular application that can be published, located, and invoked from anywhere on the Web. Its functionality is accessible via standard web protocols. Web services are the new generation of distributed computing – we think in terms of loosely coupled services that communicate via XML and HTTP, rather than components bound by a proprietary binary standard. The advent of XML has given developers a format for describing information in a structured and meaningful way, and it is this that forms the basis of web services. Clients can access and share data with a web service regardless of application type, platform, or language.

Benefits of web services

In the description above, we've made a lot of the importance of being able to interoperate between different web applications, and you might reasonably ask how important that really is. To some extent, the definitive answer to this question lies in the kind of business you're involved in, but if you need to share business documents and allow others to access the services you offer, you need interoperability.

❑ If you're a broking house, you could allow customers to request the latest prices and place online orders with you. By exposing your application as a web service, your application will become accessible not only to standard desktop users but also to mobile users, helping you to broaden your customer base.

❑ If you're an auctioneer, your customers will be placing online bids and sharing contract documents with other customers participating in the auction. Once again, the web service interface will help in achieving interoperability between applications running on different platforms and developed using different technologies.

❑ If you're a manufacturer, you may like to publish your catalog on your web site and allow the customer to browse and search through it, make enquiries, and finally place orders with you by using the provided interface.

❑ If you're an insurance company, you may want to receive and settle claims from partner insurance companies. All this requires interoperability, which is easily achieved by exposing your applications as web services.

So, how does this all work? Well, before a client can use a web service, it needs to know that it exists, and where to find it. This means that a web service provider needs to make its existence known by publishing its services to some kind of standard location. Secondly, in order for a client to be able to use the service, the latter needs to have some way of describing its methods, parameters, data types, and so on.

Locating services

Once a web service has been created, you'll need to publish it so that your customers, business partners, and others can locate it. For this purpose, there's a new standard called **universal description, discovery, and integration** (**UDDI**) that defines a common repository where web services can be registered. More than 250 companies currently support the UDDI project, which allows *any* organization to publish information about its web services, and lets third parties discover and use them. The sample implementation of the UDDI specifications is currently available at www.uddi.org.

The repository holds both descriptive and technical information about web services, and contact information for the businesses that offer them. A facility is provided to narrow your search to particular industry segments and/or specific geographic locations.

The two XML-based technologies that are mentioned most frequently in connection with web services are the **simple object access protocol** (**SOAP**), a standard that describes how XML can be used for making method calls between distributed objects; and the **web services description language** (**WSDL**), which describes web services in terms of the methods they expose in a form that potential clients can interrogate. However, while we'll certainly be making mention of these technologies as we go along, it turns out that they won't be occupying our minds to the degree you may have expected.

Web services and ATL Server

By now, you're doubtless wondering how to go about writing a web service. Do you need to code all this SOAP and WSDL by hand? Fortunately, the tools provided with Visual Studio .NET do most of the work for you, so creating a web service is nowhere near as difficult as you might imagine. The ATL Server web service architecture is shown in the diagram below; after you've had a quick look, we'll detail the steps that it contains.

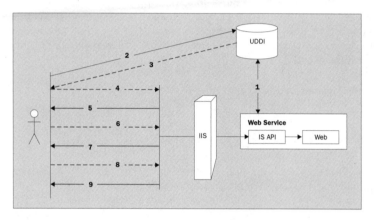

1. In the first step, we create a web service and deploy it in a UDDI registry. Here, we provide a link to our web service, along with a 'business description' that's used as a means of categorization. The idea is that if someone were looking for services related to travel, for example, they could narrow their search to that area quickly and easily.

2. An interested client searches for a web service in the registry.

3. After finding a suitable service, the client selects it and receives a link to it. This will be a URL in which the name of the target file ends in .disco, as in http://www.abcom.com/TravelDetails.disco.

4. The client browses to the URL provided in order to find the ultimate location of the web service.

5. The client receives the path to the web service in XML format. For example:

```
<?xml version="1.0" ?>
<discovery xmlns="http://schemas.xmlsoap.org/disco/">
    <contractRef xmlns="http://schemas.xmlsoap.org/disco/scl/"
        ref="http://www.abcom.com/Travel/TravelDetails.dll?Handler=GenTravelWSDL"
        docRef="http://www.abcom.com/Travel/TravelDetails.htm"/>
</discovery>
```

6. The client browses to the service link (the URL containing the string "Handler" above) in order to get the web service description file.

7. The client gets the service description and studies it – this file consists of descriptions of methods, including their names, numbers and types of parameters, and return types. The client can use this information to invoke the service and provide the correct information to it. Clients can develop an interface to access this service if they choose to do so.

8. The client invokes the service. This request comes in to IIS, which maps it (based on the URL and extension specified) to a suitable ISAPI extension DLL. This DLL in turn maps the handler specified in the request to a web application DLL, which in turn maps it to a C++ object. The difference between a web application and a web service is in the final step: in a web service, the C++ object is capable of decoding and encoding SOAP. The code to do this is inserted by the compiler when it parses the `soap_handler` attribute that we'll examine shortly.

9. The client receives the processed output in XML format.

Creating a web service

In this section, we'll take a look at the steps involved in creating a simple web service using ATL Server. Our first example will be the "Hello World" sample that's provided as part of the Wizard-generated code, but by seeing the steps involved and walking through the generated code, you'll gain a good understanding of how things fit together. Later in the chapter, we'll develop a more complex 'stock ticker' example that could be used by a stockbroker to display the latest quotes to a customer, and to accept online orders.

Creating the project

In Visual Studio .NET, begin a new C++ project and choose ATL Server Web Service from the list presented to you. (This Wizard is actually identical to the ATL Server Project Wizard that we discussed in the last chapter, except that the **Create as Web Service** option is selected by default.) Call the project `Hello`, and hit the **OK** button. Since we're going to keep the default settings for this project, we can go straight to the **Finish** button, pausing only to note how choosing to create a web service has limited some of our options:

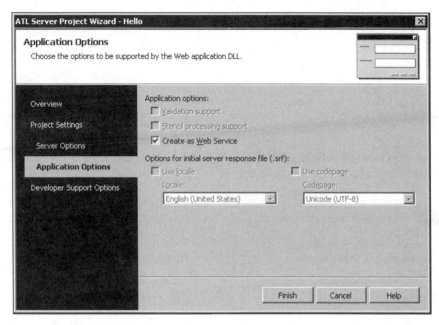

The 'restrictions' here are down to the fact that the output of this project will be in SOAP format –
there's no SRF file, and so any options connected with it become redundant. If you do now click Finish,
the Wizard will generate the following files (among several others):

❑ `Hello.cpp` and `Hello.h`
These files contain the ATL Server request handler class, the configuration of which is based
on the options selected in the Wizard.

❑ `Hello.disco`
This file contains information that allows your web service to be exposed via web servers that
support the DISCO (discovery) protocol. It's required when you start creating consumers for
the web service, and we'll be discussing its use later on.

Hello.h

Take a look at the Wizard-generated header file, `Hello.h`. The first thing you'll notice is that it defines
a namespace called `HelloService`, inside which everything else in this file is declared:

```
namespace HelloService
{
    // Rest of code here
}
```

Next, we have an interface called `IHelloService` that contains a web method (that is, a method that
uses SOAP for communicating with a client) called `HelloWorld()`. This method takes one input
parameter of type `BSTR`, and returns a `BSTR` too.

```
[
    uuid("F7CE2FE0-09E6-4DE4-8C05-94CF01E2BB9D"),
    object
]
__interface IHelloService
{
    [id(1)] HRESULT HelloWorld([in] BSTR bstrInput,
                                [out, retval] BSTR* bstrOutput);
};
```

After the interface comes the declaration of the CHelloService class, which has two attributes applied to it – request_handler and soap_handler:

```
[
    request_handler(name="Default", sdl="GenHelloWSDL"),
    soap_handler(
        name="HelloService",
        namespace="urn:HelloService",
        protocol="soap"
    )
]
```

The request_handler attribute

As in the last chapter, the request_handler attribute marks this class as an ATL Server request handler. It will implement the web method that was defined in the interface above, and objects of this class will be used to service client requests. The obvious change from Chapter 10, though, is that a second parameter called sdl is being supplied to the attribute; this specifies the name of the compiler-generated handler that returns WSDL to the client ("GenHelloWSDL" in this example). This means that if you enter the following URL into your browser, WSDL data will be returned to you:

http://ServerName/Hello.dll?Handler=GenHelloWSDL

It's worth pointing out that the sdl parameter is valid only if the soap_handler attribute has been applied to the same class.

The soap_handler attribute

Since web services use SOAP for communication with the client, any methods that are exposed to the client as web services must support SOAP. This support is added by applying the soap_handler attribute to the class that contains these methods. Once the attribute is applied, all the code that's necessary for converting between SOAP and the method's defined signature will be added automatically.

The complete definition of the soap_handler attribute is:

```
[soap_handler(name,
              namespace,
              protocol,
              style,
              use
)]
```

The name parameter specifies the name that the client will use to refer to the web service; if you don't specify it, "Service" will be added to the name of the class and used instead. The namespace parameter specifies the XML namespace to be used in identifying the service, methods, and data types; it's again optional, and will be replaced by the class name if omitted.

We'll look at this parameter again in a couple of pages' time, when we come to build this web service application.

The third parameter specifies the protocol to be used for accessing the web service; right now, the only supported protocol is SOAP, and this is the value used in the Wizard-generated code above.

The style parameter is optional, and specifies the style of operations provided by the web service – it can be either document or rpc, where the latter is both the default and the value we need to use when writing web services. Finally, the use parameter specifies whether the WSDL message parts should be encoded; the only supported values for this parameter are literal and encoded, where the second is again the default.

Returning to the Hello.h file, here at last is the handler class itself, complete with the generated implementation of the single interface method:

```
class CHelloService : public IHelloService
{
public:
    [soap_method]
    HRESULT HelloWorld(/*[in]*/ BSTR bstrInput,
                       /*[out, retval]*/ BSTR* bstrOutput)
    {
        CComBSTR bstrOut(L"Hello ");
        bstrOut += bstrInput;
        bstrOut += L"!";
        *bstrOutput = bstrOut.Detach();

        return S_OK;
    }
};
```

The supplied implementation is very straightforward, as you'd expect: it simply reads the in parameter, appends it to the string "Hello", and returns the modified string to the caller through the out parameter.

The soap_method attribute

The thing that's noteworthy about this method is that it's declared using the soap_method attribute, which indicates that the method will communicate with the client using the SOAP protocol. It has the following syntax, in which the optional name parameter specifies the WSDL name for the method:

```
[soap_method(name)]
```

Once this attribute is applied to a method, all the necessary code for handling SOAP requests and responses will be added to it. Thus, if a client calls this method using SOAP, the following will occur in sequence:

- ❑ Parameters embedded in the SOAP request will be retrieved
- ❑ Parameters will be converted to appropriate C++ data types
- ❑ Method will be invoked using these converted parameters
- ❑ XML response to the client will be created
- ❑ Response will be returned to the client

And what you have to remember, of course, is that all of this happens silently. Thanks to ATL Server, we need barely to raise a finger to arrange for this support to be present in our applications.

Building the project

When you build this solution in Visual Studio .NET, it will create the required DLLs for you, and copy them into either the root folder of your IIS web server or the folder that you specified in the Project Settings page of the Wizard. At this stage, the project DLLs are deployed, and the web service is ready for use.

Running the project

To run the application from Visual Studio .NET, just press (Ctrl-)F5, as you would for any other project type. You should find that WSDL code is generated and output to a browser window, as shown in the screenshot below:

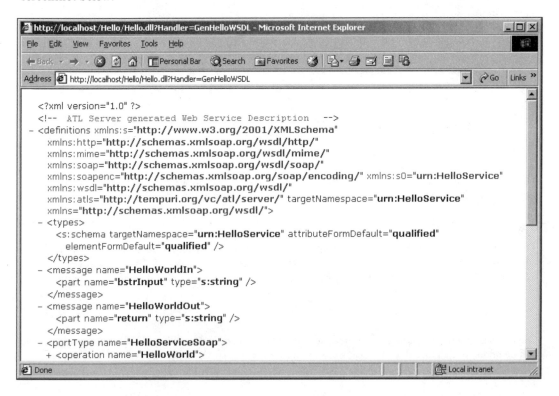

This WSDL describes the SOAP methods that were defined in the `CHelloService` class. It includes details of the method names, parameter types, and return types, and bears some further investigation. To begin with, at the top of this output, the various namespaces are imported. Notice in particular that the namespace defined in the `soap_handler` attribute of our class is added in the following line:

```
xmlns:s0="urn:HelloService"
```

After defining the namespaces and types, two messages are declared: `HelloWorldIn` specifies the input message, and `HelloWorldOut` specifies the output message:

```
<message name="HelloWorldIn">
   <part name="bstrInput" type="s:string" />
</message>
<message name="HelloWorldOut">
   <part name="return" type="s:string" />
</message>
```

The `portType` element describes our `HelloWorld` service. The input and output messages used by the `HelloWorld` operation are specified by the two corresponding attributes:

```
<portType name="HelloServiceSoap">
   <operation name="HelloWorld">
      <input message="s0:HelloWorldIn" />
      <output message="s0:HelloWorldOut" />
   </operation>
</portType>
```

Next, the `binding` element describes the transport mechanism as HTTP and the data style as `rpc`. The SOAP body is encoded using the encoding style defined by the `encodingStyle` attribute:

```
<binding name="HelloServiceSoap" type="s0:HelloServiceSoap">
   <soap:binding transport="http://schemas.xmlsoap.org/soap/http"
                 style="rpc" />
   <operation name="HelloWorld">
      <soap:operation soapAction="#HelloWorld" style="rpc" />
      <input>
         <soap:body use="encoded" namespace="urn:HelloService"
            encodingStyle="http://schemas.xmlsoap.org/soap/encoding/" />
      </input>
      <output>
         <soap:body use="encoded" namespace="urn:HelloService"
            encodingStyle="http://schemas.xmlsoap.org/soap/encoding/" />
      </output>
   </operation>
</binding>
```

Finally, at the end of the output, the WSDL code describes the `HelloService` web method in a `service` element:

```
<service name="HelloService">
   <port name="HelloServiceSoap" binding="s0:HelloServiceSoap">
      <soap:address
         location="http://localhost/Hello/Hello.dll?Handler=Default" />
```

```
        </port>
      </service>
```

Notice the use of the `Handler` attribute in the URL used by the web service. Its value is specified as `Default`, which is the same as the value of the argument we passed to the `request_handler` attribute that decorated our class.

A simple service consumer

All we need now is a proper client to consume this service. When you access a web service, your client application locates the service, obtains a reference to it, and uses the functionality it contains. That client application may be:

- ❑ A managed or unmanaged C++ application
- ❑ A browser-based application
- ❑ A COM component
- ❑ Another web service

In this section, we'll develop a Win32 console application that accesses our simple `Hello` web service. This will involve the following steps:

- ❑ Create a console application
- ❑ Add a 'web reference' to the service
- ❑ Write client code that creates an object of the web service type
- ❑ Invoke the web method by using the above reference
- ❑ Compile and run the client program

Creating the project

In Visual Studio .NET, create a new Visual C++ Win32 project called `HelloClient`. In the Wizard, choose to build a console application, and add support for ATL. This last step is necessary because the 'web reference' we'll add will depend on the ATL (Server) header files. Click Finish to generate the project.

Next, our client application needs a proxy class in order to access the web service. This will act as a stub for the service, and it contains code for marshaling the parameters used by the web method to and from SOAP. Microsoft has provided a utility called the **proxy generator** (`sproxy.exe`) for this purpose; it's a command-line utility that takes the web service's URL as an argument and generates a header file containing the client-side proxy:

```
> sproxy /out:Hello.h http://localhost/Hello/Hello.dll?Handler=GenHelloWSDL
```

Note that the URL you specify here gets embedded in the generated proxy header, so it's important to build the proxy against the real service address.

Examining the generated header

If you open the Hello.h header file that was generated by our previous action, you'll find the following class declaration:

```
template <typename TClient = CSoapSocketClientT<> >
class CHelloServiceT : public TClient, public CSoapRootHandler
```

The class constructor uses the Default handler that we defined:

```
CHelloServiceT(ISAXXMLReader* pReader = NULL)
    :TClient(_T("http://localhost/Hello/Hello.dll?Handler=Default"))
```

while in the class body, the HelloWorld() method is declared as follows:

```
template <typename TClient>
inline HRESULT CHelloServiceT<TClient>::HelloWorld(
    BSTR bstrInput,
    BSTR* __retval )
```

The HelloWorld() method takes a parameter of type BSTR and returns the result by using a BSTR*. The implementation calls InitializeSOAP() to enable SOAP handling for request and response:

```
HRESULT __atlsoap_hr = InitializeSOAP(NULL);
```

while the following statement prepares for the response from the method:

```
__atlsoap_hr = GenerateResponse(GetWriteStream());
```

And the method itself is called by calling SendRequest():

```
__atlsoap_hr = SendRequest(_T("SOAPAction: \"#HelloWorld\"\r\n"));
```

Finally, the program obtains the return value in the following assignment:

```
*__retval = __params.__retval;
```

Developing client code

Open the generated stdafx.h file and add the following declarations to it:

```
// Disable client timeout for testing. Default is 10000 milliseconds.
#define ATL_SOCK_TIMEOUT INFINITE

// Minimum system requirements are Windows 98, Windows NT 4.0, or later.
#define _WIN32_WINDOWS 0x0410
```

The default setting of ATL_SOCK_TIMEOUT is 10 seconds, after which the socket connection times out. We'll change this to INFINITE, disabling client timeout, which can be useful while you're testing. In real life, you probably wouldn't need to change this constant.

Also, the minimum (Windows) system requirement for using web services is Win 98, Win NT 4.0, or later versions. This is specified by the second definition above. Of course, the use of this constant doesn't mean that this web service can be consumed only by Windows clients. *Any* client capable of generating a SOAP request should be able to use our web service.

In `HelloClient.cpp`, we'll add a #include for `Hello.h`, and then write a new function called `Display()` that will use our simple web service to output a message to the console:

```
void Display()
{
    CComBSTR bstr(20);

    // Creating an instance of proxy class
    HelloService::CHelloService obj;
    HRESULT hr = obj.HelloWorld(CComBSTR(L"Bill"), &bstr.m_str);
    CString result(bstr.m_str);
    printf(result);
}
```

First we declare a variable for passing to the web service method, then we obtain a reference to our web service, and *then* we invoke `HelloWorld()`. Finally, we output the result to the console. Here's the code for the `main()` function that calls `Display()`:

```
int main(int argc, _TCHAR* argv[])
{
    if(SUCCEEDED(CoInitialize(NULL)))
    {
        Display();
        CoUninitialize();
    }
    return 0;
}
```

And, assuming that everything behaves as we'd like it to, here's the output you should see:

```
Hello Bill!
```

Understanding the client code

What's happening here is that this line:

```
HelloService::CHelloService obj;
```

creates an instance of the proxy class that we described above. The client then calls the `HelloWorld()` method of this object:

```
HRESULT hr = obj.HelloWorld(CComBSTR(L"Bill"), &bstr.m_str);
```

By means of this method, the string Bill will be converted to the string type that's defined in the XML Schema data types. Then, the method call is encapsulated in a SOAP request that gets sent to the server. At the server end, the server parses the request, retrieves the parameter, and invokes the method on the implementation object, returning a result in C++ string format. This is converted into an XML string at the server end before once again being encapsulated in SOAP and sent back to the client. The client parses the SOAP response, retrieves the result string in XML format, converts it to C++ format, and returns it to the C++ client code.

Stock quote service project

Having found our feet above, in this section, we'll create a sizable example: a web service for a stockbroker. The broker allows registered customers to obtain the latest stock quote for a given symbol, and to place an online order.

First, we'll write a web service that defines an interface for obtaining the stock price and placing an order. The sequence of calls will generally go like this: First, the client inputs the desired stock symbol and obtains the latest quote from the broker's web site. Second, the client places an order to buy or sell the stock through the provided interface. Third, the order will be saved in the broker's database on the server for off-line viewing.

Creating the database

Our stockbroker's service will require a database, and the one we'll create for this example contains three tables – Stock, OrderDetails, and Login – that we'll take a look at in the next couple of sections. For demonstration purposes, we used Microsoft Access as the database for this project, but you may use an engine of your choice.

Stock table

The Stock table holds the latest stock price for each stock symbol listed on the stock exchange, and has the following structure:

Field name	Data type
stockSymbol	Text
stockPrice	Currency

The stockSymbol field indicates the stock symbol, while the stockPrice field indicates the latest stock quote. If the broker service provides online trading, this table must be updated in real time to provide the latest bid price of each stock symbol. Initially, you will need to populate this table with a few records for testing, and such a database is available in the downloadable code.

OrderDetails table

The OrderDetails table stores the orders received from the customer. It has the following structure:

Field name	Data type
OrderID	Number
UserID	Text
StkSymbol	Text
StkPrice	Currency
buysell	Yes/No
Quantity	Number
Date	Date/Time
TotalAmount	Currency

The OrderID field is the primary key of the table and represents the ID of the order received. Aside from that, the UserID field designates the user ID, the StkSymbol field represents the symbol of the stock in which the trade is desired, the StkPrice field indicates the price at which the trade is requested, the buysell field indicates the type of trade, the Quantity field indicates the order quantity, the Date field indicates the timestamp of order placement, and the TotalAmount field indicates the total trade value.

Login table

The Login table stores member information – Name, UserID, and Password. It has the following structure:

Field name	Data type
UserID	Text
Password	Text
Name	Text

Relationships

The relationships between the different tables are depicted in the screenshot below:

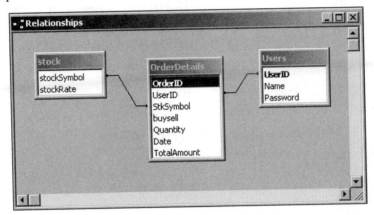

Creating the project

Once again, we'll create a new ATL Server Web Service project. Specify the name of the project as StockQuote, and from then on accept all the default options. Even for this project, we're quite happy to start with the pre-configured settings and build from those, so click on Finish to generate the project files.

Writing code

On this occasion, we'll delete the default web service method, Hello(), and add four new ones of our own:

❑   getStockQuote()

❑   placeOrder()

❑   ValidateUser()

❑   AddMemberInfo()

Adding method declarations

The getStockQuote() method will allow consumers of the service to obtain the latest stock quote for a specified symbol:

```
[id(1)] HRESULT getStockQuote([in] BSTR strSymbol,
                              [out, retval] float* stockRate);
```

This method takes a string parameter that specifies the stock symbol for which the last bid price is being requested, and returns the current stock price to the caller through its stockRate parameter.

The declaration of the placeOrder() method is shown below:

```
[id(2)] HRESULT placeOrder([in] BSTR strUserID,
                           [in] BSTR strStockSymbol,
```

```
                              [in]  float fStockRate,
                              [in]  BSTR strBuySell,
                              [in]  int Quantity,
                              [out, retval] BSTR* strMessage);
```

This method takes several input parameters:

❑ strUserID specifies the user ID

❑ strStockSymbol specifies the stock symbol in which trade is desired

❑ fStockRate specifies the price at which trade is requested

❑ strBuySell indicates whether it is a buy or sell operation

❑ Quantity specifies the desired trade quantity

The success or failure of the order placement with the broker is returned to the client through the strMessage output parameter.

Next up is the declaration of ValidateUser():

```
     [id(3)] HRESULT ValidateUser([in] BSTR strUserID,
                                  [in] BSTR strPassword,
                                  [out, retval] BSTR* strResult);
```

This method takes two input parameters:

❑ strUserID specifies the user ID

❑ strPassword specifies the user password

The success or failure of user validation is returned to the client through the strResult output parameter.

Finally, here's the declaration of AddMemberInfo():

```
     [id(4)] HRESULT AddMemberInfo([in] BSTR strUserID,
                                   [in] BSTR strPassword,
                                   [in] BSTR Name,
                                   [out, retval] BSTR* strResult);
```

The method takes three input parameters:

❑ strUserID specifies the user ID

❑ strPassword specifies the user password

❑ Name specifies the user's name

The success or failure of registering the user is returned to the client through the strResult output parameter.

Implementing the methods

Our next task is to implement the web methods. Since all four of these methods are quite lengthy in this example, we'll just look at the first two here, leaving you to examine the source code of the other two at will. If we start with getStockQuote(), the first thing we need to do is to get it exposed as a SOAP method, which means applying the soap_method attribute to it:

```
[soap_method]
```

Then, the method reads the input parameter and constructs a SQL string for selecting the record from the stock table:

```
HRESULT getStockQuote(BSTR strSymbol, float* stockPrice)
{
    CString symbol(bstrSymbol);

    // Create a query string
    CString SQLString("SELECT * FROM stock where stockSymbol='");
    SQLString += symbol;
    SQLString += "'";
```

Next, we obtain the connection to our data source and open it:

```
CDataSource ds;
CCommand<CAccessor<CStock> > cmd;
CSession session;

// Connection to database StockDB.mdb
HRESULT hr = ds.OpenFromInitializationString (L"Provider=
    Microsoft.Jet.OLEDB.4.0;User ID=Admin;Data Source=C:\\StockDB.mdb");

// Check for connection result
if(SUCCEEDED(hr))
{
    if(SUCCEEDED(session.Open(ds)))
    {
```

After that, we open the recordset, and the stock price for the requested stock is then obtained by moving to the first record:

```
hr= cmd.Open(session, SQLString);
if(SUCCEEDED(hr))
{
    cmd.MoveNext();

    // Get the stock price for the symbol
    *stockPrice = cmd.m_stockPrice;
}
```

Finally, we return an appropriate error if all has not gone according to plan:

```
        else
        {
            *stockPrice = -1;  // Query execution not successful
        }
    }
    else
    {
        *stockPrice = -2;      // Cannot open data source
    }
}
else
{
    *stockPrice = -3;          // Connection failed
}
return S_OK;
}
```

The implementation of the placeOrder() method is quite similar to getStockQuote(). Here's the complete code.

```
[soap_method]
HRESULT placeOrder(BSTR strUserID,
                   BSTR strStockSymbol,
                   float fStockPrice,
                   VARIANT_BOOL BuySell,
                   int Quantity,
                   BSTR* strMessage)
{
    CDataSource ds;
    CCommand<CAccessor<COrder> > cmd;
    CCommand<CAccessor<COrderID> > cmd1;
    CSession session;

    HRESULT hr = ds.OpenFromInitializationString = (L"Provider=
        Microsoft.Jet.OLEDB.4.0;User ID=Admin;Data Source=C:\\StockDB.mdb");

    if(SUCCEEDED(hr))
    {
        if(SUCCEEDED(session.Open(ds)))
        {
            CString stockSymbol(strStockSymbol);
            CString UserID(strUserID);
            long order_ID= 0;
            CString str("SELECT MAX(OrderID) FROM OrderDetails");
            hr= cmd1.Open(session, str);
            if(SUCCEEDED(hr))
            {
                cmd1.MoveNext();
                order_ID= cmd1.m_OrderID;
            }
```

```
        // Format date
        char date[17];
        strdate(date);

        // Calculate amount and format it
        float Amount= Quantity * fStockPrice;
        CString strAmount;
        strAmount.Format(_T("%.2f\n"), Amount);

        // Format stock price
        CString tempPrice;
        tempPrice.Format(_T("%.2f\n"), fStockPrice);

        char tempQty[20];
        char tempOrderID[20];
        char tempDate[17];
        char tempBuySell[5];
        wsprintf(tempQty, "%d", Quantity);
        wsprintf(tempOrderID, "%d", order_ID + 1);
        wsprintf(tempDate, "%s", date);
        wsprintf(tempBuySell, "%d", BuySell);

        CString SQLString("INSERT INTO OrderDetails VALUES(");
        SQLString += tempOrderID;
        SQLString += ",'";
        SQLString +=UserID;
        SQLString +="','";
        SQLString += stockSymbol;
        SQLString += "',";
        SQLString += tempPrice;
        SQLString += ",";
        SQLString += tempBuySell;
        SQLString += ",";
        SQLString += tempQty;
        SQLString += ",'";
        SQLString += tempDate;
        SQLString += "',";
        SQLString += strAmount;
        SQLString += ")";

        // Execute the query to insert records
        hr= cmd.Open(session, SQLString);
        *strMessage=L"Thank you for placing your order with us!";
    }
    else
    {
        *strMessage= L"Session failed";
    }
    }
    else
    {
        *strMessage = L"Connection failed";
    }
    return S_OK;
}
```

Here, the SQL string uses the various input parameters to the method as field values in the record. A database connection is opened, the appropriate properties are set, and the record is inserted. The success or failure of the operation is returned to the caller through the output parameter. In real life situations, you'd probably wrap code of this nature in a transaction.

Defining database mappings

Assuming that you've got hold of the implementations of ValidateUser() and AddMemberInfo() there's still one more thing that you need to do before you can build the project: you must define C++ mappings for the database tables to be used by the CCommand<> class. Create a header file called CStock.h, for mappings to the Stock table, and add the following code:

```cpp
class CStock
{
public:
    // Data elements
    float m_stockPrice;
    TCHAR m_stockSymbol[51];

    BEGIN_COLUMN_MAP(CStock)
        COLUMN_ENTRY(2, m_stockPrice)
        COLUMN_ENTRY(1, m_stockSymbol)
    END_COLUMN_MAP()
};
```

Likewise, create another header file called COrder.h, for mappings to the OrderDetails table, and add the following definition. The COrder class provides mappings for INSERT operations on this table:

```cpp
class COrder
{
public:

    // Data elements
    VARIANT_BOOL m_buysell;
    LONG m_Quantity;
    TCHAR m_StkSymbol[20];
    float m_TotalAmount;
    int m_OrderID;
    TCHAR m_UserID[50];
    DATE m_Date;
    float m_StkPrice;

    // Column binding map
    BEGIN_COLUMN_MAP(COrder)
        COLUMN_ENTRY(1, m_OrderID)
        COLUMN_ENTRY(2, m_UserID)
        COLUMN_ENTRY(3, m_StkSymbol)
        COLUMN_ENTRY(4, m_StkPrice)
        COLUMN_ENTRY(5, m_buysell)
        COLUMN_ENTRY(6, m_Quantity)
        COLUMN_ENTRY(7, m_Date)
        COLUMN_ENTRY(8, m_TotalAmount)
    END_COLUMN_MAP()
};
```

The COrderID class, defined in the same header, deals with the results of the "SELECT MAX(OrderID) FROM OrderDetails" query in the placeOrder() method.

```
class COrderID
{
public:
    // Data elements
    int m_OrderID;

    // Column binding map
    BEGIN_COLUMN_MAP(COrderID)
        COLUMN_ENTRY(1, m_OrderID)
    END_COLUMN_MAP()
};
```

Defined in CLogin.h, the CLogin class defines mappings for the INSERT query that's used while inserting member data into the database.

```
class CLogin
{
public:
    // Data elements
    TCHAR m_Name[51];
    TCHAR m_Password[51];
    TCHAR m_UserID[51];

    BEGIN_COLUMN_MAP(CLogin)
        COLUMN_ENTRY(1, m_UserID)
        COLUMN_ENTRY(2, m_Password)
        COLUMN_ENTRY(3, m_Password)
    END_COLUMN_MAP()
};
```

And finally, the CUserID class defines mappings for the SELECT query during the login process:

```
class CUserID
{
public:

    // Data elements
    TCHAR m_UserID[51];
    TCHAR m_Password[51];

    BEGIN_COLUMN_MAP(CUserID)
        COLUMN_ENTRY(1, m_UserID)
        COLUMN_ENTRY(1, m_Password)
    END_COLUMN_MAP()
};
```

All three of the header files listed here need to be included at the top of the StockQuote.h file, so that they're available to the methods defined there. In fact, this would be a good juncture at which to have another look at the downloadable files, to make sure that everything's in the right place before we progress.

Building and testing the web service

Build the project to create the DLLs. You can test the web service by running it through Visual Studio .NET; when you run it, you will see the generated WSDL that describes the various methods exposed by the web service, just as we had (on a smaller scale) for the simple web service we built earlier in the chapter.

Developing the client

To test our web service, we're going to return one last time to the issue of language interoperability and create an ASP.NET Web Application in C#. Choose this option in the New Project dialog, give it the name BrokerSite, and specify its location as http://localhost. With all of that done, click OK to generate the project files.

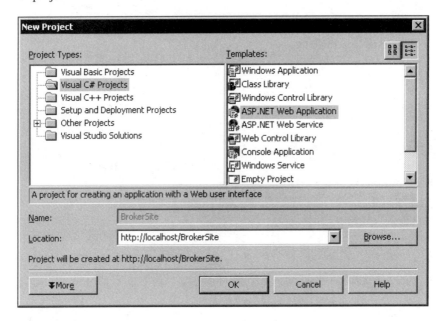

Creating the user interface

The user interface to the client application consists of three files:

- ❑ StartPage.aspx is the opening page
- ❑ Registration.aspx is the member registration page
- ❑ ServicePage.aspx is the order transaction page

StartPage.aspx

The Wizard generates one ASPX file in the project automatically, called WebForm1.aspx. The first thing you need to do is to rename it StartPage.aspx. Then, since this will be the startup page of the application, we need to configure it as such in the project: right-click on the form name in the Solution Explorer, and select the Start Page menu option.

Next, you should modify this file by using the designer and adding web components from the toolbox. The interface you're looking for is shown in the screenshot below:

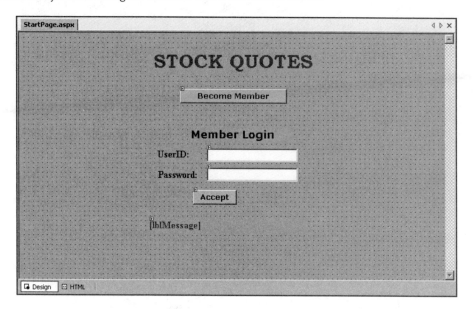

In order to achieve this, we've added the following web components to our `StartPage.aspx` file:

	Control	Type	Properties
Label	lblTitle1	HTML	Text: STOCK QUOTES
	lblTitle2	HTML	Text: Member Login
	lblUserID	HTML	Text: User ID
	lblPassword	HTML	Text: Password
	lblMessage	Web Control	
Button	btnNewMember	Web Control	Text: Become Member, ID: btnNewMember
	btnAccept	Web Control	Text: Accept, ID: btnAccept
	txtUserID	Web Control	ID: txtUserID
	txtPassword	Web Control	ID: txtPassword

Registration.aspx

In this step, we'll design the member registration form that will appear when the Become Member button is pressed. Create a new Web Form by clicking on Project | Add Web Form; the IDE displays a dialog box where we can provide a name for our form. Change the name to `Registration.aspx`. A Web Form will be added to the Solution Explorer in your project; here's how the user interface should look:

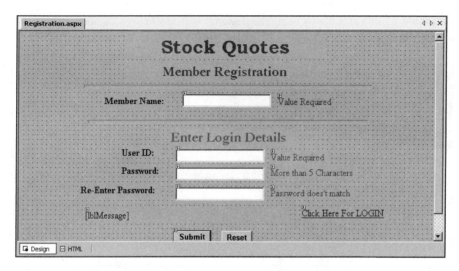

It was achieved by the addition of the following controls to the Web Form:

	Control	Type	Properties
Label	lblTitle1	HTML	Text: Stock Quotes
	lblTitle2	HTML	Text: Member Registration
	lblMemberName	HTML	Text: Member Name
	lblTitle3	HTML	Text: Enter Login Details
	lblUserID	HTML	Text: User ID
	lblPassword	HTML	Text: Password
	lblRePassword	HTML	Text: Re-enter password
	lblMessage	Web Control	
Hyperlink		Web Control	Text: Click Here For LOGIN, ID: HomePage, Visible: false
Button	btnsubmit	Web Control	Text: Submit, ID: btnSubmit
	btnReset	HTML	Text: Reset, ID: btnReset
Text box	txtName	Web Control	ID: txtName
	txtUserID	Web Control	ID: txtUserID

	Control	Type	Properties
Text box	txtPassword	Web Control	ID: txtPassword
	txtRePassword	Web Control	ID: txtRePassword
Validator	RequiredField Validator	Web Control	ID: ValidateFName, ErrorMessage: Value Required, ControlToValidate: txtName ID: ValidateUserID, ErrorMessage: Value Required ControlToValidate: txtUserID
	CompareValidator	Web Control	ID: ValidateRePwd, ErrorMessage: Password doesn't match, ControlToValidate: txtRePassword ControlToCompare: txtPassword
	RegularExpression Validator	Web Control	ID: ValidatePassword, ErrorMessage: More than 5 Characters, ControlToValidate: txtPassword, ValidationExpression: "\w{5}(\w)*"

ServicePage.aspx

Third, we design ServicePage.aspx, which is displayed to the member only after a valid login. This page allows a member to check the latest stock price by providing a stock symbol. Members can also place orders to buy or sell their stocks. The page is shown below:

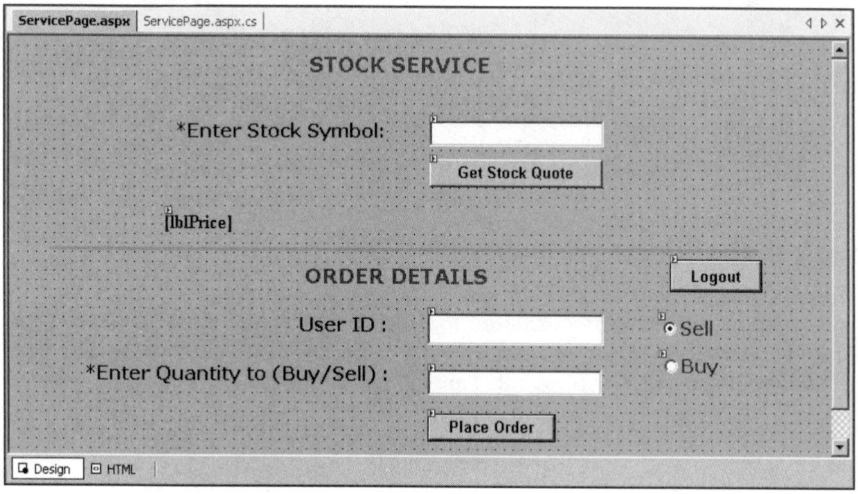

And this is the list of web controls that it uses:

	Control	Type	Properties
Label	lblTitle1	HTML	Text: STOCK SERVICE
	lblStockSymbol	HTML	Text: *Enter Stock Symbol
	lblTitle2	HTML	Text: ORDER DETAILS
	lblUserID	HTML	Text: User ID
	lblQuantity	HTML	Text: *Enter Quantity to (Buy/Sell)
	lblPrice	Web Control	
	lblConfirmation	Web Control	
Button	btnGetStockQuote	Web Control	Text: Get Stock Quote, ID: btnGetStockQuote
	btnLogout	Web Control	Text: Logout, ID: btnLogout
	btnPlaceOrder	Web Control	Text: Place Order, ID: btnPlaceOrder
Text box	txtSymbol	Web Control	ID: txtSymbol
	txtUserID	Web Control	ID: txtUserID, Enable: false
	txtQuantity	Web Control	ID: txtQuantity
Radio button	rbtnSell	Web Control	GroupName: rbtnGroup, ID: rbtnSell, Checked: true
	rbtnBuy	Web Control	GroupName: rbtnGroup, ID: rbtnBuy

Adding a reference to the web service DLL

In the Solution Explorer, right-click on the project and select **Add Web Reference**. Specify the URL for the web service (http://localhost/StockQuote/StockQuote.disco), and click **Add Reference** to add the reference for our web service DLL into the project. When this happens, the Wizard creates a localhost folder and adds a few files to it. These are shown in the screenshot opposite.

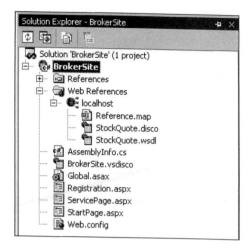

Unlike `Reference.map`, `StockQuote.disco`, and `StockQuote.wsdl`, the `StockQuote.cs` file (which contains the proxy class for the web service) is not visible in the Explorer. The file is similar to the header file that we created when we were writing C++ clients: a client program will create an instance of this proxy to invoke web methods on the remote object.

Modifying form code

With the plumbing now in place, we can add code to all three forms in order to implement the functionality we desire. As before, we'll start with the start page.

StartPage.aspx.cs

`StartPage.aspx` acts as an index page where new users can register themselves as new members. After registering, members can log in to get stock quotes and place orders. To provide all this functionality, we'll add code to our Web Form. The code for the **Become Member** button is given below.

```
private void btnNewMember_Click(object sender, System.EventArgs e)
{
    Response.Redirect("Registration.aspx");
}
```

When the user clicks on the button, they're taken to a new form as a result of the `Response.Redirect()` method, which accepts a page link as a string.

A registered member can log in by entering their user ID and password. Validation of these two items is performed in the `btnAccept` click method handler:

```
private void btnAccept_Click(object sender, System.EventArgs e)
{
    localhost.StockQuoteService obj= new localhost.StockQuoteService();
    string result= obj.ValidateUser(txtUserID.Text, txtPassword.Text);
```

```
      if(result== "Success")
      {
          Session.Add("UserID", txtUserID.Text);
          Response.Redirect("ServicePage.aspx");
      }
      else
      {
          lblMessage.Text = "Invalid UserID";
      }
  }
```

We create a web service object and invoke the `ValidateUser()` method that it defines. This attempts to validate the user, and will return either a success code or a failure code. If they entered with a valid ID and password, we'll direct them to the `ServicePage` after storing their user ID in a session variable called `UserID`. This value is then displayed on the service page.

Registration.aspx.cs

The registration form accepts values from prospective new members who have to enter their `Name`, `UserID`, and `Password`, on which we perform validation using Web Form validators. (In fact, for safety, passwords have to be entered twice.) All of the information is mandatory; when the member clicks on the Submit button, all of these values are written to the database. The code for the Submit button is given below:

```
private void btnSubmit_Click(object sender, System.EventArgs e)
{
    localhost.StockQuoteService obj= new localhost.StockQuoteService();
    string result= obj.AddMemberInfo(txtUserID.Text,
                                     txtPassword.Text,
                                     txtName.Text);

    lblMessage.Text= result;
    HomePage.Visible= true;
}
```

Here, the member data is written to the database using a web service method. All we had to do was to create a service object and then invoke its `AddMemberInfo()` method. After the record is written, a hyperlink control is made visible that points to the login screen.

ServicePage.aspx.cs

In the service page, we first write the event handler for the Get Stock Quote button:

```
private void btnGetStockQuote_Click(object sender, System.EventArgs e)
{
    if(txtStockSymbol.Text=="")
    {
        lblPrice.Text= "VALUE REQUIRED FOR FIELDS WITH (*)";
    }
    else
    {
        // Call the service method to get the StockRate
        float price= obj.getStockQuote(txtStockSymbol.Text);
```

```
      if(price == 0)
      {
         lblPrice.Text= "INVALID STOCK SYMBOL";
      }
      else
      {
         lblPrice.Text= "Stock price is $" + String.Format("{0:F2}",price);
      }
   }
}
```

To get the stock price, the member has to enter a valid stock symbol, and this is checked in our web service method getStockQuote() – it returns 0 if an invalid stock symbol is entered. We also take care of the situation when the user clicks on the button without entering a symbol.

To place an order, the user will enter the quantity they want to buy or sell, and then click on the **Place Order** button. A record of the transaction is stored in the database, along with the user ID. The code that deals with this is shown below:

```
private void btnPlaceOrder_Click(object sender, System.EventArgs e)
{
   short transaction;

   // Validate
   bool result= ValidateInput();
   if(result)
   {
      if(rbtnBuy.Checked)
      {
         transaction= 1;                 // Buy stock
      }
      else
      {
         transaction= 0;                 // Sell stock
      }


      int stkquantity = Convert.ToInt32(txtQuantity.Text);

      // Call the service method to get the stock quote
      float price= obj.getStockQuote(txtStockSymbol.Text);

      // Call the service method to place the Order
      string message= obj.placeOrder(txtUserID.Text,
                                     txtStockSymbol.Text,
                                     price,
                                     transaction,
                                     stkquantity);
      lblConfirmation.Text= message;
      txtQuantity.Text="";
   }
```

```
    else
    {
        lblConfirmation.Text="Values required for fields with (*)";
    }
}

// Validation method
public bool ValidateInput()
{
    return (txtQuantity.Test != "");
}
```

The event handler simply calls the web method `placeOrder()` to enter the input data into the broker's database. Remember that the full source code for this application is available with the code download.

Running the client

When you run the client application, the browser opens with `StartPage.aspx`, and in fact it's perfectly OK to use the following URL to open the file: http://localhost/BrokerSite/StartPage.aspx. When you do so, you'll see the following screen:

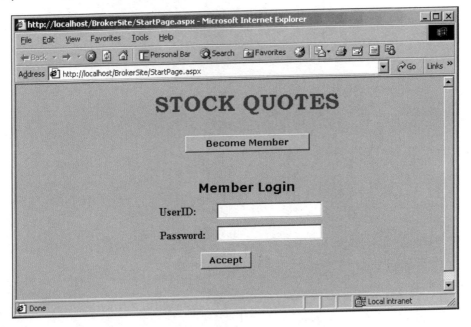

To become a member, click on the **Become Member** button. You will see a screen similar to the one below:

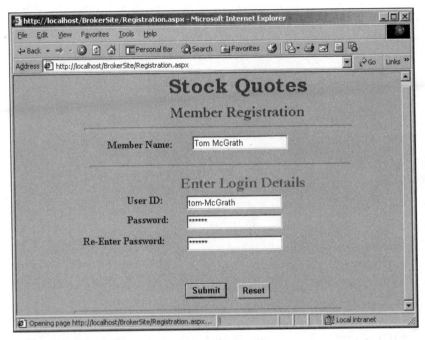

Enter the necessary information, click on the **Submit** button, and you ought to receive a confirmation message along with a link to the login page.

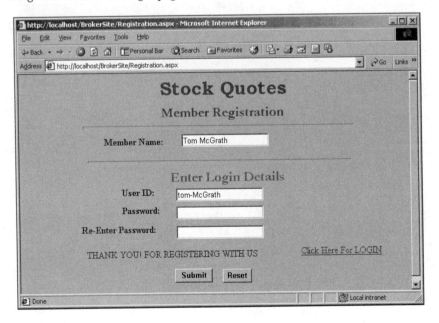

When you click on the link, you'll be taken back to the login screen:

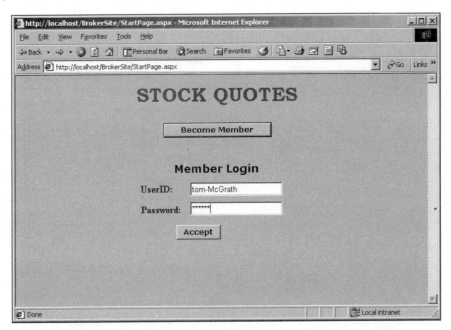

Enter the user ID and password that you configured in the previous step and click Accept. You will be authenticated by the server before you are granted access to the service page, which is shown below:

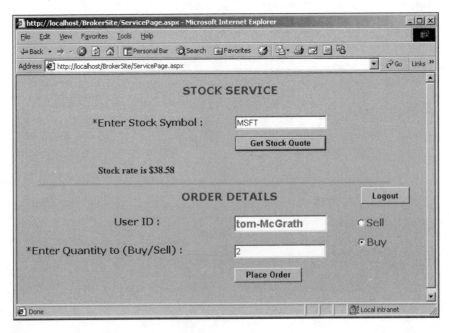

Enter the symbol of the stock you're interested in, and click on the Get Stock Quote button to retrieve the latest stock price. To place the order with the broker at this price, enter the details on the lower portion of the screen and click on the Place Order button. Note that here the user ID is taken from the session variable that we stored earlier on. The order will now be added to the broker's database, using the web method.

Finally, completing this example, you will see the order confirmation message at the bottom of the screen:

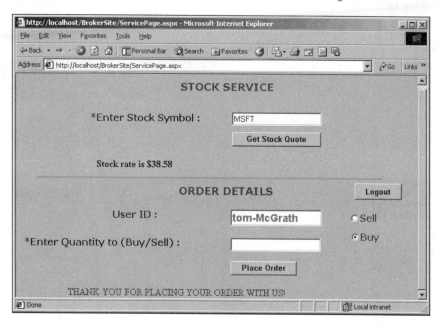

Summary

A web service is a programmable component that's accessed via standard web protocols – it exposes its interface in WSDL, and the client invokes its methods using SOAP. The web service component itself may actually be written in any language, but in the ATL Server web service architecture, component development takes place in C++.

For the final examples in this book, then, we looked at a genuinely new feature of Visual C++ – first nosing our way carefully around the default code generated by the Wizards, but later using more of our own code to get the job done. In fact, that could be an allegory for the position of Visual C++ .NET in Visual Studio .NET – at first, it's not entirely clear what's going on or what its role is. But as you experiment, you find more ways in which it can be useful, until eventually you find yourself marveling that you ever doubted it.

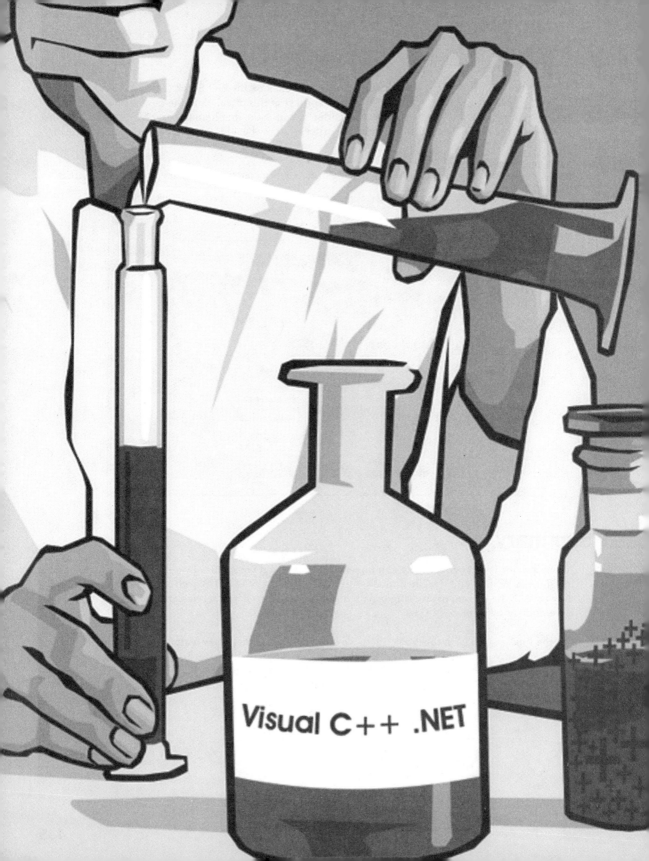

Index

A Guide to the Index

The index is arranged hierarchically, in alphabetical order, with symbols preceding the letter A. Most second-level entries and many third-level entries also occur as first-level entries. This is to ensure that users will find the information they require however they choose to search for it.

D

U

V

wrox
Programmer to Programmer™

p2p.wrox.com
The programmer's resource centre

A unique free service from Wrox Press
With the aim of helping programmers to help each other

Wrox Press aims to provide timely and practical information to today's programmer. P2P is a list server offering a host of targeted mailing lists where you can share knowledge with four fellow programmers and find solutions to your problems. Whatever the level of your programming knowledge, and whatever technology you use P2P can provide you with the information you need.

ASP Support for beginners and professionals, including a resource page with hundreds of links, and a popular ASP.NET mailing list.

DATABASES For database programmers, offering support on SQL Server, mySQL, and Oracle.

MOBILE Software development for the mobile market is growing rapidly. We provide lists for the several current standards, including WAP, Windows CE, and Symbian.

JAVA A complete set of Java lists, covering beginners, professionals, and server-side programmers (including JSP, servlets and EJBs)

.NET Microsoft's new OS platform, covering topics such as ASP.NET, C#, and general .NET discussion.

VISUAL BASIC Covers all aspects of VB programming, from programming Office macros to creating components for the .NET platform.

WEB DESIGN As web page requirements become more complex, programmer's are taking a more important role in creating web sites. For these programmers, we offer lists covering technologies such as Flash, Coldfusion, and JavaScript.

XML Covering all aspects of XML, including XSLT and schemas.

OPEN SOURCE Many Open Source topics covered including PHP, Apache, Perl, Linux, Python and more.

FOREIGN LANGUAGE Several lists dedicated to Spanish and German speaking programmers, categories include. NET, Java, XML, PHP and XML

How to subscribe
Simply visit the P2P site, at http://p2p.wrox.com/

wrox

Programmer to Programmer™

Registration Code : | 59624B2P103N7XX01 |

Wrox writes books for you. Any suggestions, or ideas about how you want
information given in your ideal book will be studied by our team.
Your comments are always valued at Wrox.

Free phone in USA 800-USE-WROX
Fax (312) 893 8001

UK Tel.: (0121) 687 4100   Fax: (0121) 687 4101

Visual C++ .NET: A primer for C++ developers – Registration Card

Name _____

Address _____

_____

_____

City _____ State/Region _____

Country _____ Postcode/Zip _____

E-Mail _____

Occupation _____

How did you hear about this book?

❐ Book review (name) _____

❐ Advertisement (name) _____

❐ Recommendation _____

❐ Catalog _____

❐ Other _____

Where did you buy this book?

❐ Bookstore (name) _____ City_____

❐ Computer store (name) _____

❐ Mail order _____

❐ Other _____

What influenced you in the purchase of this book?

❐ Cover Design ❐ Contents ❐ Other (please specify):

_____

How did you rate the overall content of this book?

❐ Excellent ❐ Good ❐ Average ❐ Poor

What did you find most useful about this book? _____

_____

_____

What did you find least useful about this book? _____

_____

Please add any additional comments. _____

_____

_____

What other subjects will you buy a computer book on soon?

_____

What is the best computer book you have used this year?

_____

Note: This information will only be used to keep you updated
about new Wrox Press titles and will not be used for
any other purpose or passed to any other third party.

wrox

Programmer to Programmer™

Note: If you post the bounce back card below in the UK, please send it to:

Wrox Press Limited, Arden House, 1102 Warwick Road,
Acocks Green, Birmingham B27 6HB. UK.

Computer Book Publishers